A MANUAL OF ETHICS

A MANUAL OF ETHICS

JOHN STUART MACKENZIE

GYAN

Published by

GYAN

Gyan Publishing House
5, Ansari Road
Daryaganj, New Delhi-110002
Phone: 011-47034999, 9811692060
E-mail: books@gyanbooks.com

Distribution Network
gyanbooks.com
India, USA, Canada, UK, Australia

ISBN: 978-93-7414-258-5 (PB)

First Published, 1901

2nd Impression 2025

Printed at: Gyan Press, Delhi.

A MANUAL OF ETHICS
Author: JOHN STUART MACKENZIE

The University Tutorial Series.

A MANUAL OF ETHICS.

The University Tutorial Series.

A

MANUAL OF ETHICS.

BY

JOHN S. MACKENZIE, M.A.,

PROFESSOR OF LOGIC AND PHILOSOPHY IN THE UNIVERSITY COLLEGE OF SOUTH WALES AND MONMOUTHSHIRE; FORMERLY FELLOW OF TRINITY COLLEGE, CAMBRIDGE.

FOURTH EDITION.

REVISED, ENLARGED, AND IN PART REWRITTEN.

HINDS, HAYDEN & ELDREDGE, INC.

NEW YORK CITY

PREFACE TO THE FOURTH EDITION.

The chief change in this edition consists in the addition of a chapter on the "Authority of the Moral Standard" (Book II., Chapter VI.). This chapter includes an account of the Sanctions, which formerly appeared as a note to Chapter VI. of Book III. I have also added a short note on the classification of the Virtues at the end of Chapter IV. of Book III. The other alterations in this edition are very slight.

I am glad to have this opportunity of acknowledging the kind expressions of appreciation that I have received from teachers of Philosophy in the United States and Canada. It is particularly gratifying to me to know that my book has been found useful in a part of the world from which so many of the most valuable and attractive Manuals of Philosophy have come. At a time when we are being somewhat acutely reminded of the essential similarity of our political problems, it is perhaps specially fitting that we should remember that we are still more profoundly united on the larger problems of life and thought.

February, 1901.

PREFACE TO THE THIRD EDITION.

THIS handbook is intended primarily for the use of private students, and especially for those who are preparing for such examinations in Ethics as those conducted by the University of London. It is hoped, however, that it will be found useful also by other classes of readers. Its design is to give, in brief compass, an outline of the most important principles of ethical doctrine, so far as these can be understood without a knowledge of Metaphysics.

To do this satisfactorily is by no means easy; and I can hardly hope that I have been successful in overcoming the difficulties. The theory of Ethics must, I believe, in the end rest on Metaphysics; and what it is possible to do without Metaphysics can be little more than a clearing of the ground, and a leading up to the metaphysical principles that are involved in the subject. The system of metaphysical truth, however, is like a city with many gates; and perhaps the student may enter it by the ethical gate as profitably as by any other. It has been my aim, at any rate, to conduct the student gradually inwards from the psychological outworks to the metaphysical foundation.

It is perhaps hardly necessary to say that the metaphysical point of view adopted in this Manual is that of the school of Idealism—*i. e.* the school founded by Kant and developed by Hegel, Green, and others. In this respect the present Text-book is similar to two other treatises which appeared a little before it—Dewey's *Outlines of a Critical Theory of Ethics*, and Muirhead's *Elements of Ethics*.[1] If these books had been published before this one was arranged for, it is probable that it would never have been undertaken. As it is, I can only plead that the subject is handled in this work in a way slightly different from that in which it is taken up by either of the other two, and that it may consequently in some respects satisfy a want which neither of them fully meets. I hope, however, that readers of my book will, as far as possible, consult the other two also. Where there is a general harmony of point of view, a comparison of the methods of treatment adopted by different writers on points of detail is often of the greatest value to the student. I think it would be especially useful for readers of this book, who have time to spare, to compare it in this way with Muirhead's *Elements of Ethics*. The latter work is designed for a slightly different purpose; and at many points it will be found to supply a very useful supplement to the present treatise by presenting the same general ideas in a somewhat different light. For the convenience of students who may use it in this way, I have inserted frequent references to Mr. Muirhead's book, and have indicated the main points of divergence.

[1] Other two books which have since appeared—Professor James Seth's *Study of Ethical Principles* and Mr. C. F. D'Arcy's *Short Study of Ethics*—are also written from a point of view which is to a large extent similar. In both of these books there is a good deal of space devoted to the discussion of the metaphysical basis; but in neither case does the discussion appear satisfactory. On the whole I have thought it best to leave such discussions to works that are expressly metaphysical in character.

My obligations to the leading exponents of the science are sufficiently obvious, and need not be specially acknowledged. In particular, how much I owe to Dr. Edward Caird will probably be evident to every one who is familiar with his writings and teaching. I must, however, make some more particular acknowledgment of the assistance I have received at various points from several friends and critics.

The proofs of this edition, as well as of the first, have been read by Mrs. Gilliland Husband, and I am indebted to her for many highly suggestive criticisms. Mr. James Welton also read all the proofs of the first edition, and Mr. Stout has read all the proofs of the present edition; and from both of these gentlemen I have received valuable assistance. I am also indebted to Professor Alexander for some useful criticisms; and, on smaller points, to Principal Lloyd Morgan, Professor Sully, Mr. W. T. Kenwood, Mr. J. A. Clarke, and others. The published criticisms by Dr. Bosanquet, Professor Ritchie, Mr. Muirhead, Miss E. E. C. Jones, and others have been very helpful. The index at the end of the first edition was prepared by Mr. H. Holman; that at the end of the present edition is the work of Mr. W. F. Trotter, of Trinity College, Cambridge, who has also given me much help in verifying references.

In conclusion, for the sake of those who have been using the previous editions, it may be well to give some indication of the principal changes that have been made in the present one. An effort has been made, in the first place, to render the method of treatment more systematic. With a view to this, the work has been divided into five parts. Of these, Book III. is the part that has been most slightly altered. The only changes in this consist in insignificant modifications of detail. The CONCLUDING CHAPTER has to do duty for the last two chapters of the former editions, and has undergone considerable transformation. The references to Art have been almost entirely omitted, while the references to Metaphysics have been made a good deal more definite. In the INTRODUCTION some further remarks have been added on the divisions into which the treatment of Ethics naturally falls, and the statements about the relation of Ethics to practical life have been considerably modified. I have found that what I said on this subject has been a good deal misunderstood; and the misunderstanding seemed to be due to want of clearness in my exposition, especially in the first chapter. I have, accordingly, added a good deal more in the way of explanation in this chapter, and have removed some passages about the general nature of moral law, which seemed specially liable to misinterpretation, and have inserted them in Book II., Chap. III., where they are perhaps more in place. I have also added a chapter at the end of Book II., dealing with the general subject of the bearing of Theory on Practice. I hope I may have succeeded in this way in removing the impression, which appears to have been created in some minds, that I thought it to be the business of ethical science to construct the moral life *in vacuo*. Nothing could well have been further from my intention; and, if I have overestimated the practical significance of philosophical reflection, I have at least not forgotten either the *dictum* of Hegel [1]

[1] "Philosophy, as the thought of the world, does not appear until reality has completed its formative process, and made itself ready. . . . When philosophy paints its grey in grey, one form of life has become old, and by such painting it cannot be rejuvenated, but only known. The owl of Minerva takes its flight only when the shades

or the epigram of Bradley,[1] or the gibe of Schiller.[2] I do not hold, with Coleridge, that "the only kind of common sense worth having is that which is based on Metaphysics;" but I do certainly believe that there is not much value in any kind of common sense that cannot be vindicated by philosophical reflection; and I think that, when it is thus vindicated, it is at the same time enlightened.

The most considerable alterations, however, occur in Book I. I have thought it desirable to add a good deal of new material on the development of the moral life and of the moral judgment. It may be held that these subjects belong more properly to Sociology and Psychology than to Ethics in the stricter sense; but I have found that their absence is a more serious defect than their presence. I have also added, at the beginning of Book II., a short historical account of the leading points of view in ethical theory.

UNIVERSITY COLLEGE, CARDIFF,
May, 1897.

of night are gathering." Preface to the *Rechtsphilosophie*. As a counterblast to this, it may be remarked, however, that several things seem to have been rejuvenated by Hegel himself.

[1] "Metaphysics is the finding of bad reasons for what we believe upon instinct." Preface to *Appearance and Reality*. But are the reasons always "bad," and are they always "for"?

[2] "Doch weil, was ein Professor spricht,
Nicht gleich zu Allen dringet,
So übt Natur die Mutterpflicht
Und sorgt, dass nie die Kette bricht,
Und dass der Reif nie springet.
Einstweilen, bis den Bau der Welt
Philosophie zusammenhält,
Erhält *sie* das Getriebe
Durch Hunger und durch Liebe."—*Die Weltweisen*.

CONTENTS.

INTRODUCTION.

CHAPTER I.—THE SCOPE OF ETHICS.

CHAPTER II.—THE RELATION OF ETHICS TO OTHER SCIENCES.

CHAPTER III.—THE DIVISIONS OF THE SUBJECT.

BOOK I.

PROLEGOMENA, CHIEFLY PSYCHOLOGICAL.

CHAPTER I.—DESIRE AND WILL.

PAGE

CHAPTER II.—MOTIVE AND INTENTION.

CHAPTER III.—CHARACTER AND CONDUCT.

CHAPTER IV.—THE EVOLUTION OF CONDUCT.

CHAPTER V.—THE GROWTH OF THE MORAL JUDGMENT.

CHAPTER VI.—THE SIGNIFICANCE OF THE MORAL JUDGMENT.

BOOK II.

THEORIES OF THE MORAL STANDARD.

CHAPTER I.—THE DEVELOPMENT OF ETHICAL THOUGHT.

CHAPTER II.—THE TYPES OF ETHICAL THEORY.

CHAPTER III.—THE STANDARD AS LAW.

CHAPTER IV.—THE STANDARD AS HAPPINESS.

BOOK III.

THE MORAL LIFE.

CHAPTER I.—THE SOCIAL UNITY.

CHAPTER II.—MORAL INSTITUTIONS.

CHAPTER III.—THE DUTIES.

INTRODUCTION.

CHAPTER I.

THE SCOPE OF ETHICS.

§ 1. Definition. *The Science of the Ideal in Conduct.*—Ethics is the science of Conduct. It considers the actions of human beings with reference to their rightness or wrongness, their tendency to good or to evil. The name "Ethics" is derived from the Greek *τὰ ἠθικά.* This again comes from ἦθος, meaning character; and this is connected with ἔθος, custom or habit. Similarly, the term "Moral Philosophy," which means the same thing as Ethics, is derived from the Latin *mores*, meaning habits or customs. Ethics, then, we may say, discusses men's habits and customs, or in other words their characters, the principles on which they habitually act, and considers what it is that constitutes the rightness or wrongness of these principles, the good or evil of these habits. These terms, however, "Right" and "Good," seem to require a little explanation.

(*a*) *Right.* The term "Right" is derived from the Latin *rectus*, meaning "straight" or "according to rule." The Greek word corresponding to it is δίκαιος, which also meant originally "according to rule."

When we say, then, that conduct is right, we mean primarily that it is according to rule. Rules, however, have reference to some result to be achieved by them; and it is this fact that is indicated by the second term, "Good."

(*b*) *Good.* The term "Good" is connected with the German *gut*, and contains the same root as the Greek ἀγαθός. A thing is generally said to be good when it is valuable for some end. Thus, particular kinds of medicine are said to be good for this or that complaint. Similarly, when we speak of conduct as good, we may mean that it is serviceable for the end we have in view.[1] It should be carefully observed, however, that the term "good" is also used (perhaps even more frequently) to signify not something which is a *means* to an end, but something which is itself taken as an end. Thus the *summum bonum*, or supreme good, means the supreme end at which we aim.

Thus, when we say that the science of Ethics is concerned with the rightness or goodness of human conduct, we mean that it is concerned with the consideration of the serviceableness of our conduct for some end at which we aim, and with the rules by which our conduct is to be directed in order that this end may be attained.[2] But if we are to consider the serviceableness of our actions to an end, and the rules by which this end is to be attained, it is evident that we must have some understanding of the nature of the end itself. Now there are many ends to which our actions

[1] *Cf.* Muirhead's *Elements of Ethics*, p. 65. Also, Spencer's *Data of Ethics*, chap. iii.

[2] This statement must be regarded as provisional. It is to some extent modified by the following paragraphs.

may be directed, *e. g.* the building of a house, the writing of a book, the passing of an examination, and so on. But since Ethics is the science of Conduct as a whole, and not of any particular kinds of Conduct, it is not any of these special ends that it sets itself to consider, but the supreme or ultimate end to which our whole lives are directed. This end is commonly referred to as the *Summum Bonum* or Supreme Good.

Now it is no doubt open to question at the outset, whether there can be said to be any one supreme end in human life. Men aim at various objects. Some desire wealth; others, independence; others, power. Some are eager for fame; others, for knowledge; others, for love; and some again find their highest good in loving and serving others.[1] Some are fond of excitement; others, of peace. Some fill their lives with many-sided interests—art and science, and the development of social and political institutions; others are tempted to regard all these as vanity, and sometimes even, turning from them all in disgust, to believe that the best thing of all would be to die and be at rest;[2] while others again fix their highest hopes on a life beyond death, to be perfected in a better world than this. But a little consideration serves to show that many of these ends cannot be regarded as ulti-

[1] "This is shown by the delight that mothers take in loving; for some give their children to others to rear, and love them since they know them, but do not look for love in return, if it be impossible to have both, being content to see their children doing well, and loving them, though they receive from them, in their ignorance, nothing of what is due to a mother."—Aristotle's *Ethics*, VIII. viii. 3.

[2] See, for instance, Shakespeare's Sonnet LXVI.—"Tired with all these, for restful death I cry," &c., and *cf.* Byron and the modern Pessimists, *passim.*

mate. If, for instance, we were to question those who are seeking for wealth or independence or power, we should generally find that they would explain their desire for these objects by enumerating the advantages which the attainment of the desired objects would bring. The possibility of such an explanation proves that these objects are not regarded as *ultimate* ends by those who pursue them, but are desired for the sake of something else. Still, we hardly seem to be justified in starting with the assumption that there is any one ultimate end in human life. The question whether any such end can be discovered is rather one that must be discussed in the course of our study. What it is necessary for us to assume is simply that there is some *ideal* in life, *i. e.* that there is some standard of judgment by reference to which we are able to say that one form of conduct is *better* than another. What the nature of this ideal or standard is—whether it has reference to a single ultimate end, to a set of rules imposed upon us by some authority, to an ideal type of human life which we are somehow enabled to form for ourselves, or in what other possible way it is determined—we must endeavour to discover as we go on. In the meantime it seems sufficient to define Ethics as *the science of the ideal involved in human life.*[1]

§ 2. THE NATURE OF ETHICS. *It is a Normative Science.*—The fact that Ethics is concerned with an end or ideal or standard serves at once to distinguish it from most other sciences. Most sciences are con-

[1] On the general nature of the science of Ethics, the reader may consult Sidgwick's *History of Ethics*, Chap. I.; Muirhead's *Elements of Ethics*, Book I.; Dewey's *Outlines of Ethics*, Introduction; and Sidgwick's *Methods of Ethics*, Book I., Chap. I.

cerned with certain uniformities of our experience—with the ways in which certain classes of objects (such as rocks or plants) are found to exist, or with the ways in which certain classes of events (such as the phenomena of sound or electricity) are found to occur. Such sciences have no direct reference to any end that is to be achieved or to any ideal by reference to which the facts are judged. The knowledge which they communicate may, indeed, be useful for certain purposes. A knowledge about rocks is useful for those who wish to build houses or to sink mines. A knowledge about electricity is useful for those who wish to protect their buildings or to form telegraphic communications. But the truth of the sciences that deal with such subjects as these is in no way affected by the ends which they may thus be made to subserve. Knowledge about the nebulæ is as much a part of the science of astronomy as knowledge about the solar system, though the latter can be directly turned to account in the art of navigation, while the former has no direct practical utility. The science of Ethics, then, is distinguished from the natural sciences, inasmuch as it has a direct reference to an end that men desire to attain, or a type to which they wish to approximate.

It is not by any means the only science, however, which has such a reference. On the contrary, there is a whole class of sciences of this character. These are commonly called the *normative* sciences—*i. e.* the sciences that lay down rules or laws or, more strictly, that seek to define a standard or ideal with reference to which rules or laws may be formulated. Of this kind are the science of medicine (*i. e.* Hygienics), which deals with the nature of the distinction between health and disease, and with the rules to be observed for the attainment of health, or for the avoidance and removal of disease ; the science of architecture, which deals with the types to be aimed at and the rules to be observed in the construction of buildings, with a view to their stability, convenience, and beauty ; the science of navigation, which deals with the aims and principles involved in the management of ships ; the science of rhetoric, which deals with the principles of persuasiveness and beauty of style ; the science of logic, which deals with the conditions of correct thinking. Most of these sciences are of a mixed character, being partly concerned with the analysis of facts, and partly with the definition of ends or ideals and with the statement of rules to be observed for the attainment of them. Thus the science of medicine deals with the facts of disease as well as with the nature and conditions of health, and the science of architecture discusses the ways in which buildings have been constructed at various periods of man's history, as well as the ways in which it is most desirable that buildings should be constructed. Sometimes, indeed, these two sides of a science are so evenly balanced, that it is difficult to say whether it ought properly to be regarded as a natural or a normative science. This is notably the case with regard to political economy. But in all such cases it is possible to separate the two sides of the science, and to consider them as forming in reality two distinct, though closely connected, sciences.

In the case of Ethics, the normative side is by far the more important ; but the other side is not entirely absent. There are ethical facts as well as ethical laws and ideals. Thus the ideas of the Thugs, who are said to regard murder as a supreme duty, constitute an important fact in the moral life of a certain section of mankind; but no scientific system of ethics is ever likely to include such a duty in its statement of the moral ideal, any more than a system of medicine is likely to express approval of extensive indulgence in alcohol or tight lacing. This is no doubt a somewhat extreme case; but there are in every community certain peculiarities of the moral sense which are in reality quite analogous. Thus, much of the conduct which is regarded as fine and noble in a modern Englishman, would probably have seemed almost unintelligible to a cultivated Athenian or to a devout Jew in the ancient world; and much of the conduct that one of the latter would have praised, would seem to the modern Englishman to lack delicacy or humanity. Now, some of the differences which occur in the moral codes of different peoples are not without meaning even for the student of the moral ideal. A reflective moralist, to whatever school of thought he might belong, would not approve of quite the same conduct under all conditions of life, any more than a thoughtful physician would prescribe the same regimen to an inhabitant of Canada as to an inhabitant of India. Different circumstances bring different obligations; and in the general progress of history, there is a progress in the nature of the duties that are imposed on men. As Lowell says—

> "New occasions teach new duties:
> Time makes ancient good uncouth."

Even the strictest of moralists, therefore, might admit differences in ethical codes at different times and places. But the differences which we actually find are not all of this nature. No system of medicine would commend opium and crushed feet; and no system of ethics would regard with equal approval the Code of Honour, the Ten Commandments, and the Sermon on the Mount. But all these are *ethical facts*, and have an equal right to be chronicled as such, though they have not an equal right to be approved. There is a marked difference, therefore, between the science which deals with the *facts* of the moral life and that which deals with the *rules* and *ideals* of the moral life. The former science is a part of that wider science which deals with the general structure of societies—the science which is usually known as Sociology. The latter science, on the other hand, is that to which the name of Ethics is more strictly appropriated; and it is with it alone, or at least mainly, that we shall be concerned in the present work. The former is a natural or positive science; the latter is a normative science. But, of course, in dealing with the latter, we can scarcely avoid touching on the former.

§ 3. Ethics not a Practical Science.—There is, however, still another distinction which it is important to draw. It will be observed that the sciences referred to in the foregoing paragraph as normative are not all of quite the same kind. Some of them are definitely concerned with the consideration of the means required for the realisation of certain assignable ends, while others are more directly interested in the elucidation of the ends or ideals involved in certain forms of activity. Perhaps it would be best to confine the term "normative" to the latter kind of science, while the former might be more appropriately described as "practical." Medicine (Hygienics) is a practical science, rather than a normative one, since its aim is not so much that of understanding the ideal of health[1] as that of ascertaining the means by which health may be best produced. Now, the science of Ethics has sometimes been regarded as a practical science in this sense. It is generally so regarded by those writers who think that it is possible to formulate some one simple end at which human beings ought to aim as the *summum bonum*. Thus, what is commonly known as the Utilitarian school regards the attainment of "the greatest happiness of the greatest number" as the end to be aimed at, and conceives that it is the business of Ethics to consider the means by which this end may be attained, just as the scientific student of public health may consider the best means for preventing the spread of an infectious disease. The extent to which, if at all, it is possible to treat Ethics in this way, will have to be considered at a later stage, after we have discussed the different views that may be taken of the nature of the moral ideal. We shall then see grounds for thinking that the moral life cannot be regarded as directed towards the attainment of any one simple result, and that consequently the means of attaining the moral ideal cannot be formulated in any definite set of rules. In so far as this is the case, the science of Ethics cannot properly be described as practical. It must content itself with understanding the nature of the ideal, and must not hope to formulate rules for its attainment. Hence most writers on Ethics have preferred to treat it as a purely speculative, rather than as a practical science. This is probably the best view to

[1] Perhaps this is more properly the function of Physiology.

take. At any rate, it is important to observe that the description of Ethics as "normative" does not involve the view that it has any direct bearing on practice. It is the business of a normative science to define an ideal, not to lay down rules for its attainment. Æsthetics, for instance, is a normative science, concerned with the standard of Beauty; but it is no part of its business to inquire how Beauty is produced. So with Ethics. It discusses the ideal of goodness or rightness, and is not directly concerned with the means by which this ideal may be realised.

Ethics, then, though a normative science, is not to be regarded as a practical science.[1]

§ 4. Ethics not an Art. If Ethics is not strictly to be classed as a practical science, it ought still less to be described as an art. Yet the question has sometimes been raised, with regard both to Logic and to Ethics, whether both these departments of study are not rather of the nature of arts than of sciences,[2] since they have both a certain reference to practice. Logic has sometimes been called the Art of Thinking,[3] and though Ethics has perhaps never been described as the Art of Conduct, yet it has often been treated as if it were directly concerned with that art. Now, it may be questioned whether it is quite correct to speak of an art of thinking or of an art of conduct at all. This is a question to which we shall shortly return. But at any rate it is now generally recognized that it is best to treat

[1] The extent to which it may be regarded as bearing on practice is discussed below, Book II., chap. vii. All the statements made in the present chapter must be regarded as provisional.

[2] *Cf.* Welton's *Manual of Logic*, vol. i. p. 12.

[3] This was, in particular, the title of the *Port Royal Logic.*

both Logic and Ethics as having no direct bearing upon these arts. It may be well, however, to notice the reasons which have led to the view that these sciences are of the nature of arts.

In the case of every practical science, the question is apt to present itself, whether we are really concerned with a science at all or rather with an art. And the answer seems to be, that if we insist on drawing an absolute distinction between a science and an art, a practical science must be regarded as lying midway between them. A science, it is said, teaches us *to know*, and an art *to do*;[1] but a practical science teaches us *to know how to do*. Since, however, such a science is primarily concerned with the communication of knowledge, it is more properly to be described as a science than as an art; but it is a kind of science that has a very direct relation to a corresponding art. There is scarcely any art that is not indirectly related to a great number of different sciences. The art of painting, for instance, may derive useful lessons from the sciences of optics, anatomy, botany, geology, and a great variety of others. The art of navigation, in like manner, is much aided by the sciences of astronomy, magnetism, acoustics, hydrostatics, and many more. But such relationships are comparatively indirect. The dependence of an art upon its corresponding practical science is of a very much closer character. The art of rhetoric is a direct application of the science of rhetoric, so far as there is any such science; and the art of fencing, of the science of fencing. Indeed, if a practical science could be completely worked out into all its details, the

[1] *Cf.* Jevons's *Elementary Logic*, p. 7; Welton's *Manual of Logic*, vol. i. p. 12; Mill's *Logic*, Introduction.

art corresponding to it would contain nothing which is not included in the science. Perhaps this is the case with such an art as that of fencing. Still, even here the science and the art are clearly distinguishable. A man may be quite familiar with the science, and yet not be skilled in the art; and *vice versa*. But in most cases the distinction is even more marked than this: for the art usually includes a great deal that we are not able to reduce to science at all. Indeed, some arts are so entirely dependent on the possession of a peculiar knack or dexterity, or of a peculiar kind of genius, that they can scarcely be said to have any science corresponding to them at all. Thus, for example, there is no science of cookery, there is no science of sleight-of-hand, there is no science of making jokes, and there is no science of poetry.[1]

Now there is no doubt a sense in which conduct, as well as thinking, may be said to be an art.[2] Both of these are activities presupposing certain natural gifts, proceeding upon certain principles, and made perfect by practice. But such an art as either of these seems clearly to be one that cannot be subjected to exact scientific treatment. Men of moral genius and large experience of life may communicate the fruits of their

[1] Poetry used to be known as "the gay science;" but the word "science" is here used in the sense of "art." The failure to distinguish between these two terms has given rise to much confusion. Thus, when Carlyle called political economy "the dismal science," he meant to contrast it with poetry. But it is now generally recognized that political economy is a science in the stricter sense, though partly a practical science, and is not to be classed with arts like poetry.

[2] A recent book by Mr. N. P. Gilman and Mr. E. P. Jackson, is entitled *Conduct as a Fine Art;* but this reminds one somewhat of De Quincey's essay on "Murder regarded as one of the Fine Arts."

experience to mankind, and may thus be said to instruct them in the art of conduct. But it is certainly not the business of a student of ethical science as such to be a prophet or preacher. Even if Ethics were in the strict sense a practical science, it could still only deal with the general principles involved in human action. But action itself is concerned with the particular, which can never be exhausted by general principles. For the communication of the art of conduct "example is better than precept," and experience is better than either; so that even if it were the business of Ethics to lay down precepts (*i. e.* if it were a practical science), these precepts would still not suffice for instruction in the art of life. But as Ethics is a normative, rather than a practical, science, it is not even its primary business to lay down precepts at all, but rather to define the ideal involved in life. How far the definition of this ideal may lead on to practical precepts, is a matter for future consideration.

§ 5. Is there any Art of Conduct?—We may, however, proceed further, and ask whether it is strictly legitimate to speak of an Art of Conduct at all. A little consideration suffices to show that such a conception is in the highest degree questionable. No doubt the term Art may be used in somewhat different senses. The Industrial Arts are not quite of the same nature as the Fine Arts. The former are directed to the production of objects useful for some ulterior end; whereas the objects produced by the latter are rather ends in themselves. But in both cases there is a definite product which it is the object of the Art to bring forth. Now in the case of morality, at least on a *prima facie* view, this is not true. There is no product in this case, but only an activity. Of course it may be said that the activity is valued with reference to a certain ultimate end, *i. e.* to the *summum bonum.* How far this is true, we shall have to consider in the course of our study; but it would, at any rate, be misleading at the outset to think of conduct as being of the same nature as the Arts, whether Industrial or Expressive. It may be convenient to sum up the differences in the following way.

(1) *Virtue exists only in activity.*—A good painter is one who *can* paint beautifully: a good man is not one who *can,* but one who *does,* act rightly. The good painter is good when he is asleep or on a journey, or when, for any other reason, he is not employed in his art.[1] The good man is not good when asleep or on a journey, unless when it is good to sleep or to go on a journey. Goodness is not a capacity or potentiality, but an activity; in Aristotelian language, it is not a δύναμις, but an ἐνέργεια.

This is a simple point, and yet it is a point that presented great difficulty to ancient philosophers. By nothing perhaps were they so much misled as by

[1] *Cf.* Aristotle's *Ethics,* I. viii. 9. Of course, we judge the goodness of a painter by the work that he does; but the point is that he may cease to act without ceasing to be a skilled artist. A good painter may decide to paint no more; but a good man cannot decide to retire from the life of virtuous activity, or even to take a rest from it. There are no holidays from virtue. Charles Lamb, indeed, has suggested that a leading element in the enjoyment of certain forms of Comedy consists in the fact that they free us from the burden of our habitual moral consciousness. This may be true; but if any one were to seek for a holiday by actually practising the modes of life depicted in these Comedies, he would, so far, have ceased to be virtuous.

the analogy of virtue to the arts.[1] Thus in Plato's *Republic,* Socrates is represented as arguing that if justice consists in keeping property safe, the just man must be a kind of thief; for the same kind of skill which enables a man to defend property, will also enable him to steal it.[2] The answer to this is, that justice is not a kind of skill, but a kind of activity. The just man is not merely one who *can,* but one who *does,* keep property safe. Now though the *capacity* of preserving property may be identical with the *capacity* of appropriating it, the *act* of preserving is certainly very different from the *act* of appropriating. The man who knows precisely what the truth about any matter is, would undoubtedly, as a general rule, be the most competent person to invent lies with respect to the same matter. Yet the truth-speaker and the liar are very different persons; because they are not merely men who possess particular kinds of capacity, but men who act in particular ways. Often, indeed, the most atrocious liars have no special capacity for the art. And so also it is with other vices. "The Devil," it is said, "is an Ass."

(2) *The Essence of Virtue lies in the Will.*—The man who is a bungler in any of the particular arts may be a very worthy and well-meaning person; but the best intentions in the world will not make him a good artist. In the case of virtuous action, on the other hand, as Kant says,[3] "a good will is good not because

[1] This does not apply to Aristotle. See the passage referred to in the preceding note.

[2] Of course, Plato intended this for a joke; but it is doubtful whether he knew exactly where the fallacy comes in.

[3] *Metaphysic of Morals,* I.

of what it performs or effects, not by its aptness for the attainment of some proposed end, but simply by virtue of the volition." "Even if it should happen that, owing to a special disfavour of fortune, or the niggardly provision of a step-motherly nature, this will should wholly lack power to accomplish its purpose, if with its greatest efforts it should yet achieve nothing, and there should remain only the good will (not, to be sure, a mere wish, but the summoning of all means in our power), then, like a jewel, it would still shine by its own light, as a thing which has its whole value in itself." In like manner, Aristotle says[1] of a good man living in circumstances in which he cannot find scope for his highest virtues, διαλάμπει τὸ καλόν, "his nobility shines through." It is true that even in the fine arts purpose counts for something; and a stammering utterance may be not without a grace of its own.[2] In conduct also, if a man blunders entirely, we generally assume that there was some flaw in his purpose—that he did not reflect sufficiently, or did not will the good with sufficient intensity. Still, the distinction remains, that in art the ultimate appeal is to the work achieved, whereas in morals the ultimate appeal is to the inner aim. Or rather, in morals the achievement

[1] *Ethics*, I. x. 12.

[2] *Cf.* Browning's *Andrea del Sarto*:—

> "That arm is wrongly put—and there again—
> A fault to pardon in the drawing's lines,
> Its body, so to speak: its soul is right,
> He means right—that, a child may understand."

But here Art is being judged almost from an ethical, rather than from a purely æsthetical point of view. "*He means* right," is not an æsthetical judgment, (though, of course, the distinction between 'body' and 'soul'—*i. e.* technique and expression—does belong to Æsthetics).

cannot be distinguished from the inner activity by which it is brought about.[1]

§ **6.** Is THERE ANY SCIENCE OF CONDUCT?—The fact that it is somewhat questionable to speak of an Art of Conduct suggests a doubt whether it is even quite proper to speak of a Science of Conduct. We generally understand by a science the study of some limited portion of our experience. Now in dealing with morals we are concerned rather with the whole of our experience from one particular point of view, *viz.*, from the point of view of activity—*i. e.* from the point of view of the pursuit of ends or ideals. Matthew Arnold has said that "Conduct is three-fourths of life;" but of course, from the point of view of purposive activity, conduct is the *whole* of life. It is common to distinguish the pursuit of truth (science) and the pursuit of beauty (fine art) from the moral life in the narrower sense; but when truth and beauty are regarded as ends to be attained, the pursuit of them is a kind of conduct; and the consideration of these ends, as of all others, falls within the scope of the science of morals. In a sense, therefore, Ethics is not a science at all, if by a science we understand the study of some limited department of human experience. It is rather a part of philosophy, *i. e.* a part of the study of experience as a whole. It is, indeed, only a *part* of philosophy; because it considers the experience of life only from the point of view of will or activity. It does not, except indirectly, consider man as *knowing* or *enjoying*, but as *doing*, *i. e.* pursuing an end. But it considers man's *whole* activity, the entire nature

[1] This point is more fully brought out in Book I., chap. vi.

of the good which he seeks, and the whole significance of his activity in seeking it. For this reason some writers prefer to describe the subject as Moral Philosophy or Ethical Philosophy, rather than as the Science of Ethics. For it is the business of Philosophy, rather than of Science, to deal with experience as a whole. Similarly, Logic and Æsthetics, the two sciences which most closely resemble Ethics, are rather philosophical than scientific. But the term Science may be used in a wide sense to include the philosophical studies as well as those that are called scientific in the narrower sense. In the next chapter we must endeavour to explain more definitely the place of Ethics among the other departments of knowledge.

§ 7. SUMMARY.—The statements in this chapter are intended to give a general indication of the nature of ethical science. The student ought to be warned, however, that different writers regard the subject in different ways. Some regard it as having a directly practical aim, while others endeavour to treat it as a purely theoretical science, in the same sense in which chemistry or astronomy is purely theoretical. I have adopted a middle course, by describing it as normative. But the full significance of this difference, as well as the grounds for adopting one or other of these views, can hardly become apparent to the student until he has learned to appreciate the distinction between the leading theories of the moral standard. In fact, in studying Ethics, as in studying most other subjects of any complexity, it should always be borne in mind that the definition of the subject and the understanding of its scope and method come rather at the end than at the beginning. With these cautions, however, the student may perhaps find the remarks made in this chapter of some service as an introduction to the study.

The main points may be summed up in this way :—

(1) Ethics is the science which deals with the Ideal, or with the Standard of Rightness and Wrongness, Good and Evil, involved in Conduct.

(2) This science is normative, not one of the ordinary Positive Sciences.

(3) It is, however, not properly to be described as a Practical Science, though it has a close bearing upon practical life.

(4) Still less is it to be described as an Art.

(5) It is hardly correct to speak of an Art of Conduct at all.

(6) Some objection may also be taken even to the term Science of Conduct, since the study of the Ideal in Conduct is rather philosophical than scientific.

NOTE ON POSITIVE AND NORMATIVE SCIENCES.

It may be well to warn the student, more fully than could well be done in the text, that the convenient distinction, here adopted, between positive and normative sciences, is not to be taken as an absolute one; still less, as exhaustive. On reflection, the student will no doubt find that many sciences which are essentially positive have in them elements that are of a normative character. In illustration of this, we might refer to the saying of the astronomer, who was questioned about the way in which the planets move: "I know nothing about the way in which the planets move; I only know how the planets ought to move—if there are any planets!" This is, of course, a paradox; but it may serve to bring out the truth that much of what is contained even in the positive sciences depends on the consideration of ideal standards. Again, the student who pursues the study of metaphysics will soon find that there is a sense in which even such principles as the law of causation may be said, as Kant put it, to be prescribed to nature. Further, there is a sense in which even purely normative sciences may be said to deal with what is. Logic is said to be concerned with correct thinking; but there is a very true sense in which it may be held that incorrect thinking is not thought; so that, from this point of view, Logic may be said to be concerned with the principles of thought as thought. Similarly, it might perhaps be urged that an object which is not appreciated as beautiful is not really appreciated; and that an action which is not good is not, in the full sense of the word, an action. Hence, the distinction between positive and normative sciences is one that may require, to a large extent, to be thrown aside as the student advances. It is one of those convenient distinctions (like that between sense and thought, knowing and willing, matter and spirit, etc.) which require to be drawn at the outset, but which may be gradually superseded. It remains true, however, that the ordinary concrete sciences, like botany or physiology,[1] make it their main aim to co-ordinate particular facts of experience, while logic and ethics deal essentially with standards of judgment. It would obviously be far beyond the scope of such a work as this to attempt any

[1] In the case of physiology, this statement is open to some qualification, in so far as physiology makes it its business to study the *normal* action of vital functions.

exhaustive classification of the sciences; but perhaps the following list may serve, roughly, to indicate the relations in which they stand to one another.

(1) The ordinary concrete sciences, *e.g.* botany, biology, anatomy, geology, &c. Of these it is on the whole true to say that they deal with particular classes of facts, and try to co-ordinate them.

(2) The ordinary abstract sciences, such as mathematics, mechanics, the more theoretical parts of astronomy, &c. These sciences also aim at the elucidation of facts; but, in order to elucidate them, they make use of hypothetical constructions, often involving a reference to ideal standards—as, in mathematics, the standard of a perfectly straight line, and the like.[1]

(3) The normative sciences, such as logic, æsthetics, ethics, which deal definitely rather with standards of judgment than with particular facts.

(4) The practical sciences, such as medicine, architecture, rhetoric, &c., which apply standards of judgment to the formulation of principles of action. All normative sciences are capable of being made practical when they are thus applied.

Arts, properly so called, seek to carry out certain forms of activity for the production of certain results. They depend on the principles laid down by the practical sciences, but generally depend on more than one of them.

It should also be carefully borne in mind that often what is commonly regarded as a single science may include elements which, if taken by themselves, would refer it alternately to several, or perhaps all, of the above classes. Thus Political Economy is a positive science in so far as it deals with the facts of commercial life, and seeks to co-ordinate them—in so far, that is to say, as it is dealt with historically and concretely. It is, however, an abstract science, in so far as it deals with hypothetical conditions, such as that of perfectly free competition, and seeks to show what would follow from these conditions. It is a normative science, in so far as it seeks to establish an

[1] It may perhaps be of some assistance to the student to point out that the names of the more purely positive sciences generally end in "logy"—geology, biology, anthropology, psychology, sociology, &c.; while those of the more abstract and normative (*i. e.* those that are, in some sense, concerned with standards or ideals) generally end in "ic" or "ics"—mathematics, mechanics, logic, æsthetics, ethics, &c. But this is only roughly true. *Cf.* Giddings's *Principles of Sociology*, p. 50.

ideal standard, such as that of industrial freedom, to which the facts of the commercial life ought to conform. It is a practical science when it uses this standard to guide the statesman, the man of business, the workman, or the social reformer. When, finally, these various people make use of it, under the guidance of common sense, it becomes an art; and the carrying of it into effect in this way involves various other forms of knowledge, as well as the knowledge of the particular science in question.[1]

It thus appears that sciences cannot be quite so simply arranged as the student might perhaps be led to suppose from the statements in the text. The broad distinction, however, between the positive and the normative—between that in which the ultimate reference is to a particular class of facts, and that in which the ultimate reference is to an ideal standard, is all that is of special importance for our present purpose. If the student will bear in mind the two sciences with which, from his previous study, he is probably most likely to be familiar, Psychology and Logic, he will find in them two very perfect types of the distinction in question. Psychology deals with the *facts* of consciousness; Logic deals with the *standard* of correctness.

[1] Cf. Keynes's *Scope and Method of Political Economy*, pp. 34-36.

CHAPTER II.

THE RELATION OF ETHICS TO OTHER SCIENCES.

§ 1. General Statement.—From what has already been stated, it appears that Ethics is to be regarded as belonging to the group of sciences that are called philosophic. Now the question as to the general nature and divisions of philosophic study is to some extent controversial; and of course it is beyond our present scope to enter on any discussion of this question; but perhaps the student may find the following statements helpful and not very misleading. He may correct them for himself, if necessary, as he advances in the study of philosophy.

Philosophy is the study of the nature of experience as a whole. The particular sciences investigate particular portions of the content of our experience; but philosophy seeks to understand the whole in the light of its central principles. In order to do this, it endeavours to analyze the various elements that enter into the constitution of the world as we know it. This part of the investigation is perhaps that which is most properly described as Epistemology. Next we may go on to trace the genesis of the various elements that constitute our experience—to examine, that is to say, the process by which experience grows up in the consciousness of individuals and races. This is the task of Psychology. Now, when we thus examine our experience and trace its growth, it is found that the content which is thus brought to light consists partly of facts presented in various ways before our consciousness and partly of ideals. The study of the particular facts that come before our consciousness has to be handed over to the particular sciences; or, in so far as philosophy is able to deal with them, they form the content of what is called the Philosophy of Nature. The ideals, again, which emerge in our experience, are found to be three in number, corresponding, it would seem, to the Knowing, the Feeling, and the Willing sides of our conscious nature. They are the ideals of Truth, Beauty, and Goodness. The study of these ideals forms the subject-matter of the three sciences of Logic, Æsthetics, and Ethics. Finally the question arises with respect to the kind and degree of reality possessed by these various elements in our experience. This inquiry is that which is properly known as Ontology. The first and the last of these departments of study—Epistemology and Ontology—tend to coalesce; and the two together constitute what is commonly known as Metaphysics, which thus forms the Alpha and the Omega of the philosophical sciences.

From this it will be seen that Ethics stands, along with Logic and Æsthetics, midway between Psychology and Metaphysics; and, in fact, whatever may be thought of the foregoing method of stating the relationship, it is generally recognized that there is a very close connection between Ethics and each of these two other philosophical sciences.

Further consideration, however, reveals a variety of other subjects to which Ethics is closely related. On some it is dependent for materials, to others it supplies assistance. It may be well to try to bring out a little more in detail some of these relationships, though of course it is only possible to indicate them here very briefly.

§ 2. Physical Science and Ethics.—The relation of Physical Science to Ethics is but slight. It has sometimes been supposed that the question of physical causation has an important bearing on Ethics. It has been thought that morality postulates the freedom of the will, and that there is a certain conflict between this postulate and the theory of the universal applicability of the law of cause and effect. This point will be referred to in a subsequent chapter. In the meantime it must suffice to say that the supposition of such a conflict appears to rest upon a misconception.

Of course, Ethics is indirectly related to Physical Science, inasmuch as a knowledge of physical laws enables us to predict, more accurately and certainly than we should otherwise be able to do, what the effect of various kinds of conduct will be. But this knowledge affects only the details of conduct, not the general principles by which our conduct is guided. A wise man in modern times will be less afraid of the sea and of the stars, and more afraid of foul air and impure water, than a man of similar wisdom in ancient times; but the general consideration of the question, what kinds of things we ought to fear, and what kinds we ought not to fear, need not be affected by this difference in detail, which is due to the advance of knowledge. Physical Science in short is chiefly useful to Ethics in the way of helping us to understand the environment within which the moral life is passed, rather than the nature of the moral life itself.

§ 3. Biology and Ethics.—The relation of Biology to Ethics is much closer than that of Physics or Chemistry, but is essentially of the same indirect character. Many of the most sacred of human obligations rest on physiological considerations; but the general principles on which these obligations rest can be discussed without any direct reference to physiological details, and would not, in their general principles, be affected by any new physiological discoveries.

Some recent writers, under the influence of the theory of evolution,[1] have represented the connection of Biology with Ethics as being of a much more fundamental character than that which has now been indicated. It has been thought that the criterion of good or bad conduct is to be found in the tendency to promote the development of life or the reverse; and that, consequently, we may speak of good or bad conduct in the lowest forms of life in quite the same sense as in man. This is a view to which some reference will have to be made at a later stage. In the meantime it seems sufficient to say that conduct, in the sense in which the term is used in Ethics, has no meaning except with reference to a being who has a rational will; and that, in the case of such a being, the development of life is but a subordinate part of the end. Consequently, Biology does not appear to have any direct bearing upon Ethics.[2] The study of animal life, however, does throw a good deal of light on the development of the moral consciousness; but it does this only

[1] See especially Spencer's *Principles of Ethics.*

[2] It is only in so far as we attribute some form of self-consciousness to the lower animals that we are entitled to speak of "sub-human" Ethics. *Cf.* Muirhead's *Elements of Ethics*, p. 212, *note*, and see below, Book I., chap. iii., § 3.

in so far as animal life is studied from the psychological, not from the purely biological, point of view.

§ 4. Psychology and Ethics.—The relation of Psychology to Ethics is much closer and more important. At the same time, the dependence of the one upon the other ought not to be exaggerated. As Logic deals with the correctness of thought, so Ethics deals with the correctness of conduct. Neither of them is directly concerned with the process by which we come to think or to act correctly. Still, the processes of feeling, desiring, and willing cannot be ignored by the student of Ethics; any more than the processes of generalizing, judging, and reasoning can be ignored by the student of Logic; and the consideration of all these falls within the province of the psychologist. Psychology, in fact, as I have already tried to indicate, leads up to ethics, as it leads up to Logic and Æsthetics.

In this connection, however, there is another important point to be noticed, to which reference has not yet been made. Human conduct, as we shall find more and more, has a social reference. Most of our actions derive their moral significance very largely from our relations to our fellow-men. Now Psychology, as commonly studied, has but little bearing on this. Psychology, as a rule, deals mainly with the growth of the individual consciousness, and only refers indirectly to the facts of social relationship. It is possible, however, to study the process of mental development from a more social point of view. The study of language, for instance, the study of the customs of savage peoples, the study of the growth of institutions, etc., throw light upon the gradual development of the human mind in relation to its social environment. The term

Sociology has been used to denote, in a comprehensive way, the study of such social phenomena; and, from the point of view of Ethics, this study of the facts of mind in relation to society has a more direct interest than purely individual Psychology.

§ 5. LOGIC, ÆSTHETICS, AND ETHICS.—These three sciences, as I have already pointed out, are essentially cognate. They are all normative, not positive: they are concerned, that is to say, not with the investigation of facts and relations between facts, but with the discussion of standards. Logic studies the standard of Truth. It is concerned with the *validity* of various processes of thought. Æsthetics and Ethics, again, may be said to be concerned with *value* or worth. Æsthetics considers the standard of Beauty, or as we may perhaps say, worth for feeling. Ethics considers the standard of goodness, *i. e.* value or worth from the point of view of action—*valour*, as we might put it. *Validity*, *Value*, *Valour*, might almost be said to be the subjects of the three sciences; but this of course is something of a play on words. At any rate they are very closely related to one other. Ethics might almost be described as the Logic of conduct—*i. e.* it considers the conditions of the consistency of conduct with the ideal[1] in-

[1] As we have had frequent occasion to use this term Ideal, and shall have to use it frequently in the sequel, it may be well to enter a caution at this point against a misconception to which it is liable. An Ideal means a type, model, or standard; and that which is ideal is that which is normal, that which conforms to its type or standard. The adjective "ideal," however, corresponds to the two nouns "Idea" and "Ideal," and there is a certain ambiguity in its use. As corresponding to "idea" (in the sense made current in English by Locke, Berkeley and Hume) it is apt to be understood as referring to that which is merely fancied, as distinguished from that which exists in fact. (The more correct philosophical use, in this sense, is

volved in it, just as Logic considers the conditions of the consistency of thought with the standards that it implies. Again, the study of the Good is also closely related to the study of the Beautiful. Indeed, so close is the connection between the two conceptions that the Greeks used the same word, τὸ καλόν, indifferently to express beauty and moral nobility. The phrase "beauty of holiness" also occurs in Hebrew literature; and in modern times we sometimes meet with such expressions as "beautiful soul," "a beautiful life," and the like—though these expressions generally refer rather to religious piety than to purely moral excellence, and even in that reference strike us perhaps as savour-

seen in such phrases as "ideal content," "ideal construction," "ideal synthesis," and the like.) Thus, when Byron speaks of "ideal woe" he means imaginary woe, woe of which the ground is purely fanciful. And indeed this meaning clings even to the noun "Ideal," and to "ideal" as an adjective corresponding to that noun. An artist's Ideal is apt to be understood as meaning a type of beauty which is nowhere to be found existing. The ideal, in fact, comes to be understood in the sense of a poetic vision,

> "The light that never was on sea or land,
> The consecration and the poet's dream."

In this sense also an Ideal state, like Plato's Republic, is contrasted with actually existing conditions. Now this use of the word is apt to be very misleading in Ethics. In order to avoid such confusion it is well for the student to think of the moral Ideal, not in relation to Ideal States or the artist's Ideal, but rather in relation to the logical Ideal. The Ideal of correct thinking is not something in the air, but is something that is realized every time we think at all; for to think wrongly is to a certain extent not to think. Similarly the moral ideal may be said to be realized every time we truly act. It is important that we should get rid of the habit of thinking of the Ideal as something "too good to be true," and learn to think of it rather as the determining principle in reality. (See Hegel's *Logic*, Wallace's Translation, p. II.) The point of this may become more apparent in the sequel.

ing a little of cant. I have already indicated that the Greek philosophers got into some trouble through their failure to distinguish clearly between moral conduct and art; and the sharper separation in modern times between the two conceptions marks an advance in scientific clearness. When the moral life is regarded as beautiful, it is looked at from a somewhat external point of view, as if it were a result rather than an act of will; and it was no doubt partly because the Greeks had not fully reached the inner point of view (for which we are largely indebted to Christianity) that they were tempted to regard the moral life as if it were simply an artistic product. When we regard morality as involving a struggle of the will, it can scarcely impress us as beautiful. In the religious sense also, when we speak of the beauty of holiness, beautiful souls, and beautiful lives, we are generally thinking of the persons referred to as if they "flourished" rather than lived, as if they were passive products rather than active producers. Still, it cannot be denied that the contemplation of a life of eminent virtue yields us a certain æsthetic satisfaction; and from certain points of view it is tempting, even for a modern writer, to regard virtue as a kind of beauty. The consideration of the relation between the Good and the Beautiful is, however, too difficult a subject to be taken up at this point; and we must, at any rate, reserve the discussion of it for the present.

§ **6.** Metaphysics and Ethics.—The consideration of validity and value leads inevitably to the problem of reality. In the case of thought we may be satisfied for a time with the mere consideration of its formal self-consistency. But this is soon found to be unsatisfactory; and we pass on, as in what is called Inductive Logic, to the question of the conditions of the consistency of thought with the facts of nature. This again leads us on to the discussion of the ultimate nature of reality. Similarly, in dealing with the Beautiful, we may at first be content to regard it as the pleasant; but we are soon led to inquire how far the pleasantness of objects is illusory and how far it rests upon their essential nature. Thus in both these cases we are led on into metaphysical inquiries. So it is in the case of Ethics. When we ask what constitutes the value or active worth of human life we are soon led into the question of the essential nature of human personality and its place in the universe of actual existence. It is possible, no doubt, to proceed a certain length in Logic, Æsthetics, and Ethics without insisting upon an answer to the ultimate problems of ontology; but they all lead us on inevitably into these problems.

§ 7. Ethics and Political Philosophy.—So far we have been referring to the sciences upon which Ethics may be said to rest. We have now to notice departments of study which rest upon Ethics. These may all be brought under the general heading of political or social Philosophy. As I have already remarked, the study of conduct leads us inevitably into the study of social life. An entirely solitary human being is inconceivable. A man is always a member of some kind of community. As Aristotle said, he is a political animal (πολιτικὸν ζῷον). Hence the science of Ethics is very closely related to that of Politics. We cannot well consider the virtues of the individual without considering also the society to which he is related, and the ways in which it may help or hinder the development of his life. The ideal also which we lay down for the individual will necessarily suggest an ideal arrangement of society, which will be best fitted to enable the individual to realize his highest aims. For this reason, Aristotle even went so far as to say that Ethics is essentially a part of Politics. If we accept this statement, however, we must employ the term Politics in a very wide sense. In this wide sense it is perhaps better to use the term Social Philosophy. But even in the narrower sense of the term, it is evident that the relation of Ethics to Politics must be a very intimate one.[1]

§ 8. ETHICS AND ECONOMICS.—Among the departments of Political Philosophy to which Ethics is thus closely related there is one to which great importance has been attached in recent times—the science of Political Economy. Economics, like Ethics, is concerned with *goods*, *i. e.* with things having value with reference to certain human ends. But while the goods with which Ethics deals are those acts which are the conditions of the attainment of the highest end of life, economic goods are merely those objects which are the means of satisfying any human want. It follows that if we are really to understand the worth of economic goods, we must consider them in close relation to the ethical good. Food, for instance, clothing, house room, and the like, are economic goods; and they serve a variety of purposes—the support of life, the development of life, the prolongation of life, the promotion of enjoyment, the attainment of independence, the furtherance of peace, decency, and security, and so on. And the

[1] *Cf.* Muirhead's *Elements of Ethics*, p. 40 *sqq.*, and see below, Book III., chaps. i. and ii.

worth of the goods will depend on the importance of these ends. Now the importance of these ends can be ascertained only by observing their relation to the supreme end of our lives. Hence a certain knowledge of Ethics is presupposed in the intelligent study of Economics. This truth has frequently been overlooked. The study of Economics has too often been conducted in such a way as to suggest that Wealth is an end in itself; and this has had the practical result of retarding social reforms, and encouraging those who are already too much prepared to pursue riches at any price. For this reason some of the leading writers on Political Economy have been severely criticised by Carlyle and Ruskin and other moralists; and it is now generally recognized that the two sciences of Ethics and Economics must be brought into closer relationship to one another, at least if Economics is to be treated as, in any degree, normative and practical.[1]

§ 9. Ethics and Pædagogics.—Ethics ought also to throw an important light on the science of Education. The reader has probably already discovered, from his previous course of philosophic study, that the science of psychology has a good deal to say that bears on Education. Psychology, however, is chiefly concerned with the various capacities of the human mind and the method of their development. The light which it throws on mental Education is similar to that which is thrown by physiology on physical Education. The question as to what qualities it is most desirable

[1] On this subject, *cf.* Keynes's *Scope and Method of Political Economy*, chap. ii. For a more extreme view, see Devas's *Political Economy*, Book IV., chap. v. Cf. *International Journal of Ethics*, Vol. III., no. 3, and Vol. VII., no. 2.

to evoke and strengthen must obviously depend on our view of the qualities which the good citizen ought to possess, and generally on our view of the nature of the ethical end.[1]

§ 10. CONCLUDING REMARK.—These notes on the relationship between Ethics and other sciences are necessarily somewhat fragmentary, and perhaps the student may not find them very enlightening, especially at the beginning of his course. They may serve, however, to indicate the wider bearings of the science, and to prepare the way for the consideration of the divisions into which the study of it naturally falls. Possibly also if the student will return upon this chapter, after having gone through the body of the treatise, he may then be better able to appreciate the points to which reference has here been made.

[1] Mrs. Bryant has written a valuable book on *Educational Ends* which brings out with considerable fulness the bearing of ethical considerations on the subject of Education. Similarly, Milton's *Tractate on Education* is written throughout with reference to an ethical ideal. *Cf.* also Bacon's *De Augmentis*, Book VII. and many other works of a similar character. The recent book by Professor MacCunn on *The Making of Character* is now probably the best work we have in English on the ethical aspects of Education.

CHAPTER III.

THE DIVISIONS OF THE SUBJECT.

§ 1. General Remarks.—If we adhered quite rigidly to the view of Ethics put forward in the first chapter, it would hardly be necessary to introduce any divisions in the treatment of it. It would all be concerned with the definition of the moral ideal, the analysis of what is involved in it, and the consideration of its validity; and this would practically be but a single inquiry. But it is hardly possible to limit the subject in this rigid way. There are a number of considerations which, on a strict view, might be held not properly to belong to Ethics, but which are so essential to the understanding of it that it is hardly possible to omit them from any book dealing comprehensively with the subject. The nature of these outlying considerations has been partly indicated in the foregoing chapter; but we have now to notice more precisely the way in which they tend to break up the study of Ethics into different departments.

In the first place, it is necessary to give some attention to the psychological aspects of the subject. The consideration of the nature of Feeling, Desire, Will, of the meaning and place of Motives and Intentions in the individual consciousness, of the origin and nature of conscience, of the elements contained in the moral judgment, and other problems of a similar character, is an almost indispensable preliminary to the study of the moral ideal. Again, the treatment of these psychological questions naturally leads us on to the more sociological aspects of the subject, *i. e.* to the study of the way in which the moral consciousness grows up in mankind in relation to the general development of civilization in its various aspects. These genetical inquiries lead us on to the consideration of the nature and significance of the moral ideal. But even the treatment of this is necessarily to some extent historical. It is hardly possible, at the present stage of the development of ethical study, to lay down the one view that is to be accepted as correct, without reference to the various more or less incorrect opinions that have been current in the course of ethical speculation. Having considered these and formed our view as to the general nature of the doctrine that is to be taken as true, we are then able, finally, to consider the application of this doctrine to the treatment of the concrete facts of the moral life. In this way there are at least four main divisions of the study :—(1) The Psychology of the Moral Consciousness, (2) The Sociology of the Moral Life, (3) The Theories of the Moral Standard, (4) The Application of the Standard to the treatment of the Moral Life. A part dealing with the Metaphysics of Ethics might also be added ; but this could hardly be separated from the discussion of the Theories of the Moral Standard, which, as we shall see, inevitably leads us into metaphysical considerations.

A few remarks may now be made on each of these divisions of the subject.

§ 2. THE PSYCHOLOGICAL ASPECTS OF ETHICS.—Most

of the points that fall under this head are discussed in treatises on Psychology, where they are more strictly in place. But it is found convenient in ethical works to recall some of the more important considerations on the subject of Desire and Will, in particular, and also to deal with the nature of conscience and the moral judgment, which are apt to be passed over somewhat slightly in purely psychological discussions. The bearing of such questions as that of the freedom of the Will on the moral judgment has also to be considered; and, though this is partly a metaphysical question, yet it is on the whole the psychological aspect of it that more directly concerns Ethics. It is, however, the more social aspects of Psychology with which Ethics is most intimately connected, and we are thus led to the second division of the subject.

§ **3.** THE SOCIOLOGICAL ASPECTS OF ETHICS.—The science of Sociology is still in its infancy, and it is perhaps premature to state precisely what it would contain; but we may say of it generally that it is nothing more than an extension of psychology to the consideration of the more social aspects of life. Such a consideration has reference to much that has very little bearing on Ethics. When we study the life of savage peoples, the primitive facts of language, the early religious ideas, the superstitious practices, the beginnings of law and government, our interest is directed to many points that do not much concern the rightness and wrongness of conduct. All these things, however, are modes of conduct, or tend to affect conduct; and it is possible to study them from this point of view. Also the tendency to pass judgment upon these and other forms of activity, as being right or wrong, good or evil, begins at a very early stage in the development of the human race; and the way in which this judgment grows up is one of the most interesting points in the study of Sociology. All this is hardly to be described as Ethics in the stricter sense; but it is an almost indispensable preparation for the study of ethical problems.

§ 4. The Theories of the Moral Standard.—The study of Ethics in the stricter sense commences with the consideration of the nature of the Ideal, Standard, or End, by reference to which Conduct is pronounced to be right or wrong, good or evil. Now there are several different theories on this subject; and, though some of these theories are now generally admitted to have been superseded, yet the leading types of theory cannot well be neglected, the more so as these leading types are seldom wholly erroneous, but nearly always bring out some important aspect of the subject. At the same time, the student should be warned against the common error of supposing that these controversies about the definition of the Standard, often rather futile and involving a good deal of misunderstanding on all sides, constitute the whole, or even the main part, of ethical doctrine. In order to guard against such a misconception, it is important to pass on to the consideration of the way in which ethical principles may be used in the treatment of the concrete moral life, even if the discussion of this subject is inevitably of a very summary and incomplete character.

§ 5. The Concrete Moral Life.—It will be found that the exact way in which the concrete moral life is to be handled by ethical science depends to a considerable extent on the nature of the theory which we finally adopt. If, for instance, we were to take the view that the moral standard consists in certain absolute and immutable laws which are intuitively known to every developed consciousness, the study of the concrete moral life could have little more than a historical interest. We should only be able to discover that at certain periods the nature of the moral laws has been obscured, for various reasons, from the consciousness of the majority of the human race ; and that at other times the laws, though fully recognized, have been very commonly disobeyed. These facts would be of sociological and psychological, rather than of strictly ethical interest. On the other hand, if we should be led to take the view that the moral standard consists in a certain end—say, happiness—which, though generally pursued by mankind, is not pursued consistently or wisely, it would then be possible to point out, at least in general terms, the ways in which improvements could be introduced into the concrete moral life of mankind. Rules could be laid down for the more complete and consistent adoption of the right means to the end that we have in view. Or, again, if we accepted the view that the Standard is of the nature of an Ideal that is more or less clearly present throughout the development of the human consciousness, it would then be possible for us to trace the ways in which this Ideal comes into clearness, to point out how it is illustrated in the concrete growth of the moral life, and to indicate to some extent the directions in which we may hope to see it more fully realized. According to the first of these views, the study of the concrete moral life would have hardly any ethical interest. According to the second view, the study of

Ethics would lead directly to certain practical recommendations for the remodelling of the concrete moral life. According to the third view, it would be the main business of Ethics to bring out the significance of the moral life in its concrete development, rather than to aim at its reform. Accordingly, it is not possible to decide on the precise way in which this department of the subject should be dealt with, until we have considered the nature of the moral Standard. This portion of the treatment of Ethics is sometimes called Applied Ethics.

§ 6. Plan of the Present Work.—A complete treatise on the Principles of Ethics would thus, as I conceive, fall naturally into four distinct parts—with, possibly, a fifth devoted to the development of the more metaphysical aspects of the subject. The present work, however, is only intended to serve the purpose of an introductory sketch; and the divisions which are here adopted need not be of quite so elaborate a character. As this book is intended primarily to be read by students who have already pursued a course in Psychology, the psychological aspects of the subject need not be very fully developed. As regards the sociological aspects, again, the whole science of sociology is in so undeveloped a condition that it would hardly be appropriate in an elementary Text-book to make any confident assertions about it. In a larger work various points might fittingly be discussed which in such a book as this are best omitted. Accordingly, all that is to be said about these two departments of ethical study is here compressed under the general heading of "Prolegomena, chiefly Psychological." The various theories of morals must be dealt with somewhat more fully;

but here also we must content ourselves with the broad distinctions, and leave the more minute historical details for future study. In dealing with the concrete moral life, we cannot attempt to do much more than indicate the main points which it would be important to consider in a more complete treatise. Finally, the metaphysical implications of ethical theory can only be referred to in a concluding chapter.

BOOK I.

PROLEGOMENA, CHIEFLY PSYCHOLOGICAL.

CHAPTER I.

DESIRE AND WILL.

§ 1. Introductory Remark.—The questions that concern us in this chapter are essentially psychological; and most of the points on which we have to touch will be found treated, with more or less fulness, in any psychological handbook. But it seems necessary here to bring out their ethical significance. What chiefly concerns us is the nature of those activities which are described by the terms Will, and Conduct, and the relation of these to that general condition of conscious life which is described as Character. But in order to understand these it is necessary also to say something about the relationship between Desire and Will; and it is to that point that the present chapter is to be devoted.

§ 2. General Nature of Desire.—Before we consider the way in which our desires are related to the will, it is necessary to determine precisely what we are to understand by the term desire. We must not, for instance, confound human desires with the mere appetites of an animal; and there are also several other minor distinctions which it is necessary to keep in view. We may say, generally, that nothing is an object of desire for a man unless it is consciously regarded as a good: but this remark is perhaps not very enlightening; for it would be difficult to define a *good* otherwise than as an object that is consciously desired.[1] The point is, however, that in all real desire there is some object that is consciously taken as an end. Such an object consciously taken as an end in desire is what we call a good. By defining in this way, we seem to be able to avoid going round in a circle. In order to understand this point, however, it is necessary to go more into the details of the distinction between desire and other modes of activity. We may conveniently begin with those forms of activity that are lowest in the scale of life, and pass upwards from these to the highest forms of human desire and will.

§ 3. Want and Appetite.—We may begin by distinguishing the appetite of an animal from the mere presence of an animal want. An animal want is in itself of the same nature as a vegetable want. It is a blind tendency towards particular ends, which are involved in the development of the life of the animal, just as they might be also in the life of a plant. We may say, if we like, that nature wills[2] the realization of these ends; but they are not consciously willed by the animal or plant itself. In the case of an appetite, on the other hand, there is not merely a blind tendency towards a particular end; but this tendency is to a

[1] *Cf.* Aristotle's *Ethics*, I. i. 1.: "The good is that at which all things aim."

[2] This conception is due to Aristotle. It is of course partly metaphorical, but suggests a teleological view of the world.

certain extent present to consciousness. This consciousness may appear partly in the form of a definite presentation of the kind of object that will satisfy a given want. The hungry lion may be more or less clearly aware of the nature of the object that it seeks. The plant, on the other hand, when it turns to the sunlight, may be said to have a want; but it cannot be supposed to have any consciousness of the nature of the object that will satisfy it. Even in the case of an animal appetite, however, the consciousness of the object is probably in most instances somewhat dim and vague.[1] The most prominent element in the consciousness is rather the feeling of pleasure or pain than any definite presentation of an object. An unsatisfied appetite is in itself[2] painful; whereas the satisfaction of any appetite brings with it the feeling of pleasure. These feelings form so characteristic and prominent an element in animal appetites that satisfactions of appetite are frequently referred to simply as pleasures, while unsatisfied appetites are called pains. A pleasure-seeker is generally understood to be one who seeks the satisfaction of his animal appetites, or of human impulses which are akin to these appetites. A certain confusion is thus apt to arise

1 Some psychologists (of whom I gather that Mr. Stout is one) would deny that this element is present at all.

2 It is necessary to say "in itself"; because the total effect of a consciousness of unsatisfied want is sometimes rather pleasurable than painful. Thus, moderate hunger in man, and perhaps even in animals, seems often to be rather agreeable than otherwise. The reason is probably in part that the feeling of hunger adds a pleasant stimulus to the vital energies generally, and in part that the anticipation of satisfaction is easily called up by the consciousness of want. See Note I. at the end of chap. ii.

between the satisfaction of an appetite and the agreeable feeling which accompanies it; since both are called pleasure. But with this confusion we need not at present trouble ourselves.[1] It is enough now to observe that pleasure and pain are the most prominent and characteristic features of animal appetite.[2]

§ 4. APPETITE AND DESIRE.—In the case of what is strictly called desire, there is not merely the consciousness of an object, with an accompanying feeling of pleasure and pain, but also a recognition of the object as a good, or as an element in a more or less clearly defined end.[3] The hunger of an animal is different from the mere want of nutriment in a plant; but desire for food in a man is scarcely less different from mere hunger. A man may be hungry and yet not desire food. In the desire of food there is involved, in addition to the hunger, the representation of the food as an end which it is worth while to secure. We may express this by saying that desire implies a definite *point of view*, whereas there is no such implication in a mere appetite. Hunger is to all intents the same phenomenon in the brute and in the sage; but the desires of the sage and the hero are very different from those of the savage, the miser, or the epicure. The desires of different men are determined by the total nature of the point of view which the men occupy. What they desire depends on what they like; and what

[1] See below, chap. ii., §§ 7 and 8.

[2] Appetite is, in the Aristotelian psychology, known as ἐπιθυμία. Desire is ὄρεξις. But Aristotle uses ὄρεξις in a wide sense, so as to include ἐπιθυμία. *De Anima*, II., iii. 2.

[3] For a full discussion of this point, see Green's *Prolegomena to Ethics*, Book II., chap. ii. *Cf.* also Muirhead's *Elements of Ethics*, pp. 51–2, and Dewey's *Psychology*, p. 360 *sqq.*

they like, as Mr. Ruskin is so fond of insisting, is an exact expression of what they are. Thus, while ordinary hunger or thirst tells us nothing about the character of him who feels it, the hunger and thirst after righteousness, or after power, or after fame, is a revelation of a whole point of view.[1] The desires of a person, therefore, are not an isolated phenomenon, but form an element in the totality, or, as we may say, the *universe* of his character;[2] and it is from this point of view that we must regard them, if we are to understand their full significance.

§ **5.** Universe of Desire.—What is meant by saying that the desires of a human being form part of a "universe" may be made somewhat clearer by reference to a similar conception in the science of Logic. It has become a familiar thing in Logic to speak of a "universe of discourse,"[3] as signifying the sphere of reference within which a particular statement is made. Thus a statement about "the gods" may be true with reference to the world as depicted in the Homeric poems, or to the world of Greek mythology generally, but may be false or meaningless if understood with reference to the world of ordinary fact. So too we may make statements about griffins and unicorns in the universe of heraldry, about fairies in the universe of romance, about Hamlet or King Lear in the universe of Shakespeare's plays, about Heaven and Hell and Purgatory in the universe of Dante's *Divine Comedy;* and our statements may be true within these several uni-

[1] *Cf.* Muirhead's *Elemets of Ethics*, p. 52.

[2] *Cf.* Dewey's *Psychology*, pp. 363–4.

[3] See Keynes's *Formal Logic*, pp. 137–8, Venn's *Empirical Logic*, p. 180, Welton's *Manual of Logic*, vol. i., pp. 59–60.

verses, though they would become false if taken out of the particular universe to which they belong. Now there is something quite analogous in the case of our desires. Each desire also belongs to a particular universe, and loses its meaning if we pass out of that universe into another. This universe to which a desire belongs is the universe that is constituted by the totality of what we call a man's *character*, as that character presents itself at the time at which the desire is felt. It is, in short, the universe of the man's ethical *point of view* at the moment in question. That there are great differences between such universes, is evident from the judgments that we habitually pass on the representations of human conduct in poems and novels and dramas. We are often aware that a desire which is attributed to a fictitious personage is not such a desire as a man of his general character and situation would feel, or at least not such as he would feel in such a degree as is attributed to him. It is not such a desire, in fact, as belongs to his particular universe. And the particular universe which we thus estimate, and which varies so widely with the characters of different individuals, is not even one that remains constant for the same person. We must all be aware of the different desires that dominate our minds in different moods, in different conditions, in different states of health. These differences constitute what we may call a difference of universe; and to each such universe a different set of desires, or at least a different arrangement of desires, belongs. This universe may even alter suddenly in the same individual, through some sudden transformation of conditions. It is such a change that is illustrated in the old fable of the cat which was transformed into a princess, but returned again to its proper shape on the sudden appearance of a mouse. The sudden change of condition caused her to drop at once from the universe of princess to the universe of cat. Of such transformations life is rich in instances. There is a German proverb that what one wishes in youth one has to satiety in age; but even from year to year and from day to day—sometimes even from hour to hour—we may find ourselves passing from one universe into another, where what we formerly desired becomes uninteresting, perhaps even disgusting. Any sudden change—the news of the death of a friend, the recollection of a promise, the suggestion of a moral principle, and the like—may carry us instantaneously from one world into another. This is illustrated in Shakespeare's play of *Love's Labour Lost*, where the announcement of the death of the King of France brings suddenly to a close the wit and levity of the preceding scenes, and introduces an entirely different tone. Such a change may fairly be referred to as a passage from one universe to another. Or again, such a change may be illustrated by the common transformation from a man's Sunday view of life to that which he takes during the rest of the week. Even a change of clothes suffices with some men to produce a change of universe; for it is not always entirely true that "the cowl does not make the monk."[1]

§ 6. Conflict of Desires.—In the preceding section we have assumed, for the sake of simplicity, that at

[1] On the nature of psychological universes the psychology of Herbart is particularly instructive. Reference may be made to Mr. Stout's Articles in *Mind* and to the same writer's *Analytic Psychology*, (especially chaps. VIII., IX., and X.)

any given moment an individual occupies a definite point of view, or is, so to speak, an inhabitant of a single universe. In reality, however, the content of an individual's consciousness is not so simple. There are nearly always several points of view present to a given individual at a given moment; or, at any rate, several points of view alternate with one another so rapidly, that they may practically be regarded as present together. A statesman, for instance, may be influenced in his conduct by motives derived from many different universes. He may occupy the universe which is constituted by the consideration of the good of his country; and from this point of view he may strongly desire to see certain measures carried out. But at the same time he may be not uninfluenced by considerations drawn from very different universes. He may occupy also a universe constituted by his own personal ambition, by the welfare of his family, by the wishes of his constituency, by a view of duty to the world (as distinguished from his own country), perhaps also by religious considerations. He may occupy alternately, and almost simultaneously, all these different points of view; and very various desires may arise in his mind in consequence. It is probable that some of these desires will conflict with others. From one point of view he may desire peace, from another war: from one point of view he may set his heart on liberty, from another on order. It then comes to be a question which of these ends the man will finally choose. Now it is often said that in such cases a man will naturally, or even necessarily, be influenced by the strongest desire or motive. But it must be observed that this mode of statement is misleading. It implies that a desire is an isolated thing; whereas in reality it forms part of a universe or system. Consequently, the real strength of a desire does not depend on its own individual liveliness or force, but rather on the force of the universe or system to which it belongs. Thus a man might be strongly desirous of war from a feeling of hatred towards a foreign power. But if the man were of such a character that the sense of duty was more dominant in him than the feeling of personal hatred, he might decide for peace, though the desire for peace in itself did not strongly influence him. The latter desire would conquer, not because it was in itself the stronger, but because it formed a part of a stronger universe or system.[1] Of course a strong desire gives strength to the universe to which it belongs; but the final triumph of a desire depends not on its own individual dominance, but on the dominance of its universe. How in particular individuals one universe comes to be dominant rather than another, is a question rather for Psychology than for Ethics. In so far as it concerns Ethics, it will be touched upon in some future sections of this book.[2] In the meantime, what it is important to note is merely that a desire is not an isolated phenomenon but a part of a system; and that consequently a conflict of desires is in reality a conflict between two or more universes of desire.[3]

[1] *Cf.* Green's *Prolegomena to Ethics*, Book II., chap. i., § 105, p. 108.

[2] See, for instance, Book III., chap. vi.

[3] *Cf.* Dewey's *Psychology*, pp. 364–5: "It is important to notice that it is a strife or conflict which goes on in the man himself; *it is a conflict of himself with himself* [*i. e.*, in our language, a conflict of him self as one universe with himself as another universe]; it is not a conflict of himself with something external to him, nor of one impulse with another impulse, he meanwhile remaining a passive spectator

§ 7. Desire and Wish.—The terms "desire" and "wish" are frequently used as synonymous; but there is a slight difference in the usage of the terms, and it seems desirable to employ them in Ethics in distinct senses. We may say briefly that a wish is an effective desire. The meaning of this will be more apparent when it is considered in relation to what has just been said with regard to universes of desire and the conflict between them. It has been stated that any given desire belongs to a system or universe, and that various such systems may exist simultaneously and come into conflict with one another. When such conflicts occur, certain desires predominate over others; some are subordinated or sink into abeyance. Now it may be convenient to limit the term "wish" to those desires that predominate or continue to be effective. A hungry man may be said to have a desire for food; but this desire may be dominant only within the universe of animal inclination. The desire may be kept in abeyance by a sense of religious obligation, by devotion to work, or by some overmastering passion. In such cases we may say that the man no longer *wishes* for food, though a desire for food continues to exist in his consciousness as an element in a subordinate universe —held, as it were, in leash. A desire, then, which

awaiting the conclusion of the struggle. What gives the conflict of desires its whole meaning is that it represents the man at strife with himself. He is the opposing contestants as well as the battle-field." This last expression was no doubt suggested to Prof. Dewey by a very striking passage in Hegel's *Philosophy of Religion* (I. 64), in which he says: "I am not one of the combatants, but rather both of the combatants and also the combat itself"; or, as Principal Caird renders it (*Philosophy of Religion*, chap. ix., p. 262): "I am at once the combatants and the conflict and the field that is torn with the strife."

has become ineffective, is not to be described as a wish.[1]

§ 8. Wish and Will.—If it is important to distinguish an effective wish from a mere latent desire, it is still more important to distinguish a wish from a definite act of will. It might seem at first that if a wish is a dominant desire it must always issue in will. But this is not the case. The reason is that a wish is often of an abstract character, directed towards some single element in a concrete event, without reference to the accompanying circumstances. In order, on the other hand, that an event may be willed, it has to be accepted in its concrete totality. When Lady Anne, in Shakespeare's *King Richard III.*, says to the Duke of Gloucester,

> "Though I wish thy death,
> I will not be the executioner,"

the contrast between wish and will is well brought out. The wish for the death is a mere abstract wish, since it does not include the means by which the death might be brought about.[2] On the other hand, when a total concrete effect is willed, it may include many elements

[1] I use the term wish, it will be observed, in a sense almost corresponding to the Aristotelian βούλησις (as distinguished from ὄρεξις). See, for instance, *De Anima*, III., ix. 3, III., x. 3, &c. E. Wallace translates βούλησις "settled wish." It should be observed, however, that "wish" is not always understood in this way by Psychologists. Often no distinction is drawn between Desire and Wish; and when a distinction is drawn, it is frequently drawn in a different way (sometimes almost in the opposite way).

[2] Often, of course, the means are entirely beyond our power. Thus, we may wish for a change of weather, or to live some part of our past lives over again. Here the wish cannot pass into will, because, as soon as we think of the means, we see that they are out of reach.

that are not in themselves wished, and even elements to which the agent's wishes are strenuously opposed. This also may be illustrated from Shakespeare. When the apothecary, in *Romeo and Juliet,* says to Romeo, on agreeing to sell him the poison,

> "My poverty, but not my will, consents,"[1]

what he means is evidently that his *wish* does not consent. He does will the sale of the poison—he accepts that concrete act—but he wishes it were not necessary for him to do so. The dominant single desire, we may say, is opposed to the sale of the poison (*i. e.* if we assume that the apothecary was honest in his declaration) ; but the dominant universe of desire is that which is constituted by his poverty, and by this he is led to will the sale. Briefly, then, we may say that a wish is a dominant single desire ; whereas the will depends on the dominance of a universe of desire.[2]

§ 9. WILL AND ACT.—Another important distinction is that between the mere Will (*i. e.* the mere *intention, purpose,* or *resolution*) and the carrying of it into act. A resolution has always reference to something that is more or less future. Sometimes it refers to the *immediate* future, and is carried into effect at once. At other times it refers to the *remote* future, and remains in abeyance till the proper time arrives. In the latter case the purpose may never be carried into effect at all. An intention or resolution is always something more than a mere wish : it is the definite acceptance of a

[1] This passage is discussed in Green's *Prolegomena to Ethics,* § 143, p. 148. "The will," Green says, "is only the strong competing wish which does not suffice to determine action."

[2] This use of the term will seems to correspond pretty closely to the Aristotelian προαίρεσις.

concrete event as an object to be aimed at. But if this event is remote, the purpose may lie within one universe and the carrying of it out within another. When the time for action comes, the conditions may have changed. At the lowest there will be this change, that what was formerly presented merely in anticipative imagination is now presented as an actual fact. To resolve to make a confession, for instance, is one thing: actually to make it, in the presence of those to whom it has to be made, is often a very different thing. In the former case the accompanying circumstances are only presented in an imaginative and partly symbolic way: in the latter case they are actually present to sense. Now, the actual facts may not correspond to the anticipation. Those to whom the confession was to be made, for instance, may be found to be in a different mood from what was expected. And even if the anticipation proves substantially correct, still, in the actual presentation we may be impressed by accessory circumstances of which we had not taken any particular account. The man who resolves to get up at an early hour may not have thought particularly about the coldness of the morning air, or about the pleasantness of lying in bed; whereas, when the time comes, these may be among the most impressive circumstances. Or, again, when Lady Macbeth intended to murder Duncan, it did not occur to her that he might resemble her father. So, too, when Hamlet resolved to carry out the behests of the Ghost, he did not think of all the doubts that might suggest themselves to his mind after the Ghost had vanished. Thus "enterprises of great pith and moment," as well as more insignificant designs, may be frustrated by a change of universe; and the "best intentions," or the worst, may lead to nothing.[1] This is especially true when the purpose is one that carries great consequences in its train, involving perhaps a complete change of the world within which we have been living. In such a case the changed world cannot be with any completeness imagined, and some very small circumstance may easily give a completely new turn to our thoughts. The "insurrection"[2] by which the universe within which we are living is to be overthrown cannot be at once carried out, and we cannot with any thoroughness think ourselves into the new conditions that are to arise. Thus a mere resolution is still far from being an *act.*[3] What is commonly called "force of will" means the power of carrying resolutions into act. This power depends largely on the habit of fixing our attention upon the salient features of an object that is aimed at, and not allowing ourselves to be distracted by subordinate conditions. Hence, narrow-minded or hard-hearted men have often more "force of will," in this sense, than those who take wider views. But a wide-minded man may also acquire "force of will" by taking a clear and decided view of the circumstances

[1] *Cf.* below, Book III., chap. vi., § 3.

[2] *Cf.* Shakespeare's *Julius Cæsar,* Act II., scene i., ll. 63 *sqq.*

> "Between the acting of a dreadful thing
> And the first motion, all the interim is
> Like a phantasma, or a hideous dream:
> The Genius and the mortal instruments
> Are then in council; and the State of man,
> Like to a little kingdom, suffers then
> The nature of an insurrection."

[3] For an admirable summary of the elements involved in an act of will, see Muirhead's *Elements of Ethics,* pp. 48–50.

that are important, and thus eliminating insignificant details.

§ **10.** THE MEANING OF PURPOSE.—When Will is regarded in relation to the end at which it aims, it is called Purpose. This term, however, is sometimes used also to describe the end itself, rather than the fact of aiming at an end. Purpose should be carefully distinguished from those tendencies to action which accompany appetite, desire, and wish. Action based on appetite is generally described as impulsive; but this term is sometimes used also with reference to actions that issue from desire. We may use the terms Blind Impulse and Conscious Impulse to mark the distinction. The tendency of a wish, again, to issue in action is most properly described by the term Inclination. When we are *inclined* to do anything, we are not merely conscious of an impulse to do it, but we to a certain extent approve the impulse; though it may be that, on reflection, we may *resolve* not to follow it. A Purpose or Resolution is thus distinguished from an Impulse (whether Blind or Conscious) and from an Inclination.

§ **11.** WILL AND CHARACTER.—"A character," said Novalis, "is a completely fashioned will." Character may be said, in the language we have just been using, to consist in the continuous dominance of a definite universe. A man of good character is one in whom the universe of duty habitually predominates. A miser is one in whom the dominant universe is that which is constituted by the love of money. A fanatic is one in whom some particular universe is so entirely dominant as to shut out entirely other important points of view. And in like manner all other kinds of character may be described by reference to the nature of the universe that is dominant in them. When Pope said that "Most women have no characters at all," he meant that the universes of desire in which they live are so continually varying that no one of them can be said to be habitually dominant. And certainly it is the case that most men, as well as most women, cannot be accounted for by so simple an explanation as the exclusive dominance of such "ruling passions" as Pope dealt with. In the case of most actual human beings what we have is not so much any one universe that decidedly predominates as a number of universes that stand to one another in certain definite relations. The different relations in which they stand to one another constitute the differences of character. How it comes that now one, and now another, predominates, is, as we have already remarked, a question rather for Psychology than for Ethics. The habitual modes of action that accompany a formed character are described by the term Conduct. The meaning of this we shall have to discuss almost immediately.[1]

[1] Mr. Stout's article on "Voluntary Action" (*Mind*, New Series, Vol. V., no. 19) will be found in the highest degree instructive on several of the points referred to in this chapter, as well as on some of those that are dealt with in the following chapters. See also the closing chapter of his *Manual of Psychology*.

CHAPTER II.

MOTIVE AND INTENTION.

§ **1.** Preliminary Remarks.—So far we have been considering the general nature of the relationship between Desire and Will. It is now necessary that we should direct our attention to the nature of the end involved in Volition; and, in particular, that we should consider the important distinction between an Intention and a Motive. This is a point on which a good deal of discussion has turned; and, owing to the great difficulties that are involved in it, it is a point that requires very careful study. First, then, we must try to understand exactly what Intention and Motive mean.

§ **2.** The Meaning of Intention.—The term Intention corresponds pretty closely to the term Purpose. Indeed, they are sometimes used as synonymous. But Purpose seems to refer rather to the mental activity, and Intention to the end towards which the mental activity is directed. Intention, understood in this sense, means anything which we purpose to bring about. Now what we thus purpose is often a very complicated result. We may aim at some external end, *i. e.* at the accomplishment of some change in the physical world—*e. g.* the building of a house; or in the social system within which we live—

e. g. the overthrow of a government; or, again, we may aim at the bringing about of some state of our own minds, or at the realization of some principle. Some distinctions between different kinds of Intention may help to make this clear.

In the first place, we may distinguish between the *immediate* and the *remote* intentions of an act. Thus, two men may both have the immediate intention of saving a third from drowning; but the one may wish to save him from drowning simply in order that his life may be preserved, whereas the other may wish to save him from drowning in order that he may be reserved for hanging.[1] In this case, while the immediate intentions are the same, the remote intentions are very different. The remote intention of an act is sometimes called the motive; but this use of the term seems to be incorrect.

In the second place, we may distinguish between the *outer* and the *inner* intention of an act. This may be illustrated by the familiar story of Abraham Lincoln and the pig that he helped out of a ditch. On being praised for this action, Lincoln is said to have replied that he did it, not for the sake of the pig, but rather on his own account, in order to rid his mind of the uncomfortable thought of the animal's distress. Here the outer intention was to rescue the animal, while the inner intention was to remove an uncomfortable feeling from the mind. The inner intention, in this instance, is evidently only a particular case of the remote intention; but it is not so in every instance. Thus if a man were to endeavour to produce

[1] *Cf.* Mill's *Utilitarianism*, chap. ii. p. 27, *note*.

a certain feeling in his mind—say, of penitence or of faith—with the view of securing the favour of Heaven, the immediate intention would be an inner one, while the remote intention would be outer. The inner intention of an act, like the remote intention, is sometimes apt to be confounded with the motive.

In the third place, we may distinguish between the *direct* and the *indirect* intention of an act. If a Nihilist seeks to blow up a train containing an Emperor and others,[1] his direct intention may be simply the destruction of the Emperor, but indirectly also he intends the destruction of the others who are in the train, since he is aware that their destruction will be necessarily included along with that of the Emperor.

In the fourth place, we may distinguish between the *conscious* and the *unconscious* intention of an act. To what extent any intention can be unconscious, is a question for psychology. By an unconscious intention is here understood simply an intention which the agent does not definitely avow to himself. A man's conduct is often in reality profoundly influenced by such intentions. Thus the intention which he avows to himself may be that of promoting the well-being of mankind, while in reality he may be much more strongly influenced by that of advancing his own reputation.

In the fifth place, we may distinguish between the *formal* and the *material* intention of an act. The material intention means the particular result as a realized fact; the formal intention means the principle embodied in the fact. Two men may both aim at the

[1] *Cf.* Sidgwick's *Methods of Ethics*, Book III., chap. i., § 2 (p. 202, note 2).

overthrow of a particular government. Their material intentions are in that case the same. But the one may aim at its overthrow because he thinks it too progressive, the other because he thinks it too conservative. The intentions of the two men are in this case very different formally, though their actions (which may consist simply in the giving of a vote) may be materially the same.

These distinctions are given here, not as being an exhaustive list, but simply with the view of bringing out the complications that may be involved in a purpose. It is important to bring them out, since, otherwise, the relation between motive and intention can hardly be explained.

Summing up, then, we may say, that an intention, in the broadest sense of the term, means any aim that is definitely adopted as an object of will; and that such intentions may be of various distinct kinds.

§ 3. MEANING OF MOTIVE.—The term "motive" is not less ambiguous than "intention." The motive means, of course, what *moves* us or *causes* us to act in a particular way. Now there is an ambiguity in the term "cause." A cause may be either efficient or final. The efficient cause of a man's movements, for instance, is the action of certain nerves, muscles, &c.; the final cause is the desired end, the reaching of a destination or the production of a result. There is a similar ambiguity in the use of the term "motive."[1] A motive may be understood to mean either that which *impels* or that which *induces* us to act in a particular way.

In the former sense, we say that we are moved by

[1] *Cf.* Muirhead's *Elements of Ethics*, pp. 58–60.

feeling or emotion. Thus we say that a man's motive was anger, or jealousy, or fear, or pity, or pleasure, or pain. Some writers[1] have even maintained that pleasure and pain are the only ultimate motives. This view we shall shortly require to consider. In the meantime we have simply to remark that it is no doubt true that men are sometimes moved to action by feeling. In conduct on which a moral judgment can be passed, however, a man is never solely moved by feeling. If a man is entirely "carried away" by feeling—by anger or fear, for instance—he cannot properly be said to *act* at all, any more than a stone acts when a man throws it at an object. We may judge the *character* of a man who is carried away by feeling or passion: we may say that he ought not to have allowed himself to be so carried away; but if he is entirely mastered by his passion, we cannot pass a moral judgment on his act, any more than on the act of a madman, or one who is drunk. Moral activity or conduct is purposeful action; and action with a purpose is not simply moved by feeling: it is moved rather by the thought of some end to be attained. This leads us to the second, and more correct, sense in which the term "motive" may be used.

The distinction may be made clear by considering the case of a man who is "moved by pity" to give assistance to a fellow-creature in distress. The mere feeling of pity is evidently not sufficient to move us to action. It may serve as an element in the efficient cause of action—*i. e.* the man who has a keen sense of pity may be more readily impelled to action than the one whose feeling is comparatively blunt. But the

[1] *E. g.* Bentham.

feeling itself is not a sufficient *inducement* to action. By itself, it moves at the utmost to tears—as, for instance, in the theatre, when we witness imaginary distresses. When a man is moved to action, he must have, besides the mere feeling, the conception of an end to be attained. He perceives a fellow-creature, for instance, in a wretched plight, and sees that, by a certain effort, the man might be put in a more favourable position. The putting of the man in this more favourable position presents itself to his mind as a desirable end; and the thought of this desirable end induces him to act in a particular way. If he feels pity, in addition, this may impel him the more readily to such an action; but the feeling of pity is not, by itself, the inducement to the action, *i. e.* the motive in the more correct sense. The motive, that which induces us to act, is the thought of a desirable end.[1]

§ 4. Relation between Motives and Intentions.—

[1] So also when, in Goldsmith's ballad,

> "The dog, to gain some private ends,
> Went mad, and bit the man,"

the motive was constituted by the gaining of some private ends, not by the mere madness. *Cf.* Tucker's *Light of Nature*, chap. v. The view of Motive given above seems to be essentially that of Aristotle, when he says (*De Anima*, III. x. 4) ἀεὶ κινεῖ τὸ ὀρεκτόν ("it is always the desired object that moves to action"). Some writers, however, still object to this use of the term. See, for instance, the discussions in the *International Journal of Ethics*, Vol. IV., Nos. 1 and 2. Professor Ritchie maintains there (p. 236) that "'desire' is the genus of which 'motive' is a species. The differentia of 'motive' is the presence of a conception of an end." But surely this must be erroneous. Surely *all* desire involves a conception of an end. It is right to add that the term "motive" seems originally to have been used for any efficient cause of movement. It appears to be used in this way in Shakespeare's description of Cressida—

From what has now been said, it is evident that the relation between motives and intentions is a very close one. The motive of our act is that which induces us to perform it. Now it is evident that this must be included in the intention, in the broadest sense of that term, but need not be, and generally will not be, identical with the whole of it.[1] What induces us to perform an act is always something that we hope to achieve by it;[2] but there may be much that we expect to achieve by it (and even that we consciously *intend* to achieve by it) which would not serve as an inducement to its performance, and which might even serve as an inducement not to perform it. The motive of a reformer may be partly that of improving the state of mankind and partly that of acquiring fame for himself. Both of these ends form part of his intention, in the widest sense of the term. But he may also be well aware that the result of his action will be, for a time, "not to send peace on the earth, but a sword." He may anticipate a certain amount of confusion and misery as the immediate result of his action, and perhaps also of persecution for himself. If he clearly

"Her wanton spirits look out
At every joint and motive of her body."

But here, as in so many other cases, the meaning of the word has been gradually modified, partly to suit the conveniences of ordinary life, and partly to meet the requirements of science.

1 *Cf.* Muirhead's *Elements of Ethics*, p. 61. When Prof. Dewey (*Outlines of Ethics*, p. 9) says that "the foreseen, the *ideal* consequences are the end of the act, and as such form the motive," he appears to identify the motive with the whole intention. This seems to me to be erroneous, or at least to be an inconvenient use of the term. For the meaning of "ideal" in this phrase of Prof. Dewey's, see above, Introduction, chap. ii., § 5, *note*.

2 Except of course when we are impelled by mere feeling or passion.

foresees that these results will ensue on his action, it can scarcely be said that he does not intend them. He deliberately accepts them as being inevitably involved in the good result which he hopes to achieve. But assuredly we may say that these evil consequences form no part of his motive in endeavouring to achieve the good result. Or, to take a still simpler case, when Brutus helped to kill Cæsar, in order to save his country,[1] he certainly intended to kill Cæsar, but the killing of Cæsar was no part of his motive.

The motive of an act, then, is a part of the intention, in the broadest sense of that term, but does not necessarily include the whole of the intention. Adopting the distinctions that have been drawn in section 2, we may say that the motive generally includes the greater part of the remote intention, but frequently does not include much of the immediate intention; that it generally includes the direct intention, but not the indirect; that it nearly always includes the formal intention, but often not much of the material intention; and that it may be either outer or inner, conscious or unconscious.

§ 5. IS THE MOTIVE ALWAYS PLEASURE?—We are now in a position to deal with the question, to which allusion has already been made, whether the motive to action is always pleasure. This question must be carefully distinguished, at the outset, from the question whether pleasure is always involved in the presentation of any motive. This distinction has been expressed as that between *taking pleasure in an idea* and *aiming*

[1] Assuming the view taken by Plutarch and Shakespeare to be correct. For a different view of Brutus, see Froude's *Cæsar*.

at the idea of pleasure. It is probably true that everything at which we aim is thought of as pleasant. We take pleasure in the idea of accomplishing our end. To say this is obviously a very different thing from saying that the idea of pleasure is the end at which we aim, or that pleasure is always that which serves as the inducement to action.[1] The former view would be generally accepted by all psychologists; the latter is the doctrine of those who are known as Psychological Hedonists. This doctrine is expressed, for instance, in the following passage from Bentham.[2] "Nature has placed man under the empire of *pleasure* and of *pain*. We owe to them all our ideas; we refer to them all our judgments, and all the determinations of our life. He who pretends to withdraw himself from this subjection knows not what he says. His only object is to seek pleasure and to shun pain, even at the very instant that he rejects the greatest pleasures or embraces pains the most acute. These eternal and irresistible sentiments ought to be the great study of the moralist and the legislator. The *principle of utility* subjects everything to these two motives." Here we have a clear statement of the view that pleasure and pain are the only possible motives to action, the only ends at which we can aim. This is the view that we have now to consider.

§ **6.** Psychological Hedonism.—Psychological Hedonism is the theory that the ultimate object of desire is pleasure. The best known exponent of this doctrine

[1] It is probably true, as Mr. Bradley has urged, that the idea of pleasure is always pleasant (see *Mind*, New Series, Vol. IV, no. 14). But this does not affect the present point.

[2] *Principles of Legislation*, chap. I.

is John Stuart Mill.[1] In the fourth chapter of his book on *Utilitarianism* he reasons in the following way. "And now to decide whether this is really so; whether mankind do desire nothing for itself but that which is a pleasure to them, or of which the absence is a pain; we have evidently arrived at a question of fact and experience, dependent, like all similar questions, upon evidence. It can only be determined by practised self-consciousness and self-observation, assisted by observation of others. I believe that these sources of evidence, impartially consulted, will declare that desiring a thing and finding it pleasant, aversion to it and thinking of it as painful, are phenomena entirely inseparable, or rather two parts of the same phenomenon; in strictness of language, two different modes of naming the same psychological fact: that to think of an object as desirable (except for the sake of its consequences), and to think of it as pleasant, are one and the same thing; and that to desire anything, except in proportion as the idea of it is pleasant, is a physical and metaphysical impossibility." This passage has been well criticised by Dr. Sidgwick in his *Methods of Ethics* (Book I., chap. iv.). He says—"Mill explains that 'desiring a thing and finding it pleasant, are, in strict-

[1] Nearly all Hedonists, however, especially egoistic Hedonists, have with more or less clearness adopted this position. For a general historical exposition of the Hedonistic point of view, the student may be referred to Lecky's *History of European Morals*, chap. i., and Watson's *Hedonistic Theories, from Aristippus to Spencer*. The chief living exponent of psychological Hedonism is Professor Bain. See his *Mental and Moral Science*, Book IV., chap. iv., and *The Emotions and the Will*, "The Will," chap. viii. Dr. Bain, however, admits that it is possible, "for moments," to aim at other things than pleasure. On the general meaning of Hedonism and its chief varieties, see below, Book II., chap. iv., §§ 1–4.

ness of language, two modes of naming the same psychological fact.' If this be the case, it is hard to see how the proposition we are discussing requires to be determined by 'practised self-consciousness and self-observation;' as the denial of it would involve a contradiction in terms. The truth is that there is an ambiguity in the word Pleasure, which has always tended seriously to confuse the discussion of this question. When we speak of a man doing something at his own 'pleasure,' or as he 'pleases,' we usually signify the mere fact of choice or preference; the mere determination of the will in a certain direction. Now, if by 'pleasant' we mean that which influences choice, exercises a certain attractive force on the will, it is an assertion incontrovertible because tautological, to say that we desire what is pleasant—or even that we desire a thing in proportion as it appears pleasant." This would mean simply that we desire it in proportion as we desire it; because "appears pleasant" means simply "is desired by us." But, as Dr. Sidgwick goes on to say, if we understand "pleasure" in a more exact sense, it is not obvious that what we desire is always pleasure. If we take pleasure to mean the agreeable feeling which attends the satisfaction of our wants, it is not by any means evident that this is always what we desire. On the contrary, it seems evident rather that this is *not* always what we desire.

§ 7. THE OBJECT OF DESIRE. (1) *The Paradox of Hedonism.*—In the part of the *Methods of Ethics* to which reference has just been made, Dr. Sidgwick goes on to argue that in fact what we desire is very frequently some objective end, and not the accompanying pleasure. He points out that even when we do desire pleasure, the best way to *get* it is often to *forget* it. If we think about the pleasure itself, we are almost sure to miss it; whereas if we direct our desires towards objective ends, the pleasure comes of itself. This is not true of all pleasures. It is true chiefly of the "pleasures of pursuit."[1] "Take, for example," says Dr. Sidgwick, "the case of any game which involves—as most games do—a contest for victory. No ordinary player before entering on such a contest, has any desire for victory in it: indeed he often finds it difficult to imagine himself deriving gratification from such victory, before he has actually engaged in the competition. What he deliberately, before the game begins, desires, is not victory, but the pleasant excitement of the struggle for it; only for the full development of this pleasure a transient desire to win the game is generally indispensable. This desire, which does not exist at first, is stimulated to considerable intensity by the competition itself." "A certain degree of disinterestedness seems to be necessary in order to obtain full enjoyment. A man who maintains throughout an epicurean mood, fixing his aim on his own pleasure, does not catch the full spirit of the chase; his eagerness never gets just the sharpness of edge which imparts to the pleasure its highest zest. Here comes into view what we may call the fundamental paradox of Hedonism, that the impulse towards pleasure, if too predominant, defeats its own aim. This effect is not visible, or at any rate is scarcely visible, in the case of passive sensual pleasures. But of our active enjoyments generally . . . . it may certainly be said that

[1] See the Note at the end of this chapter.

we cannot attain them, at least in their highest degree, so long as we concentrate our aim on them." "Similarly, the pleasures of thought and study can only be enjoyed in the highest degree by those who have an ardour of curiosity which carries the mind temporarily away from self and its sensations. In all kinds of Art, again, the exercise of the creative faculty is attended by intense and exquisite pleasures; but in order to get them, one must forget them." This "paradox of Hedonism," that in order to get pleasure it is necessary to seek something else, was to some extent recognized even by Mill; but he does not seem to have perceived that it is inconsistent with the view that desire is always directed towards pleasure. Desire can evidently be, at least temporarily, directed not towards pleasure, but towards certain objective ends.

§ **8**. THE OBJECT OF DESIRE. (2) *Wants prior to Satisfactions.*—We must next notice another point, which was brought out chiefly by Butler[1] and Hutcheson, though some subsequent writers have ignored it—*viz.* that many kinds of pleasure would not exist at all, if they were not preceded by certain desires for objects. Take, for instance, the pleasures of the benevolent affections. No one could possibly feel these pleasures unless he were first benevolent—*i. e.* had a desire for the welfare of others. In such a case, therefore, the very existence of the pleasure depends on the fact that desire is first directed towards something other than pleasure. It might even be argued that this is the case

[1] See Sidgwick's *History of Ethics*, p. 192; and *cf.* Green's edition of Hume, vol. ii., Introd., p. 26, Green's *Prolegomena to Ethics*, § 161, p. 167, Caird's *Critical Philosophy of Kant*, vol. ii., p. 230, *note.*

with all pleasures. Pleasure ensues upon the satisfaction of certain wants, and the wants must be prior to the satisfactions. We have a "disinterested" desire for food, before we can have a desire for the pleasure that accompanies the taking of food. From this consideration also it appears that there are some desires which are not desires for pleasure.

§ 9. THE OBJECT OF DESIRE. (3) *Pleasures and Pleasure.* At the same time it must be allowed that there is a certain plausibility in Mill's statements, and we must endeavour to account for this plausibility. It seems to arise from an ambiguity[1] in the word "pleasure." Pleasure is sometimes understood to mean agreeable *feeling*, or the feeling of satisfaction, and sometimes it is understood to mean an *object* that gives satisfaction. The hearing of music is sometimes said to be a pleasure: but of course the hearing of music is not a feeling of satisfaction; it is an object that gives satisfaction. Generally it may be observed that when we speak of "pleasures" in the plural, or rather in the concrete, we mean objects that give satisfaction; whereas when we speak of "pleasure" in the abstract we more often mean the feeling of satisfaction which such objects bring with them.[2] But this is not always the case.

Perhaps this distinction is more obvious in the case of pain than in the case of pleasure. Pain is generally understood as the negative of pleasure, *i. e.* as meaning disagreeable feeling, or feeling of dissatisfaction. But

[1] A *second* ambiguity. Another ambiguity, pointed out by Dr. Sidgwick, has been already referred to above.

[2] *Cf.* Dr. Ward's article on "Psychology" in the *Encyclopædia Britannica*, p. 71.

when we speak of "pains" we usually mean objects that produce a disagreeable feeling; and indeed we usually mean objects of a definite kind—*viz.* organic sensations. The pain of toothache, for instance, is not merely a feeling of disagreeableness or dissatisfaction, but a definite sensation. That sensation is an object, and it is an object which brings with it a feeling of disagreeableness. The sensation of burning is another object; the sensation of a stunning blow is another object; the consciousness of having acted wrongly is another object. All these objects bring with them a disagreeable feeling; but in all of them the object which brings the disagreeable feeling, or is accompanied by the disagreeable feeling, is quite distinguishable from the feeling of disagreeableness itself.[1]

Now when it is said that what we desire is always pleasure, what seems to be meant is that what we desire is always some object the attainment of which is accompanied by an agreeable feeling. But this is so true that it is almost a tautology. It is clear that if we desire anything, the attainment of it will bring at least a temporary satisfaction; and this satisfaction will be accompanied by a feeling of satisfaction—*i. e.* pleasure. Consequently, anything that we desire may be said to be a pleasure—*i. e.* something that will bring pleasure when attained. The man who desires the overthrow

[1] Külpe and Titchener *(Outline of Psychology)* are honourably distinguished among psychologists by the care with which they have distinguished between pain and unpleasantness. Organic pain seems to be a distinct sensation in quite the same sense in which a sweet taste or smell is a distinct sensation. The feeling or affection of pleasure and pain, though perhaps inseparable from these experiences, can be distinguished from them quite clearly.

of a political party, for instance, will be pleased if that event happens. We may consequently say that the overthrow of the party was a pleasure. It is in this sense that we use the phrase "an unexpected pleasure," and the like. But evidently the overthrow of a political party is not itself an agreeable feeling; it only brings an agreeable feeling with it. The fact that we desire *pleasures* is no evidence that we desire *pleasure.*

A passage from Mill may help to make this clear. "What, for example," he asks,[1] "shall we say of the love of money? There is nothing originally more desirable about money than about any heap of glittering pebbles. Its worth is solely that of the things which it will buy; the desires for other things than itself, which it is a means of gratifying. Yet the love of money is not only one of the strongest moving forces of human life, but money is, in many cases, desired in and for itself; the desire to possess it is often stronger than the desire to use it, and goes on increasing when all the desires which point to ends beyond it, to be compassed by it, are falling off. It may be then said truly, that money is desired not for the sake of an end, but as part of the end. From being a means to happiness, it has come to be itself a principal ingredient of the individual's conception of happiness. The same may be said of the majority of the great objects of human life—power, for example, or fame. . . . The strongest attraction, both of power and of fame, is the immense aid they give to the attainment of our other wishes; and it is the strong association thus generated between them and all our objects of desire, which gives

[1] *Utilitarianism*, chap. iv.

to the direct desire of them the intensity it often assumes, so as in some characters to surpass in strength all other desires. In these cases the means have become a part of the end, and a more important part of it than any of the things which they are means to. What was once desired as an instrument for the attainment of happiness, has come to be desired for its own sake. In being desired for its own sake it is, however, desired as *part* of happiness. . . . The desire of it is not a different thing from the desire of happiness, any more than the love of music, or the desire of health. They are included in happiness. They are some of the elements of which the desire of happiness is made up. Happiness is not an abstract idea, but a concrete whole; and these are some of its parts." The meaning of all this seems quite clear. Evidently money, power, fame, music, and health are not parts of agreeable feeling. What Mill means is that they are parts of that totality of objects which *gives* agreeable feeling. That we desire such objects, then, may show that we seek *pleasures*, but not that we seek *pleasure*. And that we seek pleasures is a mere tautology. It means simply that we seek what we seek.

§ **10.** Can Reason serve as a Motive?—Even those writers who have not committed themselves to the view that pleasure and pain are the only possible motives, have sometimes been inclined to argue that at least Reason is not capable of serving as a motive to action. This view was most clearly stated by Hume, when he said[1] that "Reason is, and ought only to be, the slave of the passions, and can never pretend to any other

1 *Treatise of Human Nature*, Book II., Part III., Section III. *Cf.* also *Dissertation on the Passions*, Section V.

office than to serve and obey them." The term Passion, as here used, is practically synonymous with Impulse; and the meaning of the statement is that all actions depend on particular impulses, while reason can at the most only indicate the means by which these impulses may be gratified. Reason, it is thus held, cannot form any new motive for us: it can only show how an existing motive may be pursued to the best advantage. This view, however, seems to rest on that false conception of the nature of desire to which reference has already been made. It proceeds on the supposition that our mental constitution is made up of a number of isolated and independent desires, among which reason works as a separate faculty. If we recognise that our desires form a universe, then they cannot be said to exist independently. The problem then is to understand the nature of the whole within which particular desires emerge. If that whole is a rational system, the desires which grow up in it will be very different from those desires that might exist in a being in whom reason is not yet developed. In this sense, therefore, reason may be said not only to guide our desires, impulses, or passions, but actually to constitute their determinate nature. Reason, that is to say, may set before us ends or motives which for an irrational being would not exist at all. In this sense, then, reason is capable of furnishing us with motives to action.

§ **11.** Is Reason the only Motive?—There is, however, an error of an opposite kind against which also we must be on our guard, though no doubt it is one into which, in modern times, we are in much less danger of falling. We must not suppose that *all* motives are rational motives, *i. e.* that the inducement to act is always for a human being what it would be if he were guided entirely by reason. This view may be better understood by a reference to the doctrine of Socrates. Socrates maintained that "virtue is knowledge," by which he meant that if we knew with perfect clearness what the nature of the moral end is we should inevitably pursue it. Now it is no doubt true that within a completely rational universe the supreme good would serve as the supreme inducement. But if it is possible that a man may know the nature of the supreme good and yet not occupy a completely rational universe, then it is possible to know the good and not to pursue it. Now it seems clear at least that it is possible to know what is good with a very tolerable degree of clearness, and yet not pursue it. This is expressed in the familiar saying, "Video meliora proboque, deteriora sequor." The reason of this is that the motive to action is not always completely rational.

§ **12.** HOW MOTIVES ARE CONSTITUTED.—The conclusion, therefore, to which we are led is that motives are neither constituted simply by pleasure and pain, nor simply by dominant desires, passions, or impulses, nor simply by reason, but that they depend upon the nature of the universe within which they emerge. A motive, we may say generally, is an end which is in harmony or conformity with the universe within which it is presented. At any given moment in our lives there are various possible ends which we may set before ourselves. There are various ways in which the content of our world might be changed, so as to be more in harmony with the system of our consciousness. Now, in so far as any such change presents itself to us as something which could be brought about by our own activity, it presents itself to us as a possible motive to action. Whether it will actually move us to act depends on the question whether the motive presented to us is compatible with other possible motives which are presented to us at the same time. The line of action that is finally willed by us is that which coheres most perfectly with the general system of our consciousness. Whether or not the line thus adopted is a reasonable line depends on the question whether or not we are living within a rational universe.[1]

At this point, however, we come definitely upon the question with respect to the relationship between Character and Conduct; and as this is a question of great importance, it seems to require a separate chapter.

[1] In connection with this point, reference may be profitably made to Dr. Sidgwick's article on "Unreasonable Action" (*Mind*, New Series, No. 6), and to Mr. Stout's *Analytic Psychology*, Vol. II., p. 267. See also Bosanquet's *Psychology of the Moral Self*, Lecture IX.

NOTE ON PLEASURE AND DESIRE.

It is assumed in this chapter that a satisfied desire brings pleasure, while an unsatisfied desire (or an unsatisfied appetite) is accompanied by pain. It should be observed, however, that this is a point on which there has been a good deal of discussion; and that the view taken in the text is not universally adopted. The chief point on which there is difference of opinion is with reference to what are called "the Pleasures of Pursuit." It is held by some writers, and notably by Professor Sidgwick, that, in consequence of the existence of these pleasures, unsatisfied desires and appetites are frequently in themselves rather pleasurable than painful. It may be well here to add a few words on this point. Professor Sidgwick's view is thus stated in the *Methods of Ethics* (Book I., chap. iv., § 2, p. 48):—"When a desire is having its natural effect in causing the actions which tend to the attainment of its object, it seems to be commonly either a neutral or a more or less pleasurable consciousness: even when this attainment is still remote. At any rate the consciousness of eager activity, in which this desire is an essential item, is highly pleasurable: and in fact such pleasures, which we may call generally the pleasures of Pursuit, constitute a considerable element in the total enjoyment of life. Indeed it is almost a commonplace to say that they are more important than the pleasures of Attainment: and in many cases it is the prospect of the former rather than of the latter that induces us to engage in a pursuit."[1] I believe that this antithesis between "Pursuit" and "Attainment" involves a fundamental misconception, and it seems to me to be of considerable importance that this misconception should be removed. There is, so far as I can see, no such thing as a pleasure of Pursuit, as opposed to Attainment. The truth appears to me to be rather that there are two kinds of attainment—what might be called *progressive* attainment and *catastrophic* attainment. The "pleasure of Pursuit" is, I think, in reality the pleasure of progressive Attainment. When it was said, for instance, "If I held Truth in my hand, I would let it go again for the *pleasure of pursuing it*," what was really intended seems to have been *the pleasure of progressively attaining it*. And I think this is

[1] For some further illustrations of Dr. Sidgwick's view, the reader may be referred to *Mind*, New Series, vol. i., No. 1 (Jan. 1892), pp. 94-101.

the case also with those pleasures that are referred to by Professor Sidgwick as "pleasures of Pursuit." He takes the case, for instance, of a game of skill. "No ordinary player, before entering on such a contest, has any desire for victory in it: indeed he often finds it difficult to imagine himself deriving gratification from such victory, before he has actually engaged in the competition. What he deliberately, before the game begins, desires is not victory, but the pleasant excitement of the struggle for it; only for the full development of this pleasure a transient desire to win the game is generally indispensable. This desire, which does not exist at first, is stimulated to considerable intensity by the competition itself: and in proportion as it is thus stimulated both the mere contest becomes more pleasurable, and the victory, which was originally indifferent, comes to afford a keen enjoyment." With the whole of this passage I agree, with the single exception of the statement that the contest becomes more pleasurable *in proportion as* the desire to win the game is stimulated. On the contrary, it seems to me that we may distinguish between two kinds of desire to win the game—*viz.* the desire to win it simply as a catastrophic result, and the desire to win it as the culminating point in a continuous process. In proportion as the former kind of desire is stimulated, it appears to me that the game ceases to be pleasurable. It is, I believe, a common experience that the gambler whose aim is fixed exclusively on the result of the game ceases to get any real pleasure from it. The man who really enjoys the game is he who desires victory, but desires it only as the culminating point in a progressive series. And the same applies in other cases. The mountaineer who *merely* wishes to reach the topmost peak, is simply annoyed by the process of climbing up: he would prefer to reach it by a balloon or by a hydraulic hoist. The man who enjoys the ascent is the one who desires the end only in so far as it gives unity and completeness to the process of attaining it. So also the man who is *merely* interested in the conclusion of a story does not enjoy the novel in which it is told: his view is rather like that of Christopher Sly—"'Tis a very excellent piece of work—would 'twere done!" The man who really enjoys the story cares for the end only in relation to the process that leads up to it. Now the man who desires an end in relation to the process of reaching it, is not, I think, correctly described as receiving pleasure from a *pursuit*, as distinguished from an *attainment*. The pursuit is, for him, a progressive attainment. From the nature of the case, he could not attain otherwise than by pursuit. A story, for instance, does not admit of any kind of attainment but that of going through it from beginning to end. In such a process the desire receives a continuous satisfaction, and is not properly regarded as waiting for its satisfaction till the end is reached.

I conceive that this view may be applied even to such a case as that of hunger. It seems to me, indeed, to be somewhat incorrect to speak of the mere *appetite* of hunger as desire. *Hunger* ought, I think, to be sharply distinguished from the *desire for food*. It seems to me to be mainly owing to the failure to draw this distinction that hunger is represented by Professor Sidgwick as forming an exception [1] to the general rule about the "Paradox of Hedonism." [2] It forms an exception, so far as I can see, only because it is not a desire at all. This, however, is a side issue, on which I do not wish to insist at present. The craving of hunger, though not properly a desire, seems to resemble certain of our desires in being susceptible of a progressive satisfaction: and it is for this reason, as I conceive, that the craving appears often to be pleasurable. It is pleasurable because it is continuously attaining its object. As far as I can judge, indeed, the satisfaction of hunger begins, under normal conditions, even prior to the taking of food at all. The "watering of the mouth" is, I think, a commencement of satisfaction; and in the case of predatory animals I suspect that there is a certain satisfaction even in the act of pursuit.[3] At any rate, the normal act of satisfying hunger does not appear to be of a catastrophic character. *Ducere cœnam* is a principle of general applicability. The satisfaction of the craving is a progressive one. Now, if this is the case, it seems clear that the mere fact that hunger is, under normal conditions, rather pleasurable than otherwise (which I believe to be true), cannot be accepted as a proof that the mere craving in itself is pleasurable, or is not painful, in so far as it remains unsatisfied. For under normal conditions it is not unsatisfied, but is progressively attaining its end.[4]

There is another point, closely connected with this one, which appears to me to be overlooked by Professor Sidgwick in his discussion on the above subject—*viz.* that our desires and appetites are capable, to a considerable extent, of an imaginative satisfaction.

1 See *Methods of Ethics*, Book I., chap. iv., § 2, p. 49: "This effect" [*viz.* that we lose pleasure by seeking it] "is not visible, or at any rate is scarcely visible, in the case of passive sensual pleasures."

2 See above, § 7.

3 It is only in *this* sense, I think, that there is any real "pleasure of pursuit."

4 See also Spencer's *Data of Ethics*, pp. 156–158.

Dickens's "Marchioness" did not by any means stand alone in the power of "making-believe very much." If it is true that

> "Cowards die many times before their deaths;
> The valiant never taste of death but once,"

it may also be said that the imaginative satisfy their desires many times before they are satisfied in fact, while the unimaginative have but a single satisfaction. The imaginative player, even if he loses, loses but once for a score of times that he has won—in fancy; and these imaginary successes may be quite as satisfying to his mind at the moment as an equal number of real ones would have been. The "pleasures of Pursuit" are to a large extent made up of these mental victories; and this fact must largely qualify our view of them as cases of unsatisfied desire, even apart from the consideration (which may not be always applicable) that the desire is in reality attaining its end by means of a continuous process.

I make these remarks merely with the view of bringing out the point of view which seems to me correct, and which I have adopted in the present handbook. They are not by any means offered with the view of giving a complete solution to the difficult question involved.[1]

---

[1] Students interested in the subject of pleasures of Pursuit will find further discussion and admirable illustrations in Tucker's *Light of Nature*, chap. vi.

CHAPTER III.

CHARACTER AND CONDUCT.

§ 1. General Remarks. We now understand, in some degree, what is meant by Will, Desire, Motive, Intention, and what is the nature of the relationship between these; and we are now prepared to consider the nature of Character and its relation to Conduct. In discussing this, we are naturally led to the famous question about the Freedom of the Will; for this concerns the relationship between Character and Conduct. And in considering this, it seems necessary also to explain the terms Circumstance and Habit. Accordingly I intend first to present four sections, dealing respectively with Character, Conduct, Circumstance, and Habit, then to explain the significance of the Freedom of the Will, and finally to sum up about the nature of Voluntary Action.

§ 2. Character. We have seen that Character means the complete universe or system constituted by acts of will of a particular kind. Character is on the whole the most important element in life from the point of view of Ethics, as we shall see more fully in the sequel.

The accidental dominance of a good purpose at this or that moment is of comparatively little consequence unless it is an indication of the habitual dominance of a certain universe. Hence Aristotle rightly laid emphasis rather on the formation of Good Habit[1]—*i. e.*, in the language we have here adopted, on the establishment of a continuously dominant universe—than on the mere presence of a Good Will at any given moment. Will is, indeed, the expression of character, but it is the expression of it under the limitations of a particular time and place; and much may remain latent in the character which it would be necessary to take into account in forming a complete moral estimate of a given individual. This is well expressed in Browning's *Rabbi Ben Ezra*—

> "Not on the vulgar mass
> Called 'work' must sentence pass,
> Things done, that took the eye and had the price;
>
> . . . . .
>
> But all, the world's coarse thumb
> And finger failed to plumb,
> So passed in making up the main account;
> All instincts immature,
> All purposes unsure,
> That weighed not as his work, yet swelled the man's amount.
> Thoughts hardly to be packed
> Into a narrow act,
> Fancies that broke through language and escaped:
> All I could never be,
> All, men ignored in me,
>
> This, I was worth to God, whose wheel the pitcher shaped."

At the same time, it is true that "the tree is known by its fruit." The good character necessarily expresses itself in good acts of will.

§ 3. CONDUCT. The term conduct is sometimes used

[1] *Ethics*, Book II. chap. v.

in a loose sense to include all sorts of vital activities, or at any rate all vital activities which are directed to an end. It is in this sense, for instance, that the term is employed by Mr. Herbert Spencer.[1] Consequently he speaks of the conduct of molluscs, &c.[2] But this seems to be an inconvenient extension of the meaning of the term. Although the activities of molluscs are no doubt adjusted to an end, yet we cannot regard them as purposeful activities. A purposeful activity is not merely directed to an end, but, as Kant put it, directed by the *idea* of an end. Now even the higher animals, in so far as they are guided by mere instinct,[3] cannot be supposed to have any such idea. They move towards certain ends, but they do not *will* these ends. They have an *end*, but they have no *purpose*.[4] Now Mr. Spencer admits that purposeless acts are not to be included in conduct. Hence it seems best to confine the term conduct to those acts that are not merely adjusted to ends, but also definitely willed. A person's conduct, then, is the complete system of such acts, corresponding to his character.

§ 4. Circumstance.—We have said that conduct corresponds to character. But of course the particular acts which are performed by an individual depend not only on the nature of the systematic unity of his con-

1 *Data of Ethics*, chap. i. 2 *Ibid.*, chap. ii.

3 It may well be doubted whether they *ever* have such an idea. Darwin, however, who is certainly a high authority, seems disposed to attribute some consciousness of the adaptation of means to end even to such very humble creatures as earthworms.

4 It might be convenient to use the term *purposive*, as distinguished from *purposeful*, to denote action (such as instinctive movements) in which an end may be seen to be involved, but in which there is no definite consciousness of the end aimed at.

sciousness, but also on the conditions or environment within which his life happens to be passed. Hence it is sometimes said that a man's conduct depends upon his character and circumstances. We must now consider what exactly is to be understood by circumstances.

In the first place, we must note that, if we are to understand the ethical significance of a man's circumstances, we must clear our minds of that view according to which circumstances are simply the external environment in which a man's life is passed. Understood in this sense, any contemporary event might be called a circumstance—*e. g.* the position of the planets, the state of the tides, the direction of the wind, &c. But for most purposes (unless we are believers in Astrology), such conditions are not to be classed as circumstances at all. Again, the geological formation of the country in which a man lives is seldom worth reckoning as a circumstance; though the presence of gold or coal or iron may be a circumstance of considerable importance. Riches or poverty, health or disease, are generally circumstances of more importance; and so are, in general, a man's social surroundings. From such considerations as this we may see that it is not so easy as it might at first appear to determine what a man's circumstances are, in any sense that is ethically significant. Circumstances in this sense are not anything external to the man, but only external conditions in so far as they enter into his life. What are to be reckoned circumstances in this sense, is a question that depends on the character of the man. Hence it is somewhat misleading to speak as if character and circumstance were two co-ordinate factors in human life;

since it depends largely on character whether anything is to be reckoned a circumstance or not.[1]

Again, are we to say that the fact that a man has a good memory, or a good temper, or a good understanding, or a good reputation, is an element in his character or in his circumstance? Such facts depend largely on the systematic constitution of a man's conscious life, and so belong to his character; yet, on the other hand, they may be regarded as circumstances by which he is helped or hindered in the conduct of his life. Even the fact that a man has already formed a good habit of action—say, a habit of punctuality—may be a favourable circumstance with reference to his future development. Thus it is to a considerable extent a question of the point of view from which a thing is regarded, whether it is to be described as an element of character or of circumstance. Probably by far the greatest part of any man's present circumstance is simply the expression of what his past character has been.

Hence, when we say that a man's actions are the result of his character and his circumstance, we must remember that two men living to all appearance in the same general conditions may in reality be in wholly different circumstances. What stimulates one may depress another, just as "the twilight that sends the hens to roost sets the fox to prowl, and the lion's roar which gathers the jackals scatters the sheep."[2] What

1 Some suggestive remarks on this point will be found in a paper on "Character and the Emotions," by Mr. A. F. Shand, in *Mind*, new series, Vol. v., No. 18. The relationship between character and circumstance has also been brought out, in a profound and suggestive way, by Mr. Bosanquet, in *Aspects of the Social Problem*.

2 Art. "Psychology" in *Encyclopædia Britannica*, p. 42.

is physically the same is in such cases, to all intents, a different circumstance.

§ 5. HABIT.—The significance of Habit has already been to some extent indicated in connection with character, and in particular reference has been made to Aristotle's view that the main thing in the moral life is the establishment of good habits. This view was put forward by Aristotle in opposition to the Socratic doctrine, that Virtue is a kind of Knowledge;[1] yet the two views are not so much opposed as might at first sight appear. Virtue is a kind of knowledge, as well as a kind of habit. It is, in fact, as we have already indicated, a point of view. The virtuous man is one who lives continuously in the universe which is constituted by duty. To live continuously in that universe is a habit; but it is at the same time a species of insight. The man who lives in a different universe sees things habitually in a different way—through a differently coloured glass, we might say. To be virtuous, therefore, is to possess habitually a certain kind of knowledge or insight. And thus both Socrates and Aristotle were right. Virtue is both a kind of knowledge and a kind of habit. Habit, in fact, in the sense in which the term is applied to moral character, is not mere custom. It is not on a level with habits such as our manner of walking or speaking or of wearing clothes. It is not, in short, of the nature of what is commonly called a secondarily automatic action. It is a *habit of willing*. Habits which have a moral signi-

[1] *Cf.* Sidgwick's *History of Ethics*, pp. 24-5 and 54; and, for a fuller account of the doctrine of Socrates, see Zeller's *Socrates and the Socratic Schools*, Part II., chap. vii.

ficance are habits of deliberate choice.[1] Now deliberate choice depends on thought or reason.[2] In order to choose the right, in the sense in which such a choice has any moral significance, we must know the right. If we simply hit on the right course by chance, we do not really choose the right. Right willing, therefore, depends on true insight. Whether it is possible to have true insight without willing rightly is a further question, which we shall have to consider shortly. In the meantime we may partly see what Sócrates meant by saying that virtue is a kind of knowledge. It depends on the occupation of a certain point of view, on the possession of a certain rational insight. At the same time, we see the truth of Aristotle's saying that virtue is habit. It is not merely a certain act of will, but a continuous state of character, a steadfast occupation of a definite universe.

Another point which it is important to notice in this connection is that action which has thus become habitual tends to be pleasant. A good character, for instance, is one whose dominant interest lies within a certain form of moral universe. Such a character will find pleasure in acting in accordance with this interest. Hence Aristotle says again[3] that "a man is not good at all unless he takes pleasure in noble deeds. No one would call a man just who did not take pleasure in doing justice, nor generous, who took no pleasure in acts of generosity, and so on." Further, habit, as is said, becomes a second nature; so that actions that

[1] Ἔστιν ἄρα ἡ ἀρετὴ ἕξις προαιρετική ("Virtue, then, is a habit of choice").—Aristotle's *Ethics*, II. vi. 15.

[2] *Cf.* Green's *Prolegomena to Ethics*, Book II., chap. ii.

[3] *Nicomachean Ethics*, I. viii. 12.

have become habitual are done almost instinctively; at least without the necessity for definite reflection. It is important to bear this in mind. Its application will become especially apparent when we are dealing with some of the theories of Kant.

§ 6. THE FREEDOM OF THE WILL.—We are now in a position to consider what is meant by human freedom, in so far as this has ethical significance.

Some views on this point may almost immediately be ruled out of court. Thus, it has been argued that there is no real freedom, since men are determined by circumstances. This was the doctrine, for instance, of Robert Owen, the Socialist. Accordingly, he made it his great aim in life to improve men's external conditions. But we have seen that mere external conditions are not circumstances in any sense that is ethically important. Before setting ourselves to improve men's conditions, we should ask ourselves how far their conditions are real circumstances to them, and what sort of circumstances they are. To ask this is at the same time to ask what sort of people they are. It is a complete mistake to suppose that men are determined by conditions that are in any true sense external to them.

Again, freedom is sometimes understood to mean the power of acting without motives. But this also is an absurdity. To act without motives, *i. e.* without reference to anything that may reasonably serve as an inducement to action, would be to act from blind impulse, as some of the lower animals may be supposed to do. But this is evidently the very reverse of what we understand by freedom.

In order to avoid such crude misconceptions as

these, it is important to consider in what sense the idea of freedom is ethically significant.

§ 7. Freedom essential to Morals.—There is involved in the moral consciousness the conviction that we ought to act in one way rather than in another, that one manner of action is good or right, and another bad or evil. Now, as Kant urged, there would be no meaning in an "ought" if it were not accompanied by a "can."[1] It does not follow, however, that the "can" refers to an immediate possibility. A man ought to be wise, for instance; but wisdom is a quality that can only be gradually developed. What can be done at once is only to put ourselves in the way of acquiring it. Similarly, we ought to love our neighbours. But love is a feeling that cannot be produced at will.[2] We can only put ourselves in the way of cultivating kindly affections. But it would be absurd to say that a man ought to add a cubit to his stature or to live for two hundred years. He cannot even put himself in the way of attaining these ends, and they cannot therefore form any part of his duty. Now if a man's will were absolutely determined by his circumstances, it would be strictly impossible for him to become anything but

[1] *Cf.* the lines of Emerson—

"So nigh is grandeur to our dust,
So near is God to man,
When Duty whispers low, *Thou must,*
The youth replies, *I can.*"

[2] For this reason Kant even denies that love is a duty. See *Metaphysic of Morals,* section I. (Abbott's translation, pp. 15–16). But love can be cultivated, though it cannot be directly produced. Kant's view on this and kindred points is due to the absolute antithesis which he makes between Reason and Feeling. *Cf.* Caird's *Critical Philosophy of Kant,* vol. ii. pp. 280–282. See also below, Book II., chap. iii., § 13.

that which he does become, and consequently it would be impossible that he ought to be anything different. There would thus be no "ought" at all. Moral imperatives would cease to have any meaning.[1] If, then, there is to be any meaning in the moral imperative, the will must not be absolutely determined by circumstances, but must in some sense be free. This is true also even if we do not, like Kant, think of the moral end as of the nature of an imperative, but rather as a Good or Ideal to be attained.[2] It still remains true that such an ideal must be, as Aristotle put it, πρακτὸν καὶ κτητὸν ἀνθρώπῳ (practicable and attainable by man).

§ 8. Necessity essential to Morals.—Nevertheless, there is a sense also in which necessity is required for the moral life. The moral life consists, as we have endeavoured to point out, in the formation of character. Now to have a character is to live habitually in a certain universe. And in any given universe desires have a definite position with reference to one another; so that there can be no doubt which is to give place to another. Hence the more decidedly a character is formed, the more uniform will be its choice

[1] Hence purely determinist writers when they are quite consistent, deny the existence of any absolute "ought," and regard Ethics not as a normative science, but as an ordinary natural history science—investigating what men do or tend to do, not what they ought to do. This is the view, for instance, which is taken by Schopenhauer (who, in spite of his emphasis on the Will, was to all intents a pure determinist). *Cf.* Janet's *Theory of Morals*, p. 138. Another good example of pure determinism, accompanied by the denial of the unity of the self, leading to a natural history view of Ethics, will be found in Simmel's *Einleitung in die Moralwissenschaft*. Bentham's attitude to some extent illustrates the same thing. See below, Book II., chap. iv., § 5.

[2] See below, Book II., chap. ii.

and its action. Nay, even in the case of characters that are imperfectly formed, any uncertainty that exists with regard to the action is due only to our imperfect knowledge. It is difficult to predict what will be done by a man who is continually shifting from one universe to another. But his action would be fully foreseen by any one who knew exactly the relation in which these universes stand to one another in his mental life. And not only is this true as a fact with regard to the moral lives of men, but it *must* be true if the moral life is to have any meaning. The moral life means the building up of character, *i. e.* it means the forming of definite habits of action. And if a habit of action be definite, it is uniform and predictable. Now necessity is often understood to mean nothing more than uniformity. In this sense, then, necessity is required for the moral life.

§ **9.** The true Sense of Freedom.—It is apt to seem as if there were a certain contradiction between these two demands of the moral life. But there is no contradiction when we observe precisely what is the nature of the freedom and what is the nature of the necessity that is demanded. The necessity means simply the uniform activity of a given character. The freedom, on the other hand, means simply the absence of determination by anything outside the character itself. A vicious man in a sense can, and in a sense cannot, do a good action. He cannot, in the sense that a good action does not issue from such a character as his. A corrupt tree cannot bring forth good fruit. But he can do the action, in the sense that there is nothing to prevent him *except his character—i. e.* except himself. Now a man cannot stand outside of himself, and regard a defect in his own character as something by which his action is hindered. If he can, *but for himself*, he *can* in the only sense that is required for morality. To be free means that one is determined by nothing but oneself.[1] What this means, however, we must endeavour to explain somewhat more fully.

§ **10**. Animal Spontaneity.—Consider in what sense an animal is free. As compared with a plant or a stone, it evidently has a certain spontaneity. It is not moved from without, as a stone seems to be, but conducts itself in accordance with its own inner feelings. It should be observed, however, that even a stone is not moved entirely from without. No rock was ever thrown to the ground without its own consent. What we call the laws of nature in obedience to which stones are raised or thrown down, are laws of the stone's nature as well as of things outside of it. "The hyssop grows in the wall, because the whole universe cannot prevent it from growing."[2] This is as true as to say that it grows there because the whole universe *makes* it grow. The law is within it quite as truly as it is without it. In this sense Hegel was no doubt right in saying that the planets run round the sun freely like the immortal gods. "The sun attracts them," it is

[1] Those writers who insist on the fact that there is determination or law in all our actions, and who on this ground deny freedom, are commonly known as Necessitarians. On the other hand, those who insist on liberty to such an extent as to deny all law or determination in human conduct, are called Libertarians or Indeterminists. It is now generally recognized that these two schools of writers simply represent opposite sides of the same truth, and that the idea of *self-determination* combines the two sides.

[2] Carlyle, I think, says this; I do not remember where.

said. But the sun could not attract them unless they were willing to be attracted—*i. e.* unless it lay in their own nature to be attracted. Still, we do not usually think of the planets, or of inanimate nature generally, as having any spontaneity in its motions. And rightly. The movements of the planets are not determined by themselves; for they have no selves. The law is as truly within them as without them; but it is also as truly without them as within them. It is, as we say, a "law of nature" generally, and does not belong to any one thing in particular. There is no centre to which the movement can strictly be referred. In the case of an animal it is different. Here there *is* a self, there is a centre of reference—*viz.* the consciousness of the animal itself. It is from that point that the movement proceeds, and we say therefore that it is spontaneous.

§ **11.** Human Liberty.—Yet a mere animal has not a self in the full sense of the term. Its self is simply the feeling of the moment. It has not a definite universe of reference. A man's self, on the other hand, is the universe in which he habitually lives. For this reason, a man is free in a sense in which an animal is not free. If an animal could be supposed to think and speak, it could not refer its actions to itself, but only to its impulse at this or that moment.[1] No doubt, there would be a certain continuity and predictability in its impulses; yet at each moment they would have a certain

[1] *Cf.* Dewey's *Outlines of Ethics*, pp. 158-9. "An animal which does not have the power of proposing ends to itself is impelled to action by its wants and appetites just as they come into consciousness. It is *irritated* into acting." See also Gizycki's *Introduction to the Study of Ethics*, chap. vi.

independence, and would not refer to a common centre. This, of course, means simply that the animal does *not* think, and consequently does not bring the moments of its consciousness to a unity. Man, on the other hand, lives within the universe of his character. In so far as his momentary impulses do not reflect and reveal that character, he does not regard them as, strictly speaking, his own. His acts are his own only when he *is himself* in doing them—*i. e.* when they flow from the centre of his habitual universe. He has thus a centre of action which has a certain relative permanence; and for this reason his acts are free in a sense in which the movements of a mere animal, though spontaneous, are not free.[1]

§ 12. THE HIGHEST FREEDOM.—We see, then, that there are higher and lower senses of freedom. Even a stone is not simply determined from without. An animal has spontaneity. But man has freedom in a higher sense than either of these. This fact naturally suggests the inquiry whether the ordinary freedom of

[1] Those writers who have insisted on determination, to the exclusion of freedom, have generally also denied the unity of the individual self or character. Thus Hume (who may be regarded as the founder of the determinist school in modern times) says (*Treatise on Human Nature*, Book I., Part IV., section vi.): "When I enter most intimately into what I call *myself*, I always stumble on some particular perception or other, of heat or cold, light or shade, love or hatred, pain or pleasure"; and he consequently concludes that the self or personality is "nothing but a bundle or collection of different perceptions, which succeed each other with an inconceivable rapidity, and are in a perpetual flux and movement." Mill also accepted this view. See his *Examination of Sir W. Hamilton*, chap. xii. For criticisms of it, see Green's edition of Hume, vol. i., Introd., § 342, and Dr. Ward's article on "Psychology" in the *Encyclopædia Britannica*, p. 39.

a man is freedom in the highest sense, or whether there is the possibility of a freedom of a still higher kind.

The answer seems clearly to be that there is a freedom of a still higher kind. This follows at once from the fact that there is a *self* of a still higher kind. This is a point which we shall have to consider more fully in the sequel. In the meantime, we may anticipate so far as to say that, in a certain sense, no form of self can be regarded as ultimately real except the rational self. If this is so, the only true or ultimate freedom will be the freedom that consists in acting from this self as a centre. This is recognised even in ordinary language. The man who acts irrationally is said to be "enslaved by his passions." He is thus not thoroughly free. And indeed, there are times when a man feels that his irrational acts are not, strictly speaking, *his own.* His true self lies deeper. This seems to have been felt by the writer in the Pauline Epistles, when he referred his shortcomings not to himself, but to "sin that dwelleth in me." Here he identifies himself with the higher or rational self. Yet in another passage he seems to identify himself rather with the lower self, when he says, "It is no longer I that live, but Christ that liveth in me." Here "I" refers to the lower self—the habitual character of the individual—while the higher or true self is referred to as "Christ," living in him and gradually coming to complete realisation. There are, in fact, we may say, three selves in every man. There is the self that is revealed in occasional impulses which we cannot quite subdue, the "sin" that, after all, dwelleth in us. On the other hand, there is the permanent character, the universe in which we habitually live.[1] And finally there is the true or rational self, in which alone we feel that we can rest with satisfaction—the "Christ" (to adopt the Pauline metaphor) that liveth in us, and in whom we hope more and more to abide. And, as it is said elsewhere, "his service is perfect freedom." It may, in a certain sense, be maintained that there is no other perfect freedom. The only ultimate self is the rational self; and the only ultimate freedom is the freedom that we have when we are rational. This, however, is a point that cannot be fully understood until we have considered the nature of the moral ideal.

The significance of all this may perhaps become more apparent as we proceed. In the meantime we may now sum up the results at which we have arrived with respect to the nature of Conduct or Voluntary Action.

§ **13.** The Nature of Voluntary Action.—A definite illustration may perhaps help to make the nature of the various elements in voluntary action clear to us.

Take the case of the desire of food. The first element involved in this is the mere animal *appetite.* This we may suppose to be at first a mere blind impulse analogous to the organic impulse by which a flower turns to the light; but it is distinguished from such a vegetable impulse by the presence of consciousness. In this consciousness there are two main elements—

1 Even this may not be quite simple. "Zwei Seelen wohnen, ach! in dieser Brust," said Faust ("Two souls, alas! live in this breast of mine"); and the same could, in some degree, be said by most men. "I am double," said Renan; "sometimes one part of myself laughs, while the other cries." In cases of madness, the two selves often become very distinctly separated.

the ideal presentation, in vague outline,[1] of the object striven towards, and a feeling of pleasure and pain, The latter feeling is twofold: there is a sense of pleasure in the anticipated satisfaction, and a sense of uneasiness connected with the consciousness of its absence. Thus in the appetite of hunger there is a peculiar craving, partly pleasant and partly uneasy, accompanied by a more or less vague consciousness of the kind of object that would yield satisfaction.[1] *Desire* is distinguished from mere appetite by the definite presence of a consciousness of the object as an end to be aimed at. The appetite of hunger involves a vague uneasiness, a vague consciousness of the kind of object that would remove the uneasiness, a vague anticipation of pleasure in its attainment. Desire of food, on the other hand, is a definite presentation of the idea of food as an end to be sought. In this presentation, as in the more vague presentation of the object in appetite, there is also involved an element of pleasure and pain. The object thus definitely presented as an end in desire is what is most properly understood by a *motive.* Such motives may conflict: the ends involved may be incompatible with one another. Hence the desires governed by these motives may remain in abeyance. The object presented as a desirable end may not be definitely chosen as an end—*i. e.* it may not become a *wish.* A wish is a desire selected. It is a desire on which attention has been concentrated, and which has thus secured a certain dominance in our consciousness. The wish for food is more than the mere desire for food. It is a concentrated desire. But even this is still not an

[1] It is open to doubt whether this element is present in the animal consciousness at all. *Cf.* above, chap. i., § 3.

act of will. An act of will involves, besides, a definite *purpose* or *intention ; i. e.* in an act of will we do not merely concentrate our attention on an end as a good to be sought ; but, in addition, we regard it as an end to be brought about by us. The purpose of procuring food—the intention, for instance, of working for a livelihood—is more than the mere wish for food, more than a mere prayer or aspiration. *Will*, however, involves, further, an actual energising. A purpose or intention refers to the future, and may not be carried out. In an act of will the idea becomes a force. How this is done is a difficult question to answer ; and, happily, it is not a problem that we require here to solve. We have merely to notice this element of active energising as involved in an Act of Will. The man who wills to procure food does not merely intend to work, but actually does exert himself. Finally, *character* is a formed habit—*e. g.* the habit of activity in some particular industrial pursuit.[1]

[1] Mr. Stout's article on "Voluntary Action," already referred to, should be consulted on several of these points.

NOTE ON RESPONSIBILITY.

In modern times the interest in the question of the Freedom of the Will has been stimulated mainly by the desire to have a clear view of human responsibility.[1] The Mediæval conceptions of Heaven and Hell gave special force to this desire. God was thought of as a supreme Judge, standing outside the world, and apportioning infinite rewards and punishments in accordance with the lives which men had led, or, as some rather thought, in accordance with the beliefs which they had entertained. This doctrine presented serious difficulties. On the one hand, if Liberty of Indifference were asserted, if men were supposed to have the power of acting "without motives," of choosing a particular line of conduct without reference to their characters—*i. e.* to the universe of desires within which they have habitually lived—this appeared to be both unintelligible in itself and to involve too strong an assertion of the freedom of a merely created, finite, and dependent being. On the other hand, if man were held to be free only in the sense that he is self-determined, it appeared as if he could not be regarded as ultimately responsible for the building up of his own character, for the selection of the universe within which he was to live. This difficulty was felt as early as the time of St. Paul; and the only solution of it seems to lie in the acknowledgment that it is a mystery. *Credo quia absurdum.*

A similar difficulty, however, comes up even at the present time with reference to the responsibility of the individual to society. How, it is asked, can any one be regarded as responsible for the formation of his own character, seeing that he is born with particular inherited aptitudes and tendencies, and that the whole development of his life is determined by the moral atmosphere in which he is placed? In a sense we choose our own universes; but the "we," the self that chooses, is not an undetermined existence. We are ushered into the world with a certain predisposition to good or to evil in particular directions. Over this "original sin," or original virtue, which lies in our disposition from the first, we have no control. It is ourselves; it constitutes the particular nature which we inherit; and the directions in which it moves us depend on the circumstances in which we grow up. How, then, is society entitled to punish us for our offences? Even so firm an upholder of personal independence, and so stern an advocate of the punishment of crime, as Thomas Carlyle, admitted, and even insisted, that a man's char-

---

[1] *Cf.* below, Book III., chap. vi., § 7.

acter is an inheritance, and that the development of it is affected by bodily qualities. Thus, notwithstanding his strenuous insistence on the doctrine that every man is the shaper of his own destiny, we find him, in his Essay on Sir Walter Scott, making this candid admission: "Disease, which is but superficial, and issues in outer lameness, does not cloud the young existence; rather forwards it towards the expansion it is fitted for. The miserable disease had been one of the internal nobler parts, marring the general organisation; under which no Walter Scott could have been forwarded, or with all his other endowments could have been producible or possible." What, then, becomes of responsibility? Have we not here a puzzle or antinomy as real as that with which the Mediæval Theology was perplexed?

But the answer to this has been partly seen already. If a man were a mere animal, the only reasonable course would be to take him as we find him. In that case, the only justification of punishment[1] would be found in the hope of effecting, by means of it, some improvement in the disposition of him who is punished. But a man cannot regard himself as a mere animal, nor can a society of men regard its members as simply animals. They must be regarded as beings animated by an ideal, which they are bound to aim at realising, and which they *can* realise as soon as they become aware of the obligation. No man could regard it as an excuse for his evil conduct, that he is a mere brute beast, who knows no better. Nor could a society accept this as an excuse for any of its members. Whether a God, sitting outside as an external Judge, ought not to accept it as an excuse, is quite another question, with which we have here no concern. Our question is merely with regard to the way in which a man or a society of men must judge human conduct. And, from this point of view, it is quite sufficient to say that men must regard themselves and others as soldiers of the ideal; that those who fail to struggle for it must be treated as deserters, and those who deny its authority as guilty of *lèse majesté* against the dignity of human nature. There is no stone wall in the way of a man's moral progress. There is only himself. And he cannot accept himself as a mere fact, but only as a fact ruled by an ideal.

I cannot hope that such remarks as these will remove all difficulties from the mind of the student. The question, however, when pressed beyond a certain point, begins to be rather of metaphysical and theological than of strictly ethical importance.[2]

---

[1] See below, Book III., chap. vi., § 6.

[2] A complete discussion of this difficult question would evidently

carry us far beyond the limits of such a handbook as the present. I have touched upon it here only so far as seemed necessary to bring out its bearing upon Ethics. For fuller discussion the reader may be referred to Green's *Prolegomena to Elhics*, Book II., chap. i., Green's *Collected Works*, pp. 308—333, Bradley's *Ethical Studies*, Essay I., Sidgwick's *Methods of Ethics*, Book I., chap. v., Caird's *Critical Philosophy of Kant*, Book II., chap. iii., Martineau's *Study of Religion*, Book III., chap. ii., Alexander's *Moral Order and Progress*, pp. 336—341, Gizycki's *Introduction to the Study of Ethics*, chap. vi., Stephen's *Science of Ethics*, pp. 278—293, and Seth's *Study of Ethical Principles*, Part III., chap. i. *Cf.* also Dewey's *Outlines of Ethies*, Part I., chap. iii., Muirhead's *Elements of Ethics*, pp. 50—54, Lotze's *Practical Philosophy*, chap. iii., and Calderwood's *Handbook of Moral Philosophy*, Part II., chaps. iii. and iv. The views of Green, Bradley, Caird, Alexander, Gizycki, Dewey, and Muirhead are in the main in agreement with that here stated. Lotze, Martineau, Calderwood, and Seth defend freedom, though generally rejecting Liberty of Indifference in its most extreme form. Sidgwick takes up a neutral position. Stephen is a Determinist, and does not fully recognise the fact of self-determination. The same remark applies on the whole to the excellent discussion of Freedom in Simmel's recent *Einleitung in die Moralwissenschaft*, Vol. II., chap. vi.

CHAPTER IV.

THE EVOLUTION OF CONDUCT.

§ 1. Introductory Statement. Conduct, like other aspects of human life, undergoes a steady process of development, both in the individual and in the race. This development is closely connected with the general development of the forms and customs of social life, and thus forms part of the material which it is the business of the young science of Sociology to investigate.

Recent writers on Sociology have tended to lay a good deal of emphasis on the class of phenomena described by the terms Imitation and Suggestion, as throwing light on the development of social customs.[1] These conceptions are probably inadequate in dealing with the higher elements in social development; but they do seem to be of value in dealing with the more primitive facts of human and animal life, and they may thus serve as a convenient point of departure.

It seems to be a general truth in Psychology that every presentation involving the idea of movement brings with it a more or less definite "suggestion" of the movement involved—*i. e.* gives rise to a certain tendency to perform the movement. This is es-

[1] French writers in particular, such as Guyau and Tarde, have laid great emphasis on facts of this class.

pecially true when the movement conveyed to an animal being in idea is one for the performance of which its bodily organs are adapted. It then gives rise to movements which may be described as "imitations" of the original movement—it being borne in mind that they are not to be regarded as conscious imitations, but rather as being of the nature of "suggestion." There can be little doubt that the facts of language and other expressive movements are to a large extent to be explained in this way; and so also, in all probability, are many of the instinctive actions[1] of the lower animals and many of the customs of primitive peoples. Some further remarks on this point may suffice as an introduction to the subject.

§ 2. Germs of Conduct in the Lower Animals.—Though it is perhaps true that Conduct, in the stricter sense of the term, is not to be found at all in the actions of the lower animals, yet it is certainly the case that we may detect in them the germs of that which becomes conduct in man. If animals can seldom be credited with any direct consciousness of an end, they are at least led by certain natural impulses to the accomplishment of ends of which they

[1] It is still an undecided question, what exactly should be understood by instinct; and any discussion of it would obviously be out of place here. Some writers limit the term to forms of activity that are innate; but if Principal Lloyd Morgan is right in thinking that nothing is innate in animals except physiological tendencies to certain forms of action when an appropriate stimulus is presented, instinct in the psychological sense would seem, on this interpretation, to be reduced to zero. (See his work on *Comparative Psychology* and his more recent book on *Habit and Instinct*). For our present purpose, I prefer to understand the term as including all movements that presuppose nothing more (from the psychological point of view) than percepts and perceptual images.

are themselves unaware. Like the makers of the cathedrals, they "build better than they know," their instincts often carry them more certainly to the attainment of the ends of their species than human reason guides us. Now the nature of instinct is largely involved in obscurity. It seems partly to depend on hereditary impulses to action under particular forms of stimulus; but to some extent also it seems to be acquired in the lifetime of the individual animal, and to be developed under the influence of suggestion. The young of a species learn by imitation of the more mature.[1] This is especially seen in

[1] Here again the facts of the case are somewhat open to dispute. The following extract may be given from Principal Lloyd Morgan, who is probably our best authority on such subjects. "If one of a group of chicks learn by casual experience, such as I have before described, to drink from a tin of water, others will run up and peck at the water, and will themselves drink. A hen teaches her little ones to pick up grain or other food by pecking on the ground and dropping suitable materials before them, the chicks seeming to imitate her actions. One may make chicks and young pheasants peck by simulating the action of a hen with a pencil-point or pair of fine forceps. According to Mr. Peal's statement, before quoted, the Assamese find that young jungle pheasants will perish if their pecking responses are not thus stimulated; and Prof. Claypole tells me that this is also the case with ostriches hatched in an incubator . . . . . . It is certainly much easier to bring up young birds if older ones are setting an example of eating and drinking; and instinctive actions, such as scratching the ground, are performed earlier if imitation be not excluded. . . . . . A number of similar cases might be given. But what impresses the observer, as he watches the early development of a brood of young birds, is the presence of an imitative tendency which is exemplified in many little ways not easy to describe in detail." (*Habit and Instinct*, pp. 166—167). No doubt in all such cases congenital aptitude (and perhaps also congenital impulse) is presupposed. How much may fairly be ascribed to heredity and how much to suggestion, is a difficult problem, with which, happily, we are not here concerned.

the case of the more gregarious animals, in which, as in the familiar case of sheep, the movements of leaders are observed, and in which certain habitual forms of activity grow up,[1] almost similar to the customary morality of human beings. Sometimes also penalties seem even to be attached to violations of the customs that have grown up within the herd. In this we see the germs both of moral action and of moral judgment, though it would probably be going too far to say that there is anything more than the germs of them.

§ 3. CONDUCT AMONG SAVAGES.—Among savages also the moral consciousness is largely still in germ. Their actions are to a great extent impulsive, and show little sign of forethought with regard to distant consequences. Yet they are by no means left to the guidance of individual caprice. The savage is a member of a tribe, and his life is hedged about by customary observances, of which the purpose is not always very apparent. In the formation of these, suggestion and conscious imitation no doubt play a considerable part; and even when an end can be detected, it must not always be assumed that it was consciously present to the minds of those who were led to adopt the means to its attainment.

§ 4. THE GUIDANCE OF CONDUCT BY CUSTOM.—Even after mankind have to a considerable extent emerged from savagery, the influence of custom in the deter-

[1] How far these grow up in the lifetime of the individual, and how far they are a result of imitation, are points still open to dispute. The action of the queen bee, in killing off her rivals as soon as she herself emerges from the cell, would almost seem to imply a congenital impulse.

mination of conduct continues for a long time to be paramount. The words ἦθος, *mores*, *Sitten*, all bear evidence to the importance of custom in the formation of the morality of nations. In English the word *manners* has become restricted to a much narrower and more insignificant sense; but even now it is sometimes capable of being used more widely and seriously, as when Wordsworth says, in his sonnet to Milton,

> "And give us manners, virtue, freedom, power."

At any rate, whatever terms we may use to express the fact, there can be no doubt that customary morality precedes that which is based on law or on reflection.

§ 5. THE GUIDANCE OF CONDUCT BY LAW.—Gradually, however, in the life of a people, definite rules of action begin to be established. To some extent these are simply customary observances made more definite; but generally in the formulation of positive laws a certain change gets introduced into the previous customs. When, for instance, definite laws with reference to criminal actions take the place of the primitive custom of revenge, the extent of the retaliation is a good deal limited, and a more definite conception of justice is introduced.

§ 6. THE GUIDANCE OF CONDUCT BY IDEAS.—When definite laws have been formulated, reflection soon begins. Rules almost inevitably conflict both with custom and with one another; and in any case they are found too rigid for the guidance of conduct. Exceptional circumstances arise, and men are led to reflect on the principles that underlie the rules, in order to see how they ought to be modified under the stress of special difficulties. Such reflection leads to a gradual supersession of the letter of the law in favour of its underlying spirit. Men learn to guide themselves by principle instead of by rule, *i. e.* by consideration of the most important aims that they have in view, and the means that are best adapted to their realisation. When this stage is reached, we have passed almost entirely beyond the region of suggestion and imitation. Reflective morality is substituted for customary observance.

§ 7. Action and Reflection.—Of course the part played by reflection even in the most fully developed forms of morality ought not to be exaggerated. The moral life, even in its most developed stages, is not passed entirely in cool reflective hours; and even if it were, the complexity of the material would prevent its complete saturation by reflective principles. Swift decisions have to be made and far-reaching plans formed; so that in the actual activities of the concrete moral life even the most thoughtful of men live to a considerable extent by faith, and do not guide themselves entirely by well developed principles. The ideas by which they are guided are partly formed by reflection, but partly also they are derived from the experience of the individual and partly from the experience of the race. Even here, then, imitation and suggestion are not entirely excluded. There is something of the nature of instinct and impulse even in our most developed conduct.

§ 8. Moral Ideas and Ideas about Morality.—This leads us to notice an important distinction, on which a good deal of emphasis has been laid in recent times

—*viz.* the distinction which has been well expressed by Dr. Bosanquet[1] as that between "Moral Ideas" and "Ideas about Morality," or, as it might be put more briefly, between Moral Ideas and Ethical Ideas. The ideas by which we are guided in our actions may be of a more or less reflective character. A man may guide himself by the conception of a clearly-defined end, such as the attainment of happiness or perfection, and may adapt his whole line of conduct to the attainment of this. In such a case he is guided by an Ethical Idea or by an "Idea about Morality," *i. e.* by an idea formed through reflection upon the nature of the moral end. But a Moral Idea need not be of this character. A moral idea may be got, as it is sometimes put, out of our "spiritual atmosphere." The idea, for instance, of the kind of conduct which fits a "gentleman" or a "Christian" is not, as a rule, derived from any definite reflection on the nature of the moral end, but is rather acquired through tradition and experience. It is important, then, to remember that a man may be guided by moral ideas though he has never definitely reflected upon the nature of morality. It may be added that a man may have reflected much, and even deeply, upon the nature of morality; and yet his stock of moral ideas may be but small and inefficient. It is no doubt possible to make too much of this distinction; and perhaps Dr. Bosanquet, who is chiefly responsible for the clear statement of it, has somewhat exaggerated the antithesis. Every moral idea is capable of reflective analysis, and may thus be said to imply an ethical

[1] In an article in *The International Journal of Ethics*, Vol. I., no. I. It has since been reprinted in *The Civilization of Christendom*, pp 160–207.

idea, and, similarly, every ethical idea naturally becomes a source of moral ideas.[1] This is a point, however, on which we shall have occasion to touch more fully when we come to deal with the bearing of ethical theory on practical conduct. In the meantime it may be sufficient to bear in mind this important distinction between moral and ethical ideas.

§ **9.** The Development of the Moral Consciousness.—From this brief sketch some general notion may be formed of the way in which the moral life develops from customary action, founded on suggestion and imitation, to the stage of independent reflective choice. In order, however, to have a complete view of the growth of the moral consciousness, it is necessary to take account not only of the way in which conduct is developed, but also of the parallel development of the judgment that is passed upon conduct. From the earliest dawn of what can be described as morality, men not only act in particular ways, but also in various ways indicate their opinion that particular kinds of action are right and others wrong. The two lines of development are closely connected, but they are also quite distinct; for it is often but too apparent that men

[1] It would be interesting to inquire how far the moral ideas of the modern Christian world are a result of unconscious growth, and how far they are due to the reflective analysis of Greek thought—to the influence of Plato and Aristotle, the Stoics, &c. Or, again, we might ask how far our modern ideas about duties towards animals can be traced to the influence of Utilitarianism, and how far they are due to a more spontaneous development of moral sentiment. But such questions would be very difficult to answer. "The wind bloweth where it listeth, and thou hearest the sound thereof, but canst not tell whence it cometh or whither it goeth." This is on the whole still true of a great part of our moral development.

do not act in the way that they judge to be right, or avoid acting in the way that they judge to be wrong. Accordingly, it is now necessary that we should take account of the other line of development—the growth of the moral judgment.

NOTE ON SOCIOLOGY.

The further discussion of the points dealt with in this chapter, and to some extent also of those dealt with in the following chapter, seems to belong most properly to Sociology. But this science is in a very undeveloped state. The beginnings of it are seen in the *Politics* of Aristotle. In more modern times it owes much to Hobbes, Spinoza, Locke, Shaftesbury, Hutcheson, Rousseau, Montesquieu, St. Simon, Adam Smith, Kant, Fichte, Hegel, and several others. But the definite foundation of it must, on the whole, be ascribed to Comte. In this country it was brought into prominence by Mr. Herbert Spencer's interesting little book on *The Study of Sociology*. *The Principles of Sociology*, by the same author, have just been completed, and constitute the most elaborate contribution to the subject in this country. In French, reference may be made to such works as De Greef's *Introduction à la sociologie*, Tarde's *Les lois de l'imitation*, the writings of Fouillée and Guyau, and many others. In German, the most elaborate contribution is Schäffle's *Bau und Leben des socialen Körpers*. The works of Simmel (*Ueber sociale Differenzierung* and *Einleitung in die Moralwissenschaft*) have a special interest from the intimate way in which he seeks to connect Sociology with Ethics. He practically regards Ethics as a department of Sociology. Some account and criticism of his views will be found in Bouglé's recent work on *Les sciences sociales en Allemagne*. See also *Mind*, New Series, Vol. I., no. 4, and Vol. III., no. 2. Several American writers have also dealt with Sociology, notably Mr. Lester F. Ward. Profs. Small and Vincent have written *An Introduction to the Study of Society*, and, more recently, two interesting handbooks have been written by Profs. Giddings and Fairbanks. There is also an *American Journal of Sociology*, published at Chicago. It thus seems clear that some beginning has been made in the study of the science. But it can hardly be said as yet that it has any recognized principles or method. The student who desires to gain some idea of its present position will probably find *The Principles of Sociology* by Prof. Giddings or *An Introduction to Sociology* by Prof. Fairbanks most helpful. Both contain good Bibliographies. The recent article by Dr. Bosanquet on Philosophy and Sociology (*Mind*, January, 1897) will also be found exceedingly instructive.

CHAPTER V.

THE GROWTH OF THE MORAL JUDGMENT.

§ **1.** The Earliest Forms of the Moral Judgment.—The germs of moral judgment, like the germs of conduct, may be found even among the lower animals. Domesticated animals, especially dogs, seem often to have a consciousness of having done wrong; at least they seem to be aware when they have rendered themselves liable to punishment. And even wild animals, of the more gregarious species, seem to exhibit certain rude beginnings of moral judgment. They seem at least to exhibit a certain discomfort at the violation of a general and settled habit of action, and even in some cases, if all tales are true, to inflict punishment on those members of the herd that violate its traditions. But the severest punishments appear to be inflicted on those whose only crime is that of being diseased or wounded; so that their action may perhaps be interpreted, if it is to have a quasi-moral interpretation at all,[1] as an instinctive defence of the herd against anything that would tend to weaken it, rather than anything of the nature of a distinctly moral judgment. But

[1] The probability is rather, as Mr. Stout suggests, that "the distress of the comrade, and especially the smell of blood, rouses blind fury, which tends to find a definite channel, and thus vents itself on the object which is the centre of attention, *i. e.*, the distressed comrade itself. If an enemy is at hand, *he* will suffer."

among primitive races of mankind also the judgment passed on conduct, and expressing itself in reward and punishment, seems to mean little more than approbation of that which strengthens and disapproval of that which weakens the tribe.[1] The important point to notice, however, is that the earliest forms of moral judgment involve reference to a tribe or form of society of which the individual is but a member. The germ of this is no doubt found in the gregarious consciousness of animals.

§ 2. THE TRIBAL SELF.—This point was brought out in an interesting way by Clifford in his account[2] of what he described as "The Tribal Self." Clifford begins by saying that the Self means essentially "a sort of centre about which our remoter motives revolve, and to which they always have regard." It is, in short, a universe of reference. "If we consider now," he goes on, "the

[1] Something of the same sort may be observed even in more developed communities under certain conditions. Thus, in Bryce's *American Commonwealth* (chap. lxiii.), the following remarks are made on some aspects of American political life: "Even city politicians must have a moral code and a moral standard. It is not the code of an ordinary unprofessional citizen. It does not forbid falsehood, or malversation, or ballot stuffing, or 'repeating.' But it denounces apathy or cowardice, disobedience, and, above all, treason to the party. Its typical virtue is 'solidity,' unity of heart, mind, and effort among the workers, unquestioning loyalty to the party ticket. He who takes his own course is a kicker or bolter; and is punished not only sternly but vindictively." Nor is this kind of moral standard wholly unknown in English party politics, or in the medical profession, or in the working of Trades Unions. But such a moral standard in modern times, being as it were a standard within a standard, is not able wholly to maintain itself against the recognized moral standard of the people. Even the professional politician sometimes finds it necessary "to pander a little to the moral sense of the community," (Bryce *op. cit.*, chap. lxviii.).

[2] *Lectures and Essays* ("On the Scientific Basis of Morals").

simpler races of mankind, we shall find not only that immediate desires play a far larger part in their lives, and so that the conception of self is less used and less developed, but also that it is less definite and more wide. The savage is not only hurt when anybody treads on his foot, but when anybody treads on his tribe. He may lose his hut, and his wife, and his opportunities of getting food. In this way, the tribe becomes naturally included in that conception of self which renders remote desires possible by making them immediate." "The tribe, *quâ* tribe, has to exist, and it can only exist by aid of such an organic artifice as the conception of the tribal self in the minds of its members. Hence the natural selection of those races in which this conception is the most powerful and most habitually predominant as a motive over immediate desires. To such an extent has this proceeded that we may fairly doubt whether the selfhood of the tribe is not earlier in point of development than that of the individual. In the process of time it becomes a matter of hereditary transmission, and is thus fixed as a specific character in the constitution of social man. With the settlement of countries, and the aggregation of tribes into nations, it takes a wider and more abstract form; and in the highest natures the tribal self is incarnate in nothing less than humanity. Short of these heights, it places itself in the family and in the city. I shall call that quality or disposition of man which consists in the supremacy of the family or tribal self as a mark of reference for motives by its old name *Piety*."

Without absolutely subscribing to everything that is stated by Clifford in this connexion, we may at least recognise the importance of the point that he here seeks to emphasise—*viz.* the solidarity of the primitive moral consciousness. Man does not at first naturally think of himself as an independent individual, but rather as a part of a system[1]; and this system may in a very real sense be called a "self," since it is the universe to which the individual refers the conduct of his life. It is here, then, that we find the earliest basis for the moral judgment; and, in stating the manner of its formation, it may still be convenient to follow the mode of statement given by Clifford.

§ 3. THE ORIGIN OF CONSCIENCE.—"We do not like a man," Clifford goes on, "whose character is such that we may reasonably expect injuries from him. This dislike of a man on account of his character is a more complex feeling than the mere dislike of separate injuries. A cat likes your hand, and your lap, and the food you give her; but I do not think she has any conception of *you*. A dog, however, may like *you* even when you thrash him, though he does not like the thrashing. Now such likes and dislikes may be felt by the tribal self. If a man does anything generally regarded as good for the tribe, my tribal self may say, in the first place, I like that thing that you have done. By such common approbation of individual acts, the influence of piety as a motive becomes defined; and natural selection will in the long run preserve those tribes which have approved the right things; namely, those things which at that time gave the tribe an advantage in the struggle for existence.

[1] It may be noted that the idea of tribal unity generally embodies itself in the image of a tribal god; and the religious bond tends to become more and more important in giving unity to the system.

But in the second place, a man may as a rule and constantly, being actuated by piety, do good things for the tribe; and in that case the tribal self will say, I like *you*. The feeling expressed by this statement on the part of any individual, 'In the name of the tribe, I like you,' is what I call *approbation*. It is the feeling produced in pious individuals by that sort of character which seems to them beneficial to the community."

"Now suppose," Clifford proceeds, "that a man has done something obviously harmful to the community. Either some immediate desire, or his individual self, has for once proved stronger than the tribal self. When the tribal self wakes up, the man says, 'In the name of the tribe, I do not like this thing that I, as an individual, have done.' This self-judgment in the name of the tribe is called Conscience. If the man goes further, and draws from this act and others an inference about his own character, he may say, 'In the name of the tribe I do not like my individual self.' This is remorse."

All this ought to present no difficulty to the student who has grasped the conception of the different Universes within which we live. The Universe, from the point of view of which the primitive moral judgment is passed, is that described by Clifford as "the tribal self." From this point of view the consciousness of the primitive savage passes judgment both on himself and others as individuals within the tribe. And on the whole, actions are judged to be good or bad, and individuals to be praiseworthy or blameworthy, according as they tend to promote or to impede the existence and the welfare of the tribe.

§ 4. CUSTOM AS THE MORAL STANDARD.—We must not, however, suppose that the procedure of the primitive man is quite so self-conscious as Clifford's manner of statement might seem to imply. He does not deliberately ask himself whether his conduct is or is not of such a kind as to promote the welfare of his tribe. Still less does he ask such a question with respect to his general character or to that of others. What happens is rather, as we have already indicated, that customary modes of action grow up in the life of a people, that those modes of action that are favourable to its welfare tend on the whole to be selected and preserved, and that those modes of action also tend on the whole to be approved. In thus approving, the individual puts himself at the point of view of his tribe, but he does so unconsciously; it does not occur to him that it would be possible for him to take up any other point of view. Of himself as an independent individual, or of others as independent individuals, he has not yet formed any clear conception. Hence also it is not quite true to say that he passes judgment on his own character or on that of others. He hardly thinks of character. He judges actions. Even in such a comparatively advanced stage of the moral consciousness as that represented in Homer, the idea of a general judgment on character has scarcely emerged. In the *Iliad*, as Seeley has remarked,[1] "the distinction between right and wrong is barely recognised, and the division of mankind into the good and the bad is not recognised at all. It has often been remarked that it contains no villain. The reason of this is not that the poet does not represent his characters as doing wicked deeds, for, in fact, there is

[1] *Ecce Homo*, chap. xix.

not one among them who is not capable of deeds the most atrocious and shameful. But the poet does not regard these deeds with any strong disapprobation, and the feeling of moral indignation which has been so strong in later poets was in him so feeble that he is quite incapable of hating any of his characters for their crimes. He can no more conceive the notion of a villain than of an habitually virtuous man. The few deeds that he recognises as wrong, or at least as strange and dangerous—killing a suppliant, or killing a father—he, notwithstanding, conceives all persons alike as capable of perpetrating under the influence of passion or some heaven-sent bewilderment of the understanding." In such a state of society there are things which "one does not do," actions which are not customary, but there is hardly anything which is regarded with strong moral disapprobation.

§ 5. Positive Law as the Moral Standard.—Gradually, however, as we have seen, Law takes the place of custom in the control of conduct. Along with this there comes a certain change in the moral judgment. When "thou shalt not do" takes the place of "one does not do," the distinction between right and wrong is made more precise; and a more definite condemnation attaches to the violation of that which is recognised as right. In the early stage of customary morality, to quote Seeley once more, "men, easily tempted into crime, flung off the effects of it as easily. Agamemnon, after violating outrageously the right of property, has but to say ἀασάμην, 'My mind was bewildered,' and the excuse is sufficient to appease his own conscience, and is accepted by the public, and even by the injured party himself, who feels himself equally liable to such temporary mental perplexities." "After the introduction of law crime could never again be thus lightly expiated and forgotten." "By the law comes the knowledge of sin. A standard of action is set up, which serves to each man both as a rule of life for himself and a rule of criticism upon his neighbours. Then comes the division of mankind into those who habitually conform to this rule and those who violate it, into the good and the bad, and feelings soon spring up to sanction the classification, feelings of respect for the one class and hatred for the other."

§ **6.** The Moral Law.—But so long as the law taken as the moral standard is not definitely distinguished from the positive law of the land, the moral judgment is not yet fully formed. The positive law of a country is directed primarily against external acts prejudicial to the welfare of society, whereas the moral judgment in its fully developed form has reference rather to men's intentions, motives, and characters, than to their mere external performances. Now in the life of a developing people this distinction gradually emerges. We see it perhaps most clearly in the case of the Jews, when the Ten Commandments become definitely distinguished from the ceremonial and civil laws of the country. These Commandments include the rule, "Thou shalt not covet," as well as "Thou shalt not steal," and thus introduce the conception of a judgment to be passed on the inner attitude of mind, as well as on the outer action. As the moral consciousness develops, this conception becomes more and more pronounced.

§ **7.** Moral Conflict.—When moral development has arrived at such a stage as this, certain conflicts almost inevitably arise, both in action and in the judgment that is passed on action. In primitive societies each man's duty is comparatively obvious. There is little division of labour, and the way in which the welfare of the tribe is to be promoted can seldom be doubtful. But when law is added to custom, and moral law added to positive law, and when at the same time a man finds himself occupying many different positions within his society (being, for instance, at once father, soldier, judge, husbandman, and the like), the right thing to do on a given occasion is not always so apparent. Law may conflict with custom, or one law with another. The classical instance of such a conflict is found in the *Antigone* of Sophocles, where the definite law of the state comes into collision with the more customary principle of family affection. Antigone prefers the latter, because it is of immemorial antiquity and its origin cannot be traced, whereas the law of the state has been made and may be unmade again. But the ultimate result of such a conflict is to give rise to reflection, and to the search for some deeper standard of judgment.

§ 8. THE INDIVIDUAL CONSCIENCE AS STANDARD.—Such a standard is sometimes sought in an appeal to the heart or conscience of the individual. An appeal may be made from the outer law of the state to the inner voice, or law of the heart. But this is soon found to be unsatisfactory, inasmuch as the conflicts found in the outer law are in reality repeated in the inner law. The heart may attach itself, for instance, to the idea of the family, but it may also attach itself to the idea of the state; and devotion, to the one may be incompatible with devotion to the other.[1] We are accordingly thrown back upon reflective analysis.

§ 9. The Growth of the Reflective Judgment.—It is thus that men are gradually led to ask themselves what is the real basis of the moral judgment. This question inevitably leads to the attempt to construct some sort of scientific ethical system. It may, however, for a time stop short of this, and merely lead to the formulation of certain fundamental principles, without any definite attempt at systematic construction. In any case universal principles, applicable to all times and peoples become gradually substituted for the customs and laws of particular tribes and nations.

§ 10. Illustrations from Ancient Peoples.—The development of the moral judgment is perhaps most

[1] *Cf.* the attitude of Blanche in Shakespeare's play of *King John*, (Act. III., scene 1) :—

> "Which is the side that I must go withal?
> I am with both: each army hath a hand;
> And in their rage, I having hold of both,
> They whirl asunder and dismember me.
> Husband, I cannot pray that thou mayst win;
> Uncle, I needs must pray that thou mayst lose;
> Father, I may not wish the fortune thine;
> Grandam, I will not wish thy wishes thrive;
> Whoever wins, on that side shall I lose;
> Assured loss before the match be played."

Here the puzzle is—On which side is the self? On which side is the deepest and most abiding interest?

Cf. also the attitude of Desdemona in *Othello*—(Act. I., scene 3) :—

> "I do perceive here a divided duty."

Indeed it is out of such conflict that all the most profoundly tragic situations arise.

easily studied in the great nations of antiquity, in which there was less interference from without than in the case of most modern peoples.

Among the Jews, for instance, it is easy to trace a development from the customary and ceremonial law, through the Ten Commandments, to the deeper and more inward principles represented by the Psalms and the later prophets. The idea of the "pure heart" gradually substitutes itself for external observances; and, in Christianity, the law is quite definitely superseded by the idea of the inner principle of love. When this takes place, the purely national character of the Jewish morality is at the same time broken down, and it becomes a morality that is applicable to all times and peoples. In the case of this line of development, however, it is to be noted that every step takes place, as it were, by a new enactment. The deeper principle is always formulated by the voice of some prophet, speaking more or less definitely in the name of "the Lord." The idea of a divine law remains fundamental throughout. Even when the inner principle of Christianity is set against the external rules of the older system, it still appears in the form of a definite enactment, a 'New Commandment.' "It was said by them of old time. . . . . But I say unto you. . . . ." The appeal is still to an authoritative law.

Among the Greeks the case is very different. Here, indeed, we start also from the idea of law, and indeed of divine law. But it is a law that is never distinctly formulated in a code of commandments; and the process of its development is different. The deeper principle is not introduced in the form of a new prophetic utterance, but in the form of a reflective interpretation. Men begin to question the validity of the old principles of action, and to ask themselves how they are to be justified; and this soon gives rise to reflective systems of Ethics. The growth of these will be briefly noticed in the following Book. What it is important to observe, however, is that, different as this course of development is from that found among the Hebrews, it leads, nevertheless, to substantially similar results. Here also the growth is one from external observances to the idea of action based on principle—from the idea of duty done in obedience to the law of the state to that of duty done τοῦ καλοῦ ἕνεκα, for the sake of the beauty or nobility of it. At the same time there is a gradual advance from the idea of a kind of life which is possible only for the Greek, and not for the Barbarian, to the idea (which becomes especially prominent among the Stoics) of a kind of life which is simply human, and which belongs to all mankind as citizens of the world.

Among the Romans nothing quite similar can be traced. In their later life they were too much influenced by Greek thought for anything quite spontaneous to arise among themselves. But we see something of the same sort in the development of their law. Roman law is at first simply Roman, and rests on no definite principle. By the help of the stoical philosophy, however, they gradually introduced an inner principle into it, and in so doing made it cease to be Roman Law, and become the Law of the world.

Thus, these three peoples gradually developed from their national institutions a universal religion, a universal science, and a universal law, at the same time as they substituted an inner principle of action for a merely external obedience to their laws.

§ **11.** GENERAL NATURE OF MORAL DEVELOPMENT.—From this brief sketch the general nature of the development of the moral judgment may be more or less apparent. The following features may be specially noted :—

(1) It develops from customs, through law, to reflective principles.

(2) It develops from the judgment on external acts to the judgment on the inner purpose and character.

(3) It develops from ideas peculiar to the circumstances of particular tribes and nations to ideas that have a universal validity.

Having thus indicated the general nature of the development of the moral judgment, we may now be in a position to consider the essential elements involved in that judgment in its fully developed form.

CHAPTER VI.

THE SIGNIFICANCE OF THE MORAL JUDGMENT.

§ **1.** The Nature of the Moral Judgment.—From the statements that have now been made, the general nature of the moral judgment ought to be to a considerable extent apparent; but there are still some questions that it is important to ask with respect to its fully developed content and significance. These questions will naturally fall under two distinct heads. It is evident, in the first place, that the moral judgment is not simply of the nature of what is called a judgment in Logic. It is not merely a judgment *about*, but a judgment *upon*. It does not merely state the nature of some object, but compares it with a standard, and by means of this standard pronounces it to be good or evil, right or wrong. This is what is meant in saying that the moral point of view is normative. Now it follows from this that there are two main questions to be asked —(1) What is the object upon which judgment is pronounced?—(2) What is the point of view from which such a judgment is possible? The consideration of these questions will naturally lead us up to the consideration of the precise nature of the standard, which is to be the subject of the following book.

The two questions which we have now to consider may be briefly expressed as follows:—(1) What is the object of the moral judgment? (2) What is the subject of the moral judgment?

§ 2. THE OBJECT OF THE MORAL JUDGMENT.—In a general way the nature of the object upon which the moral judgment is passed is clear enough. The object is voluntary action. It is with this, as we have seen, that Ethics is concerned throughout. It has to do with the right direction of the will. The moral judgments which we pass are, in like manner, concerned with the will. Whatever is not willed, has no moral quality. An avalanche rolling down a mountain may devastate a village; a shower may save a nation from famine: but we do not judge either the one or the other to be morally bad or good. In like manner, we do not pass moral judgments on tigers or horses for their ravages or for their services, so long as we regard these as dictated by mere instinct, without volition. When we praise or blame them, we do it under the tacit assumption that their acts were voluntary. Moral judgments, then, are not passed upon all sorts of things, nor even upon all sorts of activities, but only upon *conduct*.

§ 3. THE GOOD WILL.—We are thus led to the famous declaration with which Kant opened his great treatise on Ethics.[1] He begins it by saying that "there is nothing in the world, or even out of it, that can be called good without qualification, except a good will." The gifts of fortune, he said, and the happiness which they bring with them, are to be regarded as good only on condition that they are rightly used. Talents and worldly wisdom are, in like manner, good only when they are subordinated to the attainment of high aims. These things are only conditionally good. But a good will is good without condition. It is, as Kant said, the only jewel that shines by its own light.

[1] *Metaphysic of Morals*, section I.

But in thus commending the good will as supremely good, and regarding it as the ultimate object approved by the moral judgment, we must be careful to distinguish will from mere wish. "Hell," it is said, "is paved with good intentions." A good will is not merely a *good intention*, in the sense in which we distinguish an intention from a fully formed purpose,[1] but *a determined effort to produce a good result*—though it may be an effort that has still to wait for its appropriate opportunity of issuing in overt action. Such an effort is, from a moral point of view, supremely good, even if, from some unforeseen contingencies, the good result is not itself achieved. A good wish is merely the consciousness that the attainment of a certain end would give satisfaction: a good will is the identification of oneself with that end.

But again, when we say that a good will is supremely good, even if it fails to achieve a good result, it ought not to be supposed that a good will can actually fail to issue in a good action—if, at least, it issues in action at all.[2] Will and act, when there is an act at all, are but the inner and outer side of the same phenomenon. A good will issues in a good action; and, conversely, there can be no good action without a good will. But an action which in itself is good may lead, through the interference of other circumstances, to a bad result; and a bad action may lead to a good result. "The morality of an action," said Dr. Johnson,[3] "depends on the motive

[1] *I.e.*, the sense in which we distinguish Wish from Will. The term "Intention" is here used in a sense somewhat different from that explained in Chapter i. of the present Book.

[2] Cf. above, Book I., chap. i., 59.

[3] Boswell's *Life of Johnson*, Vol. I.

from which we act. If I fling half-a-crown to a beggar with intention to break his head, and he picks it up and buys victuals with it, the physical effect is good, but, with respect to me, the action is very wrong." On the other hand, an act in itself good may be perverted to evil ends. "You taught me language," says Caliban to Prospero, "and my profit on't is, I know how to curse." He who benefits another may be only nourishing a snake. What constitutes the goodness of an action is the goodness of the intention; but a good intention, though it produces a good action, need not produce a good result. A result is generally a resultant of several causes, of which the will of any particular agent is only one.[1]

§ 4. JUDGMENT ON ACT AND ON AGENT.—So far there is no difficulty. But it is necessary now to draw a distinction between two forms in which the moral judgment is passed. We may judge a man's actions, or we may judge the man himself. It can hardly be doubted that both these forms of judgment are to be found even at the most developed stage of the moral consciousness that has yet been reached. The distinction corresponds, in the main, to that between Right and Good. Some of a man's actions may be right, and yet we may not

[1] If we took account of all the effects, direct and indirect, of a man's actions, we should probably find that the amount of good in the result is much more nearly in proportion to the amount of good in the intention than is commonly supposed. Green says (*Prolegomena to Ethics*, p. 320), that "there is no real reason to doubt that the good or evil in the motive of an action is exactly measured by the good or evil in its consequences." It should be noted that, in what is said up to this point, no account is taken of the question, afterwards discussed, whether it is strictly on the intention or on the motive that the moral judgment is passed.

judge him to be a good man, and *vice versa*. We sometimes, that is to say, judge character, and sometimes will in the narrower sense. Now, with respect to the judgment on character no particular difficulty seems to arise. We judge men's characters by the degree in which the total content of their moral consciousness tends towards the realisation of the highest end, whatever that may be conceived to be. It is not so easy, however, to say what it is that we judge when we judge an act rather than an agent. We do not judge the act by its result, but by the purpose of the agent. On this all are agreed. But it remains to be asked whether we judge it by the whole intention involved in it, or rather by that part of the intention which is described as the motive. On this point there is considerable difference of opinion, and the question is further complicated by a want of uniformity in the interpretation of the terms Intention and Motive.

§ **5.** Is the Moral Judgment concerned with Motives or with Intentions?—The controversy on this subject[1] has been carried on chiefly between writers of the intuitional and the utilitarian school.[2] The former have generally maintained that the moral judgment is concerned entirely with the motives of our actions, that our actions are to be pronounced good or bad in proportion to the goodness or badness of the motives by which we are actuated in doing them. Thus Dr. Martineau, the most eminent of recent intuitionist writers,

[1] This subject is well treated by Prof. Dewey in his *Outlines of Ethics*, pp. 4-6, and more fully in Muirhead's *Elements of Ethics*, pp. 57-62.

[2] The nature of these two schools will become apparent in the sequel.

has drawn out an elaborate table of the motives of our conduct, and arranged them in order of merit.[1] He places reverence at the top, and censoriousness, vindictiveness, and suspiciousness at the bottom, while between these lie a great variety of passions, appetites, affections, sentiments, etc. ; such as love of ease, fear, ambition, generosity, and compassion. Now to discuss the merits of such a scheme as this would evidently carry us beyond the limits of such a handbook as the present. Two criticisms, however, may be passed upon it. In the first place, the list of motives, or "springs of action" (as they are also called), seems to rest on a false conception of psychological divisions. The student of psychology will probably have become familiar with this objection. Modern Psychology treats the human mind as an organic unity, and repudiates any hard and fast distinctions of faculties, such as seem to be implied in Dr. Martineau's list. The motives which he enumerates are not simple, but highly complex, phenomena ; and their merits in any particular case would depend on the way in which they are composed. Fear, for instance, is not a simple element in consciousness, but a complex state ; and its merit or demerit depends on the way in which we fear and the thing of which we are afraid. The same applies to ambition, and to most of the other motives enumerated by Dr. Martineau. But, apart from this, the list seems to involve that confusion between the different senses of the term "motive" to which refer-

[1] *Types of Ethical Theory*, Part II., Book I., chap. vi. A criticism of Martineau's doctrine will be found in Sidgwick's *Methods of Ethics*, Book III., chap. xii.

ence has already been made. Thus fear and compassion, though referring to objects, may be treated as emotional states; whereas ambition does not denote a state of feeling, but rather an object aimed at—not indeed a definite object, but a range of objects almost infinite in variety (from the desire to be Mayor of a town to the desire to be the saviour of one's country), having only in common the desire of some form of personal eminence. Now mere feelings in the mind, such as fear and compassion, do not seem, as I have already indicated, to constitute motives at all, in the proper sense of the term: they are not inducements to action. What induces us to act is the presentation of some end to be attained. Consequently, if we are to have a list of motives, this list should take the form rather of a classification of ends to be attained, than of feelings that exist in our minds. Further, these ends would have to be arranged, not under any such abstract headings as "ambition" and the like, but in accordance with their actual, concrete nature.

The antagonism of the utilitarians seems to be partly due to the inadequacy of the intuitionist theory. Thus Mill urges[1] that "the morality of an action depends entirely upon the intention—that is, upon what the agent *wills to do*. But the motive, that is, the feeling which makes him will so to do, when it makes no difference in the act, makes none in the morality: though it makes a great difference in our moral estimation of the agent, especially if it indicates a good or a bad habitual *disposition*." "The motive of an action," he says again,[2] "has nothing to do with the

[1] *Utilitarianism*, chap. ii., p. 27, *note*. [2] *Ibid.*, p. 26.

morality of the action, though much with the worth of the agent." The reasonableness of this view is apparent. If one man is animated by compassion and another by fear, we may think the former a more amiable man and the latter a more cowardly man: but if they are led to act in precisely the same way, must not their actions be regarded as equally good or bad? They are not perhaps equally good *men;* but that is not the question. A good man may do a bad action, and a bad man may do a good action. The question is simply—Are their actions good or bad? How they feel in doing the actions may affect our judgment of their characters, of their lives as a whole, but not of their particular actions. Of course if their actions are *different* in consequence of their feelings—if, for instance, the man who feels compassion does the act in a more gracious way, and the man who feels fear does it in a hurried and awkward way—our moral judgment upon the actions will be different. But the reason is that in this case the feeling has to some extent affected the nature of the act that is willed. This is Mill's view; and it is evidently a reasonable view, so far as it goes. Nevertheless, it appears to me to be erroneous.

§ **6.** The Moral Judgment is partly concerned with Motives.—So long indeed as the reference is merely to the feelings by which our actions are accompanied, there is no need to dispute Mill's position.[1] But if we understand the motive to mean that which induces us

[1] Of course the nature of our feelings is ultimately determined by the nature of the ends that we have in view, and consequently in disputing the one position we are in reality disputing the other as well.

to act in a particular way, then I think we must maintain that it is on the motive that the moral judgment is passed, or at least that the motive is properly taken into account in passing judgment. Mill's error seems to arise from this, that he supposes the moral judgment to be passed on things done, whereas the moral judgment is not properly passed upon a *thing done*, but upon a *person doing*. If it were not so, we should pass moral judgment on the instinctive acts of animals, and even on the movements of rocks, clouds, and avalanches. What we judge is *conduct*; and this means not merely an overt act, but the attitude of a person in acting; and his attitude must include his motive. Now Mill himself admits that the motive (even in the sense of the mere feeling, and surely much more in the sense of the end with reference to which we are induced to act) makes a difference in our estimation of the agent. It is true, indeed, that in passing a moral judgment upon a particular act we need not take account of the whole character of the man who does it. If a man gets drunk, or tells a lie, or defrauds his neighbour, we can say that he has done wrong, without needing to inquire whether he is in other respects a good man or a bad. But this does not imply that we judge his action simply from the outside, as a thing done. It is the man doing it that we judge; and the question, what induced him to do it, is not irrelevant to this judgment. It may be admitted that we frequently omit this inner side of a man's conduct in forming our judgments. But the reason is, that it is so difficult to ascertain what the inner side is. With regard to all men's actions (except our own),

"One point must still be greatly dark,
The moving *why* they do it."

Hence the force of the precept "judge not!" But in so far as we do judge, when we try to be thoroughly just in our moral appreciations, it seems unquestionable that we take account of the motive, and that this is what we are bound to take account of.[1]

It may be objected, of course, that a man's motives are sometimes excellent, while yet we feel bound to condemn his actions. Some fanatics, for instance, have performed acts of the utmost atrocity, "thinking that they did God service." Are we to approve these actions, it may be asked, because the end aimed at was good? In answering this question, we must be sure that we understand exactly what the question is. Are we to understand that we are asked, whether, in the case of such actions, we regard the thing done as

[1] An example may help to make this clear. It has been urged that if it is just to put a man to death, this act will not be rendered vicious by the mere fact that the execution of it is accompanied by a feeling of resentment or malevolence. Certainly, I should answer, the mere feeling of resentment will make no difference in the morality of the action, any more than a feeling of reluctance or a feeling of weariness. But it is otherwise if the gratification of the feeling was the *motive* of the act. If a judge were to condemn a criminal to death, not because it is just, but because he feels resentment, and *aims at the gratification of this feeling*, then undoubtedly his action would be wrong, though the result of it might accidentally be right—*i. e.* it might be the case that the criminal ought to have been put to death. Of course in such a case the intention is wrong as well as the motive. This is necessarily so; for the motive is part of the intention. In the case supposed, it is part of the judge's intention (his *inner* intention, as I have called it) to gratify his feeling of resentment. But if this had not been part of his *motive*, it would not have vitiated his action—*i. e.* if it had not been part of his *inducement*.

a desirable result? If so, our answer would no doubt be decidedly, No. In the same way we should say that the fall of an avalanche is not a desirable result. But in neither case is our judgment a *moral* judgment. On the other hand, if we are asked whether we consider that the fanatics in question acted rightly, then we must answer that, in so far as they were aiming steadfastly at a definite end, and in so far as that end was a good one, we must approve of their actions. As a rule, indeed, we shall not entirely approve of them; but the reason is that we do not regard their aims as perfectly good. This is implied in calling them fanatics. A fanatic is one who pursues some narrow end as if it were the supreme good. The motive of such a man is not the best possible, and the more conscientiously he is guided by that motive the more certainly will his actions not be the best possible.

§ 7. BUT THE JUDGMENT IS REALLY ON CHARACTER.—It appears from this, however, that it is only in a somewhat strained sense that the judgment can be said to be passed either on the intention or on the motive alone. The truth seems to be rather that the fully developed moral judgment is always pronounced, directly or indirectly, on the *character* of the agent. That is to say, as I have already remarked, it is never simply on a thing done, but always on a person doing, that we pass moral judgment. It is true that, in some cases, we may have regard only to the person as doing this one particular action, while in other cases we may think of him as having general habits of action. But in all cases, when we are passing a strictly moral judgment, we think of the action, not as an isolated event, but as part of a system of life. We judge its significance not in the abstract, but for the person who does it, situated as he happens to be, and viewing the world as he has learned to view it. Thus we judge the action to be good or evil according to the extent to which the various elements in the whole presented content serve as inducements to act or to refrain from acting. In thus regarding the action, we are judging the whole intention, but with reference to the extent to which the various elements in it serve, or do not serve, as motives to action. We thus judge the motives, both positively and negatively, and in so doing judge the whole intention. Hence it is somewhat misleading to say simply that we pass judgment either on the intention or on the motive.[1]

§ 8. THE SUBJECT OF THE MORAL JUDGMENT.—Having thus considered the precise nature of the object upon which the moral judgment is passed, we must now turn our attention to the subject of the moral judgment, *i. e.* to the point of view from which an action is judged to be good or bad. In a sense, every man may be said to judge his own action to be good at the moment when he does it. In deliberately choosing to do it, he pronounces it to be the course of action which offers most inducement at the time. By what right, then, we may ask, does any one else pronounce it to be wrong? Or, how does it happen that the man himself, on calm reflection, judges his action to fall short of an ideal standard? The answer is that it is looked

[1] For further discussion on this point, the student may be referred to Green's *Prolegomena to Ethics*, Book II., chap. ii., Book III., chap. i., Book IV., chap. i.; Martineau's *Types of Ethical Theory*, Part II. Book I., chap. vi., § 15; and *International Journal of Ethics*, Vol. IV. Nos. 1 and 2.

at from a different point of view, regarded within a different universe or system, from that from which the individual was regarding it when he decided to act in that particular way. But there are an indefinite number of universes within which an action might be placed, an indefinite number of points of view from which an action or an agent might be judged. What claim has any one of these to be regarded as preferable to any other?

Now to give any complete answer to this question would involve the discussion of the various theories of morals, to which our attention is to be directed in the next Book. But, without entering into this discussion at present, it may be profitable to notice some ways in which the subject of the moral judgment may be conceived.

§ 9. THE MORAL CONNOISSEUR.—One way in which we may help ourselves to understand it is by calling to our aid the analogy of the judgments which are passed on works of art. We say that a poem or a play or a novel is a good or a bad artistic product. In so saying, we are passing a judgment upon it, just as we do when we say that an action is good or bad. Now from what point of view is such a judgment pronounced? Not, it seems clear, from that of the person who happens at the time to be reading or hearing or seeing the artistic product, any more than the moral judgment is passed from the point of view of the individual who is acting. The artist appeals from the judgment of the multitude to the judgment of the skilled and sympathetic critic.[1] Now it may be said

[1] "Like Verdi when, at his worst opera's end
(The thing they gave at Florence—what's its name?)

that in like manner, when we are dealing with conduct, the appeal is to the judgment of the moral connoisseur. This is the view of the Moral Sense School, to which we shall have occasion to refer in the sequel, and in particular of Shaftesbury, its most notable exponent. Without discussing the point of view of that School at present, it suffices to say here that it hardly seems to furnish us with a satisfactory answer to the present question. A work of art aims, as we have already noted, at the production of a certain result. The skilled critic is the only judge whether such a result has been achieved. "We musicians know." But in morals, as we have seen, it is rather the action than the result that is judged. Now this action, if it is a real action at all, has been already judged by the person who acts. He has deliberately chosen to act in a particular way. Yet his action is judged to be wrong, and judged to be wrong not merely by the moral connoisseur, but by himself when he reflects upon it.

§ 10. THE IMPARTIAL SPECTATOR.—A somewhat more elaborate theory was put forward by Adam Smith. His theory rests upon the fact of sympathy, to which reference has already been made. He points out that our approval or disapproval of the conduct of others depends on the extent to which we are able to sympathise with them. "We run," he says,[1] "not only to congratulate the successful, but to condole with the

While the mad houseful's plaudits near out-bang
His orchestra of salt-box, tongs and bones,
He looks through all the roaring and the wreaths
Where sits Rossini patient in his stall."

Browning—*Bishop Blougram's Apology.*

[1] *Theory of the Moral Sentiments*, Part I., Sect. I., chap. ii.

afflicted; and the pleasure which we find in the conversation of one whom in all the passions of his heart we can entirely sympathise with, seems to do more than compensate the painfulness of that sorrow with which the view of his situation affects us." "If we hear a person loudly lamenting his misfortunes, which, however, upon bringing the case home to ourselves, we feel can produce no such violent effect upon us, we are shocked at his grief; and, because we cannot enter into it, call it pusillanimity and weakness. It gives us the spleen, on the other hand, to see another too happy, or too much elevated, as we call it, with any little piece of good fortune. We are disobliged even with his joy; and, because we cannot go along with it, call it levity and folly. We are even put out of humour if our companions laugh louder or longer at a joke than we think it deserves; that is, than we feel that we ourselves could laugh at it."

"When," he goes on,[1] "the original passions of the person principally concerned are in perfect concord with the sympathetic emotions of the spectator, they necessarily appear to this last just and proper, and suitable to their objects; and, on the contrary, when, upon bringing the case home to himself, he finds that they do not coincide with what he feels, they necessarily appear to him unjust and improper, and unsuitable to the causes which excite them. To approve of the passions of another, therefore, as suitable to their objects, is the same thing as to observe that we entirely sympathise with them; and not to approve of them as such, is the same thing as to observe that we do not entirely sympathise with them. The man who resents

[1] *Ibid.*, chap. iii.

the injuries that have been done to me, and observes that I resent them precisely as he does, necessarily approves of my resentment. The man whose sympathy keeps time to my grief, cannot but admit the reasonableness of my sorrow. He who admires the same poem, or the same picture, and admires them exactly as I do, must surely allow the justness of my admiration. He who laughs at the same joke, and laughs along with me, cannot well deny the propriety of my laughter. On the contrary, the person who, upon those different occasions, either feels no such emotion as that which I feel, or feels none that bears any proportion to mine, cannot avoid disapproving my sentiments on account of their dissonance with his own. If my animosity goes beyond what the indignation of my friend can correspond to; if my grief exceeds what his most tender compassion can go along with; if my admiration is either too high or too low to tally with his own; if I laugh loud and heartily when he only smiles, or, on the contrary, only smile when he laughs loud and heartily; in all these cases, as soon as he comes from considering the object, to observe how I am affected by it, according as there is more or less disproportion between his sentiments and mine, I must incur a greater or less degree of his disapprobation; and upon all occasions his own sentiments are the standards and measures by which he judges of mine."

It follows from this that our earliest moral judgments are passed, not upon ourselves, but upon others. "Our first ideas," he says,[1] "of personal beauty and deformity, are drawn from the shape and appearance

[1] *Ibid.*, Part III., chap. i.

of others, not from our own. We soon become sensible, however, that others exercise the same criticism upon us." "In the same manner our first moral criticisms are exercised upon the character and conduct of other people; and we are all very forward to observe how each of these affects us. But we soon learn that other people are equally frank with regard to our own. We become anxious to know how far we deserve their censure or applause, and whether to them we must necessarily appear those agreeable or disagreeable creatures which they represent us. We begin, upon this account, to examine our own passions and conduct, and to consider how these must appear to them, by considering how they would appear to us if in their situation. We suppose ourselves the spectators of our own behaviour, and endeavour to imagine what effect it would, in this light, produce upon us. This is the only looking-glass by which we can, in some measure, with the eyes of other people, scrutinise the propriety of our own conduct. If in this view it pleases us, we are tolerably satisfied. We can be more indifferent about the applause, and, in some measure, despise the censure of the world; secure that, however misunderstood or misrepresented, we are the natural and proper objects of approbation."

"When I endeavour," he goes on, "to examine my own conduct, when I endeavour to pass sentence upon it, and either to approve or condemn it, it is evident that, in all such cases, I divide myself, as it were, into two persons; and that I, the examiner and judge, represent a different character from that other I, the person whose conduct is examined into, and judged of. The first is the spectator, whose sentiments with regard to my own conduct I endeavour to get into, by placing myself in his situation, and by considering how it would appear to me, when seen from that particular point of view. The second is the agent; the person whom I properly call myself, and of whose conduct, under the character of a spectator, I was endeavouring to form some opinion. The first is the judge; the second the person judged of. But that the judge should, in every respect, be the same with the person judged of, is as impossible, as that the cause should, in every respect, be the same with the effect."

Adam Smith was thus led to the idea of what he called the "impartial spectator," from whose point of view our moral judgments are pronounced. He distinguishes this point of view as that of "the man within," whose judgments are opposed to those of the "man without." An appeal, he says,[1] lies from the opinions of mankind "to a much higher tribunal, to the tribunal of their own consciences, to that of the supposed impartial and well-informed spectator, to that of the man within the breast, the great judge and arbiter of their conduct."

§ **11.** THE IDEAL SELF.—How far this conception of an "impartial spectator" is valuable, and what exactly is to be meant by his "impartiality," we cannot here discuss. I have given this reference to Adam Smith merely on account of the clearness with which he brings out the fact that our moral judgments involve a certain reference to a point of view higher than that of the individual who acts—an appeal, so to speak, "from Philip drunk to Philip sober." The point of view to which an appeal is thus made may perhaps be most

[1] *Ibid.*, Part III., chap. ii.

fittingly described as that of the Ideal Self. At early stages of development it corresponds to what Clifford described as "the Tribal Self." The normal member of the tribe[1] may be said to be the "impartial spectator" to whose judgment the appeal is made. At more advanced stages of human development the nature of the Ideal Self becomes more complicated; and we cannot discuss it satisfactorily until we have considered the significance of the moral standard. In the meantime this much seems necessary in order to bring out the fact that in the moral judgment there is an appeal from the Universe of the individual consciousness to a higher or more comprehensive system. With this in view, we are now able to proceed to the consideration of the various theories of the moral standard.

1 This may be compared with the view of the "normal man," taken by such a writer as Dr. Simmel. A somewhat similar conception is contained in the theory of the standard of moral value, given by Meinong in his *Psychologisch-ethische Untersuchungen zur Werththeorie.*

Note on the Meaning of Conscience.

Throughout this chapter, as well as some of the preceding, we have had frequent occasion to refer to conscience; and it may be well at this point to explain more precisely the sense (or senses) in which this term is used. The term is derived from the Latin *conscire*, to be conscious (of wrong). The Greek συνείδησις, the German *Gewissen*, and the old English *Inwit*, are similar in meaning. *Conscientia* used to be employed almost indifferently for conscience and for consciousness in general; and in English, as in French,[1] the term conscience is occasionally found with the latter meaning. It is in this sense that Milton says, referring to the loss of his eyes,

> "What supports me dost thou ask?
> The *conscience*, Friend, to have lost them overplied
> In liberty's defence, my noble task,
> Of which all Europe rings from side to side."

But even here there is perhaps a certain implication of a *moral* consciousness; as there is also in Hamlet's saying,

> "Thus conscience doth make cowards of us all,"

though here it seems to mean little more than reflection. In Chaucer's description of the Prioress, where he says,

> "All was conscience and tender heart,"

it appears almost to mean sensibility. But the definitely moral sense soon became established in English, especially under the influence of such writers as Butler. Even in the moral sense of the term. however, there is some ambiguity. It sometimes means a feeling of pleasure or pain, and especially a feeling of pain, accompanying the violation of a recognised principle of duty. At other times it means the principle of judgment by which we pronounce one action or one kind of action, to be right and another wrong. In the latter sense, again, it may refer to this principle of judgment as it appears in a particular individual or in a body of men. Such phrases as "the Non-Conformist Conscience," "the Conscience of Europe," and the like, illustrate this use of the term. We shall have to make some further comments on the nature of conscience, especially in dealing with the intuitional school of morals and with the social nature of the moral consciousness. But this much seemed necessary at present by way of general explanation of the use of the term.

---

[1] Malebranche and some other French writers use the term *conscience*, more particularly in the sense of *self*-consciousness.

BOOK II.

THEORIES OF THE MORAL STANDARD.

CHAPTER I.

THE DEVELOPMENT OF ETHICAL THOUGHT.

§ 1. Early Greek Ethics.—Thought on Ethics, as on most other scientific subjects, first took definite shape among the Greeks.[1] Attention, however, was not strongly drawn to this subject till a considerable time after philosophical thought in general had begun to develop. The earliest thinkers among the Greeks directed their attention chiefly to physical inquiries—especially to the question, What is the world made of? Two of the physical philosophers, however, do appear to have touched with some definiteness upon the ethical problem—*viz.* Heraclitus and Democritus (sometimes known as the "weeping" and the "laughing" philosopher). These two may be regarded as the founders of those modes of thinking which afterwards developed into Stoicism and Epicureanism respectively. Heraclitus took Fire as his fundamental physical principle—*i. e.* the bright and dry—and he seems to have regarded this as incessantly struggling with the dark and moist principle which is opposed to it. In the life of man he

1 For a more detailed account of the way in which this took place, reference should be made to Sidgwick's *History of Ethics.*

appears to have thought that this struggle can be found going on; and the great aim of the moral life is to secure the victory for the bright and dry. "Keep your soul dry," was with him the fundamental moral law. Hence also the saying, so often quoted, that "the dry soul [or the 'dry light'] is the best." This opposition of the moist and dry—the "blood and judgment"[1]—runs through a very long period of philosophic thought. With Democritus, on the other hand, the fundamental principle of morals seems to have been pleasure.[2] But there is no evidence that either of these philosophers made any attempt to develop his ethical ideas in a systematic form.

§ 2. THE SOPHISTS.—Parmenides and the Pythagoreans, and indeed to some extent all the early philosophers, seem also to have touched, either in a purely theoretical or in a more directly practical way, upon the ethical and political side of speculation. In fact, from quite an early period, philosophy among the Greeks seems to have come to mean a way of living as well as a way of thinking.[3] But it was that remarkable group of teachers known as the Sophists who seem first to have brought the ethical problem to the front. The

1 "Blest are those
Whose blood and judgment are so well commingled,
That they are not a pipe for fortune's fingers
To play what stop she pleases."

On the views of Heraclitus, see Burnet's *Early Greek Philosophy*, pp. 138, 139, 178, 179.

2 Not, however, sensuous pleasure. It was rather peace or ἀταραξία. Perhaps his point of view might be compared with that represented, in modern times, by Dr. Stanton Coit in a paper in *Mind*, Old Series, Vol. XI., p. 324 *sqq*.

3 Thus we hear of the "Parmenidean Life," of the Pythagorean rules of conduct, &c. *Cf.* Burnet, *op. cit.*, pp. 29, 40, 182, 316.

aim of these teachers was to a large extent practical, *i. e.* it was the aim of preparing the young men of Athens to be efficient citizens. In instructing them in the duties of citizenship, they found it necessary to inquire into the basis of political obligation and of social morality in general. This seems to have been done by them in general in a serious and candid spirit; but, naturally enough, inquiries of this kind tended to be somewhat subversive of the older moral standards, and the more conservative minds were alarmed. This alarm found expression especially in the satirical drama of Aristophanes; and as Plato also shared, to a considerable extent, the unfavourable view thus taken of the tendency of the sophistic teaching, the name of the Sophists has fallen into evil odour. Probably this is in the main unjust—perhaps in pretty much the same way as the criticisms of such men as Carlyle and Ruskin on modern science were often unjust. The Sophists were probably the most enlightened men of their day, and did more than any others to awaken the intellectual life of the city.[1]

§ 3. Socrates.—Socrates was closely associated with the Sophists, and indeed was regarded by Aristophanes as the typical example of them. He was distinguished, however, from most of the others by the fact that he did not set himself up as a professional teacher, but rather regarded himself throughout his life as a student of moral science. When commended by the oracle for his wisdom, he replied that it consisted only in knowing his own ignorance. By this attitude he displayed, perhaps not more modesty (for his modesty was at

1 Reference may profitably be made to the articles on the "Sophists" and "Socrates" in the *Encyclopædia Britannica.*

least in part ironical), but at least more earnestness than his fellow-Sophists. He was less of a dogmatist, because he was more clearly aware of the difficulty of the problem. The one point on which he was fully convinced was the unsatisfactoriness of the commonly received explanations of the moral life, and the necessity for a more scientific account. He believed that this was necessary, not merely for the satisfaction of speculative curiosity, but for the sake of practical morality. For it seemed to him that there could be no true morality which did not rest on a scientific basis. "Virtue," he said, "is knowledge" (or is *science*). He believed that if any one fully understood the nature of the moral end, he could not fail to pursue it. On the other hand, he conceived that if any one did not fully understand the nature of the moral end, he could not be moral except by accident; and this is not, in the full sense, morality at all. Whatever is not of knowledge is sin.[1] As to the nature of the moral end, however, Socrates only professed to be an inquirer. The view that he suggested seems sometimes to have leaned to Hedonism;[2] but there is no reason to suppose that he had explicitly developed any theory on the subject. The fact that diverse schools arose, claiming him as

1 This is perhaps a slight exaggeration. But Socrates, like Plato, maintained that to be temperate or courageous without knowledge is to be temperate by a kind of intemperance or courageous by a kind of cowardice. He even went so far as to say that it is better to do wrong consciously than unconsciously; since the former involves at least the knowledge of right. *Cf.* Zeller's *Socrates and the Socratic Schools*, p. 147.

2 In Plato's *Protagoras* he is represented as definitely putting forward such a doctrine; and there are also indications of the same tendency in Xenophon's *Memorabilia.*

master, seems to afford some evidence that his view had not been clearly defined.

§ 4. The Schools of Ethical Thought.—Immediately after the time of Socrates, ethical speculation began to run in separate schools, which with variations may be said to have lasted even down to our own day. The two most distinctly ethical schools, among the followers of Socrates, were those of the Cynics and the Cyrenaics, which afterwards gave rise to those of the Stoics and Epicureans. The members of these schools fixed on points connected with the general character and influence of Socrates, almost as much as with his speculative activity. The Cynics were struck with his independence and freedom from want; and they made this their fundamental principle. The Cyrenaics were more impressed by his tact and skill in making the most of his surroundings. The Cynics were thus led to asceticism, and the Cyrenaics to Hedonism. These two tendencies have persisted throughout almost the whole course of ethical speculation.

§ 5. Plato and Aristotle.—But in the meantime there were other writers who made more definite efforts to connect ethical ideas with the general principles of philosophy, and so to get beyond the one-sidedness of opposing schools. Plato, in particular, put forward a metaphysical view of the world, upon which he endeavoured to rest his ethical conceptions. His general view is contained in what is known as the theory of Ideas or Types.[1] He believed that the fundamental

[1] Εἴδη. It is difficult to render this in English. The word "idea" has come to mean in English (chiefly through the influence of Locke, Berkeley, and Hume) that which exists or goes on in our heads,

reality of things is to be found in the Type to which they conform, and to which they are imperfect approximations. Among these Types he held that the most fundamental is the Type or Idea of the Good, and it is in approximating to this that the ideal of virtue is to be found. To understand this Type it is necessary to go through a course of metaphysical training; and hence the highest form of virtue is attainable only by the philosopher. Plato, however, recognised also a lower form of virtue which can be cultivated by the good citizen, and he was accordingly led to analyse the virtue of the citizen. Aristotle carried this analysis further, and even devoted a considerable part of his great work on Ethics to the description of the various aspects of the virtuous life as found in the Athenian society of his time,[1] though he agreed with Plato in thinking that the highest type of life is to be found in the contemplation of the philosopher, rather than in the active life of the citizen. The opposition thus introduced between the life of the philosopher and that of the ordinary citizen was further developed by the Stoics. They flourished at the time when the Greek City State was decaying, and were thus not able, as Plato and Aristotle had been, to see in the life of the citizen the type of an ideal self-realization. Hence they were led to seek for the highest form of human

Our word "Ideal" comes nearer to the Platonic meaning, provided we remember that he understands it to signify, not an unreal shadow-picture, but rather the most real of all things, of which the existent world is but a shadow (or, as he seems to have generally conceived it, a realization in an imperfect medium—the ὑποδοχὴ of the *Timæus*.) *Cf.* above, p. 28, *note*, and below, pp. 266–7.

[1] This species of Descriptive Ethics was further developed by Theophrastus, the chief of Aristotle's disciples. See his *Characters*.

life in the perfect independence of the Sage, rather than in the activity of the good citizen. A similar tendency appears in the schools of the Epicureans and Sceptics. It was only with the advent of Christianity that it again became possible to conceive of an ideal kingdom, of which all are members, and in which even the humblest citizen may participate by faith, though unable to understand with any fulness the nature of the unity within which his life is passed.

§ 6. Mediæval Ethics.—Mediæval ideas on Ethics[1] were much influenced by those of Plato and Aristotle, but partly also by those of the Stoics and by conceptions derived from Christianity. The more religious aspects of morals were specially developed; and a good deal of attention was also given to the application of ethical ideas to the guidance of the individual life. Casuistry owed its origin to the efforts that were made in the latter direction.

§ 7. Schools of Ethics in Modern Times.—The development of Ethics in modern times is considerably more complex, and we can only indicate some of its main lines. Descartes is generally regarded as the founder of modern philosophy; but his interests were mainly metaphysical. In Ethics he and his school did little more than develop the ideas of the Stoics, to which they were specially attracted in consequence of the opposition between mind and body involved in their metaphysics. In the meantime, however, a more materialistic school of thought was growing up, led by Gassendi and Hobbes, and the members of this school allied themselves rather with the Epicurean school of

[1] These are dealt with pretty fully in Sidgwick's *History of Ethics*.

ancient times. Gassendi was definitely a disciple of Epicurus. Hobbes worked out a more independent line, regarding the attainment of power as the great aim of human life. Hobbes was opposed by the Cambridge Platonists and by Cumberland, who endeavoured to bring out the more social, and at the same time the more rational, side of human nature. Out of their position was developed what came to be known as the Moral Sense School, represented by Shaftesbury and Hutcheson. According to these writers we have an intuitive perception of the distinction between right and wrong, similar to the æsthetic perception of the distinction between the beautiful and the ugly; but at the same time this perception is capable of explanation. It depends on the social nature of man. What is beneficial to society strikes one naturally as good; what is harmful is instinctively regarded as bad. This point of view forms a sort of watershed, from which several streams of tendency in ethical speculation emerge. Some writers tended to emphasise exclusively the fact that there is an intuitive perception of right and wrong. Out of this came the Intuitionist School of Reid and his followers. Others were specially struck by the fact that the distinction between good and bad rests on a reasonable consideration of the results of action. Hence arose the rational school, represented by Locke, Clarke, Wollaston, &c. This line of thought may be said to have culminated in Kant; and, in the works of his immediate successors, it gave rise to a point of view approximating to those of Plato and Aristotle. This view afterwards passed into English thought in the school of modern Idealism represented by Green and others. Finally, some of those who were impressed by the teaching of the Moral Sense School were led to attach special importance to the fact that the good is that which is beneficial to society, or that which promotes human happiness. From this consideration the school of modern Utilitarianism was developed. These three schools—the Intuitionist, the Rational, and the Utilitarian, were the main lines of modern ethical thought, until the school of the modern Evolutionists arose.

CHAPTER II.

THE TYPES OF ETHICAL THEORY.

§ 1. General Survey.—We are now able to take account of the leading types of ethical thought that have occurred throughout the history of speculation. In details there is wide diversity, but in their broad outlines the types are few and simple. Two types, in particular, come up again and again in the course of ethical thought as opposing points of view—the types represented by Heraclitus and Democritus, Antisthenes and Aristippus, Zeno and Epicurus, Descartes[1] and Gassendi, Cudworth and Hobbes, Reid and Hume, Kant and Bentham. This antithesis may be roughly expressed as that between those who lay the emphasis on reason and those who lay the emphasis on passion; but, as we go on, we shall have to endeavour to define it more precisely. Besides these opposing schools, however, we find throughout the course of ethical speculation another point of view which may be described as that which lays the emphasis on the concrete personality of man, rather than on any such abstract quality as reason or passion. This point of view does not usually appear in opposition to the other two, but rather as a view in which they are reconciled and transcended. It appears chiefly in the great specula-

[1] Geulincx and Malebranche represented the more ethical aspect of the Cartesian School somewhat more definitely than Descartes himself.

tive thinkers who rise above the oppositions of the schools—such as Plato and Aristotle, Hegel, and one or two others.[1] In recent times, however, it has come out more distinctly as one school (or perhaps we should say two schools) side by side with the others—the school which may be broadly characterized as that of development. Besides these main positions there are a number of others that are more transitory and less recurrent—such as the æsthetic school, represented chiefly by the Moral Sense writers and Herbart; the school of sympathy, represented by Adam Smith; and one or two others.

We must now try to make the main lines of contrast a little clearer.

§ 2. Reason and Passion.—It has already been indicated that the main line of opposition may be said to consist in the antithesis between reason and passion. We have seen that the human consciousness may be described as a Universe or system, consisting, when we regard it from the active point of view, of various desires placed within a more or less fully co-ordinated group. Now it is possible to direct special attention either to the separate desires existing within this whole or to the form of unity by which it coheres as a system. We may regard human life as essentially a struggle between desires seeking gratification, or as the effort to bring those desires into subjection to the idea of a system. The antithesis between the two schools arises,

[1] Spinoza should on the whole be classed with them. Though a Cartesian, he fully recognises the element of truth in the point of view of such a writer as Hobbes, and his final view of the highest good as being found in the "Intellectual Love of God," is to a large extent a reproduction of the teaching of Plato and Aristotle wtth regard to the Speculative Life.

in the main, from the tendency to lay emphasis on one or other of these sides. The one tendency is perhaps best represented by such a doctrine as that of Hume, that "reason is and must always be the slave of the passions," *i. e.* that reason can do nothing but guide the particular impulses to their gratification. When this view is taken, the chief good of life is almost inevitably conceived as consisting simply in the gratification of the particular impulses as they arise. This is the view of the Cyrenaics, and, in a modified form, of the Hedonists in general. The opposite view is that which recognises some law to which the particular impulses must be subjected, in order to bring them into systematic form. In the history of ethical thought, this law has generally been conceived as the law of reason, just as the attainment of the end of the particular impulses has generally been thought of as pleasure. But Hobbes thought of the end of the desires rather as Power than as Pleasure; and so also there have been thinkers who have thought of the law to which the impulses are to be subjected in some other form than as the law of reason. Hence we are led to state the opposition in a slightly different form.

§ 3. THE RIGHT AND THE GOOD.—It has been pointed out already that there are two main forms in which the moral ideal presents itself—as the Right and as the Good. We may think of morality as conformity to a rule or standard, or as the pursuit of an end. Now the distinction between the two opposing schools of Ethics connects itself, to a considerable extent, with this distinction. It is on the whole true that the line of thinkers from Heraclitus, through the Stoics, to Kant, think of the supreme standard in morality as some sort of law, rule, or imperative, from which we learn what it is *right* to do; while the line of thinkers from Democritus, through the Epicureans, to Bentham, think rather of a *Good* (generally described as Happiness) at which men aim, and by reference to which their actions are to be praised or blamed. The two schools may thus be roughly characterised as those that take Duty and Happiness, respectively, as their standards.

§ 4. DUTY, HAPPINESS, PERFECTION.—If we describe the two opposing theories as those of Duty and Happiness, the term Perfection may appropriately be used to characterise the middle theory, which, to a large extent, combines the other two.

It may be noted that these are not merely three different theories of the moral standard, but that different types of life correspond to them. It has been remarked of Kant that his life reminds us of the "categorical imperative of duty," which was for him the kernel of morals.[1] In like manner the life of Bentham may

[1] Caird's *Critical Philosophy of Kant*, Vol. I., p. 63. Dr. Caird quotes, in this connection, the following humorous account of Kant from Heine. "The life of Immanuel Kant is hard to describe: he had indeed neither life nor history in the proper sense of the words. He lived an abstract, mechanical, old-bachelor existence in a quiet, remote street of Königsberg, an old city at the northeastern boundary of Germany. I do not believe that the great cathedral clock of that city accomplished its day's work in a less passionate and more regular way than its countryman, Immanuel Kant. Rising from bed, coffee-drinking, writing, lecturing, eating, walking, everything had its fixed time; and the neighbours knew that it must be exactly half-past four when they saw Professor Kant in his grey coat with his cane in his hand step out of his house door, and move towards the little lime-tree avenue, which is called after him the Philosopher's Walk. Eight times he walked up and down that walk at every season of the year, and when the weather was bad or the grey clouds threatened rain, his servant, old Lampe, was seen anxiously

be taken as typical of the Hedonistic position—a life spent in devotion to the improvement of the mechanical conditions of existence, the means of happiness.[1] The kind of life that corresponds to Perfection would be best represented by such men as Plato and Aristotle, or by the modern Greek, Goethe.

To some extent the three great peoples, the Hebrews, Romans, and Greeks, might be taken as representing these three ideals. With the Hebrews the law of righteousness is supreme. The Romans were also devoted to law, but in a different sense. The law which interested them most was rather that by which the mechanical conditions of life are regulated, and which provide the material of happiness. The Greeks obviously represent the ideal of perfect development of personality.

§ 5. Mixed Theories.—In contrasting these different

following him with a large umbrella under his arm, like an image of Providence." "Strange contrast between the outer life of the man and his world-destroying thought. Of a truth, if the citizens of Königsberg had had any inkling of the meaning of that thought, they would have shuddered before him as before an executioner. But the good people saw nothing in him but a professor of philosophy, and when he passed at the appointed hour, they gave him friendly greetings and set their watches."

[1] Bentham's great interest was legislation. "Bentham," says Sir Henry Maine (*Early History of Institutions*, p. 400), "was in truth neither a jurist nor a moralist in the proper sense of the word. He theorises not on law but on legislation; when carefully examined, he may be seen to be a legislator even in morals. No doubt his language seems sometimes to imply that he is explaining moral phenomena; in reality he wishes to alter or rearrange them according to a working rule gathered from his reflections on legislation. This transfer of his working rule from legislation to morality seems to me the true ground of the criticisms to which Bentham is justly open as an analyst of moral facts." On this point, see below, Book II., chap. vi., § 4.

views of the supreme standard in morals, it should be remembered always that many of the theories held by the most representative writers cannot be classed quite definitely under any one head, but rather represent combinations of the different views. Thus, even the Stoics may be said to stand midway between the theory of Duty and that of Perfection; for though their ideal may be described as that of obedience to law, it is at the same time that of the attainment of the life of the perfectly wise man. The same applies to the Cartesians and to Kant. Again, in the Moral Sense School, the ideas of Duty and Happiness are to a large extent combined, as they are also, in a different way, in the views of Dr. Sidgwick. The modern Evolutionists, such as Mr. Herbert Spencer, combine the ideas of Happiness and Perfection. And in many other ways the different theories have been united. But, as we are not at present studying the history of ethical theory, but only its most typical forms, it is most convenient for us to consider the different views, as far as possible, apart.

CHAPTER III.

THE STANDARD AS LAW.

PART I.: THE GENERAL IDEA OF MORAL LAW.

§ **1.** Introductory Remarks.—In dealing with the different types of ethical theory, it seems most convenient to start with those that take as their fundamental conception the idea of Duty, Right, Law, Obligation. To the race, as to the child, morality presents itself first in the form of commandments, and even in the form of threats. It is only at a later stage of development that we learn to regard the moral life as a good, and finally as the realisation of our own nature. Hence it seems most natural to begin with those theories which are based rather on the idea of rightness than on that of the Good. From this point of view, morality presents itself as obedience to the Law of Duty. The significance of this conception, and the different forms which it may take, are what we have now to consider.

§ **2.** The Meaning of Law in Ethics.—A good deal of confusion has been caused in the study of Ethics, as well as in that of some other subjects, by a certain ambiguity in the word Law.[1] It is important, therefore, that we should try to understand exactly the sense in which it is here to be used.

It has been customary to distinguish two distinct

[1] *Cf.* Whately's *Logic*, p. 209; and Welton's *Manual of Logic*, vol. i., p. 8.

senses in which it may be used. We speak of the laws of a country and also of the laws of nature; but it is evident that the kinds of law referred to in these two phrases are very different. The laws of a country are made by a people or by its rulers; and, even in the case of the Medes and Persians, there is always a possibility that they may be changed. There is also always a possibility that the inhabitants of the country may disobey them; and, as a general rule, they have no application at all to the inhabitants of other countries. The laws of nature,[1] on the other hand, are constant, inviolable, and all-pervading. There are three respects, therefore, in which different kinds of law may be distinguished. Some laws are constant: others are variable. Some are inviolable: others are liable to be disobeyed. Some are universal: others have only a limited application. The last of these three points, however, is scarcely distinguishable from the first: for what is universal is generally also constant and necessary, and *vice versâ.* Consequently, it may be sufficient for the present to distinguish different kinds of laws as (1) changeable or unchangeable, (2) violable or inviolable—though we shall have to return shortly to the third principle of distinction. Adopting these two principles, we might evidently have four different classes of laws—(1) Those that can be both changed and violated, (2) those that can be changed but cannot be violated, (3) those that can be violated but cannot be changed, (4) those that can neither be changed nor violated.

[1] I mean such laws as those that are stated in treatises on theoretical mechanics. These laws relate to tendencies that are operative throughout the whole of nature. See following note.

Of the first and last of these, illustrations have already been given. Of the second also it is not difficult to discover examples. The laws of the solar system, of day and night, seedtime and harvest, and all the vicissitudes of the seasons, are inviolable so long as certain conditions last; but if these conditions were changed—say, by the cooling of the sun, by the retardation of the earth's velocity, or its collision with some comet or erratic meteor—the laws also would change with them.[1] Again, most of the laws of political economy are of this character. They hold good of certain types of society, and among men who are swayed by certain motives; and within these limits they are inviolable. But change the conditions of society, or the characters of the men who compose it, and in many cases the laws will break down. Such laws are sometimes said to be *hypothetical*. They are valid only on the *supposition* that certain conditions are present and remain unchanged. Some philosophers [2] have thought that even the laws of mathematics may be of this character—that there might be a world in which two and two would be equal to five; and that if a triangle were formed with the diameter of the earth for its base and one of the fixed stars for its apex, its three angles might not be equal to two right angles.[3] But this appears to be a mistake. The laws of

[1] It might be urged that *all* laws of nature are of this character, *i. e.* that they are all hypothetical, depending on the continuance of the present constitution of the universe. This is true, unless there are some laws of such a kind that no system of nature could exist without them. The consideration of this question, however, belongs to Metaphysics.

[2] *E. g.* J. S. Mill.

[3] This was the opinion of Gauss, for instance.

mathematics belong rather to the last of our four classes.

The laws of Ethics, however, must on the whole be regarded as belonging to the third class. They cannot be changed, but they may be violated. It is true, as has been already stated, that the particular rules of morals may vary with different conditions of life; but the broad principles remain always the same, and are applicable not only to all kinds of men, but to all rational beings. If a spirit were to come among us from another world, we might have no knowledge of his nature and constitution. We might not know what would taste bitter or sweet to him, what he would judge to be hard or soft, or how he would be affected by heat or sound or colour. But we should know at least that for him, as for us, the whole is greater than any one of its parts, and every event has a cause; and that he, like us, must not tell lies, and must not wantonly destroy life.[1] These laws are unchangeable. They can, however, be broken. We may, indeed, speak of ethical principles which it is impossible to violate. An ethical writer, for instance, may insist on the truth that every sin brings with it some form of punishment. This is a truth from which there is no escape; but it is rather a metaphysical than an ethical truth. It is a fact about the constitution of the world, not a moral law. A moral law states something that *ought* to happen, not something that *necessarily does* happen.

Moral laws are not the only laws that are of this

[1] Some theological writers have denied this, holding that goodness in God may be something entirely different from goodness in man. This opinion is ably refuted by Mill in his *Examination of Hamilton*, chap. vii.

character. On the contrary, the laws of every strictly normative and of every practical science are essentially similar. No one can make the fundamental principles of architecture, navigation, or rhetoric, in any way different from what they are; though in practice any one who is willing to take the consequences may defy them. No doubt the rules of these sciences might require modification if they were to be applied to the inhabitants of another planet than ours; and even on our own planet they are not absolutely rigid. A style of building which is suitable for Iceland would scarcely be adapted for the Tropics. The navigation of the Mississippi is different from that of the Atlantic. And the oratory which would awake the enthusiasm of an Oriental people might move an Anglo-Saxon audience only to derision. Still, it is possible in all these sciences to lay down broad general laws which shall be applicable universally, or at least applicable to all conditions under which it is conceivable that we should wish to apply them—laws, indeed, from which even the particular modifications required in special cases might be deduced. For example, we might take it as a principle of rhetoric that if an audience is to be moved to the performance of some action or the acceptance of some truth to which they may be expected to be disinclined, they ought to be led up to the point by an easy transition, from step to step, beginning with some things that are obvious and familiar, and in which their affections are naturally engaged. From this it might be at once inferred that the character of such an appeal ought to vary with different audiences, according to the nature of the objects to which their experience has accustomed them, to the intensity of the feelings which have connected themselves with these objects, and to the average rapidity of their intellects in passing from one point to another. The law is constant: it is only the application that varies. The science of logic gives us a still more obvious instance of such laws. The rules of correct thinking cannot be changed, though the particular errors to which men are most liable may vary with different objects of study, different languages, and different habits of mind. In this case also, as in Ethics, the laws cannot be changed,[1] but may be violated.[2]

§ **3.** Is, Must be, and Ought to be.—The distinctions expressed in the preceding section may be conveniently summed up by saying that some laws express what *is*, some what *must be* (or *shall be*), and some what *ought*

[1] It may be urged, no doubt, that some at least of the laws of logic are applicable only within certain hypothetical limits. Some of them, for instance (*viz.* those commonly discussed under the head of Formal Logic), depend on the admission of the principles of identity, contradiction, and excluded middle; and it may be maintained that there are objects to which these principles are not strictly applicable. But this point is too subtle to be more than merely hinted at in this place.

[2] This distinction between laws, which can and cannot be violated, like other distinctions of the same sort, must be interpreted with some care, and not pressed too far. In a sense it is possible to violate a natural law, *i. e.* we can evade the conditions under which it holds. In a sense also it is not possible to violate a moral law. To act wrongly is, as we shall see, to be in contradiction with ourselves; and "a house which is divided against itself cannot stand." Similarly, even the law of a nation, if it is a real law, cannot be violated. Punishment may be said to be the open expression of this impossibility. The violation recoils upon the perpetrator, and annihilates him and his act. Cf. below, Book III., chap. vi., § 5. But of course all this does not in any way interfere with the relatively true distinction between these different classes of law.

to be.[1] What we call laws of nature are simply general statements about what is. The law of gravitation simply states that bodies tend to move in certain ways relatively to one another. Even the laws recognised in the more abstract sciences are of this character. The law of demand and supply simply states that, as a general rule, prices tend to adjust themselves in particular ways.[2] Laws of nations, on the other hand, state what *must be, i. e.* what is bound to be unless certain penalties are incurred. Atoms and prices do not and cannot violate their laws, so long as the appropriate conditions hold. Their laws are nothing but statements of the way in which certain occurrences uniformly take place under certain conditions. Human beings, on the other hand, may and do violate

[1] It is one of the very few advantages, from a philosophical point of view, which the English language possesses over the German, that we have the two words *shall* and *ought*, where they have only *sollen*, which corresponds rather more closely to *shall* than to *ought.* Hegel's objection to the use of the word *sollen* (*Logic of Hegel*, Wallace's Translation, p. 11) seem to be due chiefly to the fact that it suggests (1) something future, as opposed to what is actually realised, (2) something commanded by an external authority. The English word *ought* seems to be free from both these defects.

[2] It has already been indicated (note to Introduction, chap. i.), that there is a sense in which the principles of the more abstract sciences may be said to be normative—that theoretical astronomy may be said to state the laws according to which the planets *ought* to move, that geometry may be said to state the laws that ought to hold in a perfect triangle or circle, and so forth. But "ought" in this sense means that these relationships do hold, in so far as the appropriate conditions are realised; and the significance of the sciences lies in the fact that, in the concrete world of experience, they either do approximately hold, or are determining conditions in the actual constitution of things. Truly normative principles are not of this nature. If all men were to go mad, the principles of correct thinking would still hold as before.

the laws of their country. But the law states that they *must* not do so, and attaches penalties (or sanctions) to the doing of it. A moral law, finally, is a law that states that something *ought to be.* It is the statement of an Ideal. Thus, if a Government decides to enter upon a war which is known by the citizens to be unjust, some of the soldiers may feel that it is wrong to serve, *i. e.* that it is contrary to their ideal of what is right in conduct. Here they come in conflict with what they recognise as a moral law. Nevertheless, they must not desert; *i. e.* they will be shot if they do. Here there is a law of the State. Suppose they do desert and are shot, they die by a law of nature.

§ 4. THE CATEGORICAL IMPERATIVE.—We are now in a position to understand the important conception which was introduced by Kant with reference to the moral law. He said that it was of the nature of a categorical imperative. The meaning of this may readily be made apparent. All laws which are not simply expressions of natural uniformities may be said to be of the nature of commands. The laws of nations are commands issued by the government, with penalties attached to the violation of them. Moral laws may also (subject to a certain qualification) be said to be commands, though we are not yet in a position to consider how they are issued. Now commands may be absolute in their character, or subject to qualification. The laws of a nation are laws that we must obey, *unless we are prepared to suffer the consequences of disobedience.* Again, the fundamental principles of rhetoric may be said to be of the nature of commands or rules; but the commands which are thus laid down are applicable only to rhetoricians. The laws of architecture, in like manner, apply only to those who wish to construct stable, commodious, and beautiful buildings. Some of the laws of political economy, again, are neither constant nor universal. They are not constant; for they may vary with different conditions of society. They are not universal; for they are applicable only to those who wish to produce wealth. Even the laws of formal logic are not universal. They apply only to those who wish to be self-consistent.[1] Now a man may reject this aim. He may say, with Emerson,[2] "Suppose you should contradict yourself; what then?" "A foolish consistency is the hobgoblin of little minds, adored by little statesmen and philosophers and divines. With consistency a great soul has simply nothing to do."[3] Such imperatives as these, therefore, are merely hypothetical.[4] They apply only to those who adopt the

[1] I assume of course here that logic is to be regarded as a normative science, laying down the rules of consistent thought. Some logicians have treated the subject in a different way, regarding it either as an ordinary positive science, or as an art, or as a combination of the two.

[2] Essay on "Self-Reliance."

[3] No doubt Emerson is referring here to consistency in action, rather than to consistency in thought. But the same might be said of the latter under certain conditions. "In order to think at all," as Mr. Bradley says (*Appearance and Reality*), "you must subject yourself to a standard." Thinking is a game, and "if you sit down to the game, there is only one way of playing." So the laws of morality may be said to constitute the rules of the game. But the latter is a game that we must be always playing. We may take a holiday from thinking, and feel or dream instead, and there is nothing in the laws of thinking to prevent this. Morality, on the other hand, claims a universal jurisdiction. It is not a rule of thought that you must always be thinking; but it is a rule of action that you must always be doing what is right in the given conditions.

[4] Such laws as those of political economy are thus hypothetical in a double sense—hypothetical with regard to the conditions under

end with which the particular normative science is concerned.

The laws of Ethics differ from all other laws in being not hypothetical, but categorical. It is true that Emerson's paradox about consistency has been capped by that of the preacher who bade us, "Be not righteous overmuch."[1] But if this maxim is to have any intelligible meaning, we must understand the term "righteous" in a somewhat narrow sense. It cannot be taken to mean that we should not, to too great an extent, do what we ought to do. This would be a contradiction in terms. If we are not to be too fanatical in the observance of particular moral rules, it must be in deference to other moral rules or principles that are of a still higher authority. The supreme moral principle, whatever it may be, lays its command upon us absolutely, and admits of no question. What we *ought* to do we ought to *do*. There can be no higher law by which the moral imperative might be set aside.

There are, indeed, some other laws which might seem to be scarcely less absolute, because they relate to ends that every one naturally seeks. Thus, every one would like to be happy; and consequently if there were any practical science of happiness, every one would be bound to follow its laws. Accordingly, Kant called such laws *assertorial*,[2] because although they depend on the hypothesis that we seek for happiness, yet it may be at once *asserted* of every one that he does seek

which they are applicable, and hypothetical with regard to the end with reference to which they are applicable.

[1] *Cf.* Stephen's *Science of Ethics*, p. 418. "'Be good if you would be happy,' seems to be the verdict even of worldly prudence; but it adds in an emphatic aside, 'Be not too good.'"

[2] *Metaphysic of Morals*, section II.

this end. Again, intellectual perfection is an end which a rational being can hardly help desiring. There is probably no one who would not, if he could, have the penetration of a Newton, or the grasp of a Shakespeare or a Goethe. Hence if there were any science that taught how such perfection is to be attained, its laws would have at least an almost universal application. Still, even such laws as these are not quite parallel to the laws of morals. Their universality, if they are universal, depends on the fact that every one chooses the end to which they have reference; whereas the laws of morals apply to all men irrespective of their choice. If, indeed, happiness could be shown to be necessarily bound up with virtue, and unhappiness with vice, then the obligation to follow the rules of happiness would have the same absoluteness as the obligation to obey the moral law; but only because these two things would then be identical. In like manner, if we were to accept quite literally the view of Carlyle, that all intellectual perfection has a moral root, so that a man's virtue is exactly proportional to his intelligence, in this case also the laws of intellectual perfection would become absolute, but only because they would become moral. The moral law, then, is unique. It is the only categorical imperative.[1]

Up to this point, I have, so far as possible, been following the account of Kant. There are, however, two points on which some slight criticism, or at least caution, seems to be required. (1) It is somewhat

[1] On this subject the student should consult Kant's *Metaphysic of Morals*, section II. The opening paragraphs of Clifford's Essay "On the Scientific Basis of Morals' may also be found suggestive, though he does not entirely accept the view indicated above.

misleading to describe the moral law as an imperative. At least it can only be so described on a certain view of its nature, which will have to be further considered. To call it an imperative or command is to represent it as being of the nature of a *must* rather than of an *ought*. It should rather be described as based on an ideal. (2) In saying that it is categorical, we must remember that all that can at present be seen to be categorical is the principle that we must do what is right, when we know what it is. It remains to be seen whether it is possible to lay down any rule for the determination of what is right. If there is any such rule, it will be categorical; but it may turn out that there is none. In the latter case, it is somewhat misleading to speak of a categorical imperative.

With these general remarks on the nature of moral law, we may now proceed to ask what exactly the law is which is thus categorically imposed.

PART II.: VARIOUS CONCEPTIONS OF THE MORAL LAW.

§ 5. THE LAW OF THE TRIBE.—We have already seen that the earliest form in which the idea of law presents itself is that of the law of the tribe, or of the chief of the tribe.[1] But this is soon felt not to be categorical. It often comes into conflict with itself; and the reflecting consciousness demands something more consistent. At the best it furnishes a *must*, rather

[1] An illustration of this form of law, in comparatively recent times, may be found in the well-known saying of the Highland wife, when her husband was at the foot of the gallows,—"Go up, Donald, my man; the Laird bids ye." Contrast this with the attitude of Antigone, referred to above, Book I., chap. v., § 7.

than an *ought;* and the free man soon rebels against such government from without.

§ 6. THE LAW OF GOD.—It is a stage higher when the moral law is distinguished from the law of the land, and regarded as a principle which owes its authority, not to any man or body of men, but to God or the gods. The best known instance of such a set of laws is to be found in the Ten Commandments of the Jews. But these also may come into conflict, and require qualification. Besides, the moral consciousness soon begins to ask on what authority the divine law rests. If it rest merely on the command of powerful supernatural beings, it is still only a *must*, not an *ought.* If God is not Himself righteous, His law cannot be morally binding merely on account of His superior power. But to ask whether God is righteous is to ask for a law above that of God Himself, and by which God may be judged. Hence the law of God cannot be accepted as final.

§ 7. THE LAW OF NATURE.—In order to get over this difficulty, the view has sometimes been taken that the most fundamental law of all is that which lies in the nature of things. In Greek Ethics, in particular, the conception of nature (φύσις) plays a very prominent part. The Greeks understood by nature the essential constitution of things underlying their casual appearances. It was in this sense, for instance, that the Stoics used their famous phrase to "live according to nature" (*vivere convenienter naturæ*). In modern times also, especially in the latter part of the seventeenth and the greater part of the eighteenth centuries, much was made of the idea of natural law. Perhaps in Ethics one of the most striking applications of this conception is to be found in the system of Samuel Clarke. Clarke held that certain differences and relations between things are inherent in their very nature, and that any one who observes them in a careful and unprejudiced way will become aware of these differences and relations. "The differences, relations, and proportions of things both natural and moral, in which all unprejudiced minds thus naturally agree, are certain, unalterable, and real in the things themselves."[1] To the laws of nature thus discovered "the reason of all men everywhere naturally and necessarily assents, as all men agree in their judgment concerning the whiteness of the snow or the brightness of the sun."[2] "That from these different relations of different things there necessarily arises an agreement or disagreement of some things with others, or a fitness or unfitness of the application of different things or different relations, is likewise as plain as that there is such a thing as proportion in Geometry or Arithmetic, or uniformity or difformity in comparing together the respective figures of bodies."[3] Here we have the statement of the celebrated doctrine of "the fitness of things." But in all statements of this sort, taken as the basis of moral theory, there seems to be an obvious confusion involved. There are certainly laws in nature; but these, as we have noted, are simply statements of the uniform ways in which things occur; and such laws are exhibited quite as much in what is evil as in what is good. The destruction of a building by the explosion of a bomb is as much in accordance with the fitness of things, as deduced from the laws of nature, as the

[1] *Natural Religion*, pp. 44–45.

[2] *Ibid.*, p. 66.

[3] *Ibid.*, p. 29.

movements of the planetary system.[1] Fitness, in any sense in which it can serve as the basis of moral theories, must be fitness for something—*i. e.* it must involve some reference to an end or ideal; and no alchemy can ever extract this out of the mere observation of natural laws.[2] The analysis of the

[1] As illustrating this confusion, reference may perhaps be made to those primitive conceptions of the relation between the natural and the moral order, according to which a man by committing a crime might produce an earthquake. Some interesting facts of this sort are to be found in D'Alviella's *Hibbert Lectures* (*e.g.*, p. 168). Mill's Essay on "Nature" (in his *Three Essays on Religion*) is still worth reading, with the view of clearing up this confusion. *Cf.* also Marshall's *Principles of Economics* (3d Edn.), pp. 55–57.

[2] *Cf.* Le Rossignol's *Ethical Philosophy of Samuel Clarke*, p. 43. Mr. Leslie Stephen's comment on Clarke's doctrine (*English Thought in the Eighteenth Century*, vol. ii., p. 7.) may be worth noticing here. "An obvious difficulty," he says, "underlies all reasoning of this class, even in its most refined shape. The doctrine might, on the general assumptions of Clarke's philosophy, be applicable to the 'Laws of Nature,' but is scarcely to be made applicable to the moral law. Every science is potentially deducible from a small number of primary truths. . . Thus, for example, a being of sufficient knowledge might construct a complete theory of human nature, of which every proposition would be either self-evident or rigorously deducible from self-evident axioms. Such propositions would take the form of laws in the scientific, not in the moral, sense; the copula would be 'is,' not 'ought'; the general formula would be 'all men do so and so, not 'thou shalt do so and so.' . . . The language which he uses about the moral law is, in reality, applicable to the scientific law alone. It might be said with plausibility . . . that the proposition 'all men are mortal' is capable of being deductively proved by inferences from some self-evident axioms. A denial of it would, therefore, involve a contradiction. But the proposition 'Thou shalt not kill' is a threat, not a statement of a truth; and Clarke's attempt to bring it under the same category involves a confusion fatal to the whole theory. It is, in fact, a confusion between the art and the science of human conduct." I quote this passage, because it not only brings out what seems to be the error of Clarke, in confounding natural and

'is," in any such sense as this, can never yield an "ought." Similar doctrines to that of Clarke have frequently been put forward, even in quite recent times;[1] but they all seem to labour under the same fatal defect.

§ 8. The Moral Sense.—If the laws of nature or the laws of God are to yield us moral principles, it must be because they in some way appeal to our own consciousness, because we in some way feel that obedience to them or observance of them serves to realise an ideal which we bring with us. Now an obvious way of making the connection between such external principles and our own minds is to say that we have a natural feeling which leads us to approve some things and disapprove of others. We are thus led to the conception of the moral sense.

This point of view, like most others in Ethics, has had a long history. It connects itself essentially with the Greek view of the identity between the Beautiful and the Good. In Greek τὸ καλὸν was used habitually either for beauty or for moral excellence. Thus, the Stoic maxim, ὅτι μόνον ἀγαθὸν τὸ καλόν, means that only the beautiful (*i. e.* the morally excellent) is good. A similar view has frequently appeared in modern times. Thus, the philosopher Herbart insisted strongly on the identity of Goodness with Beauty, and definitely treated

moral law, but also illustrates the other error of confounding moral law with the command of a superior. Thou shalt not kill,' as a moral, law, is not a *threat*, but the statement of a normative principle. Similarly, there seems to be an error in representing Ethics as the *art* of conduct.

1 The theory of James Hinton, for instance,—so far as he had a theory—seems to bear a considerable resemblance to that of Clarke. See an interesting account of his ideas in *Mind*, old series, Vol. IX.

Ethics as a part of Æsthetics.[1] The conception of a kind of feeling, like æsthetic feeling, accompanying the moral judgment, comes out also in some of the writers of the school known as the Cambridge Platonists, especially in Henry More. But the writers who are specially known as the representatives of the idea of a moral sense are Shaftesbury and Hutcheson.[2] "Should one," says Shaftesbury,[3] "who had the countenance of a gentleman, ask me, 'Why I would avoid being nasty, when nobody was present?' In the first place I should be fully satisfied that he himself was a very nasty gentleman who could ask this question; and that it would be a hard matter for me to make him even conceive what true cleanliness was. However, I might, notwith-

1 See, for instance, his *Science of Education*, recently translated by Mr. and Mrs. Felkin; and *cf.* Bosanquet's *History of Æsthetics*, p. 369. We may also refer, in this connection, to the saying of Ruskin, "Taste is not only a part and an index of morality; it is the *only* morality. The first and last and closest trial question to any living creature is, 'What do you like? Tell me what you like, and I will tell you what you are.'" (*Sesame and Lilies*). See also Adam Smith's *Theory of the Moral Sentiments*, Part IV., sect. II., and *cf.* the saying of Aristotle quoted above, Book I., chap. iii., § 5.

2 Shaftesbury was the founder of this school, and its subsequent development was due chiefly to Hutcheson. See Sidgwick's *History of Ethics*, p. 189. It is scarcely necessary to point out that the meaning of the term "sense," as here used, is different from that in which we speak of the sense of taste, touch, sight, &c. The latter "senses" are concerned simply with the apprehension of particular qualities of objects; whereas the moral sense or the sense of beauty passes *judgment* on such qualities. The meaning of calling it a moral *sense* is merely to imply that it is an *intuitive* faculty of judgment. Similarly, we might say that the judgments of the epicure or of the tea-taster rest upon a sense; but it is not on the mere "sense of taste" that such judgments rest, since they involve a *standard* as well as an *apprehension*.

3 *Characteristics*, "An Essay on the Freedom of Wit and Humour." Part III., sect. iv.

standing this, be contented to give him a slight answer, and say, ''Twas because I had a nose.' Should he trouble me further, and ask, 'What if I had a cold? Or what if naturally I had no such nice smell?' I might answer perhaps, 'That I cared as little to see myself nasty, as that others should see me in that condition.' But what if it were in the dark? Why even then, though I had neither nose nor eyes, my sense of the matter would still be the same; my nature would rise at the thought of what was sordid; or if it did not, I should have a wretched nature indeed, and hate myself for a beast. Honour myself I never could; whilst I had no better sense of what, in reality, I owed myself, and what became me, as a human creature." "Much in the same manner," he goes on, "have I heard it asked, *Why should a man be honest in the dark?* What a man must be to ask this question, I won't say." And so on. Shaftesbury is thus led to conceive that to be virtuous is to be a 'virtuoso,' that a cultivated taste is our only guide. "To philosophise in a just signification is but to carry good breeding a step higher."

The plausibility of this point of view arises chiefly from the fact that in a well-developed character the habit of obedience to the moral law becomes a second nature, so that the choice of the right and the avoidance of the wrong passes almost into a kind of instinct. From this point of view it may quite rightly be maintained that the moral sense is a kind of taste.[1] But

[1] Using the term "taste," of course, in that secondary sense in which we speak of "good taste." It is not a taste like that which simply apprehends savour, but a taste like that of the tea-taster (who, by the by, is properly tea-*smeller*), who *judges* the qualities of teas by a kind of intuitive perception.

it must be remembered that the sense of beauty, as well as the sense of rightness, is capable of being explained and justified. Though it is commonly said that "there is no disputing about tastes," yet we do habitually dispute about them, and pronounce them to be right or wrong. The moral taste, then, is so far quite analogous to the æsthetic taste, and it may be quite correct to refer to it as a sense.[1] But since it is not simply an inexplicable sense, but is capable of a rational explanation, no ethical theory can be regarded as thorough which simply treats it as a sense and does not endeavour to explain it. Moreover, what can be explained can usually also be criticised. When the sense of beauty, for instance, has been explained, it is possible to criticise the sense of beauty as it is found in particular individuals; and to determine that the æsthetic taste of some men is good, while that of others is defective. Similarly, when the moral sense is explained, it will naturally be possible to pass judgment on the moral tastes of different individuals and even of

[1] In this connection it may be noted that even complex intellectual processes become, after long practice, scarcely distinguishable from intuitive perceptions. A man who is highly skilled in any art seems to see at a glance what requires to be done on any given occasion. Yet we do not postulate a *sense* in such cases, because we know that the judgments of the expert rest in reality on rational grounds (though frequently he might not be able to give any clear account of the grounds of his own judgment). An illustration of a similar fact may be found in "Lord Mansfield's advice to a man of practical good sense, who, being appointed governor of a colony, had to preside in its Court of Justice, without previous judicial practice or legal education. The advice was to give his decision boldly, for it would probably be right; but never to venture on assigning reasons, for they would almost infallibly be wrong" (Mill's *Logic*, Book II., chap. iii., § 3). In such a case the reasons of the action are latent; but no one would doubt that reasons

different ages and nations. For these reasons, then, a system of ethics which simply rests content with the idea of a moral sense, can scarcely be regarded as satisfactory.

As a matter of fact, indeed, the moral sense was not accepted either by Shaftesbury or by Hutcheson as a sufficient basis for Ethics. They both sought to explain it as due to the nature of man as a social being. They both thought that what a cultivated moral taste approves is that which is beneficial to society as a whole, what tends to bring about "the greatest happiness of the greatest number."[1] All that they urged was that it is not necessary to reflect upon this principle, since it is naturally embodied in any cultivated taste.

But, of course, in morals we want some principle which will apply generally, not merely to those of cultivated taste; or at least we require to know definitely what it is that constitutes a cultivated taste, in order that it may be developed, as far as possible, in all

could be found. So in the moral life the good man seems to see instinctively in many cases what he ought to do, and frequently could not give any reason. It is this fact that makes it appear as if there were some special "moral sense" involved. But the truth is that even intellectual insight depends, from this point of view, on a kind of developed intuition. Everything that we really know, we know by directly looking at it, rather than by arguing round about it. "All the thinking in the world," as Goethe said, "does not bring us to thought; we must be right by nature, so that good thoughts may come to us, like free children of God, and cry 'Here we are.'" So it is with moral perception. It depends on a developed sense or intuition, but not an unintelligible sense, or one destitute of inner principle. "Our instinctive knowledge," says Mach (*Science of Mechanics*, Chap. I., sect. ii.), "leads us to the principle which explains that knowledge itself, and which is in its turn corroborated by the existence of that knowledge." So it is with our instinctive morality.

[1] This phrase was actually used by Hutcheson.

mankind. In this way the moral sense differs from the artistic sense. A man who is deficient in the latter may be a respected member of society; but the man who lacks the former is condemned by all who have it. It is this authoritativeness of the moral sense that is not sufficiently brought out when it is regarded as analogous to the sense of beauty.

§ 9. THE LAW OF CONSCIENCE.—Bishop Butler was strongly impressed by the unsatisfactoriness of the view of Shaftesbury in this respect; and he endeavoured to remedy the defect by substituting the idea of Conscience for that of the moral sense. In itself this is but a slight change; but by Conscience Butler understood something considerably different from what Shaftesbury had meant by the moral sense. Butler thought of human nature as an organic whole, containing many elements, some of which are naturally subordinate to others. Thus, there are in our nature a number of particular passions or impulses which lead us to pursue particular objects; but all these are naturally subordinate to Self-love, on the one hand, and to Benevolence, on the other; *i. e.* it is natural for us to restrain or guide our passions with a view to the good of ourselves or of others. But there is a certain principle in human nature which is naturally superior even to Self-love or Benevolence. This is the principle of reflection upon the law of rightness; and this is what Butler understood by Conscience. He regarded this principle as categorical, on account of its place in the human constitution. "Thus that principle, by which we survey, and either approve or disapprove our own heart, temper, and actions, is not only to be considered as what is in its turn to have some influence; which may be said of every passion, of the lowest appetites: but likewise as being superior; as from its very nature manifestly claiming superiority over all others; insomuch that you cannot form a notion of this faculty, conscience, without taking in judgment, direction, superintendency. This is a constituent part of the idea, that is, of the faculty itself: and to preside and govern, from the very economy and constitution of man, belongs to it. Had it strength, as it has right, had it power, as it has manifest authority, it would absolutely govern the world."[1]

When we ask, however, what is the nature of this authoritative principle, two different views seem to present themselves. According to one view, it is simply an inexplicable faculty which we find within us, by which laws are laid down. According to another view, it is an intelligible authority whose commands can be understood by rational reflection. It is not quite clear in which of these two ways Butler thought of Conscience; but among those who followed him the two views began to be clearly distinguished. The former view is that which is generally known as Intuitionism, in the narrower sense: the other is the view of a law of Reason.

§ **10.** Intuitionism.—Intuitionism[2] may be described generally as the theory that actions are right or wrong

1 *Sermon* II.

2 From Latin, *intueri*, to look at. The intuitionists hold that we perceive the rightness or wrongness of actions by simply looking at them, without needing to consider their relations to any ends outside themselves. It may be noted here that the term is generally written in the longer form "Intuitionalism." But the shorter form has been made current by Dr. Sidgwick, and seems more convenient.

according to their own intrinsic nature, and not in virtue of any ends outside themselves which they tend to realise. Thus, truth-speaking would be regarded as a duty, not because it is essential for social well-being, or for any other extrinsic reason, but because it is right in its own nature.[1] This theory has been held in various forms, more or less philosophical in character. For a full account of these forms reference must be made to histories of Ethics and Philosophy.[2] Here it is only possible to notice the leading points.

In the narrower sense of the term, Intuitionism is understood to mean the doctrine which refers the judgment upon actions to the tribunal of Conscience, understood as a faculty which admits of no question or appeal.

When conscience is thus referred to as the fundamental principle of morals, we must not under-

[1] It should be observed that there is a certain ambiguity in the use of the term Intuitionism. It is employed in a wider and in a narrower sense. In the narrower sense it means a doctrine which traces our moral judgments to some unanalysable form of *perception*, some purely intuitive conviction of which no rational account can be given. In this acceptation of the term, Kant and his forerunners, Clarke, Wollaston, &c., were not intuitionists; for Kant at least rested the moral judgment on the practical *reason*, not on perception. But in a wider sense all the writers of this class may be characterised as intuitionists; since they appeal to self-evident laws, rather than to any conception of a good with reference to which our moral actions may be regarded as means.

[2] For the best modern statement of the intuitionist doctrine, the student should consult Martineau's *Types of Ethical Theory*, Part II. An excellent criticism of intuitionism will be found in Sidgwick's *Methods of Ethics*, Book I., chaps. viii. and ix., and Book III. For the history of the subject, see Sidgwick's *History of Ethics*, especially pp. 224—236. Also pp. 170—204. Calderwood's *Handbook of Moral Philosophy* may also be referred to.

stand it to mean the conscience of this or that individual. The conscience of any particular individual is simply the consciousness of the harmony or disharmony of his action with his own standard of right: and if this standard is defective, the same defect will appear in the conscience. His conscience may be, in Mr. Ruskin's phrase, "The conscience of an ass." The man who does not act conscientiously certainly acts wrongly: he does not conform even to his own standard of rightness. But a man may act conscientiously and yet act wrongly, on account of some imperfection in his standard. One who acts conscientiously in accordance with some defective standard is generally known as a "fanatic."[1]

When, however, Kant says that "an erring conscience is a chimera,"[2] or when Butler says of the conscience that "if it had power, as it has manifest authority, it would absolutely govern the world," or when, in general, intuitionist writers refer to the conscience as the supreme principle of morals, what they mean by conscience is rather what may be called the universal conscience. They mean that ultimate recognition of the rightness and wrongness of actions, which is latent in all men, but which in some men is more fully developed than in others. The principles by which this recognition is made are sometimes referred to as principles of Common Sense, because they are

[1] *Cf.* above, Book I., chap. vi., § 6. It is there explained that we judge the action to be wrong because it is not done from the best motive. It may, however, appear to the agent to be the best. See also below, Book III., chap. ii., § 14.

[2] See the Preface to his *Metaphysical Elements of Ethics* (Abbott's translation), pp. 311 and 321.

supposed to be common or universal throughout the whole human race.[1]

The principles of common sense have been referred to by some writers[2] as if they were simply certain moral truths which are found unaccountably in the consciousness of mankind. Against this view there is the same objection as there is against the corresponding view with regard to intellectual truth. It conflicts with a principle which is deeper than any other principle of common sense can well be—the principle, namely, that the world must be regarded as an intelligible system of which a definite account can be given before the bar of reason. If this principle is a mistaken one, it is hard to believe that there can be any other that has a deeper claim to be regarded as of universal validity. The inadequacy of conscience as a basis of morals becomes further apparent when we endeavour to determine definitely what principles are laid down by

1 It will thus be seen that there is a certain ambiguity in the use of the term "conscience." There is another ambiguity, to which we shall have occasion to refer by and by. Conscience is frequently, perhaps even generally, understood to denote, not the principles of moral judgment, but the feeling of pain which accompanies the violation of moral law. When we speak of "the voice of conscience," and of conscience as laying down laws, we are of course not speaking of it as a mere feeling of pain, but as containing principles in accordance with which we form our moral judgments. The confusion which results from this ambiguity in the use of the term is well brought out by Mr. Muirhead in his *Elements of Ethics* pp. 78–9. *Cf.* also Porter's *Elements of Moral Science*, p. 246. And see above, Note at end of Book I.

2 Especially Reid and the other members of the so-called Scotch School. See Sidgwick's *History of Ethics*, pp. 226–233. Dr. Martineau's theory is essentially a carrying out of this view. On the other hand, such a book as Janet's *Theory of Morals* represents a more rational interpretation of the intuitional principles.

it. The content of conscience, even if we mean by it the conscience of a people or an age, rather than that of an individual, is found to vary very considerably in different times and countries; and even at the same time and place the rules that are laid down by it are of a very uncertain character.[1] Reflection shows, moreover, that these variations are not arbitrary, but have a distinct reference to the utility of actions under varying conditions for the realisation of human welfare. This has been well brought out in the very thorough examination of Common Sense Morality which is given in Dr. Sidgwick's *Methods of Ethics.*[2] From this it appears that the moral sense must not be regarded as a blind faculty, laying down principles for our guidance which are not capable of any further analysis or justification. On the contrary, the principles which it lays down can be rationally justified and explained. In fact, it is only by such justification and explanation that we can distinguish what is permanent and reliable in the decisions of conscience from what is variable and untrustworthy. But when we thus draw distinctions and pass judgment upon conscience itself, it is evident that we must somehow have a conscience behind conscience, a faculty of judgment which stands above the blind law of the heart.

§ 11. THE LAW OF REASON.—The view, however, which holds that there are certain universal principles of moral truth in the human consciousness is not necessarily pledged to regard these principles as unin-

[1] See Locke's *Essay Concerning Human Understanding*, Book I., chap. iii., and Spencer's *Principles of Ethics*, Part II.

[2] See especially Book III., chap. xi., for a summary of Dr. Sidgwick's carefully reasoned conclusions on this point.

telligible. Just as Kant held that there are certain principles of intellectual truth—what he called *categories*—which belong to the nature of all intelligent beings as such, so it may be held also that there are certain universal principles of moral truth. And just as the categories of our intellectual life may be deduced from the very nature of thought, so also the principles of our moral life may be capable of a rational deduction. There may be principles of our moral life which are as obvious to us, when we reflect upon them, as that $2 + 2 = 4$, or that every event must have a cause; and yet it may be possible, as in these latter cases it is, to see, on further reflection, why it is that these principles are obvious. If this were so, the intuitions of the moral consciousness would in reality be due to a kind of rational insight. They would be a manifestation of what might be called moral reason. This is the view of the deeper intuitionists, of whom Clarke may be taken as a type;[1] for the law of reason, in this sense, is scarcely distinguishable from what was referred to above as the law of nature. The Stoics, and most other writers who have referred to a law of nature, have also described it as the law of reason—nature being nearly always conceived by them as in some sense, a rational system.[2]

[1] See Sidgwick's *History of Ethics*, pp. 179—184. A similar view seems to be represented by Janet in his *Theory of Morals*, Book III., chap. iv. Janet holds that, in spite of the apparent diversities of moral sentiment in different peoples brought out by such writers as Locke and Spencer, there are yet certain latent principles which are the same in all men, and to which a final appeal may be made. This view seems not inconsistent with the recognition that particular individuals and races may have a very imperfect apprehension of the ultimate principles involved in their moral judgments.

[2] When the law of nature is thus conceived as a principle of reason, it comes to be thought of as normative.

When, however, the unsatisfactoriness of basing moral principles on a law of nature has become apparent, writers of this type are naturally led to lay more and more emphasis on the fact that it is in reality a law of reason with which we are concerned. Ethics thus comes to be conceived after the analogy of Logic, just as the moral sense school conceived it on the analogy of Æsthetics. Wollaston, a disciple of Clarke, represents this tendency in its most extreme form. "Moral evil, according to Wollaston, is the practical denial of a true position, and moral good the affirmation of it. To steal is wrong because it is to deny that the thing stolen is what it is, the property of another. Every right action is the affirmation of a truth; every wrong action is the denial of a truth."[1] "Thirty years of profound meditation," says Stephen,[2] "had convinced Wollaston that the reason why a man should abstain from breaking his wife's head was, that it was a way of denying that she was his wife. All sin, in other words, was lying." If a man runs another through the body, it is simply a pointed way of denying that he is a man and a brother; and the evil lies not in the pointedness but in the error. "It is worse than a crime—it is a blunder." In all this the sophistry is obvious. A bad action is inconsistent; but it is not inconsistent with fact: it is inconsistent with an ideal—the ideal, for instance, which is involved in the relationship between man and man.[3]

1 Le Rossignol's *Ethical Philosophy of Samuel Clarke*, p. 87.

2 *English Thought in the Eighteenth Century*, vol. i., p. 130.

3 What is said above refers specially to the views of Clarke and Wollaston. With Locke Ethics is conceived more definitely on the analogy of mathematics. He thinks of these as the two demonstrative sciences, starting with nominal definitions and proceeding by the law of self-consistency. This seems to involve some misconcep-

A more ingenious and suggestive form of this doctrine was put forward by Kant, who argued that bad actions are essentially inconsistent with themselves; or at least that there is an inconsistency in the principle upon which they proceed. His view on this point is so important that we must examine it at some length.

PART III. THE DOCTRINE OF KANT.

§ **12.** Kant's View of the Moral Reason.—Kant argued that, since the moral imperative is categorical, it cannot be derived from the consideration of any end outside of the will of the individual. For every external end is empirical, and could give rise only to a hypothetical imperative. We should only be entitled to say that, *if* we seek that end, we are bound to act in a particular way, with a view to its attainment. Kant held, therefore, that the absolute imperative of duty has no reference to any external ends to which the will is directed, but simply to the right direction of the will itself. "There is nothing good but the good will;" and this is good in itself, not with reference to any external facts. It must have its law entirely within itself. If the imperative which it involves were dependent on any of the facts of experience, which are by their nature contingent, it would itself be contingent, and could not be an absolute law. It follows from this that the moral law cannot have any particular content. It cannot tell

tion of the nature both of mathematics and of morals. Geometry does not start simply with nominal definitions. It starts with the conception of space. Similarly, Ethics does not start with arbitrary definitions of justice, &c., but with the conception of the concrete human ideal. This is a subject, however, into which we cannot enter with any fulness here.

us any particular things that we are to do or to abstain from doing; because all particular things have in them an empirical and contingent element, and the moral law can have no reference to any such element. Hence the moral law cannot tell us what the *matter* or content of our actions ought to be: it can only instruct us with regard to the *form*. But a pure form, without any matter, must be simply the form of law in general. That is to say, the moral law can tell us nothing more than that we are to act in a way that is conformable to law. And this means simply that our actions must have a certain self-consistency—*i. e.* that the principles on which we act must be principles that we can adopt throughout the whole of our lives, and that we can apply to the lives of others. Kant is thus led to give as the content of the categorical imperative this formula—"Act only on that maxim (or principle) which thou canst at the same time will to become a universal law."[1]

He illustrates the application of this formula by taking such a case as that of breaking promises. It is wrong to break a promise, because the breach of a promise is a kind of action which could not be universalised. If it were a universal rule that every one were to break his promise, whenever he felt inclined, no one would place any reliance on promises. Promises, in fact, would cease to be made. And of course, if they were not made, they could not be broken. Hence it would be impossible for every one to break his promise. And since it is impossible for every one, it must be wrong for any one. The essence of wrongdoing consists in making an exception.

1 *Metaphysic of Morals*, section II.

Similarly, it may easily be shown that we could not, without a certain absurdity, have universal suicide,[1] or universal stealing, or even universal indifference to the misfortunes of others. Since, then, we cannot really will that such acts should be done by every one, we have no right to will that we ourselves should do them. In fact, the moral law is—Act only in such a way as you could will that every one else should act under the same general conditions.

§ **13.** CRITICISM OF KANT. (1) *Formalism.*—It seems clear that the principle laid down by Kant affords in many cases a safe *negative* guide in conduct. If we cannot will that all men should, under like conditions, act as we are doing, we may generally be sure that we are acting wrongly. When, however, we endeavour to extract *positive* guidance from the formula —when we try to ascertain, by means of it, not merely what we should abstain from doing, but what we should do—it begins to appear that it is merely a formal principle,[2] from which no definite matter can be derived; and further consideration may lead us to see that it cannot even give us quite satisfactory negative guidance.

We must first observe, however, what was the exact

1 This is one of the most difficult points to prove in at all a satisfactory way. Kant's argument is ingenious, but hardly convincing.

2 See the criticisms on Kant in Mill's *Utilitarianism*, chap. i., p. 5, Bradley's *Ethical Studies*, pp. 139 *sqq.*, Dewey's *Outlines of Ethics*, pp. 78—82, Muirhead's *Elements of Ethics*, pp. 130-135, Adamson's *Philosophy of Kant*, pp. 119-20, &c. For a full discussion of Kant's doctrine on this point, see Caird's *Critical Philosophy of Kant*, Book II., chap. ii. Mr. Abbott, in his translation of Kant's *Theory of Ethics*, pp. xlix—lv, partly defends Kant's point of view, but does not succeed in showing that it leads to results that are practically helpful.

meaning that Kant put upon his principle. It is evident that it might be interpreted in two very different ways. It might be taken to refer to general *species* of conduct, or it might be taken to refer to *particular acts*, with all the limitations of time, place, and circumstance. It was in the former sense that the principle was understood by Kant;[1] but it is well to bear in mind that there is also a possibility of the latter interpretation. The difference between the two might be illustrated, for instance, in the case of stealing. According to the former interpretation, stealing must in all cases be condemned, because its principle cannot be universalised. According to the latter interpretation, it would be necessary, in each particular instance in which there is a temptation to steal, to consider whether it is possible to will that every human being should steal, *when placed under precisely similar conditions.* The former interpretation would evidently give us a very strict view of duty, while the latter might easily give us a very lax one.

Now if we accept, as Kant does, the former of these two interpretations, it seems clear that the principle is a purely formal one, from which the particular matter of conduct cannot be extracted. In order to apply it at all, we must presuppose a certain given material.[2]

1 The reason why Kant took this view is, that he thought that a man ought not only to be able to will that the principle of his action should be universally adopted, but that it should be made into *a law of nature.* To discuss the ground on which he held this opinion, would carry us beyond the scope of this manual.

2 Kant was partly aware of this, and in his later treatment of the subject seeks to derive the positive part of moral obligation from the consideration of the twofold end—our own Perfection and the Happiness of others—and also from the general principles of Jurispru-

Thus, in order to show that stealing leads to self-contradiction, we must presuppose the existence of property. It is inconsistent to take the property of another, if we recognise the legitimacy of private property; but if any one denies this, there is no inconsistency in his acting accordingly. In order to apply Kant's principle, therefore, it is necessary first to know what presuppositions we are entitled to make. Otherwise, there is scarcely any action which might not be shown to lead to inconsistency. For instance, the relief of distress, the effort after the moral improvement of society, and the like, might be said to lead to inconsistency; for if every one were engaged in these actions, it would be unnecessary for any one to engage in them. They are necessary only because they are neglected. The only difference between these cases and that of theft or of promise-breaking, is that in the one set of cases the abolition of the activity would lead to what is regarded as a desirable result—the cessation of distress or immorality; while in the other set of cases it would lead to what is regarded as an undesirable result—the cessation of property or of promises. But when we ask why the one result is to be regarded as desirable and the other as undesirable, there is no answer from the Kantian point of view. All that the Kantian principle enables us to say is that, assuming certain kinds

dence. See Abbott, pp. 296—302. Thus, the positive side of duty would be derived largely from utilitarian considerations, while the moral reason would simply urge us to be self-consistent. Kant's view thus approximated to that developed in recent times by Dr. Sidgwick. See below, chap. iv. But on this point, as on many others, Kant kept the different sides of his theory in separate compartments of his mind, and never really brought them together. *Cf.* Caird's *Critical Philosophy of Kant*, Book II., chaps. vi. and vii.

of conduct to be in general right, we must not make exceptions on our own behalf.

If, on the other hand, we were to adopt the second of the two possible interpretations of the principle of consistency, it would not be possible to derive from it even this very moderate amount of instruction. For to say that we are always to act in such a way that we could will that all other human beings, under exactly the same conditions, should act similarly, is merely to say that we are to act in a way that we approve. Whenever a man approves of his own course of action, he *ipso facto* wills that any one else in like conditions should do likewise. Consequently, from this principle no rule of conduct whatever can be derived. It simply throws us back upon the morality of common sense.[1]

The pure will of Kant, being thus entirely formal, and destitute of particular content, has been well described by Jacobi as a "will that wills *nothing*."[2]

§ **14.** Criticism of Kant (*continued*). (2) *Stringency.*—Not only is the Kantian principle open to the charge of being purely formal, it has also the defect of giving rise to a code of morals of a much stricter character than that which the moral sense of the best men[3] seems to demand. Of course this cannot be regarded as a fatal criticism; for it may be that that moral sense

1 Or upon utilitarian considerations. See preceding note. It may be remarked that this difficulty in Kant arises from the dualism of his philosophical point of view.

2 See Caird's *Critical Philosophy of Kant*, vol. ii., p. 216, *note*.

3 Our English moralists are fond of referring to the opinions of "the plain man." But it depends a good deal on the *character* of "the plain man" whether his opinions on moral questions are worth considering.

is deficient.[1] Still on the whole any conflict with that sense must be regarded as a *primâ facie* presumption against an ethical system in which it occurs; and, along with other criticisms, may help to overthrow it. Now there are two distinct ways in which the Kantian system appears to be much too rigorous.

(*a*) In the first place, according to the Kantian view no conduct can be regarded as truly virtuous which rests on feeling. Conduct is right only in so far as it is dictated by the moral reason; and the moral reason is a purely formal principle, which has no connection with any of the feelings or passions of human nature. But much of the conduct that men commonly praise, springs rather from feeling than from any direct application of reason.[2] This has been strikingly expressed by Wordsworth in his *Ode to Duty*—

> "There are who ask not if thine eye
> Be on them; who, in love and truth,
> Where no misgiving is, rely
> Upon the genial sense of youth:
> Glad hearts! without reproach or blot;
> Who do thy work, and know it not."[3]

1 We shall see later (chap. vi.) that few ethical writers are prepared to go against the developed moral sense of mankind; and, in particular, it is certain that Kant himself was not.

2 Kant's point of view might be illustrated by the famous declaration of Sir T. Browne in his *Religio Medici:* "I give no alms to satisfy the hunger of my brother, but to fulfil and accomplish the will and command of my God." Contrast this attitude with that of the philanthropist who is actuated simply by love of those whom he seeks to benefit, and it is at once evident, even to the plainest common sense, that the latter is immeasurably the higher of the two. Indeed, it would scarcely be a paradox to say that, in such cases, the more purely a man is guided by love, and the less conscious he is of performing a duty, the better his action is. But see next note.

3 Schiller has an even more emphatic utterance on the same point in his poem *Der Genius*, beginning, "Must I distrust my impulse?"

Kant, resting duty upon a formal principle of reason, does not recognise the possibility of such an attitude as this. This defect was early perceived by the poet Schiller, an ardent student of the Kantian system, who expressed his dissatisfaction in the form of an epigram. He supposes an ethical inquirer to bring the following difficulty before a Kantian philosopher—

> "Willingly serve I my friends, but I do it, alas! with affection.
> Hence I am plagued with the doubt, virtue I have not attained."

And he represents him as receiving the following answer—

> "This is your only resource, you must stubbornly seek to abhor them.
> Then you can do with disgust that which the law may enjoin."

Of course this is a gross exaggeration of Kant's position; for he would not demand the presence of abhorrence, nor even the absence of affection. Still, it is true that he did not recognise the possibility of the performance of duty from feeling as contrasted with

and ending, "What thou pleasest to do, is thy law." His criticism is more philosophically expressed in the treatise, *Ueber Anmuth und Würde*, where he says, among other things, that "Man not only *may* but *should* bring pleasure and duty into relation to one another; he should obey his reason with joy." Of course, it would be easy to carry all this to the opposite extreme from that represented by Kant; and perhaps Kant's is the less dangerous extreme of the two. The over-indulgent parent, for instance, cannot be justified by a mere appeal to an impulse of affection. All that we are entitled to say is that a man will often be led to the performance of duty by affection far more effectively than by the consciousness of law, and that duty so performed does not thereby cease to be duty; and further, that the highest forms of duty, involving love, are not compatible with the absence of affection, and cannot be satisfactorily done from mere respect for law. *Cf.* Janet's *Theory of Morals*, Book III., chap. V.; and see above, Book I., chap. iii., § 5.

the performance of it from the mere sense of duty given by the moral reason.

(*b*) Another respect in which the rigour of Kant's point of view appears, is this, that he permits of no exceptions to his moral imperatives. Now the moral sense of the best men seems to say that there is no commandment, however sacred (unless it be the commandment of love), that does not under certain circumstances release its claims. This objection was very forcibly put by Jacobi in an indignant protest against the Kantian system, which he addressed to Fichte.[1] "Yes," he exclaims, "I am the Atheist, the Godless one, who, in spite of the will that wills nothing, am ready to lie as the dying Desdemona lied; to lie and deceive like Pylades, when he pretended to be Orestes; to murder like Timoleon; to break law and oath like Epaminondas, like John de Witt; to commit suicide with Otho and sacrilege with David,—yea, to rub the ears of corn on the Sabbath day, merely

[1] It may be observed that Fichte himself, though a disciple of Kant, laid stress chiefly on the Kantian *dictum* that "an erring conscience is a chimera," and regarded the command to "follow conscience" as the supreme moral principle. He regarded conscience, moreover, not as a principle which lays down merely formal imperatives, but rather as one which bids us advance along the line of rational development. Fichte was thus rather a representative of the school of idealistic evolution, referred to below in chap. v. For this reason, Janet remarks (*Theory of Morals*, p. 264) that Jacobi ought to have regarded Fichte as essentially in agreement with himself. For Jacobi also appealed to the heart or moral sense of the individual. But surely what Fichte meant by the "conscience" was a *rational* and *universal* principle of guidance, very different from a mere heart or moral sense. *Cf.* Adamson's *Fichte*, pp. 193 *sqq.*; Schwegler's *History of Philosophy*, pp. 273-4; Erdmann's *History of Philosophy*, vol. ii., pp. 514-16.

because I am hungry, and because *the law is made for the sake of man and not man for the sake of the law.* I am that Godless one, and I deride the philosophy that calls me Godless for such reasons, both it and its Supreme Being; for with the holiest certitude that I have in me, I know that the prerogative of pardon in reference to such transgressions of the letter of the absolute law of reason, is the characteristic royal right of man, the seal of his dignity and of his divine nature." Jacobi held, therefore, that man is not called upon to act "in blind obedience to the law." He is entitled to appeal from pure reason to the heart, which is indeed the only "faculty of ideas that are not empty." "This heart," he says, "the Transcendental Philosophy will not be allowed to tear out of my breast, in order to set a pure impulse of Egoism in its place. I am not one to allow myself to be freed from the dependence of love, in order to have my blessedness in pride alone."

To what extent this view of Jacobi is justifiable, will probably become more apparent as we proceed. In reality, it is quite as one-sided as the view of Kant to which it is opposed. It calls attention, however, to the undue rigour of Kant's principle, in admitting of no exceptions to his moral imperatives. But indeed, even apart from such considerations as Jacobi has adduced, it must be tolerably apparent that the rigour of the Kantian system, in excluding all exceptions, overshoots the mark. For many actions in ordinary life are right simply because they *are* exceptions. Many instances of heroic self-sacrifice would be unjustifiable if every one were to perform them. When it is right for a man to devote his life to a great cause, it is usually right just because it may be assumed that no one else will do it. Or take the case of celibacy.[1] For every one to abstain from marriage would be inconsistent with the continuance of the human race on earth; consequently, any one who abstained from marriage *for the sake of some benefit to posterity* would, from Kant's point of view, be acting inconsistently; yet it seems clear that it is not the duty of every one to marry, and even that it is the duty of some to abstain,—and to abstain, too, *for the sake of posterity.*

It appears, then, that the Kantian principle, interpreted in this way, is much too stringent. On the other hand, if we were to accept the other interpretation, it would be too lax. For it would then admit of every conceivable exception that we could will to be universally allowed under precisely similar conditions; and this would include everything that human beings do,[2] except when they are consciously doing what they know cannot be justified by any rational plea.

§ **15.** REAL SIGNIFICANCE OF THE KANTIAN PRINCIPLE.—We must not, however, conclude from this that the Kantian principle is to be entirely rejected. There is a sense in which it is a quite complete criterion of the

[1] *Cf.* Sidgwick's *Methods of Ethics,* Book IV., chap. v., § 3; and Abbott's translation of Kant's *Theory of Ethics*, pp. liii., *sqq.* The student should observe carefully where the inconsistency comes in here—*viz.* in the *principle* (or maxim) itself, not in its mere *results.*

[2] For instance, a man might be dishonest in business, and justify himself by saying that the principle on which he acted was, that a shrewd man is entitled to overreach a careless one. If he had perfect confidence in his own shrewdness, he might be quite willing that this principle should be universally carried out; and at the same time he might uphold the general principle of respect for the rights of others, subject only to this particular limitation.

rightness of an action to ask whether it can be consistently carried out. Our moral action is in this respect exactly similar to our intellectual life. An error cannot be consistently carried out, and neither can a sin. But in both cases alike the test is not that of mere *formal* consistency. We may take up an erroneous idea and hold consistently to it, so long as we confine ourselves to that particular idea. The inconsistency comes in only when we try to fit the erroneous idea into the scheme of the world as a whole. It is with that scheme that error is inconsistent. In like manner in our moral life we may take up a false principle of action, and we may carry it out consistently, and even will that all others should act in accordance with it, so long as we confine our attention to that particular action and its immediate consequences. But so soon as we go beyond this, and consider its bearing on the whole scheme of life,[1] it becomes apparent that we could not will that it should be universalised. The reason is, not that the action is inconsistent with itself, but rather that it is inconsistent with *the self*—*i. e.* with the unity of our lives as a systematic whole.[2] But then we have at once to ask—How are we to know

[1] How this scheme of life is to be conceived, is a question for future consideration. We shall see, at a later stage, that life has to be thought of as a growth or development. Hence it can never stand before us as a completed scheme; and that with which we have to be consistent is rather the idea of progress. But, as the novelists say, "we are anticipating."

[2] It should be observed that Kant to some extent advanced towards the point of view here indicated; especially by his conception of Humanity as an absolute end, and still more by the pregnant idea of all rational beings as constituting a *Kingdom of ends*. *Metaphysic of Morals*, Sect. II. (Abbott's translation, pp. 46—59). But the persistent dualism of Kant's system prevented him from recognising

what is and what is not consistent with this unity? What can we, and what can we not, desire to see universally carried out? This question cannot be answered by any mere consideration of formal consistency. We must inquire into the nature of our desires—*i. e.* we must introduce *matter* as well as *form.* We must ask, in other words, what is the nature of the self with which we have to be consistent.

the full significance of the advance which he had thus suggested; and his principle remained formal after all. *Cf.* Caird's *Critical Philosophy of Kant,* vol. ii., pp. 218—226. For a more recent criticism of Kant's ethical position, see Simmel's *Einleitung in die Moralwissenschaft,* Vol. II., chap. v.

NOTE ON KANT.

Kant's view is rightly characterised by Bradley (*Ethical Studies*, Essay IV.) as that of "Duty for Duty's Sake,"[1] and is contrasted with the utilitarian view (Essay III.), which is described as that of "Pleasure for Pleasure's Sake." Professor Dewey, in like manner, describes the Kantian system (*Outlines of Ethics*, p. 78) as furnishing us with merely "Formal Ethics," and as being a "theory which attempts to find the good not only in the will itself, but in the will irrespective of any end to be reached by the will." Mr. Muirhead (*Elements of Ethics*, p. 112 *sqq.*) has also described the Kantian theory in similar terms, referring both to Bradley and to Dewey; but he has carried Bradley's antithesis between the Kantian Ethics and utilitarianism to a somewhat extreme point, even going so far as to characterise the Kantian view of the supreme good by means of the heading, "The End as Self-Sacrifice." This appears to me to be an exaggeration. Kant considered that we must do our duty out of pure respect for the law of reason, and not from any anticipation of pleasure; but he nowhere, so far as I am aware, suggests that there is any merit in the *absence* of pleasure. On the contrary, though he does not regard happiness as the direct end at which the virtuous man is to aim, he yet believes that, in any complete account of the supreme human good, happiness must be included as well as virtue—though in subordination to virtue. Indeed, he even considered that, unless we had grounds for believing that the two elements—virtue and happiness—are ultimately to be found united, the very foundation of morality would be destroyed. Thus he says, "In the *summum bonum* which is practical for us, *i. e.* to be realised by our will, virtue and happiness are thought as necessarily combined, so that the one cannot be assumed by pure practical reason without the other also being attached to it. Now this combination (like every other) is either *analytical* or *synthetical*. It has been shown that it cannot be analytical;[3] it must then be synthetical, and, more particularly, must be conceived as the connection of cause

[1] It should be noted, however, that the account given by Mr. Bradley in this chapter of the theory of "Duty for Duty's Sake" is not, and is not intended to be, an exact statement of the position of Kant.

[2] *Critique of Practical Reason*, Part I., Book II., chap. ii. § 1. Abbott's translation of Kant's *Theory of Ethics*, third edition, p. 209.

[3] *I. e.* that happiness is not directly included in virtue, or virtue in happiness.

and effect, since it concerns a practical good, *i. e.* one that is possible by means of action; consequently either the desire of happiness must be the motive to maxims of virtue,[1] or the maxim of virtue must be the efficient cause of happiness. The first is *absolutely* impossible, because (as was proved in the Analytic) maxims which place the determining principle of the will in the desire of personal happiness are not moral at all, and no virtue can be founded on them. But the second is *also impossible*, because the practical connection of causes and effects in the world, as the result of the determination of the will, does not depend upon the moral dispositions of the will, but on the knowledge of the laws of nature and the physical power to use them for one's purposes; consequently we cannot expect in the world by the most punctilious observance of the moral laws any necessary connection of happiness with virtue, adequate to the *summum bonum*. Now as the promotion of this *summum bonum*, the conception of which contains this connection, is *a priori* a necessary object of our will, and inseparably attached to the moral law, the impossibility of the former must prove the falsity of the latter. If then the supreme good is not possible by practical rules, then the moral law also which commands us to promote it is directed to vain imaginary ends, and must consequently be false."

Kant's view, then, was that the supreme aim of the virtuous man is simply that of conforming to this law of reason—*i. e.*, according to him, the law of formal consistency. He must not pursue virtue *for the sake of happiness*, but purely for the sake of duty. In this sense Kant inculcates self-sacrifice. But he does not regard self-sacrifice as the *end*. The end is conformity to law, obedience to reason. Further, Kant considers that though the virtuous man does not aim at happiness, yet the complete well-being[2] of a human being includes happiness as well as virtue. And apparently he thought that if we had no ground for believing that the two elements are ultimately conjoined, the ground of morality itself would be removed.

---

[1] *This* is what Kant denies: and it is only in this sense that he is fairly to be described as an ascetic, or as one who advocates self-sacrifice.

[2] *Complete* well-being (*bonum consummatum*) as distinguished from *supreme* well-being (*supremum bonum*). The *supreme* good is virtue: the *complete* good is virtue + happiness. See *Critique of Practical Reason*, Part I., Book II., chap. ii. (Abbott's translation, p. 206). For a discussion of Kant's view on this point, see Caird's *Critical Philosophy of Kant*, Book II., chap. v. (vol. ii. pp. 289-314)

For morality rests on a demand of reason; and the possibility of attaining the *summum bonum* is also a demand of reason. If the demands of reason were chimerical in the latter case, they would be equally discredited in the former.[1] He solves the difficulty by postulating the existence of God, "as the necessary condition of the possibility of the *summum bonum*." [2]

From this it will be seen that Kant did not really regard self-sacrifice as the end. Indeed it may be doubted whether it has ever been regarded as an end by any serious school of moralists. Bentham, indeed (at least as represented by Dumont [3]), contrasts his utilitarian theory with what he calls "the Ascetic Principle," saying of the latter that "those who follow it have a horror of pleasures. Everything which gratifies the senses, in their view, is odious and criminal. They found morality upon privations, and virtue upon the renouncement of one's self. In one word, the reverse of the partisans of utility, they approve everything which tends to diminish enjoyment, they blame everything which tends to augment it." But this description would evidently not apply to Kant,[4] nor perhaps to any school of moralists, if we except some of the extremest of the Cynics.[5] Bentham himself, in the passage from which the above extract is taken, does not refer to any philosophic writers, but only to the Jansenists and some other theologians. Even the Stoics [6] (to whom certainly Kant bears a strong resemblance [7]) did not regard

---

[1] Observe the close resemblance between Kant's view on this point and that of Butler. See Sidgwick's *History of Ethics*, pp. 195-7. Kant, however, states the difficulty in a much more precise and profound form than that in which it is put by Butler. Kant's attempted solution, in like manner, is characterised by immeasurably greater speculative depth.

[2] Kant, *loc. cit.*, section V. (Abbott, p. 221).

[3] *Theory of Legislation*, chap. ii. See also *Principles of Morals and Legislation*, chap. ii.

[4] There is, indeed, a passage in the *Methodology of Pure Practical Reason* (Abbott's translation, p. 254), in which Kant says that virtue is "worth so much only because it costs so much." But the context shows that his meaning is merely that the cost brings clearly to light the purity of the motive.

[5] See Sidgwick's *History of Ethics*, p. 33-35.

[6] For an account of the Stoics, see Sidgwick's *History of Ethics*, pp. 70-85.

[7] *Cf.* Caird's *Critical Philosophy of Kant*, vol. ii. pp. 222-3, &c.

the sacrifice of happiness as in itself a good. On the contrary, as Kant himself remarks,[1] both the Stoics and Epicureans were agreed in identifying virtue with happiness: only while the Epicureans held that the pursuit of happiness is virtue, the Stoics held, contrariwise, that the pursuit of virtue is happiness.[2]

I have thought it desirable to dwell on this slight divergence between my view on this point and that stated in Mr. Muirhead's *Elements*, not for the purpose of emphasising my disagreement, but rather to bring out the fundamental identity of our views. For if the reader will turn to the passage in Mr. Muirhead's book, I think he will easily see that the difference between us is merely superficial. Although Mr. Muirhead treats of the Kantian Ethics under the heading "The End as Self-Sacrifice," and refers to it as illustrating the ascetic principle in morals, yet his actual treatment of Kant's fundamental position does not, I think, materially differ from that suggested in the present manual. I am convinced, therefore, that our divergence on this point is little more than verbal.

It is perhaps fair to add here that a partial reply to Schiller's objections (referred to above, § 13) was made by Kant in his treatise on *Religion within the Bounds of mere Reason*.[3] Kant there admits that a thoroughly virtuous man will love virtuous activities, and perform them with pleasure; but he regards this as a mere *result* of action from the sense of duty. The man who acts from a sense of duty has a feeling of pleasure gradually superinduced. This admission obviates the grosser forms of the criticism that has been passed on Kant with regard to this point; but it still leaves a fatal dualism between the law of reason and the affections of human kindness. In short, it still has the defect of emphasising the mere isolated *good will* instead of the *good character*.[4] *Cf.* above, Book I., chap. iii., § 2.

---

[1] *Critique of Practical Reason*, Part I., Book II., chap. ii. (Abbott's translation, p. 208).

[2] Or at least that a certain form of happiness is an inseparable accident of the pursuit of virtue. See Sidgwick's *History of Ethics*, pp. 83–4.

[3] *Cf.* also *Metaphysical Elements of Ethics* (Abbott's translation), pp. 312–13.

[4] The point that it is specially important to remember is, that Kant always insists that duty must not be done *from* inclination. He never denies that it may be done *with* inclination. Consequently, he is not properly an ascetic.

CHAPTER IV.

THE STANDARD AS HAPPINESS.

§ **1.** Introductory Remarks.—We thus see that the idea of a categorical imperative breaks down, or at least lands us in sheer emptiness. It tells us only that we must judge our actions from the point of view of a universal self, not from a private standpoint of our own, and that we must act in a way that is consistent with the idea of this higher self. All this is formal:[1]

[1] In saying that it is merely formal, I do not of course mean to deny its practical importance. In concrete life we constantly tend to judge ourselves and others by standards that are not of universal application; and Kant's formula is useful as a safeguard against this. Perhaps the following passage from Bryce's *American Commonwealth* (chap. lxxv.) may serve to illustrate this danger. "All professions," he says, "have a tendency to develop a special code of rules less exacting than those of the community at large. As a profession holds certain things to be wrong, because contrary to its etiquette, which are in themselves harmless, so it justifies other things in themselves blamable. In the mercantile world, agents play sad tricks on their principals in the matter of commissions, and their fellow-merchants are astonished when the courts of law compel the ill-gotten gains to be disgorged. At the English Universities, everybody who took a Master of Arts degree was, until lately, required to sign the Thirty-nine Articles of the Church of England. Hundreds of men signed who did not believe, and admitted that they did not believe, the dogmas of this formulary; but nobody in Oxford thought the worse of them for a solemn falsehood. . . . Each profession indulges in deviations from the established rules of morals, but takes pains to conceal these deviations from the general public, and continues to talk about itself and its traditions with an air of unsullied virtue. What each profession does for itself most individuals do for themselves. They judge themselves by them-

we now wait for the content with which the form is to be filled. We have to ask, in short, what is the nature of the ideal self, and how it is constituted.

§ 2. HIGHER AND LOWER UNIVERSES.—That certain forms of will are higher or better than others, may almost be said to be the fundamental assumption of Ethics. Now it follows from this that certain desires, or certain universes of desire, are higher or better than others. Thus it becomes a problem to determine why it is that any desire or universe of desires should be regarded as higher or better than any other. The significance of this problem may perhaps be best indicated by suggesting a possible answer. It is obvious that some universes are more comprehensive than others. If a man acts from the point of view of the happiness of his nation as a whole, this is evidently a more comprehensive point of view than that from which he acts when he has regard only to his own happiness. The former includes the latter. So too, if a man acts from the point of view of his own happiness throughout the year, he acts from a more comprehensive point of view than if he has regard only to the happiness of the passing hour. Now the narrower the point of view from which we act, the more certain we are to fall into inconsistency and self-contradiction.

selves, that is to say, by their surroundings and their own past acts, and thus erect in the inner forum of conscience a more lenient code for their own transgressions than that which they apply to others. We all know that a fault which a man has often committed seems to him slighter than one he has refrained from and seen others committing. Often he gets others to take the same view. 'It is only his way,' they say: 'it is just like Roger.' The same thing happens with nations." There is perhaps some cynicism in this; but it contains sufficient truth to illustrate the present point.

If the universe within which we act is merely that of the passing hour, that universe will no longer be the dominant one when the hour is past; and then we shall find ourselves acting from some different, and perhaps inconsistent point of view. If, on the other hand, the universe within which we act is broad and comprehensive, we may be able to maintain our point of view consistently through life, and also to apply it to the actions of others. The wider universe may, therefore, be regarded as higher or better than the narrower one, since it enables us to maintain a more consistent point of view in our actions. From this consideration we may partly see why it is that one universe is to be regarded as higher or better than another. Still, this does not make it quite clear. For sometimes when we prefer one universe to another, the former does not include the latter, and is not obviously wider than it. What is the ground of preference in such cases we shall consider at a later point in this inquiry. But in the meantime, it may be well to notice a plausible explanation of the preference, which we shall see reason afterwards to reject. In such a subject as Ethics, erroneous doctrines are often almost as instructive as those that are correct.

§ **3.** Satisfaction of Desires.—When a desire attains the end to which it is directed, the desire is satisfied; and this satisfaction is attended by an agreeable feeling [1]—a feeling of pleasure, enjoyment, or happiness.

[1] I follow Dr. James Ward and others in using the term "Feeling" for pleasure and pain. It is, however, a very ambiguous term, and perhaps the term "Affection," which is used by Prof. Titchener in his *Outline of Psychology*, is in some ways preferable. See Stout's *Manual of Psychology*, Book II., chap. viii.

On the other hand, when the end of a desire is not attained, we have a disagreeable feeling—a feeling of pain, misery, or unhappiness. Now if we act within a wide universe, or within a universe that includes desires that are continually recurring throughout life, we shall be acting in such a way as to satisfy our desires with great frequency, and so to have many feelings of pleasure. On the other hand, if we act within a narrow universe, or one containing desires that do not often recur, we may have few satisfactions and a frequent occurrence of painful feelings. Now it seems plausible to say that, since what we aim at is the satisfaction of our desires, the best aim is that which will bring the greatest number of pleasures and the smallest number of pains. This consideration would supply us with a criterion of higher and lower universes. The highest universe within which we could act would be that which would supply us with the greatest number of pleasures and the smallest number of pains. The highest universe, in fact, would be that which is constituted by the consideration of our greatest happiness throughout life; or, if we consider others as well as ourselves, by the consideration of the greatest happiness of the greatest number. This leads us to the consideration of Hedonism.

§ 4. VARIETIES OF HEDONISM.—Hedonism is the general term for those theories that regard happiness or pleasure as the supreme end of life. It is derived from the Greek word ἡδονή, meaning pleasure. These theories have taken many different forms. It has been held by some that men always *do* seek pleasure, *i. e.* that pleasure in some form is always the ultimate object of desire; whereas other Hedonists confine themselves to the view that men *ought* always to seek pleasure. The former theory has been called by Prof. Sidgwick *Psychological Hedonism*, because it simply affirms the seeking of pleasure as a psychological fact; whereas he describes the other theory as *Ethical Hedonism.* Again, some have held that what each man seeks, or ought to seek, is his own pleasure; while others hold that what each seeks, or ought to seek, is the pleasure of all human beings, or even of all sentient creatures. Prof. Sidgwick has called the former of these views *Egoistic Hedonism;* the latter, *Universalistic Hedonism.* The latter has also been called *Utilitarianism*—which, however, is a very inappropriate name.[1] Most of the earlier ethical Hedonists were also psychological Hedonists; but this latter view has now been almost universally abandoned. Egoistic Hedonism has also been generally abandoned. Its chief upholders were the ancient Cyrenaics and Epicureans.[2] Some more modern writers, however,—such as Bentham and Mill —did not clearly distinguish between egoistic and universalistic Hedonism, and consequently, though in the main supporting only the latter, often seemed to be giving their adhesion to the former. The student must be careful to distinguish between these different kinds of Hedonism: otherwise great confusion will

1 See below, § 9.

2 For an account of these see Sidgwick's *History of Ethics*, pp. 32–3, and pp. 82–90. See also Zeller's *Socrates and the Socratic Schools*, and *Stoics, Epicureans, and Sceptics.* Prof. Wallace's little volume on *Epicureanism* ("Chief Ancient Philosophies") is a most delightful book, which every student ought to read. Prof. Watson's *Hedonistic Theories from Aristippus to Spencer* is also exceedingly interesting, and, though somewhat popular in its mode of treatment, is nearly always reliable.

result. Now the doctrine of Psychological Hedonism has already been considered in Book I. It is simply a statement of fact; whereas Ethical Hedonism is a theory of Value, a theory of the ground upon which one form of action ought to be preferred to others.

§ 5. ETHICAL HEDONISM.—We have seen that the theory of psychological Hedonism is unsound. Ethical Hedonism, however, does not stand or fall with this. On the contrary, as Dr. Sidgwick has pointed out,[1] ethical Hedonism is scarcely compatible with psychological Hedonism, at least in its most extreme form. If we always *did* seek our own *greatest pleasure,* there would be no point in saying that we *ought* to seek it; while, on the other hand, it would be absurd to say that we *ought* to seek the pleasure of others, except in so far as this could be shown to coincide with our own. Of course, if psychological Hedonism be merely interpreted as meaning that we always do seek *pleasure of some sort,* then ethical Hedonism may be understood as teaching that we ought to seek the *greatest* pleasure, whether our own or that of others. But, in any case, there is no necessary connection between the two doctrines.[2] The confusion that has often been made

[1] *Methods of Ethics,* Book I., chap. iv., § 1.

[2] It will be seen, therefore, that I do not agree with Mr. Muirhead (*Elements of Ethics,* p. 114) in regarding the psychological form of Hedonism as "also its logical form." At the same time, it should be observed that systems of ethical Hedonism (especially when egoistic) have nearly always been made to rest on psychological Hedonism. Nor is this necessarily inconsistent; for most Hedonists (especially egoistic Hedonists) have denied any absolute "ought" as having authority over men's natural inclinations. They have regarded Ethics as simply laying down rules for the guidance of our actions, so as to secure the greatest possible gratification to our natural impulses. They have thought that by the introduction of adequate "sanc-

between the two theories seems to be due in part to an ambiguity in the word "desirable."[1] This point also may be illustrated by a passage from Mill. "The only proof," he says, "capable of being given that an object is visible, is that people actually see it. The only proof that a sound is audible, is that people hear it. . . . In like manner, I apprehend, the sole evidence it is possible to produce that anything is desirable, is that people do actually desire it." It is here assumed that the meaning of the word "desirable" is analogous to that of "visible" and "audible." But "visible" means "able to be seen," and "audible" means "able to be heard"; whereas "desirable" does not usually mean "able to be desired." When we say that anything is desirable, we do not usually mean merely that it is able to be desired. There is scarcely anything that is not able to be desired. What we mean is rather that it is *reasonably to be desired*, or that it *ought* to be desired. When the Hedonist says that pleasure is the only thing that is desirable, he means that it is the only thing that *ought* to be desired. But the form of the word "desirable" seems to have misled several writers into the notion that they ought to

tions" (see below, Note to Book III., chap. vi.) the greatest pleasure of the community as a whole might be made coincident with the individual's greatest pleasure. Bentham was particularly explicit on this point, saying even, paradoxically, that the word "ought" "ought to be abolished." (But *cf. Principles of Morals and Legislation*, chap. i., § 10.) But this view is, of course, incompatible with the admission (now generally made by all Hedonists) that the gratification of our own inclinations may conflict with duty. If this is allowed, ethical Hedonism cannot rest on psychological. *Cf.* Gizycki's *Introduction to the Study of Ethics*, pp. 70—78.

[1] *Cf.* Sidgwick's *Methods of Ethics*, Book III., chap. xiii., § 5.

show also that pleasure is the only thing that is *capable* of being desired.[1] The latter view is that of psychological Hedonism, which seems clearly to be unsound. The former is that of ethical Hedonism, which we have still to examine.

We have already stated that there are two forms of ethical Hedonism—*egoistic* and *universalistic*. But before we proceed to consider these, it will be well to indicate more precisely what the general meaning of ethical Hedonism is.

§ **6.** QUANTITY OF PLEASURE.—Hedonism is not merely the vague theory that we ought to seek pleasure. It states definitely that we ought to seek the *greatest* pleasure. Otherwise of course it would give us no criterion of right and wrong in conduct. Pleasure may be found by acting in the most contradictory ways. But when we are told to seek the *greatest* pleasure, there can usually be but one course to follow. In estimating the quantity of pleasure, it is usually said that there are two points to be taken into account—*intensity* and *duration*.[2] Some pleasures are preferable to others because they last longer. Pains require also

[1] The fallacy here involved is that known to writers on Logic as the "Fallacy of Figure of Speech" (*figuræ dictionis*). See Whately's *Logic*, pp. 117–18, Davis's *Theory of Thought*, p. 270, Welton's *Manual of Logic*, vol. II., p. 243. Jevons (*Elementary Lessons on Logic*, p. 175) seems to have quite misunderstood this fallacy, as well as many others.

[2] In estimating the value of pleasures, there are, according to Bentham, some other qualities also which should be taken into account—*viz.* certainty, propinquity, fecundity (power of producing other pleasures), and purity (freedom from pain). He considered also that we should take account of their extent—*i. e.* the number of persons who participate in them. See his *Principles of Morals and Legislation*. He summed up his view in the following doggerel verses—

to be taken into account. Pain is simply the opposite of pleasure, and is consequently to be treated just as negative quantities are treated in mathematics. If a pleasure is represented by $+a$, the corresponding pain will be represented by $-a$; and what we are to aim at is to secure the greatest sum of pleasures or the smallest sum of pains, pleasures being counted as positive and pains as negative. If there are three pleasures, valued respectively at 3, 4, and 5; 5 is to be preferred to either 3 or 4, $3+4$ is to be preferred to 5, $3+5$ to $3+4$, and $4+5$ to $3+5$. Again, if we have pains valued at $-3, -4, -5$; -3 is to be preferred to -4, and -4 to -5. So too $5-3$ is to be preferred to $4-3$, and $3-4$ to $3-5$; while between $4-3$ and $5-4$, or between $3-3$ and $4-4$, there is no ground of preference. And so on.

§ **7.** Egoistic Hedonism.—Egoistic Hedonism is the doctrine that what each ought to seek is his own greatest pleasure. Almost the only writers who have held this doctrine in a pure form are the Cyrenaics and Epicureans. The writers of the former school, however, confined themselves to inculcating the pursuit of the pleasure of each moment as it passes—*i. e.* they did not take account of duration. The Epicureans inculcated rather the endeavour to secure the happiness

"*Intense, long, certain, speedy, fruitful, pure,*
Such marks in *pleasures* and in *pains* endure.
Such pleasures seek, if *private* be thy end;
If it be *public*, wide let them *extend.*
Such *pains* avoid, whichever be thy view;
If pains *must* come, let them *extend* to few."

Cf. Sidgwick's *History of Ethics*, pp. 240-1, and Dewey's *Outlines of Ethics*, pp. 36-7.

of life as a whole. In modern times, owing to the spirit of self-sacrifice introduced by Christianity, this doctrine has seldom been avowed in any form. Hobbes[1] and Gassendi are the chief modern writers who decidedly adopt this view; and it is by them made to rest on psychological Hedonism. It appears also in a manner in Spinoza;[2] but he subordinates it to a certain metaphysical theory, which we cannot here consider.

Egoistic Hedonism has always presented a repulsive appearance to the moral consciousness. Yet it is possible to give it a plausible appearance, and even at the present time it is recognised by Dr. Sidgwick as an inevitable element in a complete system of Ethics. The reason why this should seem to be so is evident enough. It is clear that the end at which we are to aim must be some end that will give us satisfaction. When asked why we pursue any end, the only reasonable answer that can be given, is that it satisfies some

1 For an account of Hobbes, see Sidgwick's *History of Ethics*, pp 163–170. It should be observed, however (what perhaps Dr. Sidgwick does not sufficiently bring out), that the Egoism of Hobbes is much more pronounced than his Hedonism. It is even open to question whether he is strictly to be regarded as a Hedonist at all, though on the whole the answer seems to be in the affirmative. *Cf.* Croom Robertson's *Hobbes*, p. 136. Helvetius and Mandeville may perhaps also be classed as Egoistic Hedonists. See Lecky's *History of European Morals*, p. 6 *sqq.* But Mandeville can hardly be taken seriously. It should be added that scarcely any of these writers can be regarded as *purely* (or at least consistently) egoistic. Even Hobbes is led in the end to recognise a law of Reason (though of a very derivative character) bidding us have regard to the general good. See Croom Robertson's *Hobbes*, p. 142.

2 See Principal Caird's *Spinoza*, chaps. xii. and xiii. Spinoza's highest end was rather *blessedness* than *pleasure*. See below, § 9, (c), and Chap. V., § 14.

demand of our nature; and the only finally satisfactory answer that can be given, is that it satisfies the most fundamental demand of our nature. For if we say that we pursue the end for some external reason—as, *e. g.* because we are commanded by some superior authority—there still remains the question why we are to be influenced by that external reason. The only answer that leaves no further question behind it, is the answer that has reference to an ultimate demand of our nature. Now, when we are asked what it is that satisfies the ultimate demands of our nature, it is very natural to answer "Pleasure."

On consideration, however, it appears that, in giving this answer, we are misled by the same ambiguity as that which we encountered in dealing with psychological Hedonism. It is undoubtedly true that whatever satisfies the ultimate demands of our nature will bring pleasure with it, and may consequently be described as a pleasure. But this pleasure must have some objective content, and that content is not itself pleasure. The object that gives us pleasure may be the pleasure of some one else, or it may be the welfare of our country, or it may be the fulfilment of what we conceive to be our duty. These things are *pleasures*—*i. e.* they are objects the attainment of which will bring us pleasure. But they are not themselves *pleasure*—*i. e.* agreeable feeling. Here, again, therefore, to say that we ought to seek *pleasures*, is not to say that we ought to seek *pleasure*.

Dr. Sidgwick, however, thinks[1] that "when we sit down in a cool hour" (as he says, quoting Butler), we

[1] *Methods of Ethics*, Book III., chap. xiv. § 5.

perceive that there is nothing which it is reasonable to seek—*i. e.* nothing which is desirable in itself—except pleasure. He then argues that since pleasure is the one desirable thing, the greatest pleasure must be the most desirable. A more intense pleasure is consequently to be preferred to a less intense, and a pleasure which lasts longer to one that is of shorter duration. Further, he urges that, in estimating our pleasures, a past or future pleasure ought, *cæteris paribus*, to be regarded as of equal value with a present one. For mere difference of time [1] can of itself make no difference to the value of our pleasures.[2] All this is evidently true, on the assumption that pleasure is the one desirable thing. But there seems to be no warrant for this assumption.[3]

§ 8. UNIVERSALISTIC HEDONISM.—Universalistic Hedonism or Utilitarianism is the theory that what we ought to aim at is the greatest possible amount of pleasure of all human beings, or of all sentient creatures. The chief exponents of this theory are Bentham, J. S. Mill, and Professor Sidgwick. Bentham's proof of the theory is not very explicit,[4] and may perhaps be considered to be sufficiently represented by that of Mill. Mill's argument is stated thus in the fourth chapter of his *Utilitarianism*: "No reason can be given why the general happiness is desirable, except that each person, so far as he believes it to be attainable,

1 Apart from the *uncertainty* which is generally connected with the lapse of time. Allowance would, of course, have to be made for this.

2 *Methods of Ethics*, Book III., chap. xiii., § 3.

3 *Cf.* § 5, and see below, § 10.

4 *Cf.* Sidgwick's *History of Ethics*, pp. 241–245.

desires his own happiness. This, however, being a fact, we have not only all the proof which the case admits of, but all which it is possible to require, that happiness is a good: that each person's happiness is a good to that person, and the general happiness, therefore, a good to the aggregate of all persons." He then goes on to argue that happiness is the only good, on the ground that we have already noticed—*viz.* that to desire a thing and to find it pleasant are but two ways of expressing the same thing. Now it would be difficult to collect in a short space so many fallacies as are here committed. We have already noticed the confusion in the last point, due to the ambiguity in the word "pleasure." We have also noticed the confusion with regard to the meaning of "desirable," which vitiates the first part of the argument. It only remains to notice the fallacy involved in the inference that "the general happiness is a good to the aggregate of all persons." The fallacy is that which is known in logic as "the fallacy of composition." It is inferred that because my pleasures are a good to me, yours to you, his to him, and so on, therefore my pleasures + your pleasures + his pleasures are a good to me + you + him. It is forgotten that neither the pleasures nor the persons are capable of being made into an aggregate. It is as if we should argue that because each one of a hundred soldiers is six feet high, therefore the whole company is six hundred feet high. The answer is that this would be the case if the soldiers stood on one another's heads. And similarly Mill's argument would hold good if the minds of all human beings were to be rolled into one, so as to form an aggregate. But as it is, "the aggregate of all persons" is nobody, and consequently nothing can be a good to him. A good must be a good for somebody.[1]

Dr. Sidgwick's proof is of a more satisfactory character. He considers universalistic Hedonism to be established in the very same way as Egoistic Hedonism is established.[2] He thinks that he has shown that pleasure is the only thing that is in itself desirable. This being the case, pleasure is always to be chosen. And in the choice of pleasure, reason bids us be impartial. The greatest attainable pleasure is always to be selected. In choosing our own pleasures, the future is to be regarded as of equal weight with the present. In like manner, also, the pleasures of others are to be regarded as of equal weight with our own. It might be thought that in this way Dr. Sidgwick had overthrown egoistic Hedonism, and shown universalistic Hedonism to be the only reasonable Hedonistic system. But, for some reason which it is not easy to discover, he does not consider this to be the case. So far as can be made out, the reason seems to be that what is primarily our good is our own pleasure; and it is only in a secondary way that we discover that the pleasure of others ought to be equally regarded. Now this secondary discovery cannot overthrow the first primary truth. Hence we are bound still to regard our own pleasure as a supreme good. For this reason Dr. Sidgwick considers that there is a certain contradiction or dualism in the final recommendations of reason. We are bound to seek our own greatest pleasure, and yet we are bound also to seek the greatest pleasure of the aggregate of sentient beings. Now these two ends

[1] *Cf.* Bradley's *Ethical Studies*, p. 103.

[2] *Methods of Ethics*, Book III., chap. xiii., § 3.

may not, and probably will not, coincide. There is thus a conflict between two different commands of reason. This conflict is referred to by Dr. Sidgwick as "the Dualism of Practical Reason."[1] But if there is any force in this consideration, it seems as if we might carry it further, and say that there is a similar conflict between the pursuit of our own greatest pleasure at a given moment and the pursuit of the greatest happiness of life as a whole. For it is the pleasure of a given moment that appears to be primarily desirable. At any given moment what seems desirable is the satisfaction of our present wants. Consequently, on the same principle we might say that we are bound to seek the greatest pleasure of a given moment no less than the greatest pleasure of our whole life. There would thus be three kinds of Hedonism instead of two—the Cyrenaic view being recognised as well as the Epicurean and the Benthamite. However, it is perhaps scarcely worth while to consider which form of Hedonism is the most reasonable, as they seem all to be based on a misconception.

Two points may be noted with regard to universalistic Hedonism. In the first place, it used to be described as Utilitarianism, because it was supposed to inculcate the pursuit of what is useful. But it is now seen that pleasure is not more useful than any other possible end; and the name has consequently been dropped in scientific writings—though, for shortness,

[1] For Dr. Sidgwick's view on this point, see his *Methods of Ethics*, concluding chapter. Prof. Gizycki, who is to a large extent a follower of Dr. Sidgwick, does not accept his doctrine on this point. See his criticism of the fourth edition of the *Methods of Ethics* in the *International Journal of Ethics* for October, 1890.

the term is still often used as a designation of the school. In the second place, the end of universalistic Hedonism used to be described as being the attainment of "the greatest happiness of the greatest number." The meaning of this was,[1] that if we had to choose between a great happiness of a small number and a smaller happiness of a great number, we ought to prefer the latter, even if the total happiness were less. But it is now recognised that if pleasure is to be regarded as the good, we are bound to choose the greatest pleasure, even if it should be concentrated in a single person, instead of being distributed over a large number. Accordingly, this phrase has also been abandoned.[2]

§ 9. General Criticism of Hedonism. (*a*) *Pleasure and Value.*—We see now the general foundation on which the Hedonistic theory of Ethics rests. It may be based either on a psychological theory of the object of desire or on a theory of value. The former basis has been perhaps sufficiently discussed; but on the latter some remarks must still be added.

The general point of view is that, though our desires may often be directed to other objects than pleasure, yet, when we set ourselves calmly to consider the matter, we see that pleasure is that which alone constitutes the value for us of the objects of our experi-

[1] In so far as it had any definite meaning. The phrase seems to have been frequently employed without any definite meaning being attached to it. There is an interesting discussion of this point in Edgeworth's *Mathematical Psychics*, p. 117 *sqq.*

[2] It should be observed that Bentham himself seems, in his later years, to have discarded the expression "of the greatest number.' His reasons for doing so (which are not very clearly explained) may be found in Burton's *Introduction to Bentham's Works.* pp. 18 and 19, *note.*

ence.) A psychosis (to use Prof. Huxley's term,[1] adopted by recent psychologists), *i. e.* a state of consciousness, is valuable for us exactly in proportion as it is pleasant. Consequently, though the impulse of desire may sometimes move towards the less pleasant of two possible objects; and though, therefore, we cannot say that our desires are always moved simply by the calculation of pleasure; yet, when we reflect calmly, and from a purely egoistic point of view, we see that the only reasonable ground of preference between two psychoses is that the one is more pleasurable than the other. Hence, though it is not true that we always act in such a way as to secure for ourselves the pleasantest of possible psychoses, yet we ought (*i. e.* it is reasonable) to secure for ourselves the most pleasant, so long as this does not interfere with the pleasure of any one else; and, in general, we ought to act in such a way as to make the sum of the pleasures of all psychoses, present and future, as great as possible.

Now it is true, I think, that pleasure may fairly be described as a *sense of value.*[2] Mr. Bradley has said[3]

[1] Huxley's *Hume*, p. 62.

[2] *Cf.* Dewey's *Psychology*, p. 16. I mean that it is truer to call pleasure a sense of value than to represent it as constituting value. But even to call it a sense of value involves a kind of anticipation. In sensuous pleasure, for instance, we can hardly be said to have any consciousness of value. The general subject of the relation between pleasure and value is, however, too complicated to be discussed here. I have made some attempt to deal with it in a Note on Value at the end of Chap. IV. of my *Introduction to Social Philosophy*. *Cf.* also "Notes on the Theory of Value" in *Mind*, New Series, Vol. IV., no. 16.

[3] *Ethical Studies*, p. 234. Mr. Bradley has since abandoned this view. The element of truth in it seems to lie in the fact that pleasure consists in a certain harmony of the content of conscious-

that pleasure is essentially "the feeling of self-realisedness." Exception might be taken to this, on the ground that it can scarcely be applied to the feelings of animals, or to the more animal pleasures of men. But at any rate we may say that the feeling of pleasure is the accompaniment of objects which have a certain value[1] for the consciousness to which they are presented. It is of some importance, I think, to remember that it is the objects, not the feelings of pleasure, that have value—the feeling of pleasure being the *sense* of value, not the *value* itself; but with this point we need not here trouble ourselves. It is sufficient to note that, from this point of view, it seems at least plausible to say that, though pleasure is not the direct object of desire, and though it is not even in itself that which has value for us, yet it may be accepted as the *measure of value;* just as the degrees of a thermometer, though not themselves heat, may be taken as the measure of heat; or as a token currency, though of little value in itself, may serve to measure the values of commodities.

This, I say, is a plausible view. But it evidently rests on the assumption that pleasures are all of the same sort; just as the power of money to serve as a measure of the values of goods rests on the assumption of a certain uniformity in the currency. If the sense

ness with the form of unity within which it falls. But this form of unity need not be a definite consciousness of self and its realization.

1 Wherein this value consists, we are not here called upon to decide. It may lie, as many psychologists have supposed, in a certain heightening of general vitality or of particular vital functions. On the general nature of pleasure and pain, and their place in our conscious life, the student may be referred to Mr. Stout's *Analytic Psychology*, chap. xii., or to his *Manual*, pp. 234-240.

of value which we have in pleasant feeling is to be taken as the measure of the values which we reasonably attach to the different objects that are presented to our consciousness, this implies that the values are always judged by the same standard, always presented, so to speak, before the same court of appeal. Or (taking Mr. Bradley's phrase) if pleasure is the feeling of self-realisedness, then in taking pleasure as the measure of our self-realisation, we assume that it is *always the same self that is realised.* But is this the case? Before considering this point any further, it may be well to notice the form in which it was presented by Mill.

(*b*) *Quality of Pleasures.*—We may say briefly that the Hedonistic theory proceeds on the assumption that all pleasures are capable of being quantitatively compared—that it is always possible to determine with regard to two pleasures, or two sums of pleasures, which is the greater and which is the less. On this point a serious difficulty was raised[1] by J. S. Mill, who called attention to the fact that pleasures differ not merely in quantity but also in quality—that some pleasures are preferable to others, not because as pleasures they are greater, but because they are of a more excellent kind. If this is the case, it is evident that the Hedonistic theory must be abandoned, for it is then no longer true that pleasure is the only desirable thing. One pleasure is, on this view, more desirable than another, not on account of its nature as pleasure, but on account of some other quality that it possesses, beyond its mere

1 *Utilitarianism*, chap. ii. He did not, indeed, raise the point *as* a difficulty, but rather as indicating a way out of a difficulty. But evidently it is a difficulty from the Hedonistic point of view.

pleasantness. Further, if we admit differences of quality, it becomes impossible to place pleasures, and sums of pleasure, in any precise order of desirability. Qualities cannot be estimated against quantities, unless in some way they can be reduced to quantities—and this, on Mill's supposition, is not the case. It becomes important, therefore, to consider whether there really are qualitative differences among pleasures. In order to do this, we must recur to some of the points that were discussed in a former chapter.

(*c*) *Kinds of Pleasure.*—At the beginning of Book I. we distinguished between appetites and desires, and we pointed out also that desires may belong to a great variety of distinct universes. Now just as there is a distinction between different kinds of desire, so there is a distinction between the feelings of satisfaction which accompany the attainment of their objects. When an appetite is satisfied, the feeling of satisfaction is simple and immediate. It is to this kind of feeling that the term *pleasure* is perhaps most properly applied. On the other hand, the feeling which accompanies the satisfaction of desire is of a more intellectual or reflective character, and ought perhaps rather to be described as *happiness.* Human desire involves the more or less direct consciousness of an end, and in the feeling which accompanies its satisfaction there is also a more or less direct consciousness of an end attained. These feelings vary greatly, according to the nature of the universe within which we are living at the time when the desire is satisfied. The feelings of satisfaction that belong to the universe of self-interest are very different from those that belong to the universe of duty; those that belong to the universe of animal enjoyment are very different from those that belong to the universe of poetic or religious emotion. Carlyle has suggested[1] that, in the case of such higher universes as these, the feeling ought to be described rather as *blessedness*[2] than as *happiness*. At any rate, whether or not we use different words for the different universes, it seems clear that the feelings in question are of very different characters. It is, in fact, a very different self that is realised in each of these cases; and the feeling of self-realisedness is consequently different. Or, to put it in the other form that we have used, the sense of value in each case is a sense of value for a different judge. We are estimating, as it were, sometimes in gold, sometimes in silver, and sometimes in copper. Now it might be possible, no doubt, to find a common denominator for these: but this common denominator does not seem to be supplied in the feeling of pleasure itself.

There is, however, a difficulty which is apt to present itself at this point. It is apt to be thought that what is different in these different cases is not the feeling itself, but merely the object on which the feeling depends. This is the point that we have next to consider.

(*d*) *Pleasure inseparable from its Object.*—Pleasure, it must be remembered, is not an entity, having an existence by itself, independently of the object in which pleasure is felt, or of the unity of consciousness to

1 *Sartor Resartus*, Book II., chap. ix.

2 Spinoza also seems to use the term *beatitudo* in this sense. This form of happiness is found, according to Spinoza, in the "Intellectual Love of God," *i. e.* in the appreciation of the universe as the realization of a spiritual principle. *Cf.* also Janet's *Theory of Morals*, Book I., chap. ix.

which that object is presented. It is an element in a total state of consciousness, and is entirely relative to the other elements in that state. It is the inner side of that of which the other elements may be said to form the outer side. The sharp distinction that we are apt to draw between an object of consciousness and the feeling of pleasure or pain which accompanies it, is due largely to an inadequate apprehension of the nature of the object which is presented to our consciousness. Take, for instance, the pleasure which accompanies the hearing of a musical performance. The pleasure here is evidently quite distinct from the music which we hear. But it must be remembered that the music which we hear is not the total object that is before our consciousness. The hearing of the music is accompanied by all sorts of ideas which it calls up in our minds. It is accompanied also by other ideas which were passing through our minds before the music commenced. The object which is before our consciousness is a complex total of innumerable thoughts and images. Now the feeling of pleasure is not this complex total; but neither can it be said to be anything that is separable from that total. It is the inner side to which that total corresponds as the outer side. Given that total, we could not but have that feeling of pleasure. Change that total, and our feeling of pleasure must also be changed. The total content of our consciousness in listening to a piece of music is different from the total content in reading a novel or witnessing a dramatic performance: the feeling of pleasure is also different. The feeling and the object to which it corresponds are like the two sides of a curve. They are distinguishable from one another; yet they are inseparable, and the one necessarily varies with the other.[1]

(*e*) *Pleasures cannot be Summed.*—It follows from this that there cannot be any *calculus* of pleasures—*i. e.* that the values of pleasures cannot be quantitatively estimated. For there can be no quantitative estimate of things that are not homogeneous. But, indeed, even apart from this consideration, there seems to be a certain confusion in the Hedonistic idea that we ought to aim at a greatest sum of pleasures. If pleasure is the one thing that is desirable, it is clear that a sum of pleasures cannot be desirable; for a sum of pleasures is not pleasure. We are apt to think that a sum of pleasures is pleasure, just as a sum of

[1] Dr. Sidgwick has replied to this objection, as stated by Green. "It is sometimes said," he remarks (*Methods of Ethics*, Book II., chap. ii., § 2, *note*) "that 'pleasure as feeling, in distinction from its conditions which are not feelings, cannot be conceived.' This is true in a certain sense of the word 'conceive'; but not in any sense which would prevent us from taking pleasure as an end of rational action. To adopt an old comparison, it is neither more nor less true than the statement that an angle cannot be 'conceived' apart from its sides. We certainly cannot form the notion of an angle without the notion of sides containing it; but this does not prevent us from apprehending with perfect definiteness the magnitude of any angle as greater or less than that of any other, without any comparison of the pairs of containing sides. Similarly we cannot form a notion of any pleasure existing apart from some 'conditions which are not feelings'; but this is no obstacle to our comparing a pleasure felt under any given conditions with any other, however otherwise conditioned, and pronouncing it equal or unequal: and we require no more than this to enable us to take 'amount of pleasure' as our standard in deciding between alternatives of conduct." But this reply seems to involve a misconception of the precise nature of the criticism. The length of the sides makes no difference to the size of the angle; whereas Green's argument is that the nature of the objects makes all the difference in the world to the kind of pleasure that we feel.

numbers is a number. But this is evidently not the case. A sum of pleasures is not pleasure, any more than a sum of men is a man. For pleasures, like men, cannot be added to one another. Consequently, if pleasure is the only thing that is desirable, a sum of pleasures cannot possibly be desirable. If the Hedonistic view were to be adopted, we ought always to desire the greatest pleasure—*i. e.* we ought to aim at producing the most intense feeling of pleasure that it is possible to reach in some one's consciousness.[1] This would be the highest aim. A sum of smaller pleasures in a number of different people's consciousnesses, could not be preferable to this; because a sum of pleasures is not pleasure at all. The reason why this does not appear to be the case, is that we habitually think of the desirable thing for man not as a feeling of pleasure but as a continuous state of happiness. But a continuous state of happiness is not a mere feeling of pleasure. It has a certain objective content. Now if we regard this content as the desirable thing, we do not regard the feeling of pleasure as the one thing that is desirable; *i. e.* we abandon Hedonism.

(*f*) *Matter without Form.*—We may sum up the defects of Hedonism by saying that it has the opposite

[1] Just as, if our object were to produce the greatest man (instead of the greatest pleasure), Falstaff would have to be preferred to the whole of his ragged company. We may calculate, no doubt, that nine tailors make a man; but that is only on the assumption that our object is not man as such, but the fulfilment of certain functions of a man. It might be said that in a number of men there is more flesh and blood and bone than in oue. But this is to measure flesh, blood, and bone, not men. So it is possible that in a number of pleasant experiences there is more of something than there is in one. But they are not a greater pleasure.

fault to that which we found in the system of Kant. Kant's principle of self-consistency gave us form without matter—the mere form of reason, with all the particular content of the desires left out. Hedonism, on the other hand, gives us matter without form. It takes up all the desires as they stand, and regards the satisfaction of all as having an equal right, in so far as the pleasant feeling accompanying the satisfaction is equally intense and lasts equally long. This view ignores the fact that what we really seek to satisfy is not our *desires* but *ourselves;* and the value of our satisfactions depends on the kind of self to which the satisfaction is given—*i. e.* it depends on the universe within which the satisfaction is received. It may be mere animal pleasure: it may be human happiness: it may be saint-like bliss. To consider it in this way is to consider our desires with reference to their *form* —with reference to the universe in which they have a place. Hedonism ignores this form. It looks on our desires and their gratifications simply as quantities of raw material. It regards our wants as so many mouths to be filled, and the pleasures of their satisfaction as so many lumps of sugar to go into them. It is matter without form.[1]

[1] For further criticism on Hedonism, I may refer to Bradley's *Ethical Studies*, Essay III., Green's *Prolegomena to Ethics*, Book III., chap. i., and Book IV., chaps. iii. and iv., Sorley's *Ethics of Naturalism*, Part I., chap. iii., Alexander's *Moral Order and Progress*, Book II., Part I., chap. v., § 2, Janet's *Theory of Morals*, Book I., chap. iv., Dewey's *Outlines of Ethics*, pp. 14–67, Muirhead's *Elements of Ethics*, Book III., chap. i. See also Watson's *Hedonistic Theories from Aristippus to Spencer*, and the article by Prof. James Seth, "Is Pleasure the Summum Bonum?" in the *International Journal of Ethics*, Vol. VI., no. 4. For a fuller statement of my own view on this subject, I may refer to my *Introduction to Social Philosophy*, chap. iv.

§ **10.** RELATION OF HAPPINESS TO THE SELF.—But though we thus seem bound to reject the Hedonistic theory, we must not overlook the importance of happiness. If happiness is not exactly "our being's end and aim," it is yet certain that we cannot attain the end of our being without attaining happiness. All that we have to insist on is that in seeking happiness we must observe exactly what kind of happiness it is that we seek. Happiness is relative to the nature of the being who enjoys it. The happiness of a man is different from the happiness of a beast: the happiness of a wise man is different from the happiness of a fool. What constitutes our happiness, in fact, depends on the universe in which we live. The smaller our universe, the more easily is our happiness attained.

> "That low man seeks a little thing to do,
> Sees it and does it:
> This high man, with a great thing to pursue,
> Dies ere he knows it."

"It is indisputable," as Mill says,[1] "that the being whose capacities of enjoyment are low, has the greatest chance of having them fully satisfied; and a highly endowed being will always feel that any happiness which he can look for, as the world is constituted, is imperfect. But he can learn to bear its imperfections if they are at all bearable; and they will not make him envy the being who is indeed unconscious of the imperfections, but only because he feels not at all the good which those imperfections qualify. It is better to be a human being dissatisfied than a pig satisfied; better to be Socrates dissatisfied than a fool satisfied." What is important, then, is not that we should seek the

[1] *Utilitarianism*, chap. ii.

greatest sum of happiness, but the best kind of happiness. "We can only have the highest happiness," said George Eliot,[1] "—such as goes along with being a great man—by having wide thoughts, and much feeling for the rest of the world as well as ourselves; and this sort of happiness often brings so much pain with it that we can only tell it from pain by its being what we would choose before everything else, because our souls see it is good." The nature of the highest happiness, then, depends not on its being the greatest sum, but on its belonging to the highest kind of character. That is, it depends on the nature of the self, on the nature of the universe within which we habitually live. To attain the highest happiness, then, we must live habitually in the highest kind of universe, and the desires that belong to that universe must be satisfied.

§ **11.** SELF-REALISATION AS THE END.—We seem, however, to be very little farther on than we were at the beginning of this chapter. For at the beginning of the chapter we propounded the question, how we were to distinguish a higher universe from a lower; and this question is still unanswered. We have only been enabled to see that quantity of pleasure cannot furnish the criterion, and that we must look for the criterion rather in the nature of the character itself. We see, in fact, that the end must consist in some form of self-realisation, *i. e.* in some form of the development of character—that the end, in short, ought to be described rather as *perfection* than as *happiness.* What perfection or self-realisation consists in, we must endeavour to find out in the following chapter.

[1] Epilogue to *Romola.*

CHAPTER V.

THE STANDARD AS PERFECTION.

§ 1. APPLICATION OF EVOLUTION TO MORALS.—The idea that the end at which we are to aim is the realisation of the self or the development of character, leads us at once to regard the moral life as a process of growth. Although this idea has often been applied to the moral life in former ages, yet it is chiefly in recent times that the conception has been made prominent. The whole idea of growth or development—the idea of "evolution," as it is often called—may almost be said to be a discovery of the present century. It was first brought into prominence by Hegel and Comte; it was applied by Lamarck, Darwin, and others, to the origin of species; while Mr. Spencer and others have extended its applications to the origin of social institutions, forms of government, and the like, and even to the formation of the solar and stellar systems. With these applications we are not here concerned. We have to deal only with the application of the idea of evolution to morals. And even with this application we have to deal only in a certain aspect. We are not concerned at present with the fact that the moral life of individuals and nations undergoes a gradual growth or development in the course of years or ages. This is a fact of moral history, whereas here we are concerned only with the theory of that which is essential to the very nature of morality. When we say, then, that the idea of evolution is applicable to the moral life, we mean that the moral life is, in its very essence, a growth or development. The sense in which it is so will, it is hoped, become apparent as we proceed.

§ 2. DEVELOPMENT OF LIFE.—We may say, to begin with, that what we mean is this. There is in the moral life of man a certain end or ideal, to which he may attain, or of which he may fall short; and the significance of his life consists in the pursuit of this end or ideal, and the gradual attainment of it. We may illustrate what we mean by reference to the forms of animal life. Among animals there are some that we naturally regard as standing higher in the scale of being than others. We judge them to be higher by reference to a certain (it may be a somewhat vague) standard that we have in our minds—whether it be, as with Mr. Herbert Spencer, the standard of adaptation to their environment, or the standard of approximation to the human type, or whatever else it may be. Now if we are right in supposing that there is a continuous development going on throughout the species of animal existence, the main significance of this development will lie in the evolution of forms of life that approach more and more nearly to the standard or ideal type. Similarly, the evolutionary theory of Ethics is the view that there is a standard or ideal of character, and that the significance of the moral life consists in the gradual approximation to that type.

§ 3. HIGHER AND LOWER VIEWS OF DEVELOPMENT.—In all development there is a beginning, a process, and an end. The developing thing starts from a certain level and moves onwards towards a higher level. Now in general what is presented to us is neither the beginning nor the end, but the process. The lowest forms of animal life do not often come before our notice, and the nature of the lowest of all is quite obscure. Nor do we know what possibilities there may be of still further development in the forms of animal life. The starting-point and the goal are alike concealed from us: we see only the race. So it is also with the moral life. The earliest beginnings of the moral consciousness are hidden in obscurity; and, on the other hand, we can scarcely form a clear conception of a perfectly developed moral life. We know it only in the course of its development. Nevertheless, we cannot understand the process except by reference either to its beginning or to its end. And we may endeavour to understand it by reference either to the one or to the other. Hence there are two possible methods of interpreting the moral life, if we adopt the theory of development. We may explain it by reference to its beginning or to its end. The former is perhaps the more natural method; as it is most usual to explain phenomena by their causes and mode of origination. But further consideration seems to show that this is in reality the lower and less satisfactory method. Let us consider briefly the nature and merits of the two methods.

§ 4. Explanation by Beginning.—It seems most natural at first to endeavour to explain the moral life by tracing it back to its origin in the needs of savages, or even in the struggles of the lower animals. It is in this way that we explain ordinary natural phenomena, such as the formation of geological strata, and even the growth and decline of nations. We go back to the beginning, or as near to the beginning as we can get, and trace the causes that have been in operation throughout the development of the object of our study. We do not inquire what the end of it will be. To inquire into this would, in general, throw little, if any, light upon its actual condition. Ought not the development of morals to be studied in the same way? The answer seems clear. The science of Ethics, as we have already pointed out, occupies quite a different point of view from that of the natural sciences. It is not concerned with the investigation of origins and with the tracing of history, but with the determination of ideals and the consideration of the way in which these ideals influence conduct. Now the ideal lies at the end rather than at the beginning. In dealing with natural phenomena we are concerned primarily with what *is*, and secondarily with the way in which it has come to be what it is. In Ethics, on the other hand, it is of comparatively little interest to know what is.[1] "Man partly is, and wholly hopes to be." It is what he hopes to be that determines the direction of his growth. The meaning of this, however, may become clearer if we direct attention for a little to the theory of one of the most eminent of those recent writers who have endeavoured to deal with the moral life by tracing it back to its origin.

§ 5. Mr. Herbert Spencer's View of Ethics.—Mr. Herbert Spencer's theory on this subject is contained in a very interesting book entitled *The Data of Ethics.*[2] To give any complete account of the contents of that

[1] *I. e.* what *is* in the purely natural history sense, in which we say that the lion *is*, while the unicorn *is not.* In the deeper sense, of course, Ethics *is* concerned with what is—*viz.* with what man's fundamental nature *is*. *Cf.* above, chap. iii. of the present Book, § 3.

[2] Now Part I. of his larger book, *The Principles of Ethics.*

book would be quite impossible here; but the following may be taken as indicating its drift.[1] Mr. Spencer begins by trying to determine what we mean by conduct, and what we mean by calling conduct good or bad. He examines this question by going back to the life of the lower animals. In all life there is what may be called conduct, and in all life it may be good or bad. Now the essence of life, as seen in its lowest forms, consists, according to Mr. Spencer, in "the continuous adjustment of internal relations to external relations"—*i. e.* the constant effort of an organism to adapt itself to its environment. All conduct tends either to promote or to hinder such adaptation. In so far as it tends to promote it, it is good: in so far as it tends to hinder it, it is bad. Good conduct produces pleasure, because it brings the organism into harmony with its surroundings. Bad conduct produces pain. Nearly all conduct is partly good and partly bad. Perfectly good conduct would be that which produces only pleasure with no accompanying pain. But conduct is relatively good when it tends on the whole to produce a surplus of pleasure over pain—*i. e.* when it tends on the whole to produce a more perfect adjustment of organism to environment. The supreme moral end is to help on the process of development, which consists in a more and more perfect adjustment of internal relations to external relations.

§ 6. CRITICISM OF MR. SPENCER'S VIEW.—Now this theory is in many ways suggestive. It helps to bring the study of the moral life into co-ordination with the study of life generally; and this is in harmony with the whole development of modern scientific thought,

[1] *Cf.* Sidgwick's *History of Ethics*, pp. 254-257.

which leads us to believe that there are no absolute divisions between the various objects of our knowledge, and that we are never likely to fully understand any one of these objects without bringing it into relation to all the rest. Yet a little reflection seems to show that Mr. Spencer's theory involves a kind of ὕστερον πρότερον, or putting the cart before the horse. For what is meant by saying that the development of our lives means a continuous process of adjustment to our environment? It is easy to see that in a certain sense such a process is continually going on. The progress of our knowledge means that we are constantly adjusting our ideas more and more to the objective realities of nature. In like manner, the advance of the arts means that we are gradually learning to adjust our modes of life to the necessities imposed upon us by the conditions of the external world. And so in morals, in so far as we can claim to have "sweeter manners, purer laws" than our forefathers, in so far as we have wider ideas of what is required of us, and are more conscientious in meeting these requirements, all this means that we are adjusting our modes of life more and more to the necessities of the case. But what exactly is implied in this adjustment? Does it not imply, above everything, that we have certain ends that we set before ourselves to be attained? When we say that two things are not adjusted to one another, we imply that we have some idea of a relation in which the two things ought to stand and in which at present they do not stand. In a sense everything is adjusted to everything else. Death is an adjustment. A living being is conscious of a certain want of adjustment only because it has certain definite aims. The scientific man perceives that his ideas are not fully adjusted to the facts of nature, and he pursues knowledge in order that he may adjust them more completely; but a stone is adjusted to its environment without the need of any such effort.[1] The scientific man is aware of a want of adjustment simply because he is aware of an unattained end—in other words, because he brings an ideal with him to which the world does not conform. But if this be so, then surely we ought to turn the statement the other way about. We ought not to say that the deficiency of living beings, which the development of their lives is gradually removing, consists in the fact that they are not adjusted to their environment; but rather, at least in the case of self-conscious beings, that the deficiency consists in the fact that their environment is not adjusted to them. For it is not in the environment, but in themselves, that the standard lies, with reference to which a deficiency is pronounced. If a man were content to "let the world slide," he would soon enough become adjusted to his environment; it is because he insists on pursuing his own ends that the process of adjustment is a hard one. It is because he wants to adjust his environment to himself; or rather, because he wants to adjust both himself and his surroundings to a certain ideal of what his life ought to be. Even in the case of the lower animals, indeed, it would often be as true to say that they adjust their environment to themselves as that they adjust themselves to their environment. In any case, adjustment seems to have no meaning unless we presuppose some ideal form of adjustment, some end that is consciously or uncon-

[1] *Cf.* Prof. Alexander's *Moral Order and Progress*, pp. 271–2.

sciously sought. But if so, then it is surely rather with the idea of this end that we ought to start than with the mere idea of the process of adjustment, in which the end is presupposed. Though it seems natural to begin at the beginning in our explanation and move on, through the process, to the end; yet since in this case it is the end by which the process is determined, it is rather at the end that we ought to begin.[1]

§ 7. **Views of other Evolutionists.**—Mr. Spencer's theory is distinguished from that of most other writers of the evolutionist school by the distinctness with which he recognises an ultimate and absolute end to which conduct is directed. Although he begins his explanation from below, from the beginning, from the simplest forms of life, he yet leads up to the conception of an absolute end. Hence he insists on the need of treating Ethics from a teleological point of view[2]; and indeed carries his conception of an ultimate end so far that he even propounds the idea of an absolute system of Ethics, not relating to the present world at all, but rather to a world in which the adjustment to environment shall have been completely brought about.[3] Most other evolutionists have repudiated this absolute Ethics,[4] and have also avoided the statement of any absolute end to which we are moving. Thus, Mr. Leslie Stephen seems to content

1 For a more complete discussion of Spencer's doctrine, see Sorley's *Ethics of Naturalism*, especially pp. 203–220, Alexander's *Moral Order and Progress*, pp. 266–277, Muirhead's *Elements of Ethics*, pp. 136–159, and Dewey's *Outlines of Ethics*, pp. 67–78, and pp. 142–146.

2 *Data of Ethics*, pp. 304–5.

3 See Dr. Sidgwick's account of this, *History of Ethics*, p. 256.

4 See, for instance, Stephen's *Science of Ethics*, p. 430, Alexander's *Moral Order and Progress*, p. 270.

himself with the idea of *health* or *efficiency*. "A moral rule is a statement of a condition of social welfare."[1] Virtue means efficiency with a view to the maintenance of social equilibrium.[2] This theory does not require any view of an ultimate end to which society is moving; but simply takes society as it finds it, and regards its preservation and equilibrium as the end to be aimed at.[3] Prof. Alexander adopts a view which is substantially the same. Thus he says,[4] "An act or person is measured by a certain standard or criterion of conduct, which has been called the moral ideal. This moral ideal is an adjusted order of conduct, which is based upon contending inclinations and establishes an equilibrium between them. Goodness is nothing but this adjustment in the equilibrated whole." This view of Ethics bears a close relation to the doctrine of the development of animal life which was set forth by Darwin. According to Darwin's view, the development of animal species takes place by means of a "struggle for existence," in which "the fittest" survive. This process is commonly referred to as one of "natural selection." In the same way, the view of Mr. Stephen and Prof. Alexander is that in the moral life there is a process of natural selection in which the most efficient, or the most perfectly equilibrated type of conduct is preserved. The connection between

[1] *Science of Ethics*, p. 450.

[2] *Ibid.*, pp. 79–81, &c.

[3] *Cf.* the statement of Mr. Stephen's theory in Sidgwick's *History of Ethics*, p. 257. Of course, on such a view, any actual state of society is regarded as being only partly in equilibrium; and the end aimed at may be said to be a condition of *perfect equilibrium*. But the writers referred to do not attempt to give any positive account of what would be involved in such an equilibrium.

[4] *Moral Order and Progress*, p. 399.

this theory and that of Darwin has been well worked out by Prof. Alexander in a recent article on "Natural Selection in Morals"[1]; and as this seems to me to contain perhaps the best summary statement that we have in English[2] of the attempt to explain morality from below, it may be worth while to indicate briefly its general scope and gist.

§ 8. NATURAL SELECTION IN MORALS.—"Natural Selection," says Mr. Alexander,[3] "is a name for the process by which different species with characteristic structures contend for supremacy, and one prevails and becomes relatively permanent." In the case of animal life the struggle is primarily one between different individuals or sets of individuals, some of which die out, while the "more fit" survive. It is not exactly so in morals. "The war of natural selection is carried on in human affairs not against weaker or incompatible individuals, but against their ideals or modes of life. It does not suffer any mode of life to prevail or persist but one which is compatible with social welfare."[4] What happens in the animal world is that certain individuals or sets of individuals happen to be born with peculiar natural gifts. These gifts turn out to be such as make them more fit to survive than other individuals; and accordingly they do survive, and transmit their characteristics to their descendants, while their less favoured

[1] *International Journal of Ethics*, vol. ii., No. 4 (July, 1882), pp. 409-439. *Cf.* also Prof. Alexander's *Moral Order and Progress*, Book III., chap. iv., where the same point is brought out.

[2] An even more extreme instance of an attempt to explain morality from below, and on very similar lines, will be found in a recent German work entitled *Einleitung in die Moralwissenschaft* by Dr. Georg Simmel.

[3] *Loc. Cil.*, p. 431.

[4] *Ibid.*, p. 428.

rivals die out. In the case of morals, however, we are dealing "not with animals as such, but with minds."[1] In such cases "we have something of the following kind. A person arises (or a few persons) whose feelings, modified by more or less deliberate reflection, incline him to a new course of conduct. He dislikes cruelty or discourtesy, or he objects to seeing women with inferior freedom, or to the unlimited opportunity of intoxication. He may stand alone and with only a few friends to support him. His proposal may excite ridicule or scorn or hatred; and if he is a great reformer, he may endure hardship and obloquy, or even death at the hands of the great body of persons whom he offends. By degrees his ideas spread more and more; people discover that they have similar leanings; they are persuaded by him; their previous antagonism to him is replaced by attachment to the new mode of conduct, the new political institution. The new ideas gather every day fresh strength, until at last they occupy the minds of a majority of persons, or even of nearly all."[2] "Persuasion and education, in fact, without destruction, replace here the process of propagation of its own species and destruction of the rival ones, by which in the natural world species become numerically strong and persistent." "Persuasion corresponds to the extermination of the rivals"; for "the victory of mind over mind consists in persuasion."[3] Thus, then, the origin of moral ideals, like the origin of species, is to be explained by a process of natural selection.

§ 9. NEED OF TELEOLOGY.—Now there can be no

[1] *Ibid.*, p. 420. [2] *Loc. cit.*, p. 414. [3] *Ibid.*, p. 420.

doubt that all this is very suggestive and instructive; but if it is to be taken as a complete account of the moral ideal, it labours under a fatal defect. It is a mere natural history of the growth of the moral life. Now in dealing with animal life we may be content with a mere natural history. In this case we do not want to know much more than the nature of the species that exist and that have existed, and the circumstances that have led them to survive or perish. We are not much interested to inquire what right man has to extirpate the wolf, or how we are to justify the extermination of the mammoth or the survival of the ape. We are not specially interested in the *relative values* of different species of animal life. But it is just with the question of value that Ethics is concerned. We wish to know the *ground of preference* of one kind of conduct over another; and it is no solution of this problem to say that the one kind has succeeded in driving out the other. This, indeed, is partly admitted by Mr. Alexander himself. "A new plan of life," he says, "is not made good because it succeeds; its success is the stamp, the *imprimatur* affixed to it by the course of history, the sign that it is good." [1] But this admission is of little value; for when he is asked what it is, then, that makes it good, what is the common characteristic that makes ideals morally valuable, he can only answer "that that common characteristic consists in that such a plan of life is adapted to the conditions of existence; that under it the society reacts without friction upon

[1] *Loc. cit.*, p. 418. Sometimes, I think, Mr. Alexander forgets this. Thus, in his *Moral Order and Progress*, p. 307, he says—"Evil is *simply* that which has been rejected and defeated in the struggle with the good."

its surroundings, or, as I should prefer to say, that in the conditions in which it is placed society can with this ideal so live that no part of it shall encroach upon the rest, that the society can be in equilibrium with itself."[1] But *why* should we desire that society should be in equilibrium with itself? What is it that makes this condition valuable to us? This is the question which we are forced to ask; and it is a similar question that recurs in connection with the view of Mr. Spencer, and with all similar theories. These writers answer questions of natural history instead of questions of Ethics.[2] What they say may throw considerable light on the way in which the moral life has developed, but does not answer the question—*Why* are we to choose that life? Why, we may ask, for instance, should we not seek to disturb the equilibrium of society, instead of promoting it? The answer to this could only be given by showing that that equilibrium is a *good*.

[1] *Ibid.*, p. 419. *Cf.* also Prof. Alexander's article on "The Idea of Value," in *Mind*, vol. i., No. 1 (Jan., 1892), especially pp. 44–48.

[2] This point is very fully brought out in Sorley's *Ethics of Naturalism*, Part II., chap. ix. A short passage may here be quoted (pp. 270–1). "A man might quite reasonably ask why he should adopt as maxims of conduct the laws seen to operate in nature. The end, in this way, is not made to follow from the natural function of man. It is simply a mode in which the events of the world occur; and we must, therefore, give a reason why it should be adopted as his end by the individual agent. To him there may be no sufficient ground of inducement to become 'a self-conscious agent in the evolution of the universe.' From the purely evolutionist point of view, no definite attempt has been made to solve the difficulty. It seems really to go no deeper than Dr. Johnson's reply to Boswell, when the latter plagued him to give a reason for action: 'Sir,' said he, in an animated tone, 'it is driving on the system of life.'" *Cf.* Sidgwick's *Methods of Ethics*, p. 83, Muirhead's *Elements of Ethics*, pp. 149–156.

Similarly, we may ask—Why may we not set ourselves in opposition to the stream of development which Mr. Spencer traces? Here again the answer to this question must be found by showing that the stream of development is leading to something which we recognize as *good*—something that can serve as an ideal for our moral nature. If this can be shown, then we may *start* from that ideal. That ideal then becomes the explanation of the process, instead of the process being an explanation of it. We go through the process of development *because* we are seeking that ideal. The end, and not the beginning, is thus taken as the principle of explanation.[1]

§ 10. EXPLANATION BY END.—Even in the case of the development of animal life it is not at all certain that the idea of teleology ought not to be introduced. Indeed even in Mr. Spencer's view of evolution there is a kind of teleology. The whole life of animals is regarded as a continual struggle after a perfect adjustment. That is the ideal by which the whole process is explained. And it is possible that on a deeper view of evolution the meaning of the process might be seen to have a still more profoundly teleological significance. So at least Emerson thought—

> "Striving to be man, the worm
> Mounts through all the spires of form."

So also Aristotle and Hegel thought.[2] But however

[1] This seems to be the essential point in the argument of Prof. Huxley's famous *Romanes Lecture (Evolution and Ethics)*. But Prof. Huxley partly obscures the point by drawing an unreal antithesis between the processes of nature and the activities of the moral life. *Cf.* also Principal Lloyd Morgan's *Habit and Instinct*, pp. 271 and 335, and Seth's *Man's Place in the Cosmos*, I.

[2] It is still more remarkable (though perhaps not so consistent) to

this may be with regard to animal life, and to the life of nature generally, there can be no doubt that we must apply teleological ideas in Ethics. Indeed, as we have seen, this is explicitly stated by Mr. Herbert Spencer himself. But if this is the case, then the attempt to explain the moral life *from behind* cannot be of much avail. We must explain it rather by what lies in front of us, by the ideal or end that we have in view. How this may be done, may be indicated by a brief reference to the work of the most distinguished of those thinkers in recent times who have attempted it—the late Professor T. H. Green.

§ **11.** Green's View of Ethics.—Green's doctrine is stated in his great work entitled *Prolegomena to Ethics*, probably the most considerable contribution to ethical science that has been made in England during the present century.[1] Green taught that the essential element in the nature of man is the rational or spiritual principle within him. Man has appetite, as animals have, and, like them, he has sensations and mental images; but these, and everything else in man's nature, are modified by the fact that he has reason. His appetites are not *mere* appetites: his sensations are not *mere* sensations. In his appetites there is always more or less explicitly present the consciousness of an end—*i. e.* they are desires and not mere appetites.[2] In his sensations there is always more or less

find such a pronounced materialist as Dühring objecting strongly to the Darwinian attempt to explain evolution by the mere struggle for existence, and urging the adoption of a more teleological view. See his *Cursus der Philosophie*, II. iii.

[1] The account of Green's doctrine contained in Sidgwick's *History of Ethics* (pp. 259–260) is unhappily very inadequate.

[2] I may say that Green seems to me to exaggerate the extent to

explicitly present the element of knowledge—*i. e.* they are perceptions and not mere sensations. This is due to the fact that man is rational, self-conscious, spiritual. This is the essential fact with regard to man's nature. Green points out, indeed, that even in animal life, and even in inanimate nature, we must assume the presence of a rational principle—just as Mr. Spencer points out that even in animal life there is present the principle of adjustment. But in nature the presence of this principle is implicit. We must believe that it is there, but it is concealed or imperfectly manifested. In man it is explicit; or, at any rate, it is *becoming* explicit. And the significance of the moral life consists in the constant endeavour to make this principle more and more explicit—to bring out more and more completely our rational, self-conscious, spiritual nature. How exactly this is to be done, Green admits, it is not easy to answer, just because our rational nature is not yet completely developed. The moral life is to be ex-

which animal appetites are transmuted in human consciousness. Perhaps, however, my own statement above (Book I., chap. i., § 3) contains an exaggeration on the opposite side. At any rate, the main point here is that the *essence* of man consists in his rational nature, not in anything that he has in common with a mere animal (if there is any *mere* animal). What exactly is involved in the consciousness of the higher forms of animal life, is a difficult question. It seems absurd to deny them perception. It is hard even to suppose that they are without perceptual images. Else how does the ox know his master's crib? How does the bird construct its nest? There seems to be involved in such cases not only an apprehension of the object before them but an anticipatory image of what is about to be. And indeed this seems to be required even for Darwin's earthworms (*Vegetable Mould*, chap. ii.). But all this lies beyond our present subject. Reference may be made to Lloyd Morgan's *Animal Life and Intelligence* (especially chapter ix.), to Wundt's *Human and Animal Psychology*, pp. 350-366, and to Stout's *Manual*, pp. 264-266.

plained by its end; but as we have not reached the end, we cannot, in any complete form, give the explanation. Still, we can to a considerable extent see in what way our rational nature has been so far developed, and in what direction we may proceed to develop it more fully.

This is a brief statement of Green's point of view; and it certainly appears to furnish us with an answer to the question with which we set out—*viz.* the question how we are to determine which is the higher and which is the lower among our universes of desire. Green's answer is—the highest universe is that which is most completely rational. The meaning of this, however, must be somewhat more fully considered, in relation to the point of view that we have already tried to develop.

§ 12. THE TRUE SELF.—We have seen that there are a great number of universes within which a man may live. In some of these men live only for moments at a time: in others they live habitually. Some of them are universes within which no abiding satisfaction can be found. The universe of mere animal enjoyment is of this nature. Its pleasures soon pall upon the appetite. In others we find that we have a more permanent resting-place. Now the nature of the universe within which a man habitually lives constitutes, as we have seen, his character or self. If he chances to be led into some other universe by a sudden impulse or unexpected temptation, the man scarcely considers himself to be responsible for his actions within that universe. He says that he was *not himself* when he acted so. He was not within his own universe.

But there is no limited universe within which we can

find permanent satisfaction. As we grow older, we get crusted over with habits, and go on, with little misgiving, within the universe to which we have grown accustomed. But if the universe is an imperfect one, we are not without occasional pricks of conscience—*i. e.* we sometimes become aware of a higher universe within which we ought to be living.

> "Just when we are safest, there's a sunset-touch,
> A fancy from a flower-bell, some one's death,
> A chorus-ending from Euripides—
> And that's enough for fifty hopes and fears,
> As old and new at once as nature's self,
> To rap and knock and enter in our soul."[1]

On such occasions we begin to feel that even in the life that we ordinarily live we are *not ourselves.* There is a want of permanence in our habitual universe, just as there is in those into which we find ourselves occasionally drifted by passion and impulse. Just as we do not feel satisfied in these, but escape from them as rapidly as we can, and declare that we were not ourselves when we were in them; so we become conscious at times that even in our habitual lives there is something unsatisfying, and if it were not for the frost of custom we would make our escape from these also, and declare that in them also we are not ourselves. Where, then, is the universe within which we should find an abiding satisfaction? What is the true self?

The true self is what is perhaps best described as the rational self. It is the universe that we occupy in our moments of deepest wisdom and insight. To say fully what the content of this universe is, would no doubt, as Green points out,[2] be impossible. The content of

[1] Browning—*Bishop Blougram's Apology.*
[2] *Prolegomena to Ethics*, § 288, p. 310.

the universe of rational insight is as wide as the universe of actual fact. To live completely in that universe would be to understand completely the world in which we live and our relations to it, and to act constantly in the light of that understanding. This we cannot hope to do. All that we can do is to endeavour to promote this understanding more and more in ourselves and others, and to act more and more in a way that is consistent with the promotion of this understanding. So to live is to be truly *ourselves.*[1]

§ **13.** THE REAL MEANING OF SELF-CONSISTENCY.—From this point of view we are better able to appreciate the real significance of the Kantian principle, that the supreme law of morals is to be self-consistent. This law, as we pointed out, seemed to supply us with a mere form without matter. It is not so, however, if we interpret the statement to mean not merely that we are to be *self-consistent,* but that we are to be *consistent with the self—i. e.* with the true self. For this principle has a content, though the content is not altogether easy to discover. Kant's error, we may say, consisted in this, that he understood the term Reason in a purely abstract way. He opposed it to all the particular content of our desires; whereas, in reality, reason is relative to the whole world which it interprets. The universe of rational insight is the universe in which the whole world—including all our desires—appears in its true relations. To occupy the point of view of reason,

[1] For some criticisms on the idea of self-realization, see the valuable article by Mr. A. E. Taylor in the *International Journal of Ethics,* Vol. VI., no. 3. Mr. Taylor's objections do not seem, however, to bear upon the theory as explained above and as developed in the following Book.

therefore, is not to withdraw from all our desires, and occupy the point of view of mere formal self-consistency; it is rather to place all our desires in their right relations to one another. The universe of rational insight is a universe into which they can all enter, and in which they all find their true places. Dirt has been defined as "matter in the wrong place": so moral evil may be said to consist simply in the misplacement of desire. The meaning of this will, it is hoped, become somewhat clearer as we proceed.

§ 14. The Real Meaning of Happiness.—Just as we are now better able to appreciate the significance of the categorical imperative of self-consistency, so we ought now to be able to understand more fully the true significance of the principle of happiness. The error in the conception of happiness, as formerly interpreted, lay in its being thought of simply as the gratification of each single desire, or of the greatest possible sum of desires. We now see that the end is to be found rather in the systematisation of desire. Now happiness, in the true sense of the word, as distinguished from transient pleasures, consists just in the consciousness of the realisation of such a systematic content. It is the form of feeling which accompanies the harmonious adjustment of the various elements in our lives within an ideal unity. Happiness, therefore, in this sense, though not, properly speaking, the end at which we aim, is an inseparable and essential element in its attainment.[1]

§ 15. Transition to Applied Ethics.—We have now

[1] It is in this sense, as Spinoza says, that "happiness [*beatitudo*] is not the reward of virtue, but virtue itself,"—*i. e.*, it is an essential aspect in the attainment of the right point of view.

seen, in a general way, what the nature of the moral ideal is, and how the various imperfect conceptions of this ideal find their place within what seems to be the true one. We now see, in short, at least in some degree, what is the true significance of the ethical *ought.* We see that, if it is to be described as an "imperative" at all, it is at least not to be thought of, as it is apt at first to be, as a command imposed upon us from without. It is rather to be regarded as the voice of the true self within us, passing judgment upon the self as it appears in its incomplete development. Conscience, from this point of view, may be said to be simply the sense that we are *not ourselves;* and the voice of duty is the voice that says, "To thine own self be true."

But statements of this sort are still apt to seem rather empty and unmeaning, unless we can bring them into some sort of relationship to the concrete content of life. Accordingly, what we have now to do is to consider the way in which the concrete moral life may be interpreted in the light of the general principle which has now been laid down. This, of course, can only be done in such a book as this, in the most cursory and superficial fashion. But some indication of the kind of way in which it would have to be done in a more comprehensive work, may at least be found suggestive and helpful. Before we proceed to this, however, it is necessary to consider the exact sense in which ethical principles are capable of application to the content of the practical life. This is the subject of the following chapter.

CHAPTER VI.

THE AUTHORITY OF THE MORAL STANDARD.

§ **1.** The General Problem of Authority.—In considering the nature of the moral standard, we have had to deal incidentally with the character of the authority which according to different theories is claimed for it. But it seems desirable now to add something on this particular point. As the moral standard is one that claims the absolute devotion of the human will, it is evident that its authority must be recognized as supreme and unquestionable; and we have accordingly already felt ourselves to be justified in criticizing certain views of the moral standard on the ground that they provided no adequate motive for obedience to the principles that are involved in it. This defect appears, for instance, in the view which rests moral obligation on the law of God; since the mere might of a supreme being could not be accepted as a sufficient ground for voluntary obedience. The same defect appears, in a somewhat different form, in the theory that appeals simply to the process of evolution; since it is of the very essence of the moral life to oppose itself, if necessary, to the natural tendencies of things. The consideration of such objections, however, leads us to inquire more definitely what is the nature of the authority on which moral principles must be based.

§ 2. DIFFERENT KINDS OF AUTHORITY.—In dealing with this subject, it may be convenient to recur to the distinction that has already been drawn between *is*, *must*, and *ought*. A certain kind of authority may be said to lie in each. Even in an "is" there is often a compelling power. "Facts" are said to be "stubborn things." Carlyle was particularly fond of emphasizing the absurdity of contending against actualities. It would be futile for human beings to endeavour to train themselves to walk constantly on their heads; and many other actions, not on a surface view quite so absurd, may be equally impossible. If a man offends persistently against the general conditions of health, his sin is sure to find him out; and such sin may be described as a failure to recognize the existing circumstances. But even in such instances the compelling power is perhaps more properly to be described as a "must" than as a simple "is." We do not in such instances perform actions, or abstain from actions, in mere obedience to a natural tendency, as a stone falls to the ground, or as an animal follows its instincts. Rather we do or abstain, in general, with a certain foresight of the inconvenient consequences that would otherwise result. We recognise that we *must* or that we *must not*. We do not simply feel impelled. A better illustration of the operation of the simple "is" in human action might be found in certain conventional practices—in rules of fashion, local customs, professional etiquette, and the like. The "correct thing" in such cases means little more than what the "compact majority" does. Particular people follow the custom, as a sheep follows its leader. They do things simply because they are done. But even in such cases it is probable that there is nearly always a more or less explicit consciousness of some ground for the action. It is done, it may be, from fear of public opinion, or from a conviction that eccentricity is undesirable. In the former case there is a "must," in the latter an "ought." On the whole, a careful consideration of such cases seems to show that, in all action that is distinctively human (as opposed to animal impulse or instinct), one or other of these (a "must" or an "ought") is the compelling force.

Now, taking the "must" and the "ought" as the two great moving forces in human action, there might be some convenience in limiting the use of the term "authority," at least in its ethical application, to the latter. It is in this sense that the term is chiefly used by Bishop Butler, who has perhaps done more than any one else to give it a clear meaning in ethical literature.[1] But we must remember that the term is also commonly used with reference to the "is" and the "must," as well as the "ought." An appeal to "authority" means sometimes simply an appeal to the majority of views that have been expressed on a particular point; though even in this case there is generally an implied conviction that the people whose views are referred to have some claim to be heard, that there are reasons why their opinions *ought* to be accepted as the most correct, or as the most likely to be correct, and that, if their views diverge, they should be weighed as well as counted. Again, in law

[1] Butler's second *Sermon* may be referred to as the *locus classicus* on this point.

and politics, the "authority" for an action may simply refer to the force by which it is accompanied, or the penalties which can be inflicted in connection with it. But even legal and political powers are seldom regarded as authoritative without some degree of conviction that they represent, on the whole, justice as well as might. In strictly moral matters, at any rate, it seems clear that we cannot recognize any authority that is merely of the nature of force. But the more fully this is recognized, the more urgent does it become to ascertain the exact nature of the binding power that is contained in the moral standard.

§ 3. VARIOUS VIEWS OF MORAL AUTHORITY.—We have already noticed the chief theories of the moral standard, and, in doing so, we have incidentally seen what is the kind of authority that is claimed by each. But we must now proceed to consider the different views on this particular point more definitely.

Broadly speaking, we may say that the authority claimed for the moral standard is either that of an external law, that of an inner law, or that which is contained in the idea of an end. The first is seen in views that refer us to a law of God, a law of Nature, or a law of some political or social power. The second appears in the doctrine of a law of conscience or reason. The third is found in the various doctrines that set up some form of pleasure or perfection as the end of action. But the nature of the authority does not always correspond to the nature of the standard. It is possible to maintain that the criterion of right is of one kind, while the power that binds us to its pursuit is of another. Thus, Paley regarded pleasure as the end of action, but set up the will of God as the supreme authority for its pursuit. And Utilitarians in general distinguish the ultimate end from the sanctions which bind us to follow it. Similar divergences may also be found, though perhaps in a less degree, in some other schools. Thus, Shaftesbury appears to have taken the well-being of society as the end, but the "moral sense" as the authority. Accordingly, it seems worth while at this point to consider the different theories of authority a little more in detail.

§ 4. THE AUTHORITY OF LAW.—We have already indicated the chief stages in the growth of the view which rests the authority of the moral principle on some form ot external law—a view which has not much support from ethical theory, but a great deal from popular conviction. We have traced the growth from customary obligation, through state law, to the law of a divine commandment. But there is probably no type of ethical theory in modern times that would seek to rest moral authority exclusively on any such external sources. There have, however, been several attempts in modern ethics, and especially in modern English ethics, to rest moral obligation to a large extent upon a legal basis. In recent times this tendency has been specially characteristic of the Utilitarian school, with whom the so-called "Sanctions" of morality have played a very important part. These Sanctions, whether in the rudimentary form conceived by Paley, or in the more elaborate form set forth by Bentham and Mill, are external forces, carrying an authority of that non-moral kind which we have characterised as a "must." Some special consideration of these will here be in place.

§ 5. THE SANCTIONS OF MORALITY.—This term has been introduced into Ethics in consequence of the strongly jural way in which the subject has frequently been treated.[1] A sanction means primarily a ratification.[2] Hence it comes to be applied to that which ratifies or gives force to the laws of a state—*i.e.* the punishment attached to their violation. The meaning of the term has been extended, chiefly by Utilitarian writers, to anything that gives force to the laws of Duty—*i.e.* to the *motives* by which men are induced to fulfil their obligations. According to the Utilitarian writers, the only motives are fear of pain and hope of pleasure. And the pains and pleasures may present themselves in a variety of forms. Thus, there is frequently a physical pain as a consequence of the violation of Duty. Again, there are the pains of social disapproval, and the pleasures of the approbation of our fellow-men. The pains of Hell and the pleasures of Heaven have also, at certain periods of human history, provided motives to right conduct. Now, if the view of Ethics indicated in the present handbook is to be accepted, all this is not of much ethical importance. The right motive to good conduct is the desire to realize the highest end of human life;[3] and

[1] *Cf.* Sidgwick's *History of Ethics*, pp. 8-10.

[2] *E.g.* "The Pragmatic Sanction." It is derived from the Latin *sanctio*, and means primarily "the act of binding," or "that which serves to bind a man." *Cf.* Bentham's *Principles of Morals and Legislation*, chap. iii., *note* to § ii.

[3] It is scarcely necessary to repeat that this motive need not be consciously present. (*Cf.* above, p. 197.) In a particular good action the motive is as a rule simply the interest in some particular good to be achieved. But the ultimate justification of our interest in a

what this is we have already seen. That we may be moved to act rightly in other ways is a fact rather of psychological, historical, or sociological, than of strictly ethical interest. It is also, no doubt, a fact of some importance for jurisprudence, education,[1] and practical politics. Since, however, the consideration of these external motives plays a prominent part in the Utilitarian theory of morals, some further remarks on this point seem to be called for.

If the theory of Universalistic Hedonism is accepted, and if this theory is made to rest on the basis of Psychological Hedonism, it becomes important to consider the motives by which the individual is led to seek the general happiness. His primary desire, according to this view, is for his own greatest happiness; and he can be induced to seek the general happiness only by being led to see that the conduct which leads to "the greatest happiness of the greatest number" is in the long run identical with that which leads to his own greatest happiness. Now it is chiefly by means of the Sanctions that this identity is shown. As Bentham puts it,[2] the general happiness is the *final* cause of human action; but the *efficient* cause for any given individual is the anticipation of his own pleasure or

particular good consists in the fact that it is an element in the general good; and our interest in a particular good requires frequently to be modified and corrected by reference to this.

[1] Sanctions, as already noted (above, p. 312), are of use as helping to form habits of good willing and good conduct; though this use of them should be gradually decreased till the necessity for them disappears. *Cf.* Miss Gilliland's paper on "Pleasure and Pain in Education," pp. 301–3.

[2] *Principles of Morals and Legislation*, chap. iii.

pain. "The happiness of the individuals, of whom a community is composed, that is, their pleasures and their security,[1] is the end and the sole end which the legislator ought to have in view; the sole standard, in conformity to which each individual ought, as far as depends upon the legislator, to be *made* to fashion his behaviour. But whether it be this or anything else that is to be *done,* there is nothing by which a man can ultimately be *made* to do it, but either pain or pleasure." Accordingly, Bentham proceeds to enumerate the various kinds of pain and pleasure which may be made to serve as motives to the adoption of those forms of conduct which it is desirable, with a view to the general happiness, that men should be induced to follow. These various kinds of pain and pleasure are what he calls the Sanctions.

Bentham enumerates[2] four classes of such Sanctions, which he calls the *physical,* the *political,* the *moral,* and the *religious.* If the pleasure or pain comes simply in the ordinary course of nature, and is not attached to our actions by the will of any individual, such a source of motives is called a *physical* sanction. The pains following from drunkenness are an example. It, on

[1] Bentham does not, of course, mean that the principle of security is to be regarded as an independent end in addition to pleasure. He only mentions it as the indispensable condition of the certainty, duration, and fecundity of our pleasures. *Cf.* his *Principles of the Civil Code,* Part II., chap. vii. Of all the principles subordinate to utility, there was none to which he attached so much importance as to that of security.

[2] *Principles of Morals and Legislation,* chap. iii. *Cf.* also *Principles of Legislation,* chap. vii., and Sidgwick's *History of Ethics,* pp. 240–245.

the other hand, the pleasure or pain is attached to an action by the will of a sovereign ruler or government, it is called a *political* sanction; as in the case of ordinary judicial punishment. If it is attached to an action by the will of individuals who are not in a position of authority, it is called a *moral* (*popular*) sanction; as when a man is "boycotted" or "loses caste." Finally, if it is attached to an action by the will of a supernatural power, it is called a *religious* sanction; as in the case of Heaven and Hell, or of the penalties inflicted by the Roman Catholic Church as the representative of the Divine will on earth. It may be worth while to give Bentham's own examples.[1] "A man's goods, or his person, are consumed by fire. If this happened to him by what is called an accident, it was a calamity:[2] if by reason of his own imprudence (for instance, from his neglecting to put his candle out), it may be styled a punishment of the physical sanction; if it happened to him by the sentence of the political magistrate, a punishment belonging to the political sanction; that is, what is commonly called a punishment: if for want of any assistance which his *neighbour* withheld from him out of some dislike to his *moral* character, a punishment of the moral sanction: if by an immediate act of *God's* displeasure, manifested on account of some *sin* committed by him, or through any distraction of mind, occasioned by the dread

[1] *Principles of Morals and Legislation*, chap. iii., § ix.

[2] In this case, of course, it is not a *sanction* at all; since it is not regarded as a result of any particular kind of conduct, and consequently does not serve as an inducement to the avoidance of any particular kind of conduct.

of such displeasure, a punishment of the religious sanction."

J. S. Mill accepted all these sanctions, but characterized them all as "external"; and held that we ought to recognize, in addition to them, the "internal" sanction of Conscience—*i.e.* the pleasures and pains of the moral sentiments.[1] All the other sanctions are to a large extent "physical." Indeed, Bentham himself says:[2] "Of these four sanctions the physical is altogether, we may observe, the groundwork of the political and the moral; so is it also of the religious, in as far as the latter bears relation to the present life. It is included in each of those other three. This[3] may operate in any case (that is, any of the pains or pleasures belonging to it may operate) independently of *them*[4]: none of *them* can operate but by means of this. In a word, the powers of nature may operate of themselves; but neither the magistrate, nor men at large,[5] *can* operate, nor is God in the case in question *supposed* to operate, but through the powers of nature." What Mill calls the "internal" sanction, on the other hand, does not rest on physical conditions, but is purely psychological or subjective; though the particular way in which it

[1] *Utilitarianism*, chap. iii., p. 41 *sqq.*

[2] *Principles of Morals and Legislation*, chap. iii., § xi.

[3] The physical sanction.

[4] The other three sanctions.

[5] It might be urged that the moral sanction sometimes takes the form simply of an expression of opinion. The fear of adverse public opinion is often one of the strongest forms of this sanction. But I suppose Bentham would say that even in this case the expression of the opinion takes place "through the powers of nature," *viz.* through vibrations of sound or light.

is developed is, no doubt, affected by the external environment in which our lives are passed.[1]

Though this sanction is distinguished by Mill as "internal," yet, in a sense, it is just as external as the others. All may be called internal, since all involve the subjective experience of pain, actual or prospective. On the other hand, all are external, in the sense that the pain is connected with some law not definitely recognised as the law of our own being. If, however, Conscience is definitely regarded as the law of our nature, it ceases to be merely of the nature of a sanction, and becomes a real moral authority. It is in this way that it is conceived, for instance, by Bishop Butler.[2]

§ 6. THE AUTHORITY OF CONSCIENCE.—The force of conscience, from Mill's point of view, lies simply, as we have seen, in its sting, in its power of making itself a nuisance. The Intuitionists, on the other hand,

[1] Professor Sidgwick notes (*History of Ethics*, p. 242, *note*) that even Bentham, in one of his letters to Dumont, refers separately to what are ordinarily called moral sentiments as "sympathetic and antipathetic sanctions." He thus partly anticipated Mill. But there is no official recognition of these sanctions in his published writings. The reason is probably that Bentham had a supreme contempt for such sympathetic and antipathetic sentiments. See his *Principles of Morals and Legislation*, chap. ii., § xi, *note*.

[2] An excellent account of the Sanctions will be found in Fowler's *Progressive Morality*, chaps. i. and ii. *Cf.* also Sidgwick's *Methods of Ethics*, Book II., chap. v., and concluding chapter; and Muirhead's *Elements of Ethics*, pp. 101–4. It should be observed that the use of terms is not quite uniform. Bentham's Political Sanction is sometimes described as the *Legal* Sanction; and his Moral or Popular Sanction is frequently described as the *Social* Sanction; while the term "*Moral* Sanction" is reserved for Mill's Internal Sanction. This use of the terms seems preferable to Bentham's.

represent conscience, in general, as having an authority which is independent of any such power. The attitude of Butler on this point is particularly striking. As we have already seen, he represents man's nature as a constitution, in which conscience is the supreme authority. "Thus that principle," he says,[1] "by which we survey, and either approve or disapprove our own heart, temper and actions, is not only to be considered as what is in its turn to have some influence—which may be said of every passion, of the lowest appetites—but likewise as being superior, as from its very nature manifestly claiming superiority over all others, insomuch as you cannot form a notion of this faculty, conscience, without taking in judgment, direction, superintendency. This is a constituent part of the idea, that is, of the faculty itself; and to preside and govern, from the very economy and constitution of man, belongs to it. Had it strength as it has right, had it power as it has manifest authority, it would absolutely govern the world." "But allowing," he says again,[2] "that mankind hath the rule of right within himself, yet it may be asked, 'What obligations are we under to attend to and follow it?' I answer: it has been proved that man by his nature is a law to himself, without the particular distinct consideration of the positive sanctions of that law; the rewards and punishments which we feel, and those which from the light of reason we have ground to believe, are annexed to it. The question then carries its own answer along with it. Your obligation to obey this law is its being the law of your nature. That your conscience approves

[1] *Sermon II.* [2] *Sermon III.*

of and attests to such a course of action, is itself alone an obligation. Conscience does not only offer itself to shew us the way we should walk in, but it likewise carries its own authority with it, that it is our natural guide."

If, however, we ask more definitely what is the nature of the authority of conscience, it seems impossible to give any clear account of it without reference to the idea of an end. Butler himself, in seeking to explain the nature of its authority, compares it with that which belongs to "reasonable self-love." "Suppose a brute creature," he says, "by any bait to be allured into a snare, by which he is destroyed. He plainly followed the bent of his nature, leading him to gratify his appetite: there is an entire correspondence between his whole nature and such an action: such action therefore is natural. But suppose a man, foreseeing the same danger of certain ruin, should rush into it for the sake of a present gratification, he in this instance would follow his strongest desire, as did the brute creature: but there would be as manifest a disproportion between the nature of man and such an action, as between the meanest work of art; which disproportion arises, not from considering the action singly in *itself*, or in its *consequences*, but from *comparison* of it with the nature of the agent. And since such an action is utterly disproportionate to the nature of man, it is in the strictest and most proper sense unnatural; this word expressing that disproportion. . . . Thus, without particular consideration of conscience, we may have a clear conception of the *superior nature* of one inward principle to another; and see that there really is this natural superiority, quite distinct from degrees of strength and prevalency." But it seems clear that the authority which is claimed for reasonable self-love in this instance rests on the idea of an end. It would be unnatural for us simply to follow our appetites and instincts, like brute beasts, because we have definite ideas of ends that we pursue, and know the means that may be expected to secure them. If the authority of conscience is of this nature, it is not the authority of a blind faculty, but the authority of reason itself. This view is not definitely brought out by Butler, but appears quite distinctly in Kant.

§ 7. The Authority of Reason.—Kant is the writer who has most explicitly accepted reason as the only ultimate authority in the moral life, and in this he has been followed by the school of modern idealism. But in reality the same authority was adopted, though in a somewhat less explicit form, by nearly all the Greek moralists, and especially by Socrates, Plato, Aristotle, and the Stoics; and, in more modern times, by the Cartesians and by some of our own British writers And, in recent times, there may almost be said to be a consensus of opinion that, if any ultimate authority is to be found for the moral life at all, it can only be found in reason. Even Utilitarianism, as represented by Sidgwick, Gizycki, and others, has come round to this view. The only flourishing school at the present time which does not accept this position is the school of biological evolution; and this is the kind of exception that proves the rule, since writers of this school deny in general that any ultimate authority can be found for the moral life at all. According to them, morality has merely a *de facto* justification, and the development of the species may transform and even abolish it. Simmel, for instance, represents moral principle simply as the will of the "compact majority." It is the dominant tendency of what "is," not an "ought" or even a "must." A moral scepticism of this kind seems to be the only real alternative to the doctrine of the authority of reason.

§ 8. THE ABSOLUTENESS OF THE MORAL AUTHORITY.—It is apt sometimes to seem as if the authority of the moral standard becomes less absolute the more it is refined and made strictly moral. A few written rules, whether of a state or of some divine law-giver, seem to carry a direct and indisputable authority, especially if they are sanctioned by heavy penalties, such as the prison or the gallows or hell fire. Hence writers who are specially desirous of enforcing moral principles, such as Carlyle, tend to throw them into the form of divine commandments, and to emphasize the penalties for their neglect. In comparison with such laws, a simple injunction to do what is reasonable, because it is reasonable, seems weak and ineffective. Even Kant's "categorical imperative" carries no terrors with it; for the sting of conscience may be suppressed. And still less does there seem to be any strong binding force in such an idea of an end, as we have sought to put forward in the present Manual. The realization of a rational universe seems strangely remote; and, if we fail to realize it, there seems no immediate prospect that we shall be flogged or burnt or jeered at, or suffer any serious detriment to mind or body or estate. Where, then, is the authority of this standard?

But no one who truly realizes to himself what the standard means, is likely to argue in this way. Some illustrations from similar cases of development may serve to show that the moral authority, in its highest form, is stronger, not weaker, than it was in its more primitive modes of presentment. A child who is set to draw simple lines under the guidance of a teacher, or to learn the alphabet and elementary combinations of letters, may appear to be under a strict authority, in comparison with which the great artist or poet enjoys unbounded licence. But is this really so? Has the word of the master anything like the constraining force on the child that the ideal of beauty has on the artist or poet? The one law, no doubt, is simple and definite, and carries with it, perhaps, an explicit reward or punishment. The other may be hard to define, impossible to exhaust, and it may have no reward but the joy of creation, no penalty but the pain of failure. Yet surely it is on the great artist that the sternest necessity is laid. Again, the duty of a patriotic soldier may be simple and obvious: he has but to do or die, as his officers may bid. The duty of a patriotic statesman is far more complex. He has to consider, amid the tangle of surrounding conditions, what is likely in the end to be to the highest interest of his country; and often a clear answer is nowhere to be found. Yet surely no statesman who is truly patriotic would feel the obligation to be any less real than that which is laid on the simplest soldier. Rather, the magnitude of the issues at stake must render it vastly greater. So we may say of conduct in general. The more we advance in the development of the moral life, the less possible does it become to point to any single rule that seems to carry its own authority with it, to any law that stands above us and says categorically, You must do this. What we find is, more and more, only the general principle that says, You ought to do what you find to be best. And what is best may vary very much in its external form, and even in its inner nature, with changing conditions. But this does not in any way destroy the absoluteness of the moral standard. It still remains as true as ever that we are bound to choose what is right "in the scorn of consequence," though it may be more difficult for us to say at any given point what precisely is right. The authority, indeed, must come home to us with a far more absolute power, when we recognise that it is our own law, than when we regard it as an alien force.

This much, however, is true: that, as moral principles cease to be laws of a state or of a divine lawgiver or of a definite voice of conscience within us, it becomes all the more important to have a clear view of the concrete content of the moral life. A few generalities will no longer suffice for our guidance. This is, indeed, what we find with reference to the advance of all the more distinctively human sciences. In Economics, for instance, scientific treatment began with the formulation of a few simple "laws," and it was only by degrees that it came to be recognised that what is really wanted is a concrete study of the facts of the economic system. In the case of Ethics, the science was to a large extent established on the right lines at a comparatively early point in its development by Aristotle; but, both before and after his time, there have been constant efforts to introduce an unreal simplification by appealing to some rigid abstract standard. The significance of the work of Hegel and of the recent school of development has lain largely in bringing us back again to the more concrete point of view of Aristotle. In the following Book some attempt will be made to show the value of this point of view in enabling us to deal with some of the more important problems of the moral life. Before we proceed, however, to the consideration of the moral life in the concrete, it seems desirable to raise the general question of the bearing of ethical theory on practice. The exact sense in which it is possible to apply the moral standard varies a good deal with different theories of its nature; and accordingly it seems desirable at this point to devote a chapter to the discussion of this subject.

CHAPTER VII.

THE BEARING OF THEORY ON PRACTICE.

§ **1.** Different Views.—As I have already indicated, there are different views with regard to the nature and extent of the bearing of ethical theory on the practical life of mankind. According to some, the aim of Ethics is practical throughout. According to others, it is a purely theoretical study, with just as little direct bearing on practical life as astronomy or chemistry or metaphysics. Others, again, steer a middle course, and, while holding that its aim is not directly practical, yet believe that it has important practical bearings, inasmuch as it makes clear to us the ideal involved in life. As examples of the directly practical treatment of Ethics, we may refer to most of the earlier thinkers up to Plato, to the Stoics and Epicureans, to the Mediæval Casuists, to Bentham and most of the modern Utilitarians, and on the whole to Mr. Herbert Spencer. This view corresponds also to what is probably the popular conception of the subject. Most men expect that an ethical teacher will tell them what they ought to do; and the common phrase "the Ethics of—" (Gambling, Competition, Controversy, &c.) is generally understood to mean a statement of the right attitude to be adopted with reference to certain departments of action. The more purely theoretical view is to some extent represented by the effort of Spinoza to treat morals after the manner of Geometry. It seems also to be the view taken, though in somewhat different senses, by various recent writers, among whom may be mentioned Dr. Simmel, and perhaps Mr. F. H. Bradley and Mr. B. Bosanquet,[1] and one or two others. The middle course, however, has been adopted by most of the great writers on the subject, from Aristotle downwards; *i. e.* these writers have treated the subject theoretically, but at the same time have clearly indicated its bearings upon the concrete moral life.

Now, the view which we ought to take on this point depends largely on the general theory of Ethics which we adopt. Some consideration of the way in which the nature of our theory affects its bearing on practice may, consequently, be here in place.

§ 2. Relation of Different Views to the Various Ethical Theories.—From the point of view of the Moral Sense School the bearing of ethical theory upon

[1] Simmel's views are to be found especially in his *Einleitung in die Moralwissenschaft*, vol. i., p. iii, and vol. ii., pp. 408, 409, &c. Mr. Bradley's most forcible statements on this point are to be found in his *Ethical Studies*, pp. 174–5, and in his *Principles of Logic*, pp. 247–8. For some criticisms on the statements there given, I may refer to the *International Journal of Ethics*, vol. iii., No. 4, pp. 507 *sqq.*; and to the paper by Mr. Hastings Rashdall on "The Limits of Casuistry" in the same Journal, vol. iv., No. 4, pp. 459 *sqq.* *Cf.* also *ibid.*, vol. iv., No. 3, pp. 160–173, &c. It is probable, however, that Mr. Bradley's statements are intended only as an emphatic protest against the opposite extreme of those who think that ethical science should tell us directly what we ought in particular to do. At any rate, there is ground for thinking that Mr. Bradley no longer holds to the extreme position indicated in the passages to which I have referred, and in several others throughout the *Ethical Studies.* From several indications in the writings of Mr. Bosanquet, however, it would appear that he adheres to the view expressed by Mr. Bradley; but I am not aware that he has ever given any clear statement of his position.

practical life would be exceedingly slight. For, according to this view, Ethics is on substantially the same footing as Æsthetics. Now it will be generally allowed that æsthetic theory[1] has very little direct bearing upon the cultivation of taste or the production of works of art. Of course a bad theory does sometimes corrupt the taste of a generation, and a good theory may help to set it right. But the influence of æsthetic theory in this way is probably not much greater than that of particular views on astronomy or biology might be. All knowledge affects practice, but not all knowledge guides it; and on the whole æsthetic theory does not guide taste or artistic production. Similarly, if morality were simply dependent on a kind of intuitive taste, the theory which expounded the nature of this taste would not have much effect on practical life, except in a comparatively indirect way. In like manner, it is true of most intuitional theories of morals that, if they are accepted, the bearing of Ethics on practical life must be of the slightest description. If we know what is right by an instinctive perception, or by any other kind of direct insight, the theoretical consideration of this insight can bring nothing to light which is not already involved in the practice of mankind. A rational theory, like that of Kant, on the other hand,

[1] Here, and elsewhere, I understand æsthetic theory to be concerned with the study of the Beautiful (whither found in Nature or in Art). Some writers regard Æsthetics rather as the theory of artistic production. In so far as there is any such theory, it would more nearly resemble Ethics. But I think it is better to regard Æsthetics as concerned with the apprehension of the Beautiful rather than with its creation. On the other hand, the moral life is, from the nature of this case, necessarily treated as a creative activity.

would seem to leave more scope for practical application; for, though the rational principles recognised by such a theory are implicit in the ordinary consciousness of mankind, yet the making of them explicit would bring them into greater clearness, and so might be expected to have a considerable influence upon practice. It is the Utilitarian theory, however, which lends itself most directly to practical application. According to this view there is a definite end (the greatest happiness of the greatest number) to be aimed at in life; and human beings cannot be assumed to have this end in view in their ordinary actions, except in a very vague and blundering fashion. Hence it would be the aim of ethical theory, from this point of view, to bring the end to light and to consider the means best adapted for its attainment. This would apply also to any view (such as that of Socrates), according to which there is some ascertainable end (some *summum bonum*), to which human life ought to be directed, whether this end be described as Happiness or in any other way. Finally, if we adopt the view of development, we are naturally led to take up an intermediate position with reference to the applicability of ethical theory to practice. Of course if any one were to take the view that the process of development is inevitable and not open to criticism, there would be no scope for the application of theory to practice from this point of view, any more than from the point of view of pure Intuitionism. If there are absolute laws, either of the nature of intuitive commands or of inevitable natural forces, by which the nature of the moral life is determined, the science of Ethics can only stand by and admire them. Now there are some evolutionists who appear to take this view. But, in general, the view taken by those who adopt the theory of development is that the development, at least in its higher phases, is capable of reflective guidance, and, in fact, can only take place by means of reflection. Hence, while thinkers of this school would be chary of any attempt to deal with life by a reference to some abstract end, taken up without regard to the process of its development, they would yet be ready to study this process of development with a view to ascertain how far it is adequate to the ideal that is involved in it; and this reflective criticism might be expected to have a considerable influence on practical life.

These general statements, however, are only roughly true; and we must now try to explain them somewhat more accurately in relation to the most important theories.

§ 3. THE INTUITIONIST VIEW.—According to the Intuitionist view, we apprehend immediately that certain lines of action are right and others wrong. On the most stringent interpretation this means that there can never be any real doubt as to the best course to pursue. "An erring conscience is a chimera." The study of moral principles cannot, therefore, lead us to any truth which was not known before; and scientific Ethics is simply an intellectual luxury. This stringent view, however, has seldom been taken by Intuitionists. They have generally believed that Conscience can be to some extent educated. They have also sometimes held that even intuitive moral principles may come into collision, and that reflection is required in dealing with such cases of conflict. Casuistry is not unknown among Intuitionists.

Again, I have pointed out that, according to the view of the more rational Intuitionists[1] (*i. e.* those represented by the line of thought extending from Cudworth to Kant), the function of Ethics would naturally be regarded as more directly practical; since the principle of morals is, from this point of view, one that is capable of reflective analysis. It should be observed, however, that Kant himself did not regard Ethics as being practical in this sense. For, though Kant held that the Categorical Imperative is capable of reflective analysis, yet he also held that it is so simple and obvious in its application, that it is used by all rational beings, without the need of reflective analysis. In fact, it was Kant who put forward the *dictum* that "an erring conscience is a chimera." In accordance with this view, Kant also held that there are no real cases of moral conflict, and that, consequently, casuistry is an absurdity. The laws of duty are absolute, and admit of no exceptions. Kant, indeed, is, from this point of view, quite the most stringent of all Intuitionists. In general, however, it is true that those who accept a rational principle as their standard acknowledge the importance of reflective analysis from a practical point of view.

§ 4. The Utilitarian View.—From the Utilitarian point of view, the moral life is conceived as directed towards a definite end—*viz.* the attainment of pleasure, and, more definitely, of the greatest possible pleasure of all sentient creatures. So far, then, as this end can be precisely determined, and the means to its attainment definitely ascertained, it would be possi-

[1] If they are to be called Intuitionists. See above, chap. iii., § 10.

ble to calculate what course of action is the best under any assignable conditions. The task of Ethics would thus become a quite directly practical one. But, even from the Utilitarian standpoint, this view is subject to considerable qualification. Even the Utilitarians hardly conceive that it falls within the province of Ethics to invent a morality for mankind. It would be unfair, at any rate, to attribute so crude a misconception to any of the leading exponents of the ideas of the school. J. S. Mill, in particular, has expressly guarded against it, by the statement in which he compares the results of the moral experience of mankind to the Nautical Almanack which is used in navigation. He explains that, all through the course of human life, men have been testing the consequences of various lines of action, and the results of this experience are summed up in the common sense of mankind. The ethical philosopher, as well as the "plain man," finds his Almanack already calculated, and only requires to use it. Mill conceives, however, that these calculations have been somewhat roughly made, and have not been carried, so to speak, to many places of Decimals. The ethical philosopher will endeavour gradually to revise and extend them. Dropping metaphor, we may say that there is a large body of moral truths which, from the Utilitarian point of view, may be accepted as embodying the best experience of the race; but, since the race has not been consciously guided by Utilitarian considerations, it has not always summed up its results quite accurately in the moral precepts that have come to be recognised as binding. The finer distinctions have been blurred, and the more remote consequences ignored. Hence reflection on the moral end may enable us to introduce considerable corrections into the judgment of common-sense morality.[1]

§ 5. THE EVOLUTIONIST VIEW.—When thus qualified, the Utilitarian view on this point is not substantially different from that commonly adopted by the Evolutionists—at least by those who take a definitely teleological view of the process of development. From this point of view, as from that of Utilitarianism, there is a definite end in view, though it may be an end that is a good deal more difficult to formulate. The greater complexity of the end, however, tends to introduce greater uncertainty with respect to the best means to its attainment; while, at the same time, the idea of development brings with it a greater confidence in the fruits of past experience, as embodied in the traditions and intuitions of the race. The

[1] *Cf.* Fowler and Wilson's *Principles of Morals*, Part I., pp. 118–19. "What is most of all important to the practical moralist is, that history will familiarise him with the idea of development or evolution, shewing him that institutions or habits are not accidental in their origin, or mere devices of the legislator; that they have grown up for the most part by virtue of tendencies in human nature modified and directed by external circumstances, and that these tendencies should be understood by all who seek to direct them. This consideration will teach us the precaution necessary in dealing with prevalent ideas and customs, and prevent us from making attempts to modify them without due preparation. On the other hand, by studying the circumstances in which moral ideas or rules had their origin, we shall be better able to see whether they are suitable to the present condition of mankind, or whether the necessity for them has ceased. History, in short, enables us to understand and appreciate the present; it enables us to some extent to anticipate the future, and the knowledge which it supplies is an indispensable condition of all wise attempts at moral and social improvement." It is thus that the careful Utilitarian recognises the necessity of the study of the actual course of concrete moral development.

Evolutionist is, consequently, as a rule, less prone than the Utilitarian is to imagine that it is possible by reflection to introduce definite improvements into the morality of common sense. Mr. Herbert Spencer has perhaps shown himself more ready than most to suggest practical conclusions; but this is not so much because he thinks it possible to improve upon the results of experience as because he thinks that the experience of the race has resulted in the establishment of certain quite definite intuitions as to natural rights, &c., though the perversity of the human race leads it very frequently to neglect these intuitive truths. But Mr. Spencer's views on this point do not seem to me to be quite consistent.

There are, however, as we have seen, other writers of the Evolutionist school who do not hold that it is possible to formulate any definite end to which the process of development may be regarded as tending. According to these writers, there is a gradual process of Evolution, and various forms of moral action and moral judgment arise in the course of it; but it is not possible to give any clear account of its ultimate goal. It must be taken simply as we find it; and the forms of action and of moral judgment must be taken along with the rest. The study of Ethics, from this point of view, is simply a part of the wider study of Psychology and Sociology, and hence is simply a study and interpretation of facts. This is the view, in particular, of Dr. Simmel, who ridicules the attempts of what he calls the Monistic Moralists to give an account of any single principle by which the moral life is guided. It is merely a struggle of opposing forces, and the resulting moral system expresses nothing but the tendencies of the "compact majority." But this is not so much a theory of Ethics as a theory of its impossibility. In so far, however, as such a view is taken, ethical theory would have no practical application, just as it has none according to the purely Intuitionist view. When we enter the region of absolute Law as the foundation of morals—whether it be that of God, of Conscience, of Reason, or of a blind struggle—we are beyond the possibility of regulative principles based on an ideal.

§ **6.** THE IDEALISTIC VIEW.—How does the matter stand, finally, from the point of view of the more idealistic theory of development? From this standpoint the process of development is conceived in a more distinctly teleological fashion than it is from the standpoint of biological evolution; but on the other hand the end in view is more complex and more difficult to define. The unfolding of the capabilities of mankind, the realisation of the rational Universe—phrases such as these, though they have a quite definite and intelligible meaning, hardly serve to furnish us with a clear-cut end to the attainment of which definite means may be adopted. If such an end were not one that is naturally and inevitably adopted by mankind, it would be hopeless to seek to impose it upon them. Besides, as the ideal, from this point of view, is not thought of as an external end, but as the unfolding of the essential nature of mankind, we may naturally expect to find it unfolding itself throughout the whole course of human history. If this view is correct, the ideal would be found in human life by the psychologist and the sociologist, as well as by the student of Ethics; the difference being that the former are not specially concerned with it, and find it only as one fact among others, while the student of Ethics makes it his special business to examine it. From the point of view of idealism, therefore, more than from most others, it must be clearly recognised that it is not the business of Ethics to invent a new morality for the world. If it were not true that "morality is the nature of things," no amount of reflection could ever make it so. At the same time, this ought not to be understood as meaning that the student of Ethics accepts the world as he finds it. Like the poet, he

> "Looks at all things as they are
> But through a kind of glory."

He looks at the world in the light of the ideal which is developing through it. Taking the world as it stands at any particular time, we do not find that it is a homogeneous whole. It is a struggling, developing process, in which, as the Persians put it, there is a continual conflict between Ormuzd and Ahriman, Light and Darkness. The student of Ethics, from the point of view of Idealism, is not an indifferent spectator of this struggle. He looks for the evidence of the triumph of Light. In what direction this triumph will come, he will hardly undertake to prophesy ; but, in his study of life and history, of the contest between the Family and the State, Individualism and Socialism, Law and Freedom, the ideals of the Hebrews and of the Greeks, he is interested to watch not simply the direction in which at any time things are moving, in the swaying to and fro of opposing forces, but rather in trying to bring out the *significance* of the movement, *i.e.* its bearing upon the gradual unfolding of the ideal which it involves. To study it in this way is at the same time to criticise it.

There are thus two sides in the idealistic view of Ethics. On the one hand, it looks to the experience of mankind; on the other hand, it looks to the ideal. Without the former it would be empty; without the latter it would be blind. And on the whole all the writers who have dealt with the subject from this point of view have kept their eyes upon both aspects. But some writers have tended to lay more emphasis on the one side than on the other. The typical instances of the two methods are Plato and Aristotle. Plato seems, at least to the superficial view, to be perpetually constructing ideal Republics and ideal types of life, with but little reference to the concrete facts of human development.[1] Aristotle, on the other hand, seems—again to the superficial view—to throw aside the ideal as not πρακτὸν καὶ κτητὸν ἀνθρώπῳ, and to concentrate his attention upon the virtues and institutions of the Greek State, as he found it beside him. Hegel, in more modern times, has seemed to lend himself to both forms of misunderstanding. Some have regarded him as a father of revolutionists,[2] who created a world out of his inner consciousness, without regard to fact and history; others have scoffed at him as an upholder of the *status quo*, who simply accepted the world as he found it.[3] But wisdom is justified of all her children;

[1] That Plato was not a mere dreamer of dreams, but a true interpreter of the moral life of his time, is well brought out by Hegel in his *History of Philosophy* and *Philosophy of Right*.

[2] The Socialists and Nihilists used to be fond of claiming Hegel as their founder. They seem to have abandoned this view now.

[3] Fries said of Hegel that his political views were grown "not in the garden of science, but on the dunghill of servility." In somewhat the same way Goethe was called the Friend of the powers that be (*Freund des Bestehenden*). The confusion, in the case of

and the opposition between these different aspects of truth is wholly superficial. The ethical idealist takes the world as he finds it; but he takes it to bring out its significance, and so to criticise it. He brings an ideal to bear upon it, but the ideal is one that is involved in the facts themselves. The seeming opposition is a real identity; and Aristotle is not the enemy of Plato, but his interpreter.

§ **7.** Summary of Results.—On the whole, then, we see that there are three views of the way in which Ethics bears on practical life:—

(1) There is the view that it has essentially no bearing upon it at all. This is the view of the more extreme Intuitionists, whether perceptional or rational; of those evolutionists who believe that no end can be discovered in the process of development; and perhaps also of a few idealists.

(2) There is the view that Ethics is directly practical. This is the view chiefly of the Utilitarians, but partly also of all those who think that some definite end can be formulated for mankind, which is not involved in the process of human development itself.

(3) There is the view that Ethics has for its primary function to bring out the significance of the moral life in relation to the ideal that is involved in it, and that this process is at the same time a criticism of it. The third of these views is of course the one that is here

Hegel, arises mainly from not appreciating his distinction between the Actual (*Wirklich*) and the Existent. He held that the Actual is Rational, but he meant by the Actual, not what is at any time found existing, but the underlying spirit by which the movement of history is carried on. It is the business of Ethics to bring this clearly to light.

adopted; and, in the light of what has now been said, the remarks at the beginning of this treatise on the essentially normative character of ethical science may perhaps become more intelligible.

§ 8. Comparison between Ethics and Logic.—Perhaps a comparison between Ethics and Logic, from this point of view, may help in some degree to make my meaning clearer. The essential similarity between these two sciences has been already indicated. Now, it is possible to take different views of Logic, in its bearing upon the work of the particular science, just as it is possible to take different views of Ethics, in its bearing upon practical life. It may be held that it is the business of Inductive Logic to lay down the rules to be observed by the particular sciences in the investigation of nature. This is on the whole the view suggested by Mill, just as on the whole the corresponding view of Ethics is suggested by him. Or again, such a Logic as that of Hegel, in which the, ideas, of Quantity, Substance, Cause, &c., are dealt with in their relationship to one another, may be supposed to be (and has been supposed to be) an effort to deduce these ideas *à priori*, without any reference to the way in which they emerge in our experience. Such views of Logic would be on a par with the view of Ethics according to which it is its business to invent a system of morality. But most logicians would now admit that the methods of the sciences have to be first discovered by the sciences themselves, and that the ideas used by them (Quantity, Substance, Cause, &c.), could never be known by us if they did not inevitably emerge in the course of our experience. So also it seems to be true that the content of the moral life is developed in the course of human experience, and does not wait for the science of Ethics to invent it.

But then, it may be asked, does Logic simply accept the methods of the sciences as it finds them, and simply arrange the ideas of which the sciences make use? This view also seems to be incorrect. Logic seeks to bring out the significance of those methods and ideas, and to test their validity. In this way it at once justifies them within their proper sphere, and brings out their limitations. It does not invent ideas and methods for the sciences, but it certainly criticises those that it finds, in the light of the ideas of truth and consistency which it finds in them. So with Ethics. It does not invent the Family and the State, or the ideas of Love and Trüth, or the laws about Life and Property. Still less does it seek to overturn these ideas and institutions. It finds them in the concrete world with which it deals; and it seeks to understand them in the light of the ideal of human development, to which they have reference. It thus at once shows their significance, and indicates their limitations. For the "plain man" such an institution as the Family or Private Property is apt to seem an eternal and inviolable fact in the moral life; and, if he is taught to doubt about this, by being shown that they have had a history, and have not always existed in the form in which they now appear, he is apt to become confused, and to think that the significance of those elements in human life has been destroyed. The student of Ethics should be able to see the significance and value of such institutions, while at the same time he is able to put them in their proper place as elements in a whole. It is in this form of critical insight that the study of Ethics has practical value.

§ 9. THE TREATMENT OF APPLIED ETHICS.—In the light of those observations, we are now able to proceed to the treatment of Applied Ethics. Hitherto we have been concerned with the pure theory, *i. e.* with the consideration of the nature of the standard or ideal. Now, a treatise on Ethics frequently contains nothing more than the discussion of this point; and, if our view of the nature of the standard had been somewhat different from what it is, this might possibly have sufficed for our purpose. If we had adopted an intuitional view, there could have been hardly any Applied Ethics to deal with. If we had adopted a Utilitarian view, the applications would have consisted in working out the Calculus in various directions; and however difficult (if not impossible) this might be, the general principle of it at least would have been so obvious, that we might fairly have been dispensed from the working of it out. But for any one who adopts the point of view of development a treatment of Ethics which made no attempt to interpret the concrete process of development in the light of the ideal principle involved, would be little short of an absurdity. Hence, this part of the subject has generally been a prominent one with those writers who adopt the point of view of Development. It is so, for instance, with Aristotle, in whose *Nicomachean Ethics* the concrete life of the citizen is sketched with considerable fulness, and who seeks to complete the subject by a consideration of the State and Education in his treatise on *Politics.* It is so also with Hegel, whose chief work on Ethics (the

Philosophy of Right) is almost entirely concerned with the concrete moral life.

In dealing with this concrete aspect of the subject, the student must guard against two possible misconceptions, which have perhaps already been sufficiently indicated, but which it may be well to repeat and emphasize once more.

(1) It must not for a moment be imagined that the concrete elements of the moral life are to be extracted by some sort of alchemy, out of the general principle. The task of Ethics would indeed be a hard one if it had to invent the moral life as well as to interpret it. But happily there were some good men in the world before there were books on Ethics; and even now that many books have been written, Heaven help the hapless mortal who gets his ideas of the moral life from them! We can learn what the moral life is by living it, and there is no other way. It is only after it has been lived that the science of Ethics can step in, and explain what it means. No doubt in thus explaining it, it is at the same time criticising it; and a moral life that has been subjected to criticism (like a book that has been subjected to criticism) is not quite the same thing as it was before. But the student must altogether clear his mind of any sort of notion that may linger in it, that in the chapters which follow a brand-new moral life is to be unfolded before his wondering eyes. Even a treatise on medical science does not teach us to breathe with our ears. We learn to breathe before we study physiology or hygienics, and to live before we study Ethics; and, on the whole, after we have studied them, breathe and live very much as we did before. We learn such things by action and experience. If a man is "a fool

or a physician at forty," it is certain that he is a muff or a moralist at a still more tender age; and the reflective analysis of life can only teach him to do a little more carefully and exactly (it may be, only a little more pedantically) what in the main he did before.

(2) On the other hand, the student must equally guard against the opposite misconception, that in studying the content of the moral life we regard it simply from the point of view of Sociology. To the student of Sociology the immoral life is on the whole as interesting as the moral life (Simmel says [1] it is more so), and degeneration is as interesting as development. For us, on the other hand, life is interesting only in the light of its ideal. We do not care for what it is, but for what it signifies. Hence also our method of treatment is different. We do not aim at a statement of the course through which the moral life has passed in the chequered career of its history, but rather at an account of its most significant aspects. In a complete treatment of it, we might perhaps be led to arrange it, after the manner of Hegel, in the order of its dialectical development. But in an introductory account like the present a somewhat less systematic arrangement may suffice.

At any rate, we have now had enough of these preliminary observations and warnings. Let us plunge, as best we can, into our account of the concrete moral life.

[1] See *International Journal of Ethics*, Vol. III., no. 4. So also in physiology and psychology, pathological states are often more enlightening than those that are normal.

BOOK III.

THE MORAL LIFE.

CHAPTER I.

THE SOCIAL UNITY.

§ 1. The Social Self.—We have seen that the true self is the rational self. We must now try to understand what this means. And, first of all, we have to add that the true self is the social self. Up to this point we have spoken of the individual almost as if he might be an isolated and independent unit. But every individual belongs to a social system. An isolated individual is even inconceivable. Aristotle said truly that such a being must be "either a beast or a god."[1] Such a being could have no ideal self. He must either have realized his ideal like a god, or have no ideal to realize like a beast. For our ideal self finds its embodiment in the life of a society, and it is only in this way that it is kept before us. Not only so, but even the realization of our ideal seems to demand a society. For to have a perfectly rational self would involve that our universe should have a perfectly rational content. Now the only possible universe with a rational content seems to be a universe of rational beings. Hence we

[1] *Politics*, I. ii. 14: "He who is unable to live in society, or who has no need because he is sufficient for himself, must be either a beast or a god (ἢ θηρίον ἢ θεός)."

must go even beyond the saying of Aristotle, and say that even a God must be social. Even a God must have a rational universe in relation to Himself, and must consequently create, or, in Hegelian phrase, go out of Himself into a world of rational beings. But this is perhaps too abstruse a subject to be more than hinted at here. It is sufficient for our purpose to say that it is in relation to our fellow-men that we find our ideal life. "Where two or three are gathered together, there am I in the midst of them."[1] The "I" or ideal self is not realized in any one individual, but finds its realization rather in the relations of persons to one another. It embodies itself in literature and art, in the laws of a state, in the counsels of perfection which societies gradually form for themselves.

§ 2. SOCIETY A UNITY.—Society, therefore, must be regarded as a unity—in fact, as we shall see shortly, as an organic unity. The parts of it are necessary to each other, as the parts of an animal organism are; and it is in all the parts in relation to one another, rather than in any one of them singly, that the true life is to be found. "We are members one of another." The ideal life of one requires others to complement it, and it is by mutual help that the whole develops towards perfection. This we shall see more fully in the sequel.[2]

[1] I do not mean to imply that this saying was originally intended to bear the sense here ascribed to it. But I think it has frequently been used by religious men to express that consciousness of unity, and of elevation into a higher universe, which arises when a number of men gather together in a common spirit and with a common aim for the advancement of their moral lives. Clifford's "tribal self" contains a similar idea. (See above p. 115.)

[2] See sections 11 and 12 below. The present section is intended only as a preliminary statement.

§ 3. Egoism and Altruism.—This fact leads us to introduce a certain modification into the view of the moral life that has been presented up to the present point. We have spoken of the great end of the moral life as self-realization. But since an individual is a member of a social unity, his supreme end will be not simply the perfecting of his own life, but also of the society to which he belongs. To a great extent the one end will indeed coincide with the other. Yet there appears, at least *primâ facie*, to be a certain possibility of conflict. Now when we seek simply our own individual ends, this attitude is called *Egoism;* while the term *Altruism* is used to denote devotion to the ends of others. It is of great importance to consider the precise relation of these two attitudes to one another.

§ 4. Mr. Spencer's Conciliation.—A good deal of attention has been given to this subject by Mr. Herbert Spencer,[1] and he has endeavoured to show how a conciliation may be effected between the two attitudes. He points out that either of them, if carried to an extreme, is self-destructive. If every one were to seek only his own ends, this would be a bad way of securing the ends even of any one individual. For each one stands frequently in need of help. On the other hand, if every one were to devote himself entirely to the good of others, this would be fatal to the good of others. For if each one neglected himself, he would deteriorate in his ability to help others. This point is worked out in a very interesting way by Mr. Spencer,

[1] *Data of Ethics*, chaps. xi. and xiv. *Cf.* Stephen's *Science of Ethics*, chap. vi., Dewey's *Outlines of Ethics*, pp. 70–1, and Muirhead's, *Elements of Ethics*, pp. 164–5.

and he comes to the conclusion that what we should aim at is neither pure Egoism nor pure Altruism, but a compromise between them. He thinks also that the more completely society becomes developed, the more will the two ends tend to become identical.

§ 5. SELF-REALIZATION THROUGH SELF-SACRIFICE.—The truth seems to be, however, that there is even less opposition between Egoism and Altruism than that which Mr. Spencer recognizes. We can realize the true self only by realizing social ends. In order to do this we must negate the merely individual self, which, as we have indicated, is not the true self. We must realize ourselves by sacrificing ourselves.[1] The more fully we so realize ourselves, the more do we reach a universal point of view—*i. e.* a point of view from which our own private good is no more to us than the good of any one else. No doubt it must always be necessary for us to take more thought for our own individual development than for that of any one else; because each one best understands his own individual needs, and has the best means of working out his own nature to its perfection. But when this is done from the point of view of the whole, it is no longer properly to be described as Egoism. It is self-realization, but it is self-realization for the sake of the whole. In such self-realization the mere wishes and whims of the private self have been sacrificed, and we seek to develop ourselves in the same spirit and for the same ends as those in which and for which we seek to develop others. When we live in such a spirit as this, the opposition between Egoism and Altruism ceases. We seek neither

[1] *Cf.* Caird's *Hegel*, pp. 210–218.

our own good simply nor the good of others simply, but the good both of ourselves and of others as members of a whole. Looking at the matter, therefore, from this point of view, it might be better to describe the ultimate end as the realization of a rational universe, rather than as self-realization.

§ 6. Ethics a Part of Politics.—We must recognize, in short, that man is, as Aristotle expressed it, "a political animal,"[1] and that Ethics cannot be satisfactorily treated except as a part of Politics—*i. e.* as a part of the study of Society. Our duties and our virtues are at every point dependent on our relations to one another. This fact was more clearly recognized by some of the ancient Greek thinkers than it has been by many in modern times—for, in modern times, partly on account of the influence of Christianity,[2] we have come to think more of the independence of the individual. It may be well, therefore, to glance for a moment at the way in which Ethics was regarded by Plato and Aristotle.

§ 7. Plato's View of Ethics.—Plato was so strongly impressed with the social nature of man, and with the necessity of studying his life in relation to society, that, in his study of Ethics, instead of inquiring into the characteristics of a virtuous life in an individual, he endeavoured first to determine the characteristics of a good state. Having found what these are, he considered that it would be perfectly easy to infer what are the characteristics of a good man. Accordingly, the great ethical treatise of Plato is the *Republic*, in

1 "Πολιτικὸν ζῷον" (*Politics*, I. ii. 9).

2 Partly also, no doubt, because our wider international relationships have made it impossible for us to regard any one social system as a complete and exclusive unity in itself.

which he gives a sketch of an ideal state. It seemed to him—in accordance with a classification that was current among the Greeks—that there were four great virtues required for the existence of an ideal state, *viz.* wisdom, courage, temperance, and justice; and he thought that by observing exactly the significance of these virtues in the ideal state, he was able to see also what their exact significance must be in the life of the individual.[1]

§ 8. ARISTOTLE'S VIEW OF ETHICS.—Aristotle was not less convinced than Plato of the essentially social nature of man. He began his great treatise on Ethics—perhaps the greatest that has ever been written—with a statement to the effect that Ethics is a part of Politics;[2] and the greater part of his treatise is occupied with an investigation of the virtues that are required in a good citizen of a state such as he found in Greece, and especially in Athens. He did indeed think that there was a kind of life, what he called the contemplative or speculative life (what we might call the life of science, or the life of the student), which was essentially higher than the life of political activity; but he

[1] For a fuller account of Plato's Ethics, see Sidgwick's *History of Ethics*, pp. 35-51. Plato's *Republic* is a book of such interest and importance that every student ought to find some opportunity of reading it. It has been admirably translated both by Jowett and by Davies and Vaughan. In connection with this, Dr. Bosanquet's *Companion to Plato's Republic* should by all means be used.

[2] In the wide sense in which the term Politics was used by the Greeks. Perhaps in modern times we should rather say that Ethics is a part of Social Philosophy. I have discussed this point in my *Introduction to Social Philosophy*, p. 48. On the relation between Ethics and Politics the student may profitably consult Sidgwick's *Methods of Ethics*, Book I., chap. ii. See also Muirhead's *Elements of Ethics*, Book I., chap. iii., § 14.

considered that even this higher life must be built up on a basis of civic virtue.[1]

§ **9.** Cosmopolitism.—The best Ethics of the Greeks, then, was based on the conception of the State, as the sphere within which the life of the individual is to be realized. It was only after the best days of the Greek state were over, when everything was beginning to be crushed under the iron heel of Rome,[2] that the Stoics began to speak of a *πολιτεία τοῦ κοσμοῦ*, and to think of the virtuous man (or "the wise man," as they called him) as one who is bound by no particular social ties, but lives an independent life of his own. Even the Stoics, however, recognized that the good man is a citizen; but they said that he ought to be "a citizen of the world," not of any particular community. In this way his social relations were made so vague that it almost seemed as if they might be altogether ignored. There was a great elevation in much of the teaching of the Stoics; but its want of any definite recognition of social relationships made it cold and hard, and somewhat destitute of content. And often it was inflated with a certain false pride in the independence of the individual.

§ **10.** Christian Ethics.—Christianity may be said to have gone to some extent in the same direction as Stoicism.[3] It also was essentially cosmopolitan, and it also tended to insist on the independent life of the individual.[4] Each one must "work out his own

1 See Sidgwick's *History of Ethics*, pp. 51–70.

2 See Caird's *Hegel*, pp. 204–207, Zeller's *Stoics, Epicureans, and Sceptics*, pp. 15–16, and Wallace's *Epicureanism*, chap. i

3 Sidgwick's *History of Ethics*, pp. 114–117.

4 Christianity insisted on the dignity of man as man more strongly

salvation," and must even forsake father and mother, and all other social relationships, in order to follow after the ideal life. Christianity represented the ideal life also as an imitation of a divine personality. Still, this was only one aspect of Christianity. It was no less emphatic in its insistence on the doctrine that we are "members one of another," and that in order to attain perfection we must recognise our essential unity both with each other and with God. The fact, however, that Christianity had to make its way in an adverse world rendered it necessary at first to insist somewhat strongly on the need of isolation. Its followers had to recognize that they were "not of the world," in order that they might keep their ideals pure. But after Christianity had to a great extent conquered the world, the other side—the social side—began to come out; and it is perhaps on that side now that its significance is greatest. Whether we look, therefore, to ancient or to modern systems of morals, it is not difficult to see that the recognition of the essentially social nature of man plays a prominent part in all that is best in them. This being the case, it will be well now to abandon the view of the mere individual life as that which is to be perfected, and to consider rather what is involved in the perfection of society.

§ **11.** THE SOCIAL UNIVERSE.—We must, however, first bring this point of view into relation to what has been already said with respect to the universes in which men habitually live. The life of every man, except an absolute madman, constitutes a more or less con-

than even Stoicism had done. Stoicism proclaimed the dignity only of the wise man or philosopher; whereas Christianity was preached to "publicans and sinners."

sistent whole. His actions fall within a more or less ordered scheme or plan. This whole, this plan, this totality of ends which a man pursues, we have agreed to describe as the universe within which he lives. Now this universe is always of a social character. Even the most original and even the most misanthropic of men cannot escape from the influence of the social environment by which they are formed. They inevitably imbibe something of what has been called "the ethos of their people," the moral point of view adopted by the race or nation or body of men among whom, or under the influence of whom, their lives are spent. This moral atmosphere in which they pass their lives supplies the main part of that universe within which their desires find scope. So much is this the case that a man always, except when in some abnormal state of mind, thinks of himself, not as an isolated personality, but as a member of some body. This fact is emphasized even by a writer in some respects so individualistic as Mill.[1] "The social state," he says,[2] "is at once so natural, so necessary, and so habitual to man, that, except in some unusual circumstances or by an effort of voluntary abstraction he never conceives himself otherwise than as a member of a body; and this association is riveted more and more, as mankind are further removed from the state of savage independence. Any condition, therefore, which is essential to a state of society, becomes more and more an

[1] This element in Mill's teaching is due, as he partly acknowledges two pages later, to the study of Comte. *Cf.* his *Autobiography*, chap. iv. Mill seems never to have made any serious effort to reconcile the elements which he derived from Comte with the general tenor of his philosophy.

[2] *Utilitarianism*, chap. iii., pp. 46-7

inseparable part of every person's conception of the state of things which he is born into, and which is the destiny of a human being." For this reason, when we consider any large society of human beings, bound together by a common language, a common law, a common religion, a common interest, we may say in a broad sense that they all live habitually within the same universe. They will all be distinguished no doubt by individual peculiarities; some of them will be more and some less affected by the common ties; and even from year to year and from day to day the universe of each will be liable to considerable variations. Still, speaking broadly, what the Germans call the *Sitten*, *i. e.* the moral habitudes of a man's time and place, tend to overshadow the peculiarities of his individual nature, and to have a strong determining influence on his view of life and on his conception of his own vocation. The necessity of making himself intelligible to those around him, the immense advantage of understanding them, and the need of constantly co-operating with them, would of themselves be sufficient to bring about a certain homogeneity among the members of a community. And when we add to this the influences of heredity and education, the force is overwhelming.

§ **12.** SOCIETY AN ORGANISM.—These considerations may partly enable us to understand an idea which has become prevalent in recent times among writers of very diverse schools—the idea, namely, that a society of human beings is, as we have already indicated, to be regarded as an organic unity. The meaning of this is, broadly speaking, that just as we recognize a common life animating all the members of which a living body is composed, so we must acknowledge a similar unity among the members of a human society. This idea has sometimes been presented in the form of an analogy; *i. e.* an attempt is made to draw parallels between the structures of human societies and the constitutions of animal or vegetable bodies.[1] Such analogies are no doubt occasionally suggestive; but on the whole they supply more scope for ingenuity than for insight. The essential point seems to be that a human personality is never an isolated phenomenon. It is even inconceivable apart from certain relations to other personalities. The positive content of a man's moral life depends on these relationships: apart from them it would stagnate and die, very much as a limb dies when it is cut off from its organic connection with the body of which it forms a part. The whole of a man's moral life, all its purposes, all its meaning and value, receive their tone and colour from the ideals, the institutions, the moral habits, among which his life develops. This being so, it is important, in dealing with the moral life, not merely to consider the life of an individual man, but to have regard to the unity within which the main part of his life falls.[2] That, in

[1] This has been done, for instance, by Mr. Herbert Spencer in his *Principles of Sociology*, vol. i., part ii.; and, in a still more elaborate form, by a German writer, Schäffle, in his *Bau und Leben des socialen Körpers*. Mr. Leslie Stephen (*Science of Ethics*, p. 126) thinks it preferable to speak of "social tissue" rather than of a "social organism," because there is no one abiding unity in which individuals are combined, as the parts are combined in an animal organism.

[2] On the organic nature of society, the student may be referred to Bradley's *Ethical Studies*, pp. 145-158, Bosanquet's *Philosophical Theory of the State*, especially chapters vii. and viii., and Muirhead's *Elements of Ethics*, pp. 165-172. I have expressed my own view on this subject at greater length in my *Introduction to Social Philosophy*,

spite of this unity, the individual has yet in a sense a private life of his own is a point that we shall have to consider at a later stage.

§ **13.** WHY IS THE SOCIAL UNIVERSE TO BE PREFERRED?—Now the question naturally presents itself at this point —Why should the social universe be preferred to the universe of the individual consciousness? The answer, of course, from the point of view that we have now reached, is that the individual self is in its nature incomplete, and requires a larger whole for its realization. Such a larger whole might no doubt conceivably be found in something beyond and above human society; and, if we were inventing a new morality, we might have to look about for such a larger universe. But if we accept the point of view of development, we must accept the only medium within which any actual process of moral development can be found. If it is true that the individual has no reality apart from the social whole, and that it is within that whole that his development takes place, the devotion to that whole has all the binding force which belongs to devotion to the Ideal Self. We cannot separate ourselves from the necessary medium of our evolution, and seek to perfect ourselves *in vacuo*. The further discussion of this question, however, would lead us into a metaphysical investigation of the nature of the self, its relation to the social whole within which it develops, and to the universe in general. Such a discussion would be necessary for the complete establishment of the validity of the moral ideal. But it lies beyond the province of

chap. iii. The student of the present handbook will probably understand this conception better after reading some of the following chapters.

a work which does not profess to enter into metaphysics. We can only hint a little further, in our concluding chapter, at the nature of the problem involved. In the meantime, we must content ourselves with the effort to bring out the general significance of the social universe in its bearings on the moral life.

§ **14.** Relation of Conscience to the Social Unity. The importance of the social environment in the formation of what is commonly known as Conscience, has been noticed by a number of recent writers. This is emphasized, for instance, by Mill[1] in his treatment of the moral sanctions.[2] Without endorsing all that has been said on this subject by him and others, it may at least be convenient to sum up at this point what has to be said on the nature of Conscience, and to indicate its relations to our social universe.

It has been pointed out already that there is a certain ambiguity—indeed a twofold ambiguity—in the use of the term "Conscience."[3] It is sometimes used to express the fundamental principles on which the moral judgment rests: at other times it expresses the principles adopted by a particular individual: at other times it

[1] *Utilitarianism*, chap. iii. *Cf.* also Bradley's *Ethical Studies*, p. 180 Stephen's *Science of Ethics*, chap. viii., Clifford's *Lectures and Essays* ("On the Scientific Basis of Ethics"), and Dr. Starcke's article on "The Conscience" in the *International Journal of Ethics*, vol. ii. No. 3 (April, 1892), pp. 342–372. Hegel, in his *Rechtsphilosophie*, was, I think, the first writer who clearly brought out the social bearing of Conscience. Much of what Hegel says on this point will be found reproduced, in an excellent form, in Dewey's *Outlines of Ethics* pp. 182–199.

[2] On the meaning of the moral sanctions, see the Note at the end of chap. vi.

[3] See above, Book I., chap. VI. *Cf.* also Hegel's *Philosophy of Right*, §§ 136–139.

means "a particular kind of pleasure and pain felt in perceiving our own conformity or non-conformity to principle."[1] The last seems to me to be the most convenient acceptation of the term,[2] except that I should prefer to say simply that it is a feeling of pain accompanying and resulting from our non-conformity to principle.[3] This sense of the term is evidently closely connected with the second sense; for the principles in connection with which an individual feels pain are of course the principles recognized by him. Nevertheless, the first sense also is not entirely excluded: for even if an individual is not clearly conscious of the deeper principles of reason on which the final moral judgment depends, he will yet often feel a vague uneasiness when he goes against them. It is difficult to believe, for instance, that St. Paul's conscience was entirely at rest in the midst of his persecuting zeal, even if he did think that he was "doing God service." However, in general no doubt the pain of Conscience accompanies only the violation of clearly recognized duty.

1 Starcke, *loc. cit.*, p. 348.

2 Chiefly because it gives the most definite meaning. When we go beyond this, we land ourselves in almost hopeless ambiguities.

3 The element of mystery so often thought to attach to Conscience is, I think, largely due to the fact that it is often not accompanied by any direct *perception* of "conformity or non-conformity to principle." A man has often simply an uneasy feeling of having gone wrong, without being able to say precisely what principle he has violated. Further, I am doubtful whether it is correct to speak of a *pleasure* of Conscience. Conformity to moral principle is the normal state; and this may be regarded as the neutral point. Any violation of principle, on the other hand, brings pain. The performance of duty leaves a man still in the position of an "unprofitable servant." "Spiritual pride," of course, is accompanied by a certain pleasure; but should this be described as a pleasure of Conscience? I think Carlyle was right on this point: "To say that we have a clear con-

Now we have seen that the principles of duty which an individual recognizes are largely determined by the social universe which he inhabits. Hence his conscience also must be largely determined by this.[1] A man's conscience, we may say broadly, attaches itself to that system of things which he regards as highest. There is, indeed, a certain feeling of pain, analogous to that of Conscience, in connection with every universe in which a man lives, whether he regards it as the highest or not. Thus, there is a feeling of pain or shame[2] accompanying the violation of rules of etiquette or good taste, or even accompanying the consciousness of any physical defect or awkward-

science is to utter a solecism; had we never sinned, we should have had no conscience." See his Essay on "Characteristics." Of course, there is a certain gratification accompanying the fulfilment of unaccustomed duties. If a man gets drunk only twice in the course of the week, instead of three times as usual, or if he tells the truth when there was a strong temptation to lie, he may feel pleased in reviewing his action. But there does not appear to be the same spontaneity and immediacy in this feeling as there is in the case of the corresponding pain; nor is its character so purely moral. It is more akin to the pleasure of solving a difficult problem. I suspect that, just as there is no pleasure of the teeth, corresponding to toothache; so there is, strictly speaking, no pleasure of the conscience, corresponding to its characteristic pain.

1 Hence Clifford's idea of a "tribal self"—a self which belongs to a man's tribe or society, and to which his mere individual self is subordinate. Clifford says, as we have seen, that a man's conscience is "the voice of his tribal self." The pain of his conscience is equivalent to his saying to himself, "In the name of my tribe, I hate myself for this treason which I have done." See above, Book I., chap. V., and *cf.* Muirhead's *Elements of Ethics*, pp. 157–9.

2 The Greek word αἰδώς, usually translated "shame," seems to be very nearly equivalent to what we understand by Conscience, at least in one of its aspects. *Cf.* Stephen's *Science of Ethics*, p. 321, and Caird's *Critical Philosophy of Kant*, vol. ii., pp. 285–6.

ness, even if we are aware, not only that the universe within which these things lie is not of supreme importance, but even that it does not lie within the power of our will to avoid such deficiencies. Such a feeling might be called a *quasi*-Conscience.[1] On reflection we perceive either that we are not responsible for such shortcomings, or that they are not of serious moral importance; but the feeling at the moment is scarcely distinguishable from that of Conscience proper. Sometimes such a feeling may even conflict with Conscience. Thus, the performance of duty may involve a violation of etiquette; so that, in whichever way we act, we are bound to have the pain either of Conscience or of *quasi*-Conscience. Again, Conscience sometimes attaches itself to a universe which has been transcended. When we have recently passed from one universe to another, Conscience will generally be found to have lagged a little behind, and to attach itself to the older universe rather than to the newer one. "Feeling," as Mr. Muirhead says,[2] "is the conservative element in human life." It does not attach itself to a new

[1] An excellent illustration of this is given by Mr. Muirhead (*Elements of Ethics*, p. 77) in an extract from Prof. Royce's *Religious Aspect of Philosophy* (pp. 53–4): "You ride, using another man's season ticket, or you tell a white lie, or speak an unkind word, and conscience, if a little used to such things, never winces. But you bow to the wrong man in the street, or you mispronounce a word, or you tip over a glass of water, and then you agonize about your shortcoming all day long; yes, from time to time for weeks. Such an impartial judge is the feeling of what you ought to have done.' For similar illustrations, see Stephen's *Science of Ethics*, p. 323, and Spencer's *Principles of Ethics*, p. 337.

[2] *Elements of Ethics*, p. 80. *Cf.* the saying of Mr. Jacobs, quoted by Miss Wedgwood (*The Moral Ideal*, p. 233), "The thoughts of one generation form the feelings of its successor."

universe, until we have thoroughly lived into it and made ourselves at home in it; nor does it sever itself from an old universe, until we have thoroughly broken off our connection with it. Hence a man will often feel a pain of Conscience, or *quasi*-Conscience, in doing an action which his reason has taught him to regard as perfectly allowable [1] or even as a positive duty; while, on the other hand, he will often be able to violate a recently discovered obligation without feeling any pain. [2] In general, however, the pains of Conscience attend any inconsistency with the principles which we recognize as highest; and these, in general, are the principles recognized as binding within the social universe in which we habitually live. [3]

With these remarks, we may pass on to the more detailed consideration of social ethics—*i. e.* to the consideration of the moral order within which the life of

1 "The contradiction between reason and feeling which some of us will recollect, when first we permitted ourselves to take a row or attend a concert on Sunday, is a good example from contemporary life" (Muirhead's *Elements of Ethics*, p. 80).

2 Hence, partly, the frequency of "back-sliding" in converts to new principles. Conscience does not respond to their shortcomings with sufficient readiness. It may be noted here also that it is often possible to stifle Conscience by transferring ourselves from one universe to another. Thus, a man may perform, under the influence of fanatical zeal, acts of cruelty from which, in his normal state, he would shrink in horror. He stifles Conscience by escaping from the universe in which such acts are condemned into one in which they are rather approved. A good illustration of this is given by Macaulay in his account of the state of mind of the Master of Stair in sanctioning the massacre of Glencoe (*History of England*, chap. xviii.).

3 For general discussion of the subject of Conscience, see Porter's *Elements of Moral Science*, Part I., chap. xvi., Dewey's *Outlines of Ethics*, pp. 182–206, and Muirhead's *Elements of Ethics*, pp. 73–84 and 238–242

the individual is spent, and of the relation of the individual life to that moral order. Of course this can be done, in such a work as this, only in the most sketchy fashion. But some remarks on the ethical significance of the recognized moral institutions, duties and virtues, may be found helpful.

CHAPTER II.

MORAL INSTITUTIONS.

§ 1. THE SOCIAL IMPERATIVE.—We have seen to some extent what the nature of the "ought" is. It is, as we may say, the law imposed by our ideal self upon our actual self. Since, however, the ideal self is the rational self, and since the rational self is not realized in isolation, but in a society of human beings, it follows that this "ought" is imposed on societies as well as on individuals. As Mr. Herbert Spencer says,[1] "we must consider the ideal man as existing in the ideal social state"; and in considering such an ideal we pass a criticism not only on existing men, but on existing social states. Not only can we say that an individual *ought* to act in such and such a way, but we can also say that a society *ought* to have such and such a constitution.[2] In so far as an individual acts as he ought to act, we say that his conduct is right, and that he is a good, upright, or moral man. In so far as a society is constituted as it ought to be, we say that it is a well-ordered society, and that its constitution is just. In each case we compare actually existing men or states with the ideal of a rational man and a rationally

[1] *Data of Ethics*, chap. xvi., § 106.

[2] It may be asked, On whom is this "ought" imposed? The answer is, on the society as a whole, and more particularly on its politicians and other "active citizens."

constituted state. The latter of these we must now briefly consider.[1]

§ 2. JUSTICE.—"Blessed," it is said, "are they that hunger and thirst after justice."[2] But perhaps it is more easy to hunger and thirst after it than to define precisely what it means. Here, at any rate, we can only indicate its nature in the vaguest and most general way. For a fuller treatment reference must be made to works on Politics.

A just arrangement of society may be briefly defined as one in which the ideal life of all its members is promoted as efficiently as possible. The constitution of a society is, therefore, unjust when large classes in it are so enslaved by others as to be unable to develop their own lives. It is unjust, for instance, when there is any class in it so poor, or so hard-worked, or so dependent on others, as to be unable to cultivate their faculties and make progress towards the perfection of

[1] A complete discussion of this subject belongs rather to Politics or Social Philosophy than to Ethics. But it seems necessary to consider it here, in so far as it can be dealt with from a purely ethical point of view. Some of the points dealt with here are somewhat more fully discussed in my *Introduction to Social Philosophy*, chaps. v. and vi. English writers on Ethics have, as a rule, not given much attention to the subjects referred to in this chapter. Reference may, however, be made to Stephen's *Science of Ethics*, chap. iii., Porter's *Elements of Moral Science*, Part. II., chaps. xiii.—xvi., Rickaby's *Moral Philosophy*, and Clark Murray's *Introduction to Ethics*, Book II., Part II., chap. i. For fuller treatment the student must consult such works as those of Höffding and Paulsen. Some of the points are also referred to by Prof. Gizycki, whose work has been adapted for the use of English readers by Dr. Stanton Coit. Hegel's *Philosophie des Rechts* must, however, still be regarded as the model for the treatment of this whole subject. It has recently been translated into English by Professor Dyde.

[2] The Greek word δικαιοσύνη, translated "righteousness," may equally well be rendered by "justice."

their nature.[1] It is unjust when the idle are protected and set in power, and the laborious are crushed down and degraded.

To free society from such arrangements as these has been one of the chief efforts, perhaps the chief effort, of the wise and good in all ages; and there are certainly few things to which a student of Applied Ethics should give more attention than the methods by which this has been and may still be done. The subject is, however, much too complicated for such an elementary treatise as this, or indeed for any treatise; and all that we can here do is to indicate some of the main points that have to be attended to in constructing a just order of society.[2]

§ 3. LAW AND PUBLIC OPINION.—The first thing to be observed is that a just arrangement of society can be only to a certain extent *enforced*. The saying has often been quoted—

> "How small of all that human hearts endure
> That part which kings or laws can cause or cure!"

And it is partly true, if it be taken to apply simply to that which can be directly and immediately accomplished by positive laws. Laws are inefficient when a

1 In a just social state, every human being must be treated as an absolute end. It follows from this, however, that no one can be treated as *the* absolute end: otherwise every one else would be treated only as a means with reference to this one. Hence every one must be treated at once as means and as end.

2 The accounts of Justice given by Plato and Aristotle (*Republic* and *Ethics*) have never been surpassed. For more modern discussions, the student may be referred to Mill's *Utilitarianism*, chap. v., Sidgwick's *Methods of Ethics*, Book III., chap. v., and *Principles of Political Economy*, Book III., chaps. vi. and vii., and Stephen's *Science of Ethics*, chap. v., §§ 35–39. See the Note at the end of this chapter.

people is by nature lawless; and when a people has become orderly or wise, laws may often be allowed to sink into abeyance. The conditions of life are continually changing, and positive laws which were beneficial at one time begin gradually to have a pernicious effect. It is, consequently, in many departments of life of far more importance to try to develop good habits of action and of opinion in a people than to furnish it with hard and fast positive enactments.[1] Nevertheless, the sphere of positive law is a great one. Public opinion grows very slowly, and there are always considerable bodies in a community who are unaffected by it, unless it takes the form of definite laws, with punishments attached. Sometimes, after such laws have fulfilled their purpose, it becomes desirable to repeal them. St. Paul said of the Jewish law that it was "a schoolmaster to lead men to Christ"; meaning that as soon as men grasped the true meaning of the moral ideal they could dispense with the narrow injunctions of the law, which, nevertheless, were necessary as a preparation. So it is with nearly all laws. They are too rigid and formal for human beings, as soon as they attain to true freedom; but they are necessary at first as a check upon licentiousness. What men do at first from fear, they learn by and by to do from habit, and afterwards from conscious will. Law comes first, then habit, then virtue.[2]

[1] This seems to express the element of truth in much of what is said by Mr. H. Spencer in his famous, but extremely one-sided book, *The Man* versus *the State*. Some aspects of the same point are brought out, in a more guarded way, in *Aspects of the Social Problem*, edited by Dr. Bosanquet.

[2] Mr. Muirhead quotes (*Elements of Ethics*, p. 93, note), a story about Connop Thirlwall. "who on one occasion became involved in a

§ 4. Rights and Obligations.—The forces of law and of public opinion are mainly concerned with the establishment of men's rights and obligations. These terms are strictly correlative. Every right brings an obligation with it; and that not merely in the obvious sense that when one man has a right other men are under an obligation to respect it, but also in the more subtle sense that when a man has a right he is thereby laid under an obligation to employ it for the general good. This fact is concealed from many men's minds through a certain confusion between legal and moral obligation. It is generally convenient to enforce the observance of rights by positive laws; whereas it is not generally convenient to enforce the corresponding obligation. Hence it comes to be thought that there is no obligation at all. For instance, it is convenient to protect property; whereas it would be very troublesome and dangerous to try to compel men to use their property wisely—and indeed any such attempt, beyond certain narrow limits, is almost bound to defeat its own ends. Hence it comes to be said that a man "may do what he likes with his own." *Legally*, he may; but *morally*, he is under the obligation to use his own for the general good, just as strictly as if it were another's. A man's rights, in fact, are nothing more than those things which, for the sake of the general good, it is convenient that he should be allowed to possess.

discussion with the late Dr. Christopher Wordsworth, Bishop of Lincoln, when the latter was residing at Trinity College, about the retention of enforced attendance at chapel. 'It is a choice,' said the Bishop, between compulsory religion and no religion at all.' 'The distinction,' replied Thirlwall, 'is too subtle for my mental grasp, The same might be said of compulsory morality · it is equivalent

And since it is for the sake of the general good that he possesses them, he is bound to use them for that end. By himself, a man has no right to anything whatever. He is a part of a social whole; and he has a right only to that which it is for the good of the whole that he should have. Let us consider very briefly the nature of some of the more important of these rights.

§ 5. THE RIGHTS OF MAN. (*a*) *Life.*—The first of human rights is the right to live. This right follows at once from the fact that the moral end is a personal one—a form of self-realization. If the end which men sought were some impersonal object, life might reasonably be sacrificed to that. And, indeed, as the self to be realized is the social self, the individual will sometimes be justified in sacrificing his life for the sake of his society. But such cases are exceptional. As a rule, the human good requires the continuance of life for its realization. Hence it is important that the sacredness of life should be recognized. In some primitive forms of society even this fundamental right is not acknowledged. Children are frequently exposed, and captives in war are put to death without hesitation. And even in partly civilized communities the sacredness of life is sometimes very lightly treated—*e. g.* where the practice of duelling is permitted. Indeed if the value of life were fully appreciated, there can be little doubt that even war would soon be abolished among civilized nations. At present, however,

to no morality at all." This is of course true; yet compulsory morality may form an education towards true morality. This would also have been at least a partial answer to Thirlwall. *Cf.* Höffding's *Outlines of Psychology*, p. 76. Mr. Muirhead notices the qualification at a later stage, pp. 179–180.

it remains a true maxim, *Si vis pacem para bellum.* Again, it must be observed that the right of life cannot be said to be really secured to all the citizens of a community unless the means of obtaining a livelihood are secured. The right to live thus seems to involve the right to labour.[1]

The right of life, like all rights, brings an obligation with it—*viz.* the obligation of treating life, both one's own and that of others, as a sacred thing. He who violates this obligation—*e. g.* by murder—forfeits the right of life, and may legitimately be deprived of it.

(*b*) *Freedom.*—The next right is that of freedom. The necessity of this rests mainly on the fact that the moral ideal has to be realized by the individual will. Hence the individual, in order to realize his supreme end, must be free to exercise his will. The recognition of this right usually comes much later than that of life.[2] Slavery existed long after the stage at which prisoners

1 This point was emphasized by Louis Blanc and some other socialistic writers. The question how far, and by what means, such a right is to be secured, must be left to writers on Politics and Economics, who again must probably hand it over in the end to the practical good sense of mankind.

2 Hegel remarked (*Philosophy of History*, Introduction) that the Oriental nations recognized only that *one* is free—*i. e.* the Despot: the Greeks, on the other hand, recognized that *some* are free—*viz.* the Greek citizens themselves—while Barbarians were thought to be naturally fitted for slavery: while it has been reserved for modern times, under the influence of Christianity, to demand that *all* shall be free. This demand has been especially prominent since the time of the Reformation. Sometimes it is even pushed to an extreme—*e. g.* by Rousseau and by the Economists of the *laissez faire* school. For extreme views in recent times, see *A Plea for Liberty* and Spencer's *The Man* versus *the State;* and for a criticism of these views, see Ritchie's *Principles of State Interference.*

of war were put to death; and even now, after the abolition of slavery, the conditions of contract with regard to labour and to property are often of such a kind as seriously to interfere with men's liberty in the conduct of their lives. Of course freedom in any absolute sense is not possible, and ought not to be aimed at. It can never be permissible in any well-ordered community that its members should do as they please. The right which it is desirable to secure is the right of having the free development of one's life as little interfered with as is possible, consistently with the maintenance of social order.

The right of freedom brings with it the obligation of using one's freedom for the attainment of rational ends. Milton rightly said of liberty, "who love that must first be wise and good."[1] It is only on this assumption that liberty can be granted in a well-ordered state. Hence the slowness in the acquisition of freedom is not without justification. Freedom is not a commodity that can be bought or given: it must be earned.

(*c*) *Property.*—The right of property may almost be regarded as part of the right of freedom. Nearly all the ends at which a man can aim require instruments; and if a man has not the right to use these instruments, his liberty of pursuing the ends is practically rendered void. Since, however, instruments—especially such instruments as the soil of a country—are limited in amount, it becomes a difficult question to

[1] *Cf.* also what Milton says on this point in his *Tenure of Kings and Magistrates*, § 1: "None can love freedom heartily, but good men: the rest love not freedom, but licence; which never hath more scope or more indulgence than under tyrants."

decide how the use of them is to be apportioned among the members of a community. If their use is reserved for a few, the great majority of the citizens are to a certain extent deprived of their liberty. The discussion of this question, however, must be left to writers on Politics. From a purely ethical point of view, we can only insist on the importance of the right of property, as a means of securing the possibility of a free development of life.

The right of property involves the obligation to use it wisely for the general good. In communities where the fulfilment of this obligation cannot in the main be relied on, the right of property cannot be granted. In primitive communities there is practically no such right. Everything is possessed in common. It is only as men become civilized and educated that they begin to be capable of being entrusted with property; and even then it is usually necessary that the right should be carefully guarded against misuse.[1] Some writers (*e. g.* Plato) have thought that in an ideal state there ought to be a community of goods, and no right of private property.[2] But this appears to be a mistake.

1 Strictly speaking, from a purely ethical point of view, it may be said that a man has no right to any kind of property except that which he has made an essential part of his own being. Hence a German writer, G. Simmel, says pointedly, "Ich habe wirklich nur das was ich bin" ("Strictly speaking I possess nothing but what I am") (*Einleitung in die Moralwissenschaft*, p. 172). But of course it would be impossible to observe this principle in practical politics. This does not, however, make it any the less important to take account of it.

2 See his *Republic*, Books IV. and V. The precise extent to which Plato intended to carry out the principle of community is not altogether clear. For a recent advocacy of communism, see Morris's *News from Nowhere.*

Aristotle was probably right in thinking[1] rather that in an ideal state every one should have the free use of the necessary instruments,[2] but should be taught to use them for the common good.

(*d*) *Contract.*—Another important right is the right to the fulfilment of contracts. If one man engages to render certain services to another, the second has the right to receive these services. In primitive societies there is scarcely any such thing as contract. The relations of men to one another are fixed almost from their birth, and are altered only by force.[3] Hence it has been said[4] that societies develop "from status to contract."

The right of contract involves the obligation to enter into no contracts except those that can be reasonably fulfilled. A man is not at liberty, for instance, to contract himself into slavery.[5] Nor is any one entitled, even if he were able, to enter into such a contract as that of Faust with Mephistopheles. Hence the right of contract, like that of property, is possible only in a

[1] *Politics*, II., v.

[2] Whether land, and other forms of property that are not capable of being indefinitely multiplied, can be dealt with on the same principle, is a much more difficult question.

[3] On the other hand, in modern times, contract has become so common a method of entering into relationship, that some writers have been tempted to think that all relationships are founded on such engagements. The State, for instance, was said to rest on a "social contract." Hobbes and Rousseau were the chief upholders of this view. An eloquent attack was made on it by Burke in his *Reflections on the Revolution in France.* See Muirhead's *Elements of Ethics*, p. 177, *note.* There is a good criticism in Hume's *Essays* ("Of the Original Contract").

[4] Maine's *Ancient Law*, chap. v.

[5] Hence the fallacy of Carlyle's view, that slavery consists simply in hiring a man's services for life. See his *Latter-Day Pamphlets.* A man has no right to contract away his own freedom.

highly-developed community, and even then requires considerable safeguards.[1]

(*e*) *Education.*—The last right which it seems necessary to notice here, is the right of education. In this case the right and obligation are so closely united that it is scarcely possible to distinguish them. Every one, we may say, has both the right and the obligation of being educated according to his capacity; since education is necessary for the realization of the rational self. This is a right which has been but tardily recognized even in some highly-civilized countries; and even now in many of them the highest kinds of education are practically inaccessible to the mass of the people. But it is clear that in a well-ordered state every one ought to have the means of developing his faculties to the best advantage.

§ 6. Ultimate Meaning of Rights and Obligations.—A little reflection may convince us that the ultimate significance of rights and obligations is simply this. We have a right to the means that are necessary for the development of our lives in the direction that is best for the highest good of the community of which we are members; and we are under the obligation to use the means in the best way for the attainment of this end.[2]

1 Men who are in a disadvantageous position (owing to poverty, for instance) are apt to be induced to form contracts on unfair conditions. It is desirable that they should be, as far as possible, guarded against this.

2 Of course I refer here to rights and obligations in the ethical sense. To what extent, and by what means, these rights and obligations are to be acknowledged and enforced in actual states, are questions for the political philosopher. On these subjects reference may be made to Sidgwick's *Elements of Politics*, especially chaps. iii.—vi., and chap. x.

§ 7. Social Institutions.—There are various ways in which men group themselves together in a society; and the relations in which they are thus brought to one another are often of so much ethical significance that it is desirable to notice briefly some of the more important of them.

(*a*) *The Family.*—The family is based on natural affection. Its chief objects are to provide adequate protection and care for the helplessness of childhood, and at the same time to provide an adequate sphere for the highest forms of friendship and love. It is thought that as a rule the former object can be better secured by the affection of the parents than it could be by any state arrangements;[1] and that the latter object is best fulfilled within a narrow circle.[2] The control of parents, however, requires to be in many ways limited. Thus it seems necessary to enforce the proper education of children, and to prevent them from being employed in unsuitable work at too early an age. The relation of husband and wife in the family is properly one of equality; but where this is not secured by mutual affection, it seems impossible for any state regulations to prevent the subordination of one to the other, without an intolerable interference with indi-

[1] Plato, however, thought otherwise. See his *Republic*, Book V.

[2] Among the Greeks, in the classical age, the highest forms of friendship were practically always between men. The low position of women prevented them from sharing in the higher life of the citizen. Greek views of the family life are almost entirely vitiated by this fact; just as their views of industrial life are vitiated by their acceptance of slavery, and by their contempt for all forms of manual labour except agriculture. On the Family, see Hegel's *Philosophy of Right;* also Rickaby's *Moral Philosophy*, Part II., chap. vi., and Devas's *Studies of Family Life*. Aristotle's treatment of the subject in the first two Books of the *Politics* is still highly suggestive.

vidual liberty. This is, therefore, a matter on which it is important to develop a strong public opinion. A good deal, however, can be done by law in removing disabilities which stand in the way of the recognition of perfect equality.[1]

(*b*) *The Workshop.*—Industrial relations are strongly contrasted with those of the family. They are not based on mutual affection but on contract; and they are not relations of equality but of subordination. No doubt, in the family also there is the subordination of children to their parents; but this is the subordination of the undeveloped to the developed, of the helpless to their natural protectors; whereas in the industrial life the subordination which exists is not with a view to the protection or development of those who are subordinated, but simply with a view to external ends. In these circumstances it is important to make such regulations as will secure fairness of contract, and prevent subordination from becoming slavery. It has sometimes been made a matter of regret that, as civilization advances, the relations of men in industrial life depart more and more from the type of the family. Formerly the relation between master and apprentice was almost

[1] Mr. Leslie Stephen has objected (*Science of Ethics*, chap. iii., §§ 36–39) to the common practice of classing the family along with other forms of social organization, on the ground that it rests on physiological necessities, and that it is rather a basis than a result of political unity. For a student of sociology or politics this contention would, I think, have some force. The ethical significance of the family, however, does not appear to me to be affected by it. Besides, the existence of the family, in any developed sense of the term, seems to require some kind of legal or *quasi*-legal sanctions, enforcing acknowledged rights of marriage, whether in the form of polyandry, polygamy, or monogamy. It thus presupposes social organization, and varies with the growth of that organization.

of a paternal character; whereas now, as Carlyle used to say,[1] there is nothing but the "cash *nexus*." But it is doubtful whether this ought to be made a matter for regret. A paternal relationship easily passes into tyranny when there is no basis of natural affection. It is probably best that business relationships should be made a matter of pure contract. This may to some slight extent interfere with the development of relations of mutual kindness and loyalty; but there can be little doubt that to a much greater extent it helps to prevent injustice. The feelings of kindness are more likely to arise in men as neighbours and fellow-citizens than as masters and servants;[2] and the practical offices of help can probably be better undertaken by society as a whole than by particular employers.

At the same time it cannot be doubted that anything that can be done to make the relation of subordination less harsh is in the highest degree desirable. For this reason all forms of co-operation that are practicable ought to be earnestly promoted. The question, What kinds of industry ought to be encouraged or discouraged? is also largely an ethical question; though the methods by which industries may advantageously be promoted or impeded, must be left to be discussed by economists and political philosophers. Under modern conditions of industrial life, industries are promoted or retarded chiefly[3] by changes in the demand for the objects produced by them; and these again are brought

[1] See his *Past and Present;* and *cf.* below, pp. 346, 410.

[2] At least in the former relationship they are more likely to become widely diffused: perhaps when they do arise in the latter relationship, they are apt to be more intense.

[3] Setting aside changes in natural conditions, and changes pro-

about mainly by changes in men's tastes, fashions, and habits of life. Now in so far as the objects brought into demand by such changes are necessary for the preservation or maintenance or advancement of human life, and in so far as the industries by which they are produced are not injurious to human life, there can be no question about their moral justification. The ethical question, therefore, arises chiefly with regard to the use of what are called luxuries, and to the use of objects which can be produced only by means of dangerous or deleterious processes. And the question which thus arises can be answered only by balancing the advantages which such objects bring towards the advancement of the supreme end of life against the loss occasioned by their injurious effects.[1]

(c) *The Civic Community.*—If men's business relations are to be purely a matter of contract, it is necessary that the community as a whole should undertake those more paternal functions which cannot conveniently be left to the care of individuals. This is partly the business of the central government; but to a great extent it can be more conveniently managed by each district for itself. The care which has to be exercised over the citizens consists in such matters as the provision of sanitary arrangements (including baths, and

duced by new discoveries and inventions, with which Ethics is only very indirectly concerned (since the question, how far men should be allowed to make and utilize new discoveries can scarcely at the present time be regarded as a practical one).

[1] There have been several interesting discussions of Luxury in recent times. See, for instance, Bosanquet's *Civilization of Christendom*, MacCunn's *Ethics of Citizenship*, L. Stephen's *Social Rights and Duties*, Smart's *Studies in Economics*, and the article by Professor Sidgwick in the *International Journal of Ethics*, Vol. V. no. 1.

the like), the means of education (including well-furnished public libraries), the enforcement of precautions against accidents, the prevention of adulteration of foods and other forms of deception, and the securing of the means of livelihood to those who are incapacitated for labour. The discussion of the details of such provisions, and of the question whether they can be best managed by a central authority or by local administrations, must be left to writers on Politics.

(*d*) *The Church.*—The paternal care of the citizens, however, cannot be fully provided by any form of civic machinery. There must always be a certain hardness in all such machinery, which must be managed on a basis of law and not of affection. Hence it is necessary that it should be supplemented by more personal relations among the citizens. A centre for such personal relationships is furnished by the Church, whose function it is to secure the carrying out of the highest moral ideal in human relationships. It is greatly to be regretted that differences of religious opinion prevent the Church from being so efficient in this way as it might otherwise be. There can be little doubt that in the Middle Ages, under the sway of Catholicism, its work was more efficiently done—if it is in reality possible to compare the action of institutions under very different conditions of social life. Perhaps it may be found necessary to supplement the work of the Churches by unsectarian ethical institutions. But the discussion of this question would not be suitable for an elementary text-book;[1] and indeed it could

[1] It is, however, discussed at considerable length by Prof. Gizycki in his *Introduction to the Study of Ethics* (Dr. Coit's adaptation), chap. ix.

scarcely be satisfactorily answered without introducing considerations that are not of a purely ethical character. The same remark applies to the discussion of the important question of the right relation of the Churches to the State.

(*e*) *The State.*—The State is the supreme controller of all social relationships. It makes laws and sees that they are enforced. It also carries on various kinds of work that cannot conveniently be left to private enterprise. It undertakes, for instance, the provision of the means of national defence, the conveyance of letters, and in some countries the conducting of railways. The extent to which it is desirable that such work should be undertaken by the State, cannot be discussed in an ethical treatise. But it is important to insist that any one who seeks to answer this question, must answer it by a consideration of the degree to which such action tends to promote the highest life of the citizens of the State.

(*f*) *Friendship.* These are some of the leading forms of social unity, but the relationships between human beings, through which the moral life is developed, are not exhausted by these. Such a relationship as that of individual friendship has also to be noted. This was a form of unity to which the ancient Greek writers on Ethics gave special attention, and, in particular, it rose into the highest degree of prominence in the speculations of the Epicureans, with whom it may almost be said to have taken the place of the State. In modern times the expansion of man's social universe through books, travel, &c., may have somewhat diminished the significance of these closer personal ties; but it still remains true that in a friend a man may find an *alter ego* through whom the universe of his personality is enlarged in a more perfect way than is possible by any other form of relationship, especially in cases of ideal friendship like that of Tennyson and Hallam, when it can be said, "He was rich where I was poor." This also, however, is a form of relationship to which we can do nothing more than allude.[1]

§ 8. SOCIAL PROGRESS.—All the institutions to which reference has now been made, are continually undergoing changes, which are rendered necessary by the progressive civilization of mankind. In carrying out such changes it is important to see that they are not made with a view to merely temporary advantages, and that the advantages which they secure are not bought with any loss of human efficiency. The ultimate standard by which all progress must be tested is the realization of the rational self. Material and social progress is valuable only in so far as it is a means to this. The nature of this progress will be somewhat more fully considered in a succeeding chapter.

§ 9. INDIVIDUALISM AND SOCIALISM.—In recent times discussions with regard to social progress have appeared chiefly in the form of the question, whether we ought to move in an individualistic or in a socialistic direction. Individualists think that it is chiefly important to secure, as far as possible, the freedom of action of the individual citizens. Socialists, on the other hand, think that what is chiefly desirable is to regulate the actions of individuals so as to secure the good of all. It does not appear, however, that there is any

[1] The discussion of Friendship in Aristotle's *Nicomachean Ethics* is perhaps still the best that we have. See also MacCunn's *Ethics of Citizenship*, II.

real opposition between the principles of Individualism and of Socialism.[1] The good of all can certainly not be secured if the nature of each is cramped and underfed; nor can freedom be allowed to each except on the assumption that that freedom will on the whole be used for the good of all. The question that ought to be asked is—In what directions is it desirable to give men more freedom, and in what directions is it desirable that their actions should be more controlled? It is a question of detail, and it must be answered differently at different stages of human development. Perhaps at the present time it is chiefly in the socialistic direction that advance is demanded. But the reason is simply that in recent generations the individualistic side has been too strongly insisted on. This again is mainly due to the fact that in recent times the main social advance has consisted in the emancipation of highly-skilled labour from cumbersome restraints. The problem of the next age is rather that of providing a truly human life for those who are less skilled and capable, and who are consequently less able to look after their own interests. The former advance could be made by individualistic methods: the latter seems to demand a certain degree of Socialism.[2] But here again we can do no more than indicate, quite generally and roughly, the nature of the problem involved.

1 From the point of view of Ethics, we may say that both Individualism and Socialism supply us with economic commandments. The commandment of Individualism is—Thou shalt not pauperize; or Every one must be allowed to work out his own salvation. The commandment of Socialism is—Thou shalt not exploit, or No one must be used as a mere means to any one else's salvation.

2 This subject is treated with considerable fulness by Prof. Paulsen in his *System der Ethik*, vol. ii. Book IV. iii., 3. On the general sub-

ject of Socialism as a question of practical politics, the student may consult Sidgwick's *Principles of Political Economy*, Book III., chaps. ii—vii., and *Elements of Politics*, chap. x. See also his *Methods of Ethics*, Book III., chap. v. Reference may also be made to Montague's *Limits of Individual Liberty*, Ritchie's *Principles of State Interference*, Schaffle's *Quintessence of Socialism*, Gonner's *Socialist State*, Kirkup's *Inquiry into Socialism*, Rae's *Contemporary Socialism*, Graham's *Socialism New and Old*, Rickaby's *Moral Philosophy*, Gilman's *Socialism and the American Spirit*, McKechnie's *The State and the Individual*, Donisthorpe's *Individualism*, &c. A singularly searching examination of the ideas underlying Individualism and Socialism has lately appeared in Mr. Bosanquet's *Civilization of Christendom*. The recent discussions in the *International Journal of Ethics*, Vols. VI. and VII. are also valuable.

NOTE ON JUSTICE.

Anything like a complete discussion of the difficult conception of Justice would evidently be quite beyond the scope of such a text-book as this. But a few remarks seem to be called for.

Much confusion has arisen in the treatment of this subject from a failure to observe an ambiguity in the term which was well known even to Plato and Aristotle, but which some modern writers seem to have forgotten. The term "Justice" is used in two distinct senses. We speak of a "just man," and we speak of a "just law" or a "just government." Just, in the former sense, means almost the same as morally good: it means morally good in respect to the fulfilment of social obligations. Justice, then, in this sense is equivalent to all virtue in its social aspect.[1] On the other hand, when we speak of a just law or a just government, we mean one that is fair or impartial[2] in dealing with those to whom it applies or over whom it rules.[3] This ambiguity in the use of the term is partly concealed by the fact that we sometimes speak of a man as being just in the same sense as that in which the term is applied to a law or government—*viz.* in those cases in which a man occupies a position of authority (as a judge, a king, or even a parent), so as to be a representative of law or government. Hence many writers have failed to perceive that there are two senses in which the term is used. The confusion between these two senses vitiates, for example, nearly all that is said about Justice in the fifth chapter of Mill's *Utilitarianism*. The influence of the same ambiguity seems, moreover, to be not without effect even on some

---

[1] See Aristotle's *Ethics*, Book V., chap. i. Sometimes, however, when we speak of a "just man" we mean merely one who fulfils those obligations that are enforced by positive law. *Cf.* below, chap. iii., § 12. But I do not think that this use of the term is common, or to be commended.

[2] *Ibid.*, chap. ii.

[3] Justice is derived from the Latin *jus*, law. This again is cognate with *jussum*, meaning what is *ordered*. A just man means one who obeys orders, *i. e.* the moral orders or laws. A just law or government on the other hand, means one that possesses the qualities that belong to, or ought to belong to, a law (*jus*)—*viz.* in particular, the quality of fairness or impartiality.

more recent writers. Dr. Sidgwick carefully distinguishes [1] between the two senses of Justice now referred to, and states that he intends to confine himself to the second. Nevertheless, one of his illustrations appears to refer to Justice rather in the first sense. He remarks [2] that we cannot say, "in treating of the private conduct of individuals, that *all* arbitrary inequality is recognized as unjust: it would not be commonly thought unjust in a rich bachelor with no near relatives to leave the bulk of his property in providing pensions exclusively for indigent red-haired men, however unreasonable and capricious the choice might appear." When it is said that this is not unjust, does not this mean simply that it is not contrary to any recognized moral obligation? And is not the term, therefore, used in its first sense? If a law, or a government, or even a parent in dealing with his children, were to exhibit any similar caprice to that here supposed by Dr. Sidgwick, would not this be at once regarded as unjust? In such a case, we should be using the term in its second sense. The person supposed by Dr. Sidgwick is not said to be unjust, apparently simply for the reason that he is not in a position in which Justice, in this sense, can be predicated of him at all. A man cannot, in this sense, be either just or unjust, unless he represents some form of law or government.

But there is a still further ambiguity in the use of the term. And this also was pointed out by Aristotle.[3] In speaking of Justice in the sense of fairness, we may be referring either to the apportionment of goods or to the apportionment of evils. Now evil can be fairly apportioned only to those who have done evil—*i. e.* as punishment. Justice, then, may be either distributive or corrective. But sometimes the term is used emphatically in the latter sense as if this were its exclusive use. To "do justice" is frequently understood as meaning simply to award punishment. Thus, there is an ambiguity between the broader sense of the term, including distributive and corrective Justice, and the narrower sense in which it is confined to the latter. Mill seems to have been misled by this ambiguity also. Thus, when he says that "the two essential ingredients in the sentiment of Justice are, the desire to punish a person who has done harm, and the knowledge or belief that there is some definite individual or individuals to whom harm has been done," he seems to

---

[1] *Methods of Ethics*, p. 264–5, *note* 2.

[2] *Ibid.*, p. 268–9, *note*.

[3] *Op. cit.*, Book V., chap. ii.

be referring exclusively to corrective Justice, without being aware that he is dealing only with a part of the subject.

As far as I can judge, Aristotle's treatment of the whole subject of Justice is still the best that we have. Dr. Sidgwick's treatment, however, to which reference has just been made, has of course the advantage of being more fully adapted to modern conditions of knowledge and practice.

CHAPTER III.

THE DUTIES.

§ 1. Nature of Moral Laws.—The Jews, by whom the moral consciousness of the modern world has been perhaps mainly determined,[1] summed up their view of duty in the form of ten commandments. And we find in other nations also a certain more or less explicit recognition of definite rules to which a good man must adhere—rules which say expressly, Do this, Abstain from that.[2] Now, in the moral "ought," as we have so far considered it, there are no such explicit com-

[1] It is hard to say whether the Jews or the Greeks have had most influence on us in this respect. See Hatch's *Hibbert Lectures;* and *cf.*, for a vigorous but very paradoxical view of the same subject, Duhring's *Ersatz der Religion.*

[2] The Greeks had no definite code of moral rules. Their earliest moral wisdom was expressed rather in brief proverbial sayings, such as μηδὲν ἄγαν ("nothing to excess"). Among the Greeks, however, as among all early peoples, the laws of the State furnished a basis for moral obligation, just as a child's first ideas of duty are derived from the commands of its parents. The dawning of the consciousness that there is a deeper basis of moral obligation than State laws is illustrated in the *Antigone* of Sophocles. It was largely because the early Greeks had no clear distinction between the moral law and the laws of the State that the criticisms of the Sophists (and to some extent of Socrates) were felt to be subversive of morality. See Zeller's *Pre-Socratic Philosophy*, vol. ii., p. 404, and *Socrates and the Socratic Schools*, pp. 219—221. It is noteworthy also that the absoluteness of the Jewish Law showed signs of breaking down, as soon as the Jews had lost their national independence. *Cf.* above, Book I., chap. V.

mands contained. There is only the general command to realize the rational self. We must now consider what is the place of particular rules within this general commandment.

What has been said in the last chapter may help us to do this. For we have seen there that there are certain definite, though at the same time somewhat elastic and modifiable, rights that come to be gradually recognized in human societies; and these definite rights bring definite obligations along with them. Such obligations may be expressed in the form of commandments.

It is not merely, however, in connection with these recognized rights that such obligations arise. Obligations arise in connection with all the institutions of social life, and in connection with all the relationships into which men are brought to one another. No doubt there is a certain right corresponding to all such obligations, just as there is an obligation corresponding to every right.[1] But sometimes it is the right that is obvious, and the obligation seems to follow it, whereas in other cases it is the obligation that is more easily recognized. In the preceding chapter we have considered some of the more prominent rights and institu-

1 Rights are also for the most part connected with definite institutions, or forms of social organization. Hence duties also tend to cluster round them. Thus, Mr. Alexander says (*Moral Order and Progress*, p. 253) that "Duties are the conduct . . . by which institutions are maintained": "the duty of recording a vote . . . gives effect to the institution of parliamentary franchise." It seems an exaggeration, however, to say that all duties are related to institutions in this way. The duty of regard for life, for instance, seems to be independent of any special institutions—unless we are to describe life itself as an "institution," which would be somewhat paradoxical.

tions that have grown up in social life. In this chapter we are to consider the more prominent obligations that have come to be recognized among men, as presenting themselves in the form of commandments, and to try to bring out the precise ethical significance of these elements in the moral consciousness. In the one case, as in the other, it would probably be useless to attempt to give an exhaustive classification.

§ 2. RESPECT FOR LIFE.—The first commandment is the commandment to respect life, corresponding directly to the right of life. This commandment is expressed in the form, Thou shalt not kill; and its meaning is so obvious that it requires little comment. We must merely observe that the commandment which bids us have respect for life enjoins much more than the mere passive abstinence from the destruction of another's physical existence. It involves also the care of our own, and the avoidance of anything likely to injure either our own or another's physical well-being. How much this implies, we are only gradually learning. Mr. Herbert Spencer has done admirable service in emphasizing this side of moral law.[1]

§ 3. RESPECT FOR FREEDOM.—The second commandment corresponds to the right of Freedom. It forbids any interference with the development of another man's life, except in so far as such interference may be required to help on that development itself. It may be expressed in the form, Treat every human being as a person, never as a mere thing. In this form, it may

[1] See especially his *Data of Ethics*, chap. xi., and *The Principles of Ethics*, Part III. *Cf.* also Clark Murray's *Iutroduction to Ethics*, Book II., Part II., chap. ii., and Adler's *Moral Instruction lo Children* Lecture XII.

be regarded as forbidding slavery, despotism, exploitation, prostitution, and every other form of the use of another as a mere means to one's own ends. This commandment and the preceding one are closely connected together. They might, in fact, be regarded as one; for the destruction of the life of another is simply an extreme form of interference with his free development. There is also a third commandment which is closely connected with these two, and which we may notice next.

§ 4. Respect for Character.—This may be stated as the commandment to respect character. It is the positive of which the two preceding are the negative. It not merely forbids us to injure our neighbour or to do anything that will interfere with his free development, but also positively bids us observe, as far as we can, what will further him. It was of this commandment that St. Paul was thinking when he said, "All things are lawful for me, but all things are not expedient." By the ordinary negative law he was permitted to do anything that did not positively injure another; but he was conscious that, in addition to this, he ought to abstain from anything that would tend to prevent the furtherance of another in his development. To partake of certain meats would not interfere either with the life or with the freedom of any one; but, having regard to the stage of development at which they stand, we may be aware that it would be injurious to them. Of course, we might regard this principle as simply an extension of the negative principle of respect for freedom. But perhaps it is better to regard it as positive; for when we thus have regard for the stage of development at which any one stands, we shall be led not merely to abstain from that which will injure him, but also to do that which will help him. The simplest way of summing up this commandment is perhaps to say, in Hegel's[1] language, "Be a person, and respect others as persons."

§ 5. RESPECT FOR PROPERTY.—The next commandment is, Thou shalt not steal. This is simply a carrying out of the preceding. It forbids any appropriation of the instruments of another's well-being, whether they be material things that belong to him, or such goods as time, reputation, and the like. This commandment is, as I say, involved in the preceding. For the development of a man's personality involves the use of instruments; and the right of an individual to appropriate these involves the obligation on the part of all others of leaving his possession of them inviolate. The commandment to respect property ought, however, to be regarded as involving something more than the mere condemnation of theft. It involves regard for our own property as well as that of others. It condemns, therefore, any neglect or abuse of the instruments which an individual has appropriated. It may also be regarded as condemning all forms of idleness that imply living on the work of others, and so appropriating what belongs to them.

§ 6. RESPECT FOR SOCIAL ORDER.—To avoid unnecessary details, we may next consider what is rather a group of commandments than a single rule—*viz.* those commandments that are connected with respect for social institutions and the various forms of social order. Such respect is pretty nearly equivalent to what the

[1] *Philosophie des Rechts.* § 36

Greeks used to call *αἰδώς*, shame or reverence.[1] This feeling forbids us to interfere unnecessarily with any established institution. It forbids, for instance, any violation of the sanctities of the family; it enjoins that we should "honour the king" and all constituted authorities;[2] and the like. The authority of this group of commandments rests on the importance of maintaining the social system to which we belong. The soldier feels himself in general bound to carry out the commands of his superior, even if he knows very well that "some one has blundered"; and in the same way the citizen feels bound in general to give his support to the constituted authorities of his state, even if he sees clearly that their laws are not altogether wise. Occasionally also a politician may feel himself bound to act with his party, even if he does not approve of some detail in its policy. Evidently this group of commandments might be split up into a number of separate rules. But it is so easy to do this, that it is scarcely worth while to attempt it here.

§ 7. Respect for Truth.—The next commandment is, Thou shalt not lie. This rule has a double application. On the one hand, it may be taken to mean that we should conform our actions to our words—

[1] It has already been remarked (p. 287, *note* 2) that αἰδώς is almost equivalent to conscience. Since, however, the moral obligations of the early Greeks were connected entirely with social laws and institutions, it was almost entirely with these that the feeling of αἰδώς was associated.

[2] I need hardly say that this rule is not to be understood as excluding the right of revolution. As we shall shortly see, none of these rules is to be regarded as absolutely binding. Just as a Nelson may look at the signals of his superior officer with his blind eye, so a far-seeing social reformer may defy the laws of his state. But it is only in exceptional circumstances that such conduct is justifiable.

that, for instance, we should fulfil our promises, and observe the contracts into which we have entered. On the other hand, it may be taken to mean that we should conform our words to our thoughts—*i. e.* that we should say what we mean. Evidently, these two interpretations are quite different. A man may make a promise which he does not mean to keep. In that case, he lies in the second sense. But it does not follow that he will necessarily lie in the first sense. For, having made the promise, he may keep it. Still, both senses are concerned with respect for the utterance of our thoughts—though the latter is concerned with care in the utterance of them, the former with care in conforming our actions to that which has been uttered. Lying, however, ought not to be understood as referring merely to language. We lie by our actions, if we do things in such a way as to imply that we intend to do something else, or that we have done something else, which in fact we neither have done nor intend to do. The commandment, then, Thou shalt not lie, may be taken to mean that we must always so speak and act as to express as clearly as possible what we believe to be true, or what we intend to perform; and that, having expressed our meaning, we must as far as possible conform our actions to it.

§ 8. RESPECT FOR PROGRESS.—The last commandment of which it seems necessary to take notice, is the commandment—too often overlooked in moral codes—which bids us help on, as far as we can, the advancement of the world. It may be expressed in this form, Thou shalt labour, within thy particular province, with all thy heart and with all thy soul and with all thy strength and with all thy mind.[1] It is not without reason that I express this commandment in the same form as that in which the love of God has been enjoined. It was wisely said, *Laborare est orare*, Work is Worship. The love of God is perhaps most clearly shown by faith in human progress; and faith in it is shown most clearly by devotion to it.[2] With this great positive commandment, we may conclude our list.

§ 9. Casuistry.—I have made no great effort to reduce these commandments to system. It might be a good exercise for the student to work them out more in detail, and show their relations to one another. But it seems clear that no system of commandments can ever be made quite satisfactory. There can be but one supreme law—the law which bids us realize the rational self or universe; and if we make any subordinate rules absolute, they are sure to come into conflict. Such a conflict of rules gives rise to casuistry. Casuistry consists in the effort to interpret the precise meaning of the commandments, and to explain which is to give way when a conflict arises.[3] It is evident enough that conflicts must arise. If we are always to respect life, we must sometimes appropriate property—*e. g.* the knife of a man about to commit murder. If we are always to do our utmost

[1] This is Carlyle's commandment—"Know what thou canst work at; and work at it, like a Hercules" (*Past and Present*, Book III., chap. xi.).

[2] "All true work is religion" (Carlyle, *ibid.*, chap. xii.).

[3] See Dewey's *Outlines of Ethics*, p. 88, Muirhead's *Elements of Ethics* p. 69–70. Caird's *Critical Philosophy of Kant*, vol. ii., pp. 186—190, and p, 215, and Bradley's *Ethical Studies*, p. 142.

for freedom, we shall sometimes come into conflict with order. So in other cases. We have already quoted the emphatic utterance of Jacobi on this point;[1] and though it may be somewhat exaggerated, yet it cannot be denied that there are occasions in which we feel bound to break one or more of the commandments in obedience to a higher law. Now casuistry seeks to draw out rules for breaking the rules—to show the exact circumstances in which we are entitled to violate particular commandments. This effort is chiefly associated historically with the teaching of the Jesuits.[2] It was called "casuistry" because it dealt with "cases of conscience." It fell into disrepute, and was severely attacked by Pascal. And on the whole rightly. It is bad enough that we should require particular rules of conduct at all,[3] but rules for the breaking of rules would be quite intolerable. They would become so complicated that it would be impossible to follow them out; and any such attempt would almost inevitably lead in practice to a system by which men might justify, to their own satisfaction, any action whatever.[4] The way to escape from the limitations of the commandments, is not to make other commandments more minute and subtle, but rather to fall back upon the great fundamental law, of which

[1] See above, pp. 198–9.

[2] See Sidgwick's *History of Ethics*, pp. 151—154.

[3] The expression of the moral law in the form of particular rules belongs to an early stage in moral development. It naturally comes immediately after that stage in which morality is identified with the laws of the State. *Cf.* Muirhead's *Elements of Ethics*, pp. 68—73.

[4] Hence Adam Smith says (*Theory of Moral Sentiments*, Part VI., sect. IV.) that "books of casuistry are generally as useless as they are commonly tiresome."

the particular commandments are but fragmentary aspects.

§ **10.** THE SUPREME LAW.—What is that fundamental law? It is, as we have already seen, the commandment that bids us realize the rational self. This commandment is so broad, and is apt to seem so vague, that it is certainly well that it should be supplemented, for practical purposes, by more particular rules of conduct. But when these rules come into conflict, and when we feel ourselves in a difficulty with regard to the course that we ought to pursue—when, in short, a "case of conscience" arises—we must fall back upon the supreme commandment, and ask ourselves: Is the course that we think of pursuing the one that is most conducive to the realization of the rule of reason in the world? No doubt this is a question which it will often be difficult to answer.[1] But,

[1] Sometimes it may be easier to answer in the form of feeling. The commandments in which the Jewish Law was summed up—"Thou shalt love the Lord thy God with all thy heart, &c., and thy neighbour as thyself"—express the right attitude of feeling, that of love for the supreme reason and for all rational beings. In the form of feeling, however, there is the disadvantage that the definite duties to be performed are not suggested, whereas the command to pursue the advancement of the rational life suggests at once the means that must be adopted for this end. At the same time, it is important to insist that the right attitude of mind necessarily brings with it the right form of feeling. To this point we have already referred (Book I., chap. iii, § 5, and Book II., chap, iii., § 13). We have seen that Kant refused to regard love as a duty, interpreting the Christian injunction as meaning merely that we should treat others *as if* we loved them. But, as Adam Smith remarked (*Theory of Moral Sentiments.* Part III., sect. III., chap. iv.); this could scarcely be described as loving our neighbour as ourselves; since "we love ourselves surely for our own sakes, and not merely because we are commanded to do so." On the same point, Janet has well quoted (*Theory of Morals*, p. 354) the emphatic utterance of St. Paul, "Though I bestow all my goods

in general, a man who keeps his conscience unclouded, and sets this question fairly before himself, will be able to keep himself practically clear from errors, without resorting to casuistical distinctions.[1]

§ 11. Conventional Rules.—Besides the commandments, or strict moral laws, we find in every community a number of subordinate rules of conduct, inferior in authority, but often superior in the obedience which they elicit. Such are, for instance, the rules of courtesy, those rules that belong to the "Code of Honour," the etiquette of particular trades and particular classes of society.[2] There is often a certain absurdity in these rules; and some of them are frequently laughed at under the name of "Mrs. Grundy." Certainly a superstitious devotion to them, a devotion which interferes with the fulfilment of more important duties or with the development of independence of character, is not to be commended. Yet sometimes such rules are not without reason. Schiller tells us, in a wise passage of his *Wallenstein*,[3] that we ought not to despise the narrow conventional laws; for they were often invented as a safeguard against various forms of wrong and injustice. *Pectus sibi permissum* is not less to be distrusted than *intellectus sibi permissus*; and it is often well that the impulses of a man's own heart should be checked by certain generally understood con-

to feed the poor, and though I give my body to be burned, and have not charity, it profiteth me nothing."

1 See, on this point, Green's *Prolegomena to Ethics*, Book IV. chap. ii.

2 Sometimes referred to as "minor morals."

3 *Die Piccolomini*, Act I., scene iv.—

"Lass uns die alten engen Ordnungen
Gering nicht achten!"

ventions.[1] The law of respect for social order, at any rate, will generally lead a man to follow the established custom, when no more important principle is thereby violated. Still, this is not a matter of supreme importance. A scrupulous adhesion to petty rules is no doubt as foolish as a total neglect of them. Eccentricity has its place in the moral life; and there are certainly many customs which are "more honoured in the breach than the observance." Perhaps the tendency at the present time—a result of our individualistic modes of thought—is to attach too little importance to general rules of life. The Chinese, however, under the influence of Confucius, seem to have gone to the other extreme.

§ 12. Duties of Perfect and Imperfect Obligation.—The impossibility of drawing out any absolute code of duties has led some writers to draw a distinction between that part of our obligations which can be definitely codified and that part which must be left comparatively vague. This distinction has taken various forms. Sometimes those obligations which are capable of precise definition are called duties; while that part of good conduct which cannot be so definitely formulated is classed under the head of virtue—as if the virtuous man were one who did more than his duty, more than could reasonably be demanded of him.[2] Again,

[1] Indeed, such rules are often more useful in small matters than in great; just because the small matters interest us less. *Cf.* below, § 13, *note*.

[2] There can be no doubt that this is a common use of the term "Virtue" in ordinary language. Perhaps it is even the original sense of the word. It certainly seems to have been at first applied to those qualities that appeared most eminent and praiseworthy. See Alexander's *Moral Order and Progress*, p. 243: "The distinctive mark of

Mill [1] classifies strict duties under the head of Justice; and adds that "there are other things, on the contrary, which we wish that people should do, which we like or admire them for doing, but yet admit that they are not bound to do; it is not a case of moral obligation." But surely we have a moral obligation to act in the best way possible. Another distinction is that given by Kant [2] between Duties of Perfect and Imperfect Obligation. According to this classification, Duties of Perfect Obligation are those in which a definite demand is made upon us, without any qualification—as, Thou shalt not kill, Thou shalt not lie, Thou shalt not steal. These are, for the most part, negative. On the other hand, most of our positive obligations cannot be stated in this absolute way. The duty of beneficence, for instance, is relative to time, place, and circumstance.

virtue seems to lie in what is beyond duty: yet every such act must depend on the peculiar circumstances under which it is done, of which we leave the agent to be the judge, and we certainly think it his duty to do what is best." *Cf.* Muirhead's *Elements of Ethics*, p. 190, *note*. See also Adam Smith's *Theory of Moral Sentiments*, Part I., sect. II., chap. iv., Sidgwick's *Methods of Ethics*, Book III., chap. ii., Rickaby's *Moral Philosophy*, p. 70,

1 *Utilitarianism*, chap. v. Some other writers have limited the application of the term Justice to those actions which can be enforced by national law. Thus Adam Smith says (*Theory of Moral Sentiments*, Part II., sect. II., chap. i.): "The man who barely abstains from violating either the person, or the estate, or the reputation of his neighbours, has surely very little positive merit. He fulfils, however, all the rules of what is peculiarly called justice, and does everything which his equals can with propriety force him to do, or which they can punish him for not doing. We may often fulfil all the rules of justice by sitting still and doing nothing." *Cf.* the Note at the end of chap. x.

2 *Metaphysic of Morals*, section II. (Abbott's translation, p. 39) Observe what is said in Mr. Abbott's note. *Cf.* also Caird's *Critical Philosophy of Kant*, vol. ii., pp. 382-3.

No man can be under an obligation to do good in all sorts of ways, but only in some particular ways, which he must in general discover for himself. Hence this may be called an Imperfect Obligation, because it cannot be definitely formulated.

Now it is no doubt true that there is a distinction of this kind. There is, indeed, a threefold distinction between duties of different kinds. There are, in the first place, those duties that can be definitely formulated, and embodied in the laws of a State,[1] with penalties attached to their violation. In the second place, there are those duties that cannot be put into the form of national laws, or that it would be very inconvenient to put into such a form, but which, nevertheless, every good citizen may be expected to observe. In the third place, there are duties which we may demand of some, but not of others; or which different individuals can only be expected to fulfil in varying degrees.[2] But the distinction between these different classes of duties is not a rigid one. The duties that can be made obligatory by law vary from time to time, according to the constitution of the State concerned, and the degree of the civilization of its people. The same applies to those duties that every good citizen may fairly be expected to observe. Consequently, while at any given time and place it might be possible to draw out a list of the

[1] This was the original meaning of Duties of Perfect Obligation. Kant altered the use of the phrase. Some points in connection with the relation between Ethics and Jurisprudence will be found well brought out in Adam Smith's *Theory of Moral Sentiments*, Part VI., sect. IV.

[2] The fulfilment of these in an eminent degree might be said to constitute Virtue, as distinguished from Duty, in the sense explained above. But this is on the whole an inconvenient usage.

Duties of Perfect Obligation, and to express them in a code of Commandments, yet the tables of stone on which these were engraved would require to be periodically broken up.[1] And many of the most important duties for any particular individual would remain unformulated.

§ **13.** My Station and its Duties.—The determination of a man's duties, therefore, must be left largely to his individual insight. Ethics can do little more than lay down commandments with regard to his general attitude in acting. In the details of his action, however, a man is not left entirely without guidance. Human beings do not drop from the clouds. Men are born with particular aptitudes and in a particular environment; and they generally find their sphere of activity marked out for them, within pretty narrow limits. They find themselves fixed in a particular station, helping to carry forward a general system of life; and their chief duties are connected with the effective execution of their work. Hence the force of Carlyle's great principle, "Do the Duty that lies nearest thee."[2] The

1 This of course is no sufficient reason for not formulating them as well as we can. As Hegel says (*Philosophy of Right*, § 216), "The universal law cannot be forever the ten commandments. Yet it would be absurd to refuse to set up the law 'Thou shalt not kill' on the ground that a statute-book cannot be made complete. Every statute-book can of course be better. It is patent to the most idle reflection that the most excellent, noble, and beautiful can be conceived of as still more excellent, noble, and beautiful. A large old tree branches more and more without becoming a new tree in the process; it would be folly, however, not to plant a new tree for the reason that it was destined in time to have new branches."

2 *Sartor Reeartus*, Book II., chap. ix.: "The situation that has not its Duty, its Ideal, was never yet occupied by man." See also the admirable chapter by Mr. Bradley on "My Station and its Duties"

prime duty of a workman of any kind is to do his work well, to be a good workman.[1] Of course he must first have ascertained that his work is a valuable one, and one that he is fitted to do well. Having thus found his place in life, he will not as a rule have much difficulty in ascertaining what are the commandments that apply within that sphere. Hence the important point on the whole is not to know what the rules of action are, but rather the type of character that is to be developed in us. A well-developed character, placed in a given situation, will soon discover rules for itself.[2] Thus, we

(*Ethical Studies*, Essay V.). *Cf.* Dewey's *Outlines of Ethics*, Part II.: "The moral endeavour of man takes the form not of isolated fancies about right and wrong, not of attempts to frame a morality for himself, not of efforts to bring into being some praiseworthy ideal never realized; but the form of sustaining and furthering the moral world of which he is a member." Thus we agree, after all, with the view of Dr. Johnson, that a good action is one that "is driving on the system of life." But for this view we now have a rational justification.

[1] *Cf.* Muirhead's *Elements of Ethics*, p. 47: "An artisan or an artist or a writer who does not 'do his best' is not only an inferior workman but a bad man." Mr. Muirhead quotes Carlyle's saying about a bad joiner, that he "broke the whole decalogue with every stroke of his hammer." See also Dewey's *Outlines of Ethics*, p. 112: "The good artisan 'has his heart in his work.' His self-respect makes it necessary for him to respect his technical or artistic capacity; and to do the best by it that he can without scrimping or lowering."

[2] It may be worth while to note here that rules of conduct are, in general, valuable for us in proportion as our interest in the concrete matter concerned is small. A man does not want rules for the performance of anything which he has deeply at heart. Thus, a serious student has little need of rules for study. His own interest is a sufficient guide. On the other hand, a man whose main work does not lie in study, but who is able to devote a few hours to it now and then, may find it advantageous to have definite rules for the performance of the uncongenial task. So it is in life generally. Christianity abolished the external rules of Judaism, by enjoining upon us an

are naturally led from the consideration of the commandments to the consideration of the virtues.[1]

interest in life instead. Such an interest is the only safe final guide. But so long as such an interest cannot be pre-supposed, particular rules retain a certain relative value. Some very suggestive remarks on this point will be found in Adam Smith's *Theory of Moral Sentiments*, Part III., sect. IV. He there gives some interesting examples of actions which are naturally done in obedience to rule, because our interest in them is slight; and of others which are naturally done rather from an interest in the object to be attained.

[1] Prof. Dewey says (*Outlines of Ethics*, p. 231): "It is a common remark that moral codes change from 'Do not' to 'Do,' and from this to 'Be.' A Mosaic code may attempt to regulate the specific acts of life. Christianity says, 'Be ye perfect.' The effort to exhaust the various special right acts is futile. They are not the same for any two men, and they change constantly with the same man. The very words which denote virtues come less and less to mean specific acts, and more the spirit in which conduct occurs." *Cf.* Muirhead's *Elements of Ethics*, p. 71, *note*.

Note on Rules of Conduct.

I have no doubt that some readers will be a good deal disappointed by the results of this chapter. Many of those who take up the study of Ethics expect to find in it some cut-and-dried formulas for the guidance of their daily lives. They expect the ethical philosopher to explain to them, as I once heard it put, what they ought to get up and do to-morrow morning. And no doubt it is true enough in a sense that the ethical philosopher, if he is good for anything, will explain this. He will explain to them the spirit in which they ought to apply themselves to the particular situation before them to-morrow morning. But most people, and especially most English people, are not content with this. The cause of this discontent is no doubt partly that most of us have become accustomed in our youth to a code of Ten Commandments, generally accompanied by certain subordinate rules deduced from them. Partly, again, it is that most of the English schools of Ethics have connected themselves closely with Jurisprudence,[1] and have thus given encouragement to the notion that a set of moral laws might be devised similar to the laws of a nation. Now I admit of course that it is possible to draw out certain rules of conduct, founded on the general nature of human life and the conditions under which it has to be carried on; and it is part of the task of the moral philosopher to explain the general nature of these rules, and to show their place in the conduct of life. This I have endeavoured to do. But to suppose that Ethics is called upon to do more than this appears to me to be a most fatal error. Happily life cannot yet be reduced to rule. A moral genius must always, like Mirabeau, "swallow his formulas" and start afresh. Pedantry will not carry one far in life,[2] any more than in literature.

At the same time, while emphasizing this point, I have certainly no wish to rush to the opposite extreme. There has been so strong a tendency in former times to lay down an absolute "ought" in

---

[1] The chaotic state of English law led men like Bentham to seek for a rational basis of Jurisprudence in ethical principles. This application of Ethics has reacted on the study of Ethics itself. On the Continent the prevalence of Roman Law has perhaps made the demand for a fresh ethical basis less urgent.

[2] There are some good remarks on this point in Adler's *Moral Instruction of Children*, pp. 19-23.

Ethics, with a rigid scheme of obligations hanging from it, that now, by a not unnatural reaction, we find a number of our ethical writers treading very gingerly, hesitating to say that there is any such thing as duty, apologizing for the use of the word "ought," and mildly conceding that Ethics is of no practical value. This extreme appears to me to be quite as pernicious as the other. It is the function of the ethical philosopher to discover and define the supreme end of life. This is what all the great ethical writers have done, from Plato and Aristotle to Spinoza, Kant, Hegel, and Green. As soon as this end is clearly seen, the duty of pursuing it becomes an absolute imperative, from which there is no escape. And with this end in view, the whole of our life falls into shape. Hence, as Aristotle puts it,[1] "from a practical point of view it much concerns us to know this good; for then, like archers shooting at a definite mark, we shall be more likely to attain what we want." Undoubtedly, in this sense, Ethics is of the greatest practical value. Nor is its value in any way diminished by the fact that the moral genius, or even the man of ordinary good sense, may act well without any knowledge of Ethics. The human end is involved in man's very existence. No one can exist at all without being in some degree conscious of it. The task of the moral philosopher is only that of bringing it to clear consciousness. *Only* that! In the same way, the task of the poet is *only* that of making clear to us the beauty that is everywhere around us. The task of the metaphysician is *only* that of bringing out the meaning and connection of the principles made use of in the sciences. This "only" is a little out of place.

While we must insist, then, that it is not the task of Ethics to furnish us with copy-book headings for the guidance of life, we must equally insist that it *is* its task to furnish us with practical principles—to bring the nature of the highest good to clear consciousness, and to indicate the general nature of the means by which this good is to be attained. It thus tells us, not indeed the particular rules by which our lives are to be guided, but what is of infinitely greater practical importance—the spirit in which our lives are to be lived.

I am well aware that all this will seem unsatisfactory to many minds. The military spirit is deeply rooted in human nature. Men are eager to catch the word of command, and are disappointed when they are only told, as by Jesus, to "love one another," or, as by Hegel, to "be persons," or, as in the vision of Dante, to "follow their star." And, indeed, as I have already said, Ethics does supply some-

[1] *Ethics*, I. ii. 2.

thing more than this. It does interpret for us the meaning and importance of some more special rules. But assuredly neither Ethics nor anything else will tell a man what in particular he is to do. There would be an end of the whole significance of life if any such information were to be had. All action that is of much consequence has reference to concrete situations, which could not possibly be exhausted by any abstract methods of analysis. It is the special business of every human being to find out for himself what he is to do, and to do it. Ethics only instructs him where to look for it, and helps him to see why it is worth while to find it and to do it. Like all sciences, it leaves its principles in the end to be applied by the instructed good sense of mankind.[1]

---

[1] It may perhaps appear that this point has been somewhat over-emphasized; but I think there is a real danger of misconception here, and I have been anxious to guard against it. On the general question involved, it may be well to refer, in addition to the authorities already cited, to Mill's *System of Logic*, Book VI., chap. xii., Sidgwick's *Methods of Ethics*, Book IV., chaps. iv. and v., Green's *Prolegomena to Ethics*, Book IV., Hegel's *Philosophy of Right*, Introduction, Bosanquet's *Civilization of Christendom*, p. 160 *sqq.*, and the article by Mr. Muirhead on "Abstract and Practical Ethics" in the *American Journal of Sociology* for November, 1896.

CHAPTER IV.

THE VIRTUES.

§ 1. RELATION OF THE VIRTUES TO THE COMMANDMENTS. When we have ascertained what are the most important commandments, we have at the same time discovered to a considerable extent what are the most important virtues.[1] The virtuous man will be on the whole the man who has a steadfast habit of obeying the commandments. There are, however, many virtuous habits which do not correspond to any commandments that can be definitely formulated.[2] Moreover, as the virtues are concerned mainly with inner habits of mind, whereas the commandments deal with overt acts,[3] the

1 Virtue (from Latin *vir*, a man or hero) meant originally manliness or valour. The Greek ἀρετή (from the same root as Ares, the god of war) and the German Tugend (connected with our English word "doughty") have a somewhat similar origin. The term is here employed to denote a good habit of character, as distinguished from a Duty, which denotes rather some particular kind of action that we ought to perform. Thus a man *does* his Duty; but he *possesses* a Virtue, or *is* virtuous. Another sense in which the term "Virtue" is used, has been already noticed above (chap. iii., § 12).

2 Mr. Alexander (*Moral Order and Progress*, p. 253) definitely connects the virtues, as well as the duties, with social institutions. In both cases there seems to be some exaggeration in this. *Cf.* Muirhead's *Elements of Ethics*, p. 188.

3 The Jewish commandments, as interpreted in the Sermon on the Mount, and by modern Christian thought, are of course concerned with the heart as well as with outer acts. Also the summary of the commandments in terms of love refers entirely to an inner habit of mind. But when the commandments are thus summed up, they

lines of cleavage in dealing with the virtues are naturally somewhat different from those that we find in dealing with the commandments. Hence it seems desirable to devote a separate chapter to the subject of the virtues.

§ 2. Virtues relative to States of Society.—The virtues which it is desirable for human beings to cultivate vary considerably with different times and places. They are more variable even than the commandments[1]; because the latter confine themselves to those broad principles of conduct which are applicable to nearly all the conceivable conditions of life. At the same time, even the virtues are less changeable than they are apt at first sight to appear. The Greek virtue of courage, confined almost entirely to valour in battle, has but little correspondence to anything that is supremely important in modern life. Yet the temper of mind which it indicates is one for which there is as much demand now as ever.[2] And so it is also with most of the other virtues. The precise conditions of their exercise change; but the habit of mind remains intrinsically the same. Still, even the habit of mind does undergo some alteration. The kind of fortitude which is required for valour in battle is, even in its most inward aspect, somewhat different from that

cease to be particular rules. Particular rules relate to particular modes of action. *Cf.* Muirhead's *Elements of Ethics*, p. 70. For a discussion of the relation of Virtue to Duty, see Sidgwick's *Methods of Ethics*, Book III., chap. ii. The following chapters of the same book contain interesting analyses of most of the particular virtues. *Cf.* Rickaby's *Moral Philosophy*, Part I., chap. v.

1 In that broad sense in which alone, as we have seen, universally significant commandments can be laid down.

2 See Green's *Prolegomena to Ethics*, Book III., chap. v.

fortitude which sustains the modern man of science, politician, scholar, or philanthropist. Hence this side of ethical study is one which each generation of writers requires almost to reconsider for itself. However instructive the great work of Aristotle may still remain on this point (and there is perhaps nothing more instructive in the whole range of ethical literature), it is yet not quite directly applicable to the conditions of modern life. In order to understand what are the most important virtues for us to cultivate in modern times, it is necessary to consider them in relation to the structure and requirements of modern society.

§ 3. THE ETHOS OF A PEOPLE.—It is for this reason that it is so important, from an ethical point of view, to study carefully what the Germans call the *Sitten*[1] (the moral habitudes of thought and action) of different times and peoples. We have no English word that quite expresses this idea; but, instead of having recourse to the German, we may use a Greek term, and speak of the *ethos* of a people.[2] The ethos of a people is partly constituted by definite rules or precepts. The Ten Commandments formed a very important element in the ethos of the Jews; and they have continued,

[1] The English word "Manners" used to have a meaning closely approximating to this, but it has deteriorated. See *International Journal of Ethics*, Vol. VII., no. I.

[2] *Cf.* Bradley's *Ethical Studies*, chap. v., especially p. 156, where the following is quoted from Hegel: "The child, in his character of the form of the possibility of a moral individual, is something subjective or negative; his growing to manhood is the ceasing to be of this form, and his education is the discipline or the compulsion thereof. The positive side and the essence is that he is *suckled at the breast of the universal Ethos.*" Similarly on p. 169: "The wisest men of antiquity have given judgment that wisdom and virtue consist in living agreeably to the Ethos of one's people."

with certain modifications and enlargements, to form an important element in the ethos of modern European peoples. The precepts contained in the Sermon on the Mount have perhaps never been sufficiently appropriated by the world in general to be made definitely into a part of the ethos of any people; but they have undoubtedly exercised a most profound influence on the ethos of nearly all civilized nations. The ethos of a people, then, is partly expressed in definite commands and precepts. But partly also it consists in recognized habits of action and standards of judgment which have never been precisely formulated. Thus, in England there is a general idea of the kind of conduct which is fitting in a "gentleman"; and though it might be difficult to reduce this standard to the form of definite rules, yet it has undoubtedly exercised a great influence in forming the ethos of our people.

The ethos of a people, then, we may say, constitutes the atmosphere in which the best members of a race habitually live; or, in language that we have previously employed, it constitutes the universe of their moral activities. It is the morality of our world; and on the whole the man who conforms to the morality of that world is a good man, and the man who violates it is a bad man. Mr. Bradley has even said emphatically[1]

[1] *Ethical Studies*, p. 180. So also on p. 181 he says: "We should consider whether the encouraging oneself in having opinions of one's own, in the sense of thinking differently from the world on moral subjects, be not, in any person other than a heaven-born prophet, sheer self-conceit." There is, however, some paradox in this. A man may be a moral reformer in a small way, without being exactly a "heaven-born prophet." The suffering or witnessing of wrong in some particular form, for instance, often makes a man sensitive to an evil to which most men are callous. Also the

that the man who seeks to have a higher morality than that of his world is on the threshold of immorality. But this is an exaggeration. For the ethos of a people is not a stationary thing.[1] It develops, like social life generally; and its development is brought about mainly by the constant effort of the best members of a race to reach a higher standard of life than that which they find current around them. The καλοκἀγαθός of the Greeks might occasionally permit himself to do many things, and to abstain from doing many things, which would scarcely be thought becoming in a modern "gentleman"; while the teachings of Christianity hold up to us an ideal of life which has not yet been fully embodied in the current morality of the world. While, then, it is on the whole true that the ethos of our people furnishes us with our moral standard, it must yet be remembered that it is often desirable to elevate that standard itself.[2]

disciples of the "heaven-born prophets" will for a time hold opinions different from those of the world. But what Mr. Bradley means is simply, Try to be as good as your world *first:* after that you may seek to make it better. His meaning is similar to that of Burke (*Reflections on the Revolution in France*): "We are afraid to put men to live and trade each on his own private stock of reason; because we suspect that the stock in each man is small, and that the individuals would do better to avail themselves of the general bank and capital of nations and of ages."

[1] Sometimes, indeed, it is a highly artificial thing, brought into being by the accidental circumstances of a particular time and place. Thus Adam Smith remarks (*Theory of Moral Sentiments*, Part V., sect. II.) that "in the reign of Charles II. a degree of licentiousness was deemed the characteristic of a liberal education. It was connected, according to the notions of those times, with generosity, sincerity, magnanimity, loyalty, and proved that the person who acted in this manner was a gentleman, and not a puritan."

[2] *Cf.* below, chap. vii.

Now the virtues that are current among a people at a given time are the expression in particular forms of the ethos of that people; and their significance can be appreciated only in relation to the general life of the times.

§ 4. VIRTUES RELATIVE TO THE SOCIAL FUNCTIONS.—Not only, however, are the virtues relative to different times and different social conditions: they are also relative to the functions that different individuals have to fulfil in society. Here again it is true that the differences are not so great as one is apt to think. We are apt to say that a poor man cannot exercise the virtue of liberality; and that a man who is rich and prosperous has little need for the virtue of patience. This is to a large extent true; yet the habit of mind which with a rich man leads to liberality may equally well be present, and is equally admirable, in one who is poor. And the same applies to other qualities. Still, it remains on the whole true that the virtues which we respect and admire in a man are not quite the same as those of a woman; that those of the rich are not quite the same as those of the poor; those of an old man not quite the same as those of a young man; those of a parent not quite the same as those of a child; those of a man in health not quite the same as those of one who is sick; those of a commercial man not quite the same as those of a man of science; and so in other cases. In describing the virtues, therefore, we must either go somewhat minutely into the consideration of different circumstances of life, and of the qualities that are most desirable under these varying conditions; or else we must confine ourselves to statements that are very general and vague. The limits of space and the difficulties of the subject both lead us to adopt the latter alternative.

§ 5. THE NATURE OF VIRTUE.—The virtues, as was admirably pointed out by Aristotle, are habits of deliberate choice. To be virtuous means to have a character so developed that we habitually choose to act in the right way. Now as the right action nearly always stands between two possible bad actions—one erring by excess and the other by defect—Aristotle considered[1] that virtue consists essentially in a habit of choosing the mean. He well added, however, that it is the choice of the *relative* mean—*i. e.* of the particular intermediate course which is appropriate to the particular individual in question, and to the particular circumstances in which he is placed. That mean must be determined in each case by a consideration of its conduciveness to the general development of social life. To hit upon it rightly is often a problem for individual tact and insight; but a study of the greatest examples in human history is in many cases a valuable aid in deciding on the most fitting conduct in a given case.

§ 6. THE CARDINAL VIRTUES.—From the earliest periods of ethical speculation, attempts have been made to enumerate the various forms of virtues. The most celebrated of these lists are those given by Plato and Aristotle. The former seems to have been current among Greek moralists even before the time of Plato. It has at least the merit of simplicity, containing only four cardinal[2] virtues—Wisdom (or Prudence), Courage

1 *Ethics*, Book II., chaps. vi.—ix. *Cf.* Sidgwick's *History of Ethics*, p. 59.

2 From *cardo*, a hinge. The Cardinal Virtues are supposed to be

(or Fortitude), Temperance (or Self-Restraint), and Justice (or Righteousness). This classification, however, simple as it appears, was soon found to give rise to considerable difficulties. It began to be perceived, for instance, that in a certain sense the first of the virtues includes all the others; for every virtuous activity consists in acting wisely in some particular relationship. Again, Justice (or Righteousness) seems to be made somewhat too comprehensive in its meaning when it is used to include (as, on this acceptation, it must) all the social virtues. Perceiving these and other defects in the catalogue of the virtues, Aristotle was led to a considerable expansion of the list.[1] But his expansion had so constant a reference to the virtues that were expected of an Athenian citizen that its direct interest for modern life is comparatively slight. And it would perhaps be somewhat futile to attempt to draw up any similar catalogue specially adapted for

those on which the others hinge or depend. *Cf.* the Cardinals in the Roman Catholic Church.

[1] It might be held, however, that Plato and Aristotle were in reality engaged on distinct problems. Plato sought to give an account of the Cardinal Virtues—*i. e.* the general elements involved in *all* virtuous activities; whereas Aristotle sought to give a list of special virtues, exhibited not in all virtuous activities, but in particular kinds of virtuous activity. But this view seems to me to be scarcely tenable. The distinction here referred to is clearly drawn by Prof. Dewey in his *Outlines of Ethics*, p. 230. I am doubtful, however, whether his interpretation of the term "cardinal virtue" is sanctioned by the best usage. He means those general characteristics of a virtuous attitude, such as purity of heart, disinterestedness, conscientiousness, and the like, which belong to the very essence of virtue as such. The relation of such qualities of the "inner life" to the virtues proper is partly dealt with in the next chapter. For the origin of the phrase "cardinal virtue," see Sidgwick's *History of Ethics*, p. 133. *Cf.* Rickaby's *Moral Philosophy*, p. 84.

modern times, with their complicated problems and varied relationships.[1] Nevertheless, a few suggestions towards such a catalogue may be found useful.

We may note, to begin with, the distinction which is commonly drawn between self-regarding virtues and those that are altruistic, or have reference to the good of others. This distinction is apt to be misleading. The individual has no life of his own independent of his social relations; and any virtue which has reference to the good of the individual, must have reference also to social well-being. This fact, however, need not prevent us from distinguishing between the life of an individual and the wider world to which it is related; and some virtues may be said to bear specially on the former, while others bear more particularly on the latter. It may be convenient to look at these two classes of virtues separately.

(*a*) Taking the four Platonic virtues as a convenient starting-point, it is evident that courage and temperance are the two that bear specially[2] on the life of the individual. If we understand courage (or fortitude) in the wide sense of resistance to the fear of pain, and temperance in the equally wide sense of resistance to the allurements of pleasure, these two virtues will include all forms of opposition to temptation in the individual life. Temptation appears either in the form of some pain to be avoided or some pleasure to be

[1] An interesting list has been drawn up, in the form of a table, by Mr. Muirhead, in his *Elements of Ethics*, p. 201. Some suggestive remarks on the particular virtues required in modern life will be found in Adler's *Moral Instruction of Children*, Lectures XI.—XV.

[2] Wisdom, as we shall see immediately, is also directly concerned in the guidance of the individual life. But it applies equally to our social relationships.

secured; and he who is proof against these will lead a steadfast life along the lines that he has chosen. It is evident, however, that a man may be courageous and temperate in the conduct of his life, and yet be living foolishly. A wise choice of the line to be pursued is a necessary preliminary. If we understand the Platonic virtue of wisdom (or prudence) in this sense, we shall have in a manner a complete list of the virtues required for the conduct of the individual life. But it is evident that each of these virtues must be understood in such a sense as to comprehend under it a great variety of qualities not always found together in the same individual. Thus wisdom would require to be understood as including care, foresight, prudence, and also a certain decisiveness of choice. Courage, again, would include both valour and fortitude, *i. e.* both the active courage which pursues its course in spite of the probability of pain, and the passive courage which bears inevitable suffering without flinching.[1] But these are not the same virtues, and are indeed perhaps not often found together in any high degree. Again, courage would have to be understood as including perseverance; and this seems a somewhat unnatural extension of its meaning; just as it is somewhat un-

[1] Mrs. Bryant (*Educational Ends*, pp. 71–2) regards fortitude as a higher virtue than the more active courage which goes to meet danger; because the former bears *actual* pain, the latter only the *fear* of pain. This is so far true. Courage is a blinder virtue than fortitude. The courageous man sets pain aside and forgets it whereas the man who shows fortitude is one who endures an actually present pain which cannot be set aside. But on the other hand courage is a more active and voluntary virtue than fortitude. It not merely endures pain, but goes to meet it in the fulfilment of a purpose. In this respect courage seems to be the higher virtue of the two.

natural to include decision under wisdom. Perhaps the qualities of decision, diligence, and perseverance would come most naturally under a separate heading by themselves. These qualities are concerned not so much with the resistance to the solicitations of pleasure and pain, as with the resistance to the natural inertia of human nature. The Christian virtues of faith and hope are closely connected with valour and fortitude, in so far as they supply the latter virtues with an inner ground. A confident and cheerful view of life seems to be presupposed in the highest forms of courage.[1] With reference to temperance, again, this virtue would require to be understood as including the resistance to all kinds of solicitation from pleasures, whether sensual or intellectual, in so far as these tend to interfere with the conduct of life along the lines that have been chosen. Broadly speaking, then, we should be led in this way to recognize four distinct classes of virtues as bearing directly on the conduct of the individual life—wisdom in the choice of its general course, decisiveness in pursuing it, courage and temperance in resisting the solicitations of pain and pleasure.[2]

1 Browning's portraiture of Hercules in *Balaustion's Adventure* well illustrates the qualities involved in the highest forms of active courage.

2 Mr. Muirhead remarks (*Elements of Ethics*, p. 198–9) that the virtues of courage and temperance involve one another. "In order to be temperate a man must be courageous: in order to be able to resist the allurements of pleasure he must be willing to endure the pain that resistance involves. Similarly, in order to be courageous, he must be temperate." But this is perhaps a needless subtlety. The man who temperately abstains from a bottle of wine must no doubt be courageous enough to face the difficulties and dangers involved in going without it. But does not this mean simply that temperance is a kind of *negative* courage? And does not the distinction between positive and negative still remain?

(*b*) The virtues that relate to the individual's dealings with his fellow-men are perhaps best summed up under the head of justice. At the same time, this term, as commonly understood, is much too narrow to include all the virtues that arise in such relationships. It must be understood, for instance, to include not merely the fulfilment of contracts, and the performance of every duty required by the laws, express or understood, of the community to which one belongs, but also perfect honesty and fidelity in all one's relationships with others. Mr. Ruskin has taught us to look for honesty even in modes of artistic expression; and this kind of honesty, as well as others,[1] must be included in our idea of justice, if that idea is to be made to comprehend all the virtues connected with our social obligations. Further, the Christian ideal of life has taught us to expect something beyond the mere satisfaction of obligations in our dealings with our fellow-men; and indeed more than this was expected even by the moral consciousness of the Greeks. We commonly say that generosity is expected as well as justice; and in Christian communities love also is required. In a sense, however, we may say that all this ought to be included in our idea of justice.[2] For it is part of what is due from one individual to another that

[1] Other instances of honesty, going beyond mere truthfulness, might easily be given. Thus the student who "crams" for an examination may be said to be dishonest, because his knowledge is not genuine. Again, what Mr. Bosanquet calls (*History of Æsthetic*, p. xiii) "the scholar's golden rule—never to quote from a book that he has not read from cover to cover," is a good instance of the extension of the idea of honesty.

[2] Thus, generosity, as Mr. Muirhead says, "is only justice adequately conceived" (*Elements of Ethics*, p. 200).

the latter should be treated not as a mere thing to which certain specifiable obligations are owed, but as a person, an absolute end, with infinite claims. It is true that as a general rule such ideal relationships are only partly attainable ; but the thoroughly just man will endeavour to realize them as far as possible, and will be glad when the external relationships of mere contract can be transmuted into the relationships of friendship or Christian love.[1] Hence also such ideas as those of courtesy, and even of a certain cheerfulness and good humour in social intercourse ; such efforts as that of being, as far as possible, all things to all men, of avoiding all appearance of evil, of abstaining from that which is lawful when it is not expedient, and in general all the chivalries of the Christian gentleman, are not foreign to the conception of justice. They are part of what we owe to one another as persons and as absolute ends.

We see, then, that, by giving a broad interpretation to each of the terms used, we may accept the old Greek classification of the virtues with but slight modifications. The only positive addition that we have to make is the recognition of a virtue of decisiveness and perseverance. Perhaps it was natural that the Greeks should omit this, partly because their plan of life was more mapped out for them beforehand than it is with us, and partly because with their simpler method of life steady persistence in any particular line was less essential. Perhaps also the light inconstancy of the

[1] Here we are in agreement with Carlyle. *Cf.* above, chap. ii., § 7. We doubt only whether the abolition of contract would of itself produce this desirable result. Justice must on the whole precede generosity.

Athenian character, its perennial youthfulness, made the omission of this stern virtue easy. A Roman would scarcely have forgotten the idea of disciplined application;[1] an Englishman would not naturally omit decision of character: a German would remember *Daurbarkeit.*[2] Besides this, however, it must not be forgotten that we have been extending the meaning of the four Greek virtues to senses which the Greeks themselves would not have acknowledged.[3] But such an expansion of the conception of duty is inevitable as the world advances.

Having made this classification, however, we may at once add that any attempt to draw out such a list, like an attempt to make a list of the commandments, is of very slight importance. There is essentially but one virtue (what we may, if we like, call practical wisdom[4]), just as there is essentially but one commandment. The particular virtues, like the particular commandments, are only special forms in which

[1] The decisiveness of such a man as Cæsar, for instance (*cf.* below, chap. v., § 11. *note*), seems to be a virtue which cannot be identified either with wisdom, courage, or temperance.

[2] *Persistence. Cf.* also the peculiarly German virtue of *Treue* (*fidelity*). These virtues were all somewhat foreign to the Athenian character.

[3] This was habitually done by the early Christian moralists who accepted the Platonic classification. See Sidgwick's *History of Ethics*, p. 133.

[4] It might be urged, of course, that there is a great difference between what Bacon calls "wisdom for a man's self" and that wisdom which manifests itself in a just regard for others. But wisdom for a man's self, in the sense of mere selfish prudence, is not virtue at all. Wise care of a man's own interests, in the sense in which that is a virtue, is precisely the same quality as that which leads, when extended, to a wise care of the interests of others. The only difference lies in the extension of our universe.

the right attitude of mind manifests itself. The effort to make a list of these forms is almost frivolous. I have thought it worth while to say so much as I have done on the subject, only in order to make it clear what such an effort would mean. Perhaps the best way of regarding the virtues is to treat them as those forms of character that are implied in the fulfilment of the duties or commandments; while those duties or commandments, again, depend on the elements involved in the social unity.

§ 7. EDUCATION OF CHARACTER.—Having ascertained what are the types of character to which we wish to approximate, we have next to inquire into the means by which these types are to be developed. Here, however, it would be necessary to trespass on the province of Psychology, and especially on that part of Psychology which is concerned with the theory of Education. This subject is still in a somewhat undeveloped state;[1] and there are only one or two remarks that seem to have any practical value for our present purpose. It is scarcely necessary to refer to what every moralist has noticed, the influence of example in the development of character. "As iron sharpeneth steel, so a man sharpeneth the countenance of his friend." But all the forms of social relationship have a similar value. Perhaps we may say generally that the important thing,

[1] Reference, may, however, be made to Herbart's *Science of Education.* Some good points will be found also in Guyau's *Education and Heredity*, Fouillée's *L'Enseignement au Point de Vue National*, Mrs. Bryant's *Educational Ends*, Rosenkranz's *Philosophy of Education*, and Dr. Adler's *Moral Instruction of Children.* Herbart's chief point is that the great work of education is to extend the "circle of thought." By a "circle of thought" he means very nearly what has been described in this handbook as a "universe."

from this point of view, is the influence that comes from connecting oneself with some organization that has a certain completeness in itself. Schiller said that a man must either be a whole in himself or else join himself on to a whole. To this Mr. Bradley has added,[1] "You cannot be a whole, *unless* you join a whole." Complete development of character can be attained only by devoting ourselves to some large end, in co-operation with others. Such an attachment comes to different men in different ways. Some find it in the pursuit of science, others in particular practical interests, others in the political life of the State, others in poetry or religion. It matters little what the form may be; but unless a man has, in some form, a broad human interest which lifts him out of himself, his life remains a fragment, and the virtues have no soil to grow in. The first requisite, then, for the development of the virtues, is to unite ourselves with others in the pursuit of some end or ideal. In the second place, we may observe that a certain amount of ascetic discipline is sometimes found valuable. As Aristotle put it,[2] when a man's character has been twisted in one direction, it may be straightened by bending it in the other. Also, even apart from this, a certain check to the gratification of our natural propensities helps to waken up the will:[3] it prevents us from living on by rote, and thus serves

[1] *Ethical Studies*, p. 72. Mr. Bradley attributes the saying to Goethe. It is one of the *Xenien*, and was probably of joint authorship.

[2] *Ethics*, II. ix. 5.

[3] *Cf.* James's *Principles of Psychology*, vol. i., p. 126. Prof. James lays down the maxim: "Keep the faculty of effort alive in you by a little gratuitous exercise every day." He adds, "Be systematically ascetic or heroic in little unnecessary points; do every day or two something for no other reason than that you would rather not do it."

as a stimulus to the development of character; so that, like Rabbi Ben Ezra, we may

> "welcome each rebuff
> That turns earth's smoothness rough,
> Each sting that bids nor sit nor stand but go."

It is best, however, when such a rebuff comes to us in the ordinary course of nature. When it is consciously administered, it is apt to involve too much attention to our own inner development, which almost always leads to the production of a morbid habit of mind.[1] On the whole, it is generally better to escape from our defects, not by thinking about them and trying to elude them, but by fixing our attention on the opposite excellences. Dr. Chalmers used to speak of "the expulsive power of a new affection";[2] and it certainly seems a more effectual method as a rule to expel our evil propensities by developing good ones rather than by seeking directly to crush the evil ones. At the same

I venture to doubt the wisdom of this. A man who is living with serious ends in view will, I think, always find sufficient occasions for ascetic discipline—

> "Room to deny himself, a road
> To bring him daily nearer God"—

without artificially seeking them out (except perhaps in the way indicated by Aristotle). See the whole passage from James quoted in Muirhead's *Elements of Ethics*, p. 129, *note*. *Cf.* also Miss Gilliland's Essay on "Pleasure and Pain in Education" in the *International Jonrnal of Ethics*, vol. ii., No. 3 (April, 1892), pp. 303-4.

[1] *Cf.* below, p. chap. v., § 11.

[2] So also Mrs. Humphry Ward says in *Robert Elsmere:* "This, indeed, is the only way in which opinion is ever really altered—by the substitution of one mental picture for another"; and again: "An idea cannot be killed from without—it can only be supplanted, transformed, by another idea, and that, one of equal virtue and magic." These quotations are due to Mr. Welton.

time, it must be allowed that it is seldom possible to develop the moral life, like a flower, by a simple process of steady growth. Usually a certain amount of attention to the inner life is necessary; and often a man has to pass through crises, such as used to be called, in religious language, conversion or new birth, in which the attention is turned inwards, and the man is occupied, as it were, in feeling his own pulse and fingering the motives of his conduct. This is an attitude from which we ought to escape as rapidly as possible; but it is so characteristic a feature in the development of the moral life that it seems worth while to devote a separate chapter to the consideration of it —the more so, as it will lead us to a further study of what may be called the inner side of virtue.[1]

§ 8. The Moral Syllogism.—Before we conclude this chapter, it may be convenient to take note of a highly significant conception of Aristotle, which seems here in place. In the present and the two preceding chapters we have briefly indicated the various forms

[1] With reference to moral education, it may be noted here that a certain confusion is frequently fallen into between the culture of the moral nature and the acquisition of knowledge about morals. The former is all-important: the latter frequently leads to nothing more than that form of spiritual pride which is vulgarly known as "priggishness." In the former sense, *all* real education is moral education. It is in this sense that Herbart says (*Science of Education*, p. 57), "The one and the whole work of education may be summed up in the concept—Morality.' In the latter sense, on the other hand, a moral education would generally be a bad education, leading to nothing but self-conscious introspection. *Cf.* the important distinction between "moral ideas" and "ideas about morality" drawn by Mr. Bosanquet in his article on "The Communication of Moral Ideas" in the *International Journal of Ethics* vol. I., No. 1 (Oct. 1890), p. 86. See also Miss Gilliland, *loc. cit.*, pp. 294–5.

in which the moral atmosphere (if we may so call it) affects the individual consciousness. The moral ideal involved in social life presents itself to him in the three forms of institutions to be maintained, duties to be fulfilled, and a type of life to be realized. At different stages of social development, and in different races of mankind, it tends to present itself more distinctly in one or other of these forms. Thus the Jews thought chiefly of Commandments, the Greeks chiefly of Virtues, and perhaps the Romans attached most importance to the maintenance of social institutions. But, in whatever form the moral life is conceived, the good citizen may be said to derive from these general conceptions of its nature the principles by which his life is guided. It is then his business to apply these principles in detail. This process was described by Aristotle as the formation of a practical syllogism. The major premiss consists of the general statement, that a particular social institution is to be maintained, that a particular commandment is to be obeyed, that a particular type of life is to be realized. The minor premiss consists in the apprehension that an action of a particular kind would be one that fulfilled these conditions. Then the conclusion would consist in the carrying out of the action in question.

The power of thus apprehending the general principle to be followed, and of bringing the particular action under it, was called by Aristotle practical wisdom (*φρόνησις*); and the man who possessed this quality was called a *φρόνιμος* (a wise or prudent man). The excellence of the good citizen is of this nature; and, having reached this point, it may now be convenient to give Aristotle's complete definition of Virtue as it appears in the good citizen. Most of the points in the definition have already come up in the course of our exposition; and it may be well now to have it before us in its entirety. "Virtue," says Aristotle,[1] "is the habit of choosing the relative mean, as it is determined by reason, and as the man of practical wisdom would determine it." This is apt to strike us at first as defining in a circle; but if we remember what is meant by the man of practical wisdom—*viz.* the man who has fully entered into the spirit of his moral environment; and if we remember further that the spirit of his moral environment is the product of the human ideal—*i. e.* of reason—as it has so far expressed itself; we may be able to see that it is not really defining in a circle, but the expression of a profound truth. It furnishes us, however, only with an account of the virtue of the good citizen; and though this is an important element in the life of the good man, it is not quite the whole of it. Accordingly, Aristotle proceeds from the consideration of the virtue of the *φρόνιμος* to the consideration of that of the *σοφὸς* (the man of speculative wisdom), which he declares to be higher. This raises the general question how far the highest life of the individual can be regarded as something to be realised apart from the life of the community, or as something that contains elements that are not adequately expressed in his relations to the social unity to which he belongs. It is this question that we have now to consider.

[1] *Nicomachean Ethics*, II., vi., 15. Ἔστιν ἄρα ἡ ἀρετὴ ἕξις προαιρετική, ἐν μεσότητι οὖσα τῇ πρὸς ἡμᾶς, ὡρισμένῃ λόγῳ καὶ ὡς ἂν ὁ φρόνιμος ὁρίσειεν.

NOTE ON THE CLASSIFICATION OF THE VIRTUES.

Students who desire a more complete classification of the Virtues than that which has been given in the foregoing chapter might find it advantageous to study them genetically, *i.e.*, to consider how they grow up and come to be recognised in the development of human life. From this point of view, it would probably be found that the earliest virtues to be recognized are those of Courage and Loyalty, as being the most important for the maintenance of the tribe. Courage at first means Valour in battle, but gradually comes to include Fortitude, Hopefulness, etc. In Aristotle's treatment of the virtue of Courage we see the beginnings of this process of expansion. Loyalty, in like manner, means at first simple Fidelity to the tribal unity, but gradually comes to include Perseverance and Enthusiasm in any work that may be undertaken. As we go beyond the tribal consciousness, and pass to the stage at which there is a more definite recognition of the individual life, the virtues of Temperance and Prudence make their appearance, and these also become by degrees more and more comprehensive. The growth of the individual consciousness leads to the establishment of personal relations between individuals; and with these the virtues of Fairness (Justice) and Friendliness soon acquire importance. The deepening of the individual consciousness leads to the recognition of the virtue of Reverence in its various forms of Self-Respect and Respect for others. Finally, Wisdom comes to be seen as the Virtue that underlies all others. From this point of view, then, the Cardinal Virtues would be Courage, Loyalty, Temperance, Prudence, Fairness, Friendliness, Reverence, and Wisdom. But from different points of view different results might be reached. What is important is not to have a classification of the virtues, but to understand the general significance of Virtue as the habit of acting in a suitable way in situations of a particular kind, and then to have a fairly complete view of the kinds of situation that arise in communities at different stages of development. Such a list of virtues as that given by Aristotle in the *Nicomachean Ethics* cannot be regarded as much more than a collection of specimens of some of the most important types to be found in his own age and country. The attempt to be exhaustive on such a subject would be apt to lead to a result more voluminous than luminous. On the other hand, if one tries to give simply a general classification of the different directions in which the moral life becomes specialised, such as is generally understood by a list of Cardinal Virtues, it is almost impossible to devise any principle of division that is really satisfactory. In Plato's fourfold list it is pretty clear that Wisdom is on a different footing from the other three, being rather the underlying principle of all than one of the special applications of it; while again Temperance and Justice cannot be very clearly distinguished from one another. The common division of Virtues into the self-regarding and the other-regarding is similarly unsatisfactory; and so is Aristotle's distinction of moral and intellectual virtues. On the whole, the genetic order of study seems the most satisfactory.

CHAPTER V.

THE INDIVIDUAL LIFE.

§ **1.** THE HIGHER INDIVIDUALISM.—While it is true that the life of the individual is relative throughout to the social unity to which he belongs, it is none the less true that it is in the personality of individuals that the social unity is realized. Consequently, though it is an error to think of an individual as having a life of his own independent of society, it is not an error to think of the individual life (realized within a social unity) as an absolute and supreme end in itself. Hence the efforts of such a man as Goethe after the highest culture of his individual nature are not to be classed (as shallow critics have sometimes classed them) with the strivings of egoism. The development of such a personality is at once a good in itself and a benefit to the whole of humanity. Nor is this less true, though the benefit is smaller, in the case of less comprehensive and significant personalities. What Mr. Ruskin calls "the manufacture of souls" [1] is the greatest of all industries. This is a kind of work, however, in which men are apt to be unsuccessful in proportion as they consciously set themselves to it. *Crescit occulto velut arbor ævo*, is in some measure true of most great characters. Even Goethe seems to have been somewhat injured by his

[1] *Cf.* Walt Whitman's question, "Do they turn out *men* down your way?" quoted by Dr. Adler in his *Moral Instruction of Children*, p. 270.

too deliberate self-culture. "The unconscious," says Carlyle, "is alone complete"; the reason being that a perfect character is one that is objective, that loses itself in the world with which it deals, one that knows much and loves much, not one that is much occupied in the contemplation of itself.[1] Still, this objective point of view is capable of being cultivated, and the cultivation of it involves a certain amount of self-study. Some points in connection with this may now be noted.

§ 2. Conversion.—The religious experience known as conversion seems to be a normal fact in our moral development. Recurring to the mode of expression which we have so frequently made use of, we may say that this phenomenon occurs when a man is made aware of a higher universe than that within which he is living, and at the same time becomes conscious that that higher universe is one within which he ought to live. Such an experience occurs in its intensest form only when the higher universe that is presented to us is recognized as the highest of all—*i. e.* it occurs mainly in the religious life. But even apart from this, there is frequently a crisis in the moral life, in which we pass from some lower universe to a higher. The moment, for instance, at which a man decides to devote himself to poetry, or art, or science, or philosophy, or the time

[1] There is, in fact, what we may call a Paradox of Duty, analogous to the Paradox of Pleasure referred to above (Book I., chap. ii., § 7). Just as, in order to get pleasure, a man must interest himself rather in particular objects than in his own personal feelings; so, in order to act rightly, a man must interest himself in some object that is to be accomplished rather than in his own attitude in accomplishing it. Even the wealth of our inner life depends rather on the width of our objective interests than on the intensity of our self-contemplation.

at which he hears of the death of a friend, or loses or gains a fortune, or goes to college, or falls in love, will often be such a period. Life takes on a new aspect; and the mind turns in criticism upon the life that is past. In the case of the religious life, there is often a violent reaction against the past, a condemnation of its acts and even of its ideals, repentance and remorse. In less extreme cases there is only a certain shame for the low level of our former existence, accompanied frequently by contempt for those who remain at it, together with a fixed determination to follow higher things in the future. At such times a man is intensely conscious of himself. He perhaps keeps a diary to record his inner feelings. He withdraws probably in some degree from general intercourse with the world, and becomes somewhat cynical in his estimate of it.[1] He thinks he has discovered a new world which no one has ever explored before him. It is at such times especially that the inner life becomes prominent.

§ 3. CONSCIENTIOUSNESS.—Apart, however, from any such special periods as this, one who is careful about his moral conduct frequently finds himself called upon to reflect upon his inner life, in the way of inquiry whether his conduct conforms to his highest ideals. Carlyle has commended[2] times of action in contrast with times of reflection; but in the practical moral life it is impossible to keep the two long asunder. After action we must reflect upon our activities and criticise them, with a view to improving upon them in the future. Now in so far as we merely consider our overt acts, this involves no entrance into the inner

1 See Carlyle's *Sartor Resartus*, for instance.

2 Especially in his Essay on "Characteristics."

life. But a man who is careful about his conduct will generally reflect not merely upon his actual conduct, but upon the motives by which he was led to it.[1] The habit of reflecting upon them has been called by Green conscientiousness.[2] It is doubtful whether this is a quite correct use of that term.[3] Conscientiousness seems properly to mean simply extreme care with regard to our external conduct. But, for lack of a better word, we may employ the term here in Green's sense. "A man may ask himself," Green says, "Was I, in doing so and so, acting as a good man should, with a pure heart, with a will set on the objects on which it should be set?—or again, Shall I, in doing so and so, be acting as a good man should, goodness being understood in the same sense?" This question is somewhat different from the question whether one's action has in itself been right. It is rather the question whether I, in doing an action in itself right,[4] was occupying a right attitude, or whether I did it from a wrong motive.[5] If a man is much occupied with such a

[1] As a rule, we do not do this. Although, as already remarked (above, p. 135), the moral judgment is passed on a *person doing*, not on a *thing done*, yet the interest of the agent is normally centred in a thing to be done, not in himself as doing it. *Cf.* also p. 355, *note*.

[2] *Prolegomena to Ethics*, pp. 269–271, and 323–327.

[3] See Dewey's *Outlines of Ethics*, p. 202.

[4] *I. e.* right as an overt act. A man, in acting, is primarily interested in the question, whether he is bringing about a desirable result. In *judging* his action, as we have already remarked (above, p. 135), we take account of the motive by which he is led to bring about this result. But the man himself, in acting, does not normally think of this. He simply sees the thing to be done and does it.

[5] I suspect that when men inquire into their motives in this way, they are frequently using the term "motive" in the more inaccurate sense formerly referred to (above, p. 62). They are thinking of the *feelings* that *accompany* their actions rather than of the *ends* that

question as this, it is generally a sign either of a morbid state of mind or of the fact that one has not found his true vocation in life; for when a man has found his work and is doing it, he has little time left for such inquiries.[1] Moreover, if a man's mind is honest and clear, he can generally answer the question at once, without any elaborate investigation. Consequently, when a man enters upon such inquiries, they have seldom reference to any single action that he has performed, but rather to his general attitude in life.

§ 4. SELF-EXAMINATION.—Such self-examination is often a direct result of a new awakening to a sense of the moral imperative such as we have already described as conversion; but it may be carried on by men periodically, without any such reawakening. A man may ask himself whether his life is being lived on that level which answers to his ideal of what life should be. In asking this, he will generally mean partly to ask whether his actions, viewed as external facts, are exactly such as they ought to be—whether he has actually accomplished what was required of him in the given situation; and this is a question with regard to overt fact. But frequently he will mean more than

induce them to perform these actions. But even in the stricter acceptation of the term, the inquiry into the purity of our motives is not irrelevant. See below, p. 359, *note* 1, and p. 368, *note* 1.

[1] *Cf.* Dewey's *Outlines of Ethics*, p. 201. That very wise man, Goethe, has a remark on this, as on most other things. Referring to a boy who could not console himself after he had committed a trifling fault, "I was sorry to observe this," said Goethe, "for it shows a too tender conscience, which values so highly its own moral self that it will excuse nothing in it. Such a conscience makes hypochondriacal men, if it is not balanced by great activity." (*Conversations with Eckermann.*)

this. He will frequently wish to ascertain whether the general principles of his conduct are right, whether he habitually acts in the best spirit as well as in the best manner—whether, for instance, he is perfectly disinterested in his conduct. No doubt such an inquiry, as well as an inquiry into the spirit in which particular actions have been done, is often an evidence of a morbid habit of mind. A man's interests ought for the most part to be concentrated in the objects which he is seeking to accomplish rather than in his own inner state.[2] And even if one wishes to view his acts with reference to the spirit in which they are done, it will generally be best to do this by studying some ideal type of the moral life, and endeavouring to follow in his path, rather than by a direct contemplation of one's own impulses and motives. The latter course has nearly always a tendency to paralyze action and promote egoism. Still, there are times when the study of one's own motives in particular actions is beneficial, and also times at which it is desirable to take a survey

[1] It is in such inquiries that we become aware of what may be called the inner side of the virtues. The qualities involved in this inner side of virtue—purity of heart and the like—seem to be what Prof. Dewey understands by the "Cardinal Virtues." See above, p. 341, *note* 1. It is probably true, as Green insists, that the inner and outer side of virtuous action are in the long run exactly proportioned to one another. "There is no real reason to doubt," says Green (*Prolegomena to Ethics*, Book IV., chap. i., § 295), "that the good or evil in the motive of an action is exactly measured by the good or evil in its consequences, as rightly estimated." But he admits that this correspondence would be fully apparent only to omniscience. *For us*, a certain act may be evidently the right one in a given situation (*e. g.* the killing of a tyrant, the passing of an Act of Parliament, the relief of a destitute widow, *etc.*), even if we do not know what motive has led to its being done.

[2] *Cf.* above, p. 355, *note*.

of one's general attitude in life. This is a part of self-knowledge; and though, as Carlyle says, the motto *Know thyself* is an impossible one to carry out with any completeness, yet it is important to make a certain approximation to the carrying of it out. One reason of this is, that it is not always possible in our actions to go fully into the reasons of what we do. We often require to let ourselves go, relying on the intuitions that have been acquired in the course of our lives. On such occasions it is important that we should know how far we can trust ourselves to go. For this purpose it is necessary to have an insight into the nature of our "besetting sins," and these cannot always be discovered from our overt acts. There are few, however, who carry this kind of self-knowledge very far. "The heart is deceitful," and even those who observe it most carefully are apt to miss some secret chambers. The advice of an intimate friend will often help one more than self-observation; and even self-observation is generally more successful in the form of a study of our acts and habits than in that of a study of our secret motives.

§ **5.** THE STUDY OF THE IDEAL.—I have already remarked that it is usually a more profitable way of developing the inner life rather to fix our attention on some external type than to attend to our own motives. Such types have frequently been selected and set up for the imitation of whole nations and peoples—*e. g.* Buddha, Jesus, Socrates, and the various Roman Catholic saints. And, on a smaller scale, we have innumerable biographies of heroes held up as examples not only of right action, but of a right attitude of mind and heart. Novelists also and poets have created for us imaginary types to serve the same end.[1] Indeed, this may be said to be the end of all poetry, in so far as poetry has an end at all. It is a "criticism of life," inasmuch as it presents to us higher ideals of what life might be and ought to be—and that chiefly on its inner side.[2]

§ 6. THE MONASTIC LIFE.—The importance of the study of the inner life, whether by direct self-examination, or by the contemplation of ideal patterns, has at certain times been so keenly felt that men have set themselves apart, like the Eastern mystics or the monastic orders of Catholic Christianity, for the express purpose of making this their study. We must regard this, in general, as an undesirable form of the Division of Labour. It had a certain justification in lawless times, when most men were so much occupied with violent action that they had no time for reflection. In such times men who led a contemplative life had the task of acting as the inner life for the whole community to which they belonged. And perhaps in some Oriental countries the nature of the climate renders it difficult to carry on the active and the contemplative life together.[3] The existence of a monastic order has in fact somewhat the same justification as the setting apart of a special day for religious worship. But just as, when the Sabbath is too rigidly divided from the rest of the week, it tends to become a mere ceremonial

1 On the moral and æsthetic significance of "types," the student may be referred to Stephen's *Science of Ethics*, pp. 74-76. Reference may also be made to Bacon's *De Augmentis*, Book VII., chap. iii.

2 *Cf.* the famous passage in Goethe's *Wilhelm Meister*, Book II., chap. ii., ending, "Who but the poet was it that first formed gods for us; that exalted us to them, and brought them down to us."

3 See Marshall's *Principles of Economics*, p. 12.

observance, with little reference to actual practice, so when the priestly or monastic order is too rigidly divided from the rest of the community, the inner life comes to be regarded as their special province, with which the rest of mankind have no concern.[1] This has a pernicious effect on general morals, and ultimately on the morals of the monastic order itself. No order of men can confine their attention exclusively to the inner side of life; and the pretence of doing so turns rapidly into cant and hypocrisy. Just as it is desirable that secular interests should not be entirely forgotten on Sunday, nor the religious spirit throughout the remainder of the week, so it is desirable as a general rule that "all the Lord's people should be prophets," or at any rate that prophets should retain sufficient contact with the world to enable men of the world to catch something of the spirit of the prophets.

§ 7. BEAUTIFUL SOULS.—Apart, however, from the existence of any special order for the cultivation of the inner life, we occasionally find individuals who

[1] *Cf.* the amusing account, in Milton's *Areopagitica*, § 55, of the man whose religion has become "a dividual movable": "A wealthy man . . . finds religion to be a traffic so entangled, and of so many piddling accounts, that . . . he cannot skill to keep a stock going upon that trade. . . What does he therefore, but resolves to give over toiling, and to find himself out some factor, to whose care and credit he may commit the whole managing of his religious affairs; some divine of note and estimation that must be. To him he adheres, resigns the whole warehouse of his religion, with all the locks and keys, into his custody; and indeed makes the very person of that man his religion. . . . His religion comes home at night, prays, is liberally supped, and sumptuously laid to sleep; rises, is saluted, and after the malmsey, or some well-spiced bruage . . . his religion walks abroad at eight, and leaves his kind entertainer in the shop trading all day without his religion."

set themselves apart for this purpose. It has been customary to describe these as "beautiful souls" (schöne Seelen); and Goethe has given a striking account of one in his *Wilhelm Meister.*[1] They are usually people who have been prevented in some way from taking part in the active affairs of life. The lives of such individuals have often a singular charm, and the good effects of their influence are sometimes felt over a wide circle; but this is especially the case when they do not entirely withdraw themselves from contact with active life. If they do this, their contemplation is apt to become emptied of all real content; their fine feelings turn into hysterical dreaming; and it is well if they do not end in madness.

§ **8.** Asceticism.—The development of the study of the inner life is generally accompanied by a contempt for pleasure. This sometimes goes so far, as in the case of the Indian mystics and the Mediæval monks, as to lead to the positive infliction of torture. The ostensible reason for this is frequently the idea that torture is pleasing to the gods; but the fundamental reason seems to lie in the desire of suppressing the flesh and its lusts. This is of course in some degree an essential of the moral life in any form; but asceticism seems to commit the error of turning the means into an end. It is important to repress our lower desires, in order that we may be able to devote ourselves, without let or impediment, to the highest ends of life. But the ascetic regards the suppression of desire as the end in itself. And the effort thus to suppress all

[1] Carlyle erroneously translated *schöne Seele* "fair Saint." For some very suggestive remarks on the attitude of the "beautiful soul," see Caird's *Hegel*, pp. 28–31.

natural desire frequently defeats its own aim. It concentrates attention on the objects of desire, and in a sense makes a man the slave of his desires as truly as in the case of him who yields to them. The best way to free ourselves from our lower desires is, as we have already indicated,[1] to interest ourselves in something better. It is only into a mind swept and garnished that the devils can enter: when it is well furnished and occupied they can find no room.

§ 9. THE CONTEMPLATIVE LIFE.—The study of the inner life is, in truth, but a part of the general life of speculation as distinguished from action. The distinction between the active and the contemplative life has impressed men in all ages; and different thinkers have attached importance to the one or the other. Aristotle placed the contemplative life (meaning by that the pursuit of scientific and philosophic truth) above the practical life in which the ordinary social virtues are exercised.[2] It is essentially the same point of view[3] that we find among many Eastern mystics and Mediæval saints, and, in more modern times, in such men as Wordsworth, who withdraw from the struggle of ordinary labours and find a higher life and a serener wisdom in the contemplation of nature. Wordsworth says of nature that,

> "She has a world of ready wealth
> The mind and heart to bless,
> Spontaneous wisdom breathed by health,
> Truth breathed by cheerfulness";

---

[1] See above, p. 350.

[2] *Ethics*, Book X., chaps. vii. and viii.

[3] Except (a very important qualification) that Aristotle regarded the active life of social duty as an indispensable preparation for the higher life of thought. Moreover, even the life of thought he re-

and the same thought finds utterance, in more homely fashion, from Walt Whitman, when he says, "I loaf and invite my soul." Ruskin also has sung the praises of rest and contemplation, and William Morris has found his earthly paradise in "a century of rest," in which the turmoil of modern civilization shall have been appeased, and men shall find a more worthy existence in a closer walk with nature. Similar ideas dominate Emerson and Thoreau. All these seem to think that the contemplative life is essentially higher than the active, and that this higher life is to be reached simply by withdrawing from the life of action. On the other hand, Carlyle preached a gospel of labour, and was fond of quoting the words of Sophocles that "the end of man is an action and not a thought," or the exclamation of Arnauld—"Rest! Shall I not have all eternity to rest in?" This view fits in well also with the robust philosophy of Browning, who cannot even accept the orthodox view of the rest of eternity, but conceives of it as the most fitting address to his departing spirit—

> "'Thrive and strive' cry, 'Speed! Fight on, fare ever, there as here!'"

The truth seems to be that an ordinary healthy human existence requires both sides. There are energetic natures, like Cæsar or Napoleon, that seem able to go on with a perpetual activity, scarcely requiring rest or reflection. But the activity of such men is not usually the wisest or the most beneficial. There are others whose special mission it seems to be to withdraw from the world of action and bring messages to

garded as essentially a higher form of activity, to which the life of the good citizen leads up.

mankind from the inner world of feeling and reflection. But the wisdom of such men is apt to be deficient in the depth of universal applicability which a wider contact with life can give. The Wordsworths and Emersons are not equal to the Shakespeares and Goethes. For the majority of men, at any rate, times of action naturally alternate with times of reflection, times of creation with times of re-creation. In retirement we criticise the acts of life; in life we criticise the ideas of retirement. Action and reflection are the gymnastic and music of moral culture.[1]

§ **10.** RELATION OF THE INNER TO THE OUTER LIFE.—Looking at it in a more speculative light, we may express the relation of the inner to the outer life in this way. The life of unreflective action takes place entirely within the universe with which we have identified ourselves. In the contemplative life we bring ourselves into relation with the broader universe, whether revealed in the form of the moral ideal within us, some ideal exemplar without us, the beauty and suggestiveness of nature, the discovery of scientific law, or in any other shape. Now, since the life of all

[1] *Cf.* Goethe's famous lines—

> "Es bildet ein Talent sich in der Stille,
> Sich ein Character in dem Strom der Welt."
> ("A genius forms itself in solitude;
> A character, in struggling with the world.")

"Music" and "Gymnastic" were the names of the two elements in Greek education—"Music," of course, including what used to be called "polite literature" and a good deal more. Plato points out in his *Republic* (Book III.) that both these elements are required for the development of character. See Nettleship's admirable essay on "The Theory of Education in Plato's *Republic*" (*Hellenica*, pp. 67-180).

of us involves progress, or, at the very lowest, re-adjustment to new conditions, it is impossible that it should be carried on successfully without a periodic reference to the principles on which it is based. Like chronometers, we can go on for a time by the mere impulse of our moral springs, but if we are to be kept in permanent order we must readjust ourselves by the stars. On the other hand, it would be a poor chronometer which was perpetually being set, and never could be let go. A life of pure reflection would never acquire any positive content. It would have principles, but no facts to apply them to ; yet it is by contact with such facts that the principles themselves grow. It is experience that tests them, and that sends us back again to improve them. "Best men are moulded out of faults"; for it is our errors of conduct that reveal to us the defects of our principles, and show us where they need improvement.[1]

There are, then, these two sides in every healthy moral life. It is a mistake, on the one hand, to suppose that all the worth of our life lies in its outer acts. This is not even the only part of us that affects those with whom we come in contact. "Men imagine," says Emerson, "that they communicate their virtue or vice only by overt actions, and do not see that virtue or vice emit a breath every moment." Of course, this means in reality that the virtuous man acts a little differently from the vicious man even where the external act appears to be the same. The beauty of the inner life, in Aristotle's phrase, "shines through." Hence the importance of having the heart right. On the other

[1] Hence the element of truth in the popular view about the necessity of "sowing wild oats." See below, p. 381.

hand, it is a mistake to suppose that we should be perpetually fingering our inner motives. If we do this, we shall always find that they are somewhat wrong. The impulse of the moment can never quite rise to the dignity of the eternal ideal; and the more we watch it, the less likely is it so to rise. If we make sure that our overt action is thoroughly right, the right motive will soon become habitual to us;[1] and it is a man's habitual motives that are important, not the motives that may happen to enter into a particular act.

§ 11. The Virtuous Man and the World.—If our life is to be one both of action and reflection, it must also in a sense be one that is both in the world and not of it. A life of activity cannot be one of entire withdrawal from the world and its ways; yet the man who guides himself by reflection will not simply be carried along by its currents. The man who is simply reflective and not active is sometimes characterized as

[1] It might be thought, from what has been already said in chap. iii., that, if we are resolutely setting ourselves to do good actions, the motive of them must *necessarily* be good. But this is only partly true. If a statesman devotes himself persistently to the passing of beneficial laws, this must be because he takes the benefit of his country as *part* of his motive. But he may also be influenced by the desire of personal fame, or even by that of spiting a rival. A man can seldom be quite sure that some such lower motives do not form part of his inducement to the performance of an action which he clearly sees to be in itself desirable. But the best practical course is evidently that of habituating ourselves to the performance of actions which we perceive to be desirable. By doing this, we accustom ourselves to the point of view of the "universe" within which the actions are good. We forget the lower universe of personal ambition, or of personal spite; and, by forgetting it, we gradually cease to live in it. We lose ourselves in the pure interest in our objective end; and this is the highest motive—*i. e.* on the assumption that our objective end is really a desirable one, forming an element in human progress.

"over-conscientious."[1] Sometimes this reproach is merely an indication of prejudice on the part of "men of the world"; but often it is a mark of a real want of decision of character, like that of Hamlet, or a want of appreciation of the limits within which our moral life has to be lived.[2] It is a man of this type who is sometimes said to be "so good that he is good for nothing" ("si buon che val niente"). On the other hand, the commoner defect is that of living entirely within the universe of the society in which we find ourselves, and following a multitude to do evil. The good man adapts himself to his environment, but tries at the same time to make his environment better. He does not simply try to keep himself "unspotted of the world," but also to clear the world of spot. Such a man will in a sense be "not of the world." He will live in the light of principles which are not fully embodied in the modes of action around him. But he will not withdraw into himself, and abstain from taking part in the activities of his world. This attitude of the virtuous man is strikingly depicted by Wordsworth in his sonnet to Milton,[3] in

[1] See Green's *Prolegomena to Ethics*, p. 323, and Dewey's *Outlines of Ethics*, p. 201.

[2] Froude says of Julius Cæsar (*Cæsar*, p. 339), "His habit was to take facts as they were, and when satisfied that his object was just, to go the readiest way to it." A very conscientious man can seldom bring himself to do this, and hence lacks "force of will." *Cf.* above, pp. 82–3. Descartes was so much afraid of the indecision due to a reflective habit, that he thought it necessary to make it a special practical rule for himself, never to hesitate when once he had come to the conclusion that a particular line of conduct was on the whole the best. See his *Discourse on Method*, Part III. (Veitch's translation, p. 25).

[3] *Cf.* also Milton's own emphatic declaration in the *Areopagitica*:

which he expresses both his aloofness and his readiness to serve.

> "Thy soul was like a star and dwelt apart;
> . . . . And yet thy heart
> The lowliest duties on herself did lay."

§ 12. THE MORAL REFORMER.—This twofold attitude is perhaps best seen in the case of great moral reformers. Every good man, no doubt, is a moral reformer on a small scale; but occasionally in the history of a nation there arises a man who holds up new ideals of the moral life, and induces men in some degree to adopt them, thus advancing the general moral ideas of mankind. Types of such reformers are Buddha, Socrates, and Jesus. These are generally men who have a profound appreciation of the moral life of their peoples, and who by reflection upon it are led to transcend its limitations. There was no better Athenian citizen than Socrates, none more attached to his native state, none more ardent in the performance of civic duties, few more thoroughly at home in its customs and traditions.[1] But he was more than this. He had his hours of reflective abstraction, in which he went beneath the moral traditions of his nation and examined the fundamental principles on which they rested. This reflective examination enabled him to transcend the limitations of Greek morality, and to prepare the way for deeper conceptions

"I cannot praise a fugitive and cloistered virtue, unexercised and unbreathed, that never sallies out and seeks her adversary, but slinks out of the race, where that immortal garland is to be run for, not without dust and heat." See also Bacon's *De Augmentis*, Book VII., chap. i.

[1] See Zeller's *Socrates and the Socratic School*, Part II., chap. v.

of duty. Similarly, Jesus was no ascetic or recluse. He "came eating and drinking," and was familiar with the ideas and habits of his people, even of those that were regarded as outcast and degraded. But he had also his times of retirement, temptations in the wilderness, and withdrawal to mountains. This combination of active participation and reflective withdrawal enabled him to sum up the morality of his nation, and by summing it up to set it upon a deeper basis, which fitted it to become the morality of the modern civilized world. So it is with most great moral reformers. They hold, in a sense, the mirror up to their times and peoples. They show them clearly what is already stirring dimly within their own consciences. They often seem to proclaim something entirely new and contrary to the whole spirit of the age; and consequently they often become martyrs to their convictions, as both Socrates and Jesus did. And no doubt they often do, like Moses, bring down a new law from heaven. But the new law was nearly always contained implicitly in the current morality of their time. They only interpreted that morality more carefully and strictly, freed it from self-contradictions, and pressed it back to the fundamental principles on which it rested.[1] When they do more than this, their work is seldom entirely beneficial. It is too much in the air, and has too little reference to the actual condition of things, to have much practical effect. Perhaps we may venture to blame our own great moral reformers of recent times, Carlyle and Ruskin, and, still more, Tolstoi, that they have made too little

[1] See Green's *Prolegomena to Ethics*, pp. 323—330, Muirhead's *Elements of Ethics*, pp. 253-4, and Dewey's *Outlines of Ethics*, pp. 189-90.

effort to understand what is best in the spirit of their times, and that their censures, consequently, are too much like the voice of one crying in the wilderness, an external accusation instead of an internal criticism. But even this would be only partly true. Carlyle and Ruskin are on the whole no exception to the general nature of moral reformers. Much of what is best in the spirit of the age finds in them its best expression, and their criticisms are to a very large extent organic to the thing criticised. They are to a certain extent the criticism of the age upon itself, its condemnation by its own principles, strictly interpreted ; and this is perhaps the only kind of criticism that is permanently beneficial.

CHAPTER VI.

MORAL PATHOLOGY.

§ 1. Moral Evil.—So far we have been mainly occupied with the consideration of the moral life in its positive aspect as a development towards goodness and perfection of character and social activity. We must now dwell for a little on its more shady aspects. Man's life is not a simple struggle towards virtue and holiness: it is quite as often a lapsing into vice and sin. This aspect we have on the whole neglected; and we must now give a little consideration to it.

Each man's moral life may, as we have seen, be regarded as a universe in itself. This universe may be a broad one or a narrow one. In the case of the majority of men it is sufficiently narrow to exclude many human interests. This narrowness is a source of conflict. It causes the individual good to appear to be in opposition to the general good of humanity. There is a sense in which no one ever seeks anything except what he regards as good. *Quidquid petitur petitur sub specie boni.* Evil is not sought as evil, but as a good under particular circumstances.[1] But

[1] Many of the acts that we regard as vices were at one time scarcely vices at all. They are the virtues of a lower stage of civilization, a lower universe which has been superseded, but in which some men still linger. Thus, Prof. Alexander says (*Moral Order and Progress*

the good sought is only the good of the universe concerned at the particular moment. This need not even be what the individual himself, taking a survey of his life, would regard as good for him: still less is it necessarily identical with or conformable to the general good. It may be the good of a very narrow universe —the universe of a man who is making no serious efforts to reach that rational point of view in which alone, as we have seen, true freedom is to be found; one who, remaining in servitude to his passions and animal propensities, prefers "bondage with ease to strenuous liberty." Indeed, there are even cases in which opposition to the general good becomes almost an end in itself; in which an individual is inclined to say, like Milton's Satan, "Evil, be thou my good." Social duty presents itself as a continual menace to a man who has not learned to identify the good of society with his own; and he is thus tempted to take up arms

p. 307): "Murder and lying and theft are a *damnosa hereditas* left us from a time when they were legitimate institutions: when it was honourable to kill all but members of the clan, or to lie without scruple to gain an end, and when there was promiscuity of property." *Cf.* Dewey's *Outlines of Ethics*, pp. 215–16. In this connection, Bentham refers to a passage in Homer where "Menelaus, courteously addressing a stranger, seeks to learn his occupation, and asks him what his business may be, whether by chance it is that of a pirate or what other." In Aristotle's *Politics* (I., viii. 7, 8.) pirates are mentioned along with fishermen, hunters, etc., as classes of workers who maintain themselves without retail trade. In Sparta, again, it was not thought dishonourable to steal, though it was thought dishonourable to be found out. *Cf.* Muirhead's *Elements of Ethics*, p. 210. Perhaps some forms of action which are popularly approved at the present day will seem equally surprising in future generations. Indeed, it would seem that even the pirate or filibuster has not ceased to be honoured in certain quarters among ourselves. And we can hardly even say *laudatur et alget.*

against it.[1] He cannot simply set it aside, as he can narrower goods that lie outside his own: it is a wider circle that includes his own, and he must either identify himself with it or fight against it. This war against society seldom indeed presents itself in the extreme form in which it is depicted in Milton's *Satan* or Shakespeare's *Timon of Athens*; but on a smaller scale we see it often enough in the wilful mischief of children, or in the anti-social delight that gives its edge to scandal.

But apart from any such war against the social good, even the best of men show at times "the defects of their qualities," *i. e.* the limitations connected with the particular kind of universe in which they live; and the more definite that universe is, the more marked are likely to be the defects. Hence the shortcomings which are often noticed in men of strong and original characters. A weak character has no definite limits. It flows vaguely over the boundaries of many universes, without distinctly occupying any. It excludes little because it contains little. It takes on, like a chameleon, the colour of any universe with which it comes in contact. Such a person is not likely to offend profoundly against any laws of his social surroundings. He will rather be "faultily faultless," drifting securely because he is making for nowhere, carried safely by wind and tide without any force of seamanship. It is to such that the proverb applies that "Fortune favours fools." No one can find any fault

[1] *Cf.* Shakespeare's *King Richard III.*:—

> "And therefore, since I cannot prove a lover,
> To entertain these fair well-spoken days,
> I am determined to prove a villain,
> And hate the idle pleasures of these days."

with one who has "no character at all."[1] On the other hand, one who has great strength of character in some particular direction has generally some accompanying weakness. His universe is a clear-cut circle, and excludes many elements of a complete moral life. Thus, the great poet, tenderly sensitive and full of high aspirations, is often deficient in steadiness of will and in attention to the more conventional rules of morals. The great reformer is apt to be inconsiderate of the weakness of others, and sometimes even unscrupulous in selecting the means to secure his purposes. The man who is devoted to great public achievements is often, like Socrates, unsuccessful in his domestic life. And so in many other cases. Hence in our moral judgments on individuals it is very necessary to consider not merely where they fell short, but also what they positively achieved or endeavoured.[2] A man's sins are the shadows of his virtues; and though a life of transparent goodness would cast no shadow, yet, so long as men fall short of this, the strongest virtues will often have the deepest shades.

§ 2. VICE.—Moral defects may be regarded either from the inner or from the outer side—as flaws of character or as issuing in evil deeds. From the former

[1] "Nothing so true as what you once let fall,
Most women have no characters at all."—POPE.

It is perhaps scarcely necessary to say that I do not mean to express agreement with this *dictum*.

[2] *Cf.* Carlyle's Essay on Burns: "Granted, the ship comes into harbour with shrouds and tackle damaged; the pilot is blameworthy; he has not been all-wise and all-powerful: but to know *how* blameworthy, tell us first whether his voyage has been round the Globe, or only to Ramsgate and the Isle of Dogs."

point of view, we may describe them as vices—vice[1] being the term that corresponds to virtue, and that denotes the inner stain of character rather than the overt act. From the outer side, we may speak of them rather as sins and crimes. The inner side is more extensive than the outer; for stains in the inner character may be to a large extent concealed, and not issue definitely in evil deeds—though they can scarcely fail to give a certain colour to our outer acts. It is chiefly Christianity that has taught us to attach as much weight to the evil in the heart as to the evil in outer deeds.[2] The more superficial view is to regard the latter as alone of importance. Such sayings as "whoever looketh on a woman to lust after her, has committed adultery with her already in his heart," gave a new extension to the conception of morals. Similarly, the conception of morality was deepened when it was recognized that an action which is externally good may in reality be evil if it is not done from the highest motive. "Whatever is not of faith is sin."[3] It was from this point of view that some of

[1] From Latin *vitium*, a defect or blemish. Sin appears to come from a root meaning a breach of right. The corresponding Greek word, ἁμαρτία, means an error. Crime is from the Latin *crimen*, an accusation or judgment.

[2] The term generally employed by Christian writers, however, is rather Sin than Vice. And thus Sin, though properly referring to an outer act rather than to a stain of character, has acquired the sense of Vice, and indeed has come to bear an even more inward meaning than Vice. For Vice corresponds to Virtue, and means a general habit of character issuing in particular bad acts; whereas Sin, as used by Christian writers, refers more often to the inner disposition of the heart, want of purity in the motive, and the like. It is in this sense, for instance, that St. Paul speaks of "sin dwelling in him."

[3] *Cf.* Sidgwick's *History of Ethics*, pp. 114-115.

the early Christian writers spoke of the virtues of the heathen as only "splendid vices."[1]

If we were to attempt to classify vices, the subdivisions of them would naturally correspond to those of the virtues. Thus we should have vices arising from our yielding to pleasure, or failing to endure pain, or not being sufficiently wise in our choice or strenuous in our purposes. We should also have various vices connected with imperfections in our social relationships. But into the details of such a classification we need not here enter.

§ **3.** Sin.—Although it is true, however, that the inner side of an evil character is quite as important, from a moral point of view, as the evil acts that flow from it, yet it must be remembered that there is a considerable difference between vice that remains in the heart and vice that issues in an evil deed; just as there is a difference between virtue that remains mere "good intention" and virtue that issues in deed. Mr. Muirhead remarks on this point[2]: "How far the resolution is from the completed act has become a proverb in respect to *good* resolutions. It is not, perhaps, very creditable to human nature that a similar reflection with regard to bad resolutions does not make us more charitable to persons who are caught apparently on the way to a crime. Höffding (*Psychology*, Eng. ed., p. 342) quotes a case of a woman who, having got into a neighbour's garden for the purpose of setting fire to her house, and been taken almost in the act, swore solemnly in court

1 Green, however, rightly insists that the best Greek writers were perfectly aware of the importance of the inner motive. See his *Prolegomena to Ethics*, Book III., chap. v., § 252; and *cf.* below, p.407

2 *Elements of Ethics*, p. 50, *note.*

that she knew she would not have perpetrated the act, but hesitated to state upon oath that she had abandoned her intention when she was surprised. With this we may compare the passage in Mark Rutherford's story of *Miriam's Schooling*, where, speaking of Miriam's temptation to take her own life, he says: 'Afterwards the thought that she had been close to suicide was for months a new terror to her. She was unaware that *the distance between us and dreadful crimes is much greater often than it appears to be.*'"[1] Perhaps we should say, then, not merely that "Hell is paved with good intentions," but that Heaven is paved with bad ones. It should be remembered, however, that there is an important difference here between good intentions and bad intentions. Bad intentions, like good intentions, are often frustrated by infirmity of purpose. In this case the good intention is not so good as the good act; whereas the bad intention is on the whole *worse* than the bad act. We do not think the better of Macbeth for his hesitation in committing murder; and often we feel almost an admiration for a determined crime. On the other hand, if a crime is prevented by genuine moral scruples, which arise often just at the moment when we have the opportunity of actually performing

[1] *Cf.* Carlyle's *French Revolution*, vol. iii., Book I., chap. iv.: "From the purpose of crime to the act there is an abyss; wonderful to think of. The finger lies on the pistol; but the man is not yet a murderer: nay, his whole nature staggering at such a consummation, is there not a confused pause rather—one last instant of possibility for him?" This distinction is, indeed, generally recognized in our ordinary moral judgments—though perhaps it is not so much dwelt upon as the corresponding distinction in the case of good actions. *Cf.* Adam Smith's *Theory of Moral Sentiments*, Part II., sect. III., chap. ii.

the deed, the hesitation which then arises is partly an exculpation. Thus we think on the whole the better of Lady Macbeth for her exclamation—

> "Had he not resembled
> My father as he slept, I had done't."

While, then, it is the case that a good intention is always inferior to the corresponding good deed,[1] it depends on circumstances whether a bad intention is or is not less evil than a bad deed.[2]

So also, from the point of view of the development of the character of the agent, a bad deed is often less evil than a stain in the character which does not go forth in action. An overt act brings, as a rule, an overt punishment. At any rate, the wickedness of the act is made openly apparent, in a way in which an evil thought is not made apparent. And when a man thus sees plainly the consequences of his action, he is often led to repent of it and amend his life. It is here that we see the element of truth in the common idea of the

[1] Even this, no doubt, is subject to some qualification. A comparatively unscrupulous man may often perform an action on the whole good, where a more conscientious man would hesitate. In such a case we should not always regard the conscientious man as blameworthy. Still, even here, the good intention of the conscientious man is not so good as his good action would have been, if only he could have brought himself to do it—though it may be as praiseworthy as the good action of a man who is more unscrupulous.

[2] Of course evil thoughts may also pass through a man's mind without getting the length even of intentions. In this case they are not morally culpable. *Cf.* Milton's *Paradise Lost*, Book V.—

> "Evil into the mind of God or man
> May come and go, so unapproved, and leave
> No spot or blame behind."

Even such evil, however, may be taken as evidence of the existence

benefit of "sowing wild oats." Here also we see the force of Luther's *Pecca fortiter.*[1] If there is evil in a man's heart it is generally best that it should come out plainly. There is more hope of a straightforward sinner than of one who is neither cold nor hot.[2]

§ 4. Crime.—The term Crime is generally used in a narrower sense than sin. It denotes only those offences against society which are recognized by national law, and which are liable to punishment. It is impossible that all moral offences should be brought under this category. Ingratitude, for instance, cannot be made punishable by law, because it would be practically impossible to specify the offences that come under this head. Again, the moral sense of conscientious persons is constantly outrunning the ordinary moral code of the society to which they belong, and thus inventing

of some lower universe within a man's nature—some extinct volcano, as it were—which may at some time or other burst forth into action. Milton, I suppose, would scarcely have admitted this—at least with regard to God.

[1] *Cf.* Browning's *The Statue and the Bust*—

> "The sin I impute to each frustrate ghost
> Is, the unlit lamp and the ungirt loin,
> Though the end in view was a vice, I say."

See Jones's *Browning as a Philosophical and Religious Teacher*, pp. 111—118.

[2] Similarly, in the life of a state, it is often desirable that an evil should be brought to a head. For this reason, it has often been observed that it is generally better to have a thoroughly bad despot than a half good one. Thus Hallam remarks (*Constitutional History of England*), "We are much indebted to the memory of Barbara, Duchess of Cleveland, Louisa, Duchess of Portsmouth, and Mrs. Eleanor Gwyn. . . . They played a serviceable part in ridding the kingdom of its besotted loyalty." *Cf.* Buckle's *History of Civilization*, vol. i., p. 338, where this passage is more fully given.

sins which are not recognized as crimes. Also when the evil effects of a sin fall mainly on the perpetrator of it, it is generally thought unnecessary to have a special law against it.

§ 5. PUNISHMENT.—Sin always brings evil consequences with it, and these evil consequences always react in some way upon the perpetrator. It was one of the paradoxes of the Socratic teaching that it is worse for a man to do wrong than to suffer wrong. In a sense this is true. The consequences of suffering wrong are external. They do not hurt the soul; whereas when a man does wrong, he lowers himself in the scale of being, and thus wrongs himself worse than any one else could wrong him. Still, the evil effects of a man's wrongdoing upon himself are not always apparent either to himself or to others. He often seems to have got off scot-free. Now this is contrary to our natural sense of justice. We naturally think that a man should be rewarded according to his deeds. And this idea seems to have a rational justification. The virtuous man is fighting on the side of human progress, and we feel it natural to expect that the gods will fight with him, and that his labours will prosper. The vicious man, on the other hand, is fighting against the gods, against our ideals of right; and it seems unnatural and unreasonable that his course should prosper. If for a time the virtuous man is unsuccessful, we yet feel bound to believe that his ultimate reward cannot "be dust."[1] His cause at least must prosper, unless the world is founded on injustice; and it is natural to expect and hope that he will prosper along with it. On

[1] See the concluding paragraphs in Sidgwick's *Methods of Ethics.*

the other hand, if the wicked for a time seems to flourish, we cannot help believing that his triumph is ephemeral, that in the long run the wages of sin must be death. It is here that the natural feelings of gratitude and revenge find their rational basis. Of course, we are not here maintaining that these feelings derive their *origin* from any such rational consideration. The psychological question of the development of these feelings is not now under consideration.[1] But these feelings could scarcely maintain their ground in the developed consciousness of mankind unless they had support in reason; and it is this rational support that we have now to take notice of.

Now it is out of these natural feelings that reward and punishment take their origin. In the case of revenge, indeed, and to some extent even in the case of gratitude, there is a certain tendency for the feeling to grow weaker as the race develops, so far as merely personal relationships are concerned. The primeval man resents keenly every wrong done to himself or to those who are intimately connected with himself, and seeks to return it at the earliest opportunity upon the head of the perpetrator. As the moral consciousness develops, this feeling of personal resentment becomes less keen. Men begin to learn that their merely personal wrongs are not of infinite importance; and under certain circumstances forgiveness becomes possible. They see that a wrongdoer to them is not necessarily a wrongdoer to humanity; and it is only this last that

1 On this point, see Mill's *Utilitarianism*, chap. v. See also Adam Smith's *Theory of Moral Sentiments*, Part II., sect. II., chap. iii., where the distinction between an inquiry into the origin of revenge and an inquiry into its rational basis is clearly drawn.

is of moment. As regards society, however, there is not anything like the same weakening of the sense of injury. A wrong against social law *is* a wrong against humanity, and cannot be forgiven until the offended majesty of the law has been appeased, *i. e.* until the wrongness and essential nullity of the act has been made apparent. It is here that the justification of punishment is to be found.

§ 6. THEORIES OF PUNISHMENT.—Three principal theories of the aims of punishment have been put forward. These are generally known as the preventive (or deterrent), the educative (or reformative), and the retributive theories. According to the first view, the aim of punishment is to deter others from committing similar offences. It is expressed in the familiar *dictum* of the judge—"You are not punished for stealing sheep, but in order that sheep may not be stolen." If this were the sole object of punishment, it seems probable that, with the development of the moral consciousness, it would speedily be abolished : for it could scarcely be regarded as just to inflict pain on one man *merely* for the benefit of others. It would involve treating a man as a *thing*, as a mere means, not an end in himself. The second view is that the aim of punishment is to educate or reform the offender himself. This appears to be the view that is most commonly taken at the present time;[1] because it is the one which seems to fit in best with the humanitarian sentiments of the age. It is evident that this theory could hardly be used to justify the penalty of death; and many other

[1] Though perhaps it is most often held in conjunction with the preceding view (the deterrent).

forms of punishment also would have to be regarded from this point of view as ineffective. Indeed it is probable that in many instances kind treatment would have a better effect than punishment. The third view is that the aim of punishment is to allow a man's deed to return on his own head, *i. e.* to make it apparent that the evil consequences of his act are not merely evils to others, but evils in which he is himself involved.[1] This is the view of punishment which appears to accord best with the origin of punishment among early peoples: but in later times, especially in Christian countries, there has been a tendency to reject it in favour of one or other of the two preceding theories, because it seems to rest on the unchristian passion of revenge. In this objection, however, there seems to be a misunderstanding involved. Revenge is condemned by Christianity on account of the feeling of personal malevolence which is involved in it. But retribution inflicted by a court of justice need not involve any such feeling. Such a court simply accords to a man what he has earned. He has done evil, and it is reasonable that the evil should return upon himself as the wages of his sin—the negative value which he has produced. Indeed there would in a sense be an inner self-contradiction in any society which abstained from inflicting punishment upon the guilty. Suppose a society had a law against stealing and yet allowed a thief who was unable to make restitution to escape scot-free.

[1] For an emphatic statement of this view, see Carlyle's *Latter-Day Pamphlets*, No. 2. See also Adam Smith's *Theory of Moral Sentiment*, Part II., sect. I., chap. iv., *note*, Bradley's *Ethical Studies*, Essay I., and Dühring's *Cursus der Philosophie*, sect. IV., chap. ii.

The laws of such a society would be little more than injunctions or recommendations to its citizens. They would not have the force of imperatives, or at least they would be imperatives which are liable to exceptions. Absolute imperatives must either be able to prevent any violation of their commands, or else must in some way vindicate their authority when they are violated.[1] This seems to be the primary aim of punishment. It should be observed however, that this aim in a sense includes the other two. If the aim of punishment is to vindicate the authority of the law, this will be partly done in so far as the offender is reformed, and in so far as similar acts are prevented. And indeed neither reformation nor prevention is likely to be effected by punishment *unless it is recognised that the punishment is a vindication of the law—i. e.* a revelation of the fact that the law holds good although it has been broken, that, in a sense, the breaking of it is a nullity. It is only when an offender sees the punishment of his crime to be the natural or logical outcome of his act that he is likely to be led to any real repentance; and it is only this recognition also that is likely to lead others to any real abhorrence of crime, as distinct from fear of its consequences. We may regard the retributive theory, then, when thus understood, as the most satisfactory of all the theories of punishment.[2]

1 *Cf.* above, p. 167, note 2.

2 A complete discussion of the theory of Punishment must be left to writers on the Philosophy of Law. I have here noticed only those points that seemed most important. The most original and suggestive treatment of the whole subject is that contained in Hegel's *Philosophy of Right*, §§ 96–103. Besides the theories above referred to, there are other possible views of Punishment. For in-

§ 7. Responsibility.—In considering the subject of punishment, it is necessary to ascertain to what extent a man is to be regarded as responsible for his actions. The plea of insanity is always held to exempt a man from punishment; but some thinkers go much further than this. Some hold, in fact, that all crime ought to be regarded as an evidence of insanity, and consequently that no one is to be regarded as responsible for his evil deeds. Instead of punishing men for their crimes, therefore, we ought rather to try to cure them of their distempers.[1] This view, of course, rests on the purely determinist conception of human conduct. It regards a man's acts not as the outcome of himself but of his circumstances. If the view of freedom which we have already taken is correct, this idea is false. A man's acts, when he is fully aware of what he is doing, are the expression of his own character; and it is impossible to go behind this character and fix the blame of it on some one else.[2] The case of insanity is different. Here the man is alienated from himself, and his acts are not his own. Of course, we must recog-

stance, there is the view that a main object of Punishment is to get rid of the offender, so as to prevent him from working further mischief. This is a preventive theory in a somewhat different sense from that already referred to under that name. But this view would evidently apply only to some forms of Punishment. For an interesting treatment of the whole subject, the student may be referred to Green's *Collected Works*, Vol. II., pp. 486—511. Discussions on this subject will also be found in Stephen's *Social Rights and Duties* and in the *International Journal of Ethics*, Vol. II., No. 1, pp. 20—31 and 51—76, and No. 2, pp. 232-239; also Vol. IV., No. 3, pp. 269-284, Vol. V., No. 2, pp. 241-243, Vol. VI., No. 4, pp. 479-502, and Vol. VII., No. 1, pp. 95-6.

[1] This is amusingly illustrated in S. Butler's *Erewhon*.

[2] *Cf.* above, Book I, chap. iii, especially the Note at the end.

nize in the sane man also a certain part of conduct for which he is not entirely responsible. Ignorance excuses much, unless the ignorance is itself culpable. Any condition in which a man is not fully master of himself removes his responsibility, except when—as in drunkenness—he can be blamed for the condition in which he is. When an act is done impulsively, also, a man has not the same full responsibility as he has for a deliberate action; except in so far as he is to be blamed for having habitually lived in a universe in which impulsive acts are possible.[1]

§ 8. REMORSE.—When an evil deed has been done, and when the wickedness of it has been brought home to the actor, it is accompanied by what is known as the pain of conscience. This pain arises from the sense of discord between our deeds and our ideals. It is proportioned, therefore, not to the enormity of our sins, but to the degree of discrepancy between these and our moral aspirations. In the "hardened sinner" it is scarcely felt at all, because he has habituated himself to live within a universe with whose ideals his acts are in perfect harmony. It is only in the rare moments in which he becomes aware of the larger universe beyond, that he is made conscious of any pang. On the other hand, in a sensitive moral nature, habituated to the higher universe of moral purpose, an evil deed is not merely accompanied by a pang of conscience, but, if it is an evil of any considerable magnitude, by a recurrent and persistent sense of having fallen from one's proper level. This persistent feeling of degradation is known as remorse. In its deepest form, it is not merely a grief for parti-

1 On this whole subject, see Aristotle's *Ethics*, Book III., chap. v.

cular acts but a sense of degradation in one's whole moral character—a sense that one has offended against the highest law, and that one's whole nature is in need of regeneration. The best expression of this in all literature, is, I suppose, that contained in the 51st Psalm: "Against thee, thee only, have I sinned, and done this evil in thy sight. . . . Behold, I was shapen in iniquity, and in sin did my mother conceive me," etc.

§ 9. Reformation.—The natural effect of remorse [1] is to lead to a reformation of character. This effect may be prevented by "stifling the conscience," *i. e.* by persistently withdrawing our attention from the higher moral universe and endeavouring to habituate ourselves to a life in a lower one. This endeavour may easily be successful. There is nothing inevitable about the higher point of view. *Facilis descensus Averni.* But if we do not thus abstract our attention from the voice of conscience, the natural result is that we make an effort to regain the level from which we have fallen, to bring our own actions once more into accordance with the ideals of which we are aware. This rise often requires a certain renewal of our whole nature. It requires a process of conversion like that to which we have already referred. Such a process is brought out in the Psalm which we have already quoted.

1 Some writers limit the application of the term "remorse" to those cases in which it does *not* lead to repentance. Sometimes the sense of aberration from the right path is so strong, that a return to it seems impossible, and the mind sinks into absolute despair. But there seems to be no sufficient reason for confining the term to such cases as these. It applies properly to any case in which there is a *gnawing pain* of Conscience. The word is derived from the Latin *remordeo* meaning "to bite again and again."

"Purge me with hyssop, and I shall be clean. . . . Create in me a clean heart." What is here figuratively referred to is the process of habituating ourselves to a higher universe, involving a transformation of our whole nature. When such a transformation is effected, it becomes almost impossible to act upon the lower level. Our habits of action become adjusted to the ideal within us, and go on almost without an effort. The will becomes to some extent "holy." Indeed some religious enthusiasts have even thought that such a process of "sanctification" may go so far as to make sin an impossibility.[1] But this is an exaggeration; "for virtue," as Hamlet says, "cannot so inoculate our old stock but we shall relish of it." What actually is possible is that we should definitely identify our wills with the highest point of view, and habituate ourselves by degrees to action that is in accordance with this. In this way we may asymptotically approximate to a state of perfect holiness of will.

§ **10.** Forgiveness.—The place of punishment has been indicated as the recoil of guilt upon the offender, thereby asserting the majesty of law, and leading on, through this, to repentance and reformation. In this way "the wheel comes full circle": the crime is wiped out—*i. e.* its essential nullity is exhibited—within the universe occupied by the criminal. It is possible, however, that this revolution may be effected without the intervention of punishment. The guilt may be brought home to the mind, not by the working of it out within the universe in which it has

[1] *Cf. First Epistle of John*, chap. iii., 9.: "Whosoever is born of God doth not commit sin; for his seed remaineth in him; and he cannot sin, because he is born of God."

arisen, but by rising to a higher universe. Education, for instance, may bring about this result. Modern humanitarian sentiment leads us, as far as possible, to seek to deal with criminals—especially young criminals—in this way, rather than by way of punishment. Where this is possible, the offence can be forgiven, because it no longer exists at the higher point of view. It must be remembered, however, that to say this is not to deny the validity of the preceding account of punishment.[1]

§ **11.** SOCIAL CORRUPTION.—So far we have been looking at moral evil only as it appears in the individual life. But a society, as well as an individual, may have moral excellence or defect. It may have its customs and its institutions so framed as to give encouragement to its citizens at every turn to live at the highest human level; or it may have them so devised as to obstruct the moral life and make virtue, in certain aspects, almost an impossibility.[2] Civilization ought to mean the arrangement of social conditions so as to make virtue as easy and vice as difficult as possible. But civilization, as it actually exists, is partly a product of the vices as well as of the virtues of mankind; and is adapted to the former as well as to the latter. It is not arranged for the extinction of vice, but at most, in Burke's language, that vice may "lose half its evil by losing all its grossness." It is arranged not for the promotion of virtue but only of respectability. Heroic

1 Some highly suggestive remarks on the relation between Punishment and Forgiveness will be found in Caird's *Hegel*, pp. 28–30.

2 Mr. Muirhead enumerates, as illustrations of such institutions (*Elements of Ethics*, p. 174), "brothels, gambling dens, cribs, and cramming establishments."

virtue is in many ways made difficult rather than easy.[1] Among the rich luxury is encouraged. Wants are multiplied, and go on multiplying themselves, and men are tempted to seek the satisfaction of them by dishonourable means. The poor, on the other hand, are exploited—*i. e.* used as a mere means for the advantage of others. They have no leisure for culture and are exposed to many temptations. When a nation has reached such a stage as this, it often declines and falls. Indeed it must do so, unless it is reawakened by a reformer, such as in our own time Carlyle and Ruskin. Sometimes also it is saved by a revolution; but this generally involves almost as much moral evil as the corrupt state of society itself. Sometimes, again, a nation wanders so far from the ways of righteousness that other nations feel justified in stepping in for its punishment. It is in such cases that an offensive warfare seems to be justified. But it is seldom that one nation is thus entitled to make itself the judge of another. The Jews seem to have regarded themselves in this way in ancient times. In modern times, as a general rule, only a combination of nations could feel themselves to represent the side of right reason against the corruptions of some particular society.[2]

[1] See Carlyle's view on this point in his Essay on "The Opera."

[2] This chapter is of course concerned only with the *ethical* aspect of moral pathology. For other aspects see the interesting books by Mr. W. D. Morrison on *Juvenile Offenders* and *Crime and its Causes;* also Enrico Ferri's *Criminal Sociology*, Maudsley's *Body and Mind*, and other works on morbid psychology, criminology, &c.

CHAPTER VII.

MORAL PROGRESS.

§ 1. Social Evolution.—Although we have frequently referred, throughout the preceding chapters, to the fact that the moral life is to be regarded as a process of development, yet our treatment of it has been to a large extent statical. What has been said, however, in the closing paragraphs of the last two chapters, with reference to the work of the moral reformer, seems to lead us naturally to a more explicit consideration of the conditions of moral development. That there is a certain "increasing purpose through the ages," is a truth that is now in some form generally admitted, however much we may be tempted at times to doubt it. This is on the whole an entirely modern conception, and is somewhat contrary to the impressions of the natural man. It is not only to the graceful pessimism of a Horace that the present generation seems a degenerate offspring of heroic sires. The idea of a Golden Age behind us, of the "good old times," when men were uncorrupted by the luxuries and follies of a later age, of the "wisdom of our ancestors," when men looked at the world with a fresher and deeper glance, has a certain natural fascination for the discontented spirit of man. Nor is it entirely without a basis in fact. If "new occasions bring new duties," they also bring new opportunities for vice. Looking, for instance, at the commercial morality of the present time, and comparing it with the practices of more primitive peoples, we have often a difficulty in determining whether, in the root of the matter, we have advanced or receded. If in some respects our actions seem more trustworthy and based on broader and more reasonable principles, in other respects we seem to have grown more selfish and dishonest than men ever were before.[1] It is only when we pass from the actions of individual human beings to the consideration of the principles on which men are expected to act—the codes of duty and ideals of virtue which have grown up among us—that we gain any firm assurance of progress. When we reflect, however, that those higher conceptions of conduct which prevail among us could scarcely hold their ground if there were not some individuals who habitually acted in accordance with them, we may be led to believe that even in the individual life there must on the whole have been a certain advancement. And, indeed, this conviction ought to be rather strengthened than otherwise by the recognition that, in our modern system of life, there are depths of degradation which to a ruder state of existence are scarcely known. *Corruptio optimi pessima.* The grass, as Mr. Ruskin somewhere remarks, is green every year: it is only the wheat that, on account of its higher nature, is liable to a blight. So, too, a mere animal is incapable of such a fall as we find in man. As Walt Whitman says,—

"They do not sweat and whine about their condition,
They do not lie awake in the dark and weep for their sins,
They do not make me sick discussing their duty to God;
Not one is dissatisfied, not one is demented

---

[1] *Cf.* Marshall's *Principles of Economics*, pp. 6—8 and 361.

With the mania of owning things;
Not one kneels to another, nor to his kind that lived thousands of years ago;
Not one is respectable or unhappy over the whole earth."

All this is, no doubt, very creditable to the lower animals; yet it need not induce us to envy their condition. Man's relative unhappiness, as Carlyle says, is due to his greatness. "The assertion of our weakness and deficiency," as Emerson puts it, "is the fine innuendo by which the soul makes its enormous claim." "A spark disturbs our clod;" and this disturbance brings with it the possibility of new forms of evil. Animals are not *capable* of the higher forms of sin. "The advantages which I envy in my neighbour, the favour of society or of a particular person which I lose and he wins and which makes me jealous of him, the superiority in form or power or place of which the imagination excites my ambition—these would have no more existence for an agent not self-conscious, or not dealing with other self-conscious agents, than colour has for the blind."[1] So it is also, in some measure, with the growth of civilization. Knowledge is power for evil as well as for good. The depth of our Hell measures the height of our Heaven; and when we are conscious of special degradation and misery in the midst of a high civilization, we may reflect, with Milton's Satan, "No wonder, fallen such a pernicious height." There seems, therefore, to be no real reason

[1] Green's *Prolegomena to Ethics*, p. 131. It should, however, in fairness be noted, that practically all the evils here alluded to are to be found in a rudimentary form even among the lower animals. What is peculiar to man is not so much the presence of new forms of evil as the clear consciousness that they *are* evil, and the consequent degradation in yielding to them. Still, it is also true that civilization creates more subtle forms of evil.

for doubting that in the general improvement of the conditions of life there is also a certain moral advance.[1] To the consideration of this advance we may now appropriately devote a few paragraphs.

§ 2. THE MORAL UNIVERSE.—We have seen already that the moral life of an individual is lived within what may be described as a social or moral universe. Such a universe is constituted by various elements. It consists, on the one hand, of a moral ideal, generally recognized by the society in which the individual lives. This ideal may be expressed in a code of commandments, in a series of injunctions, or in the form of a life which is set up as a model for our imitation. This is the ideal side of our moral universe. On the other hand, it consists of definite social institutions, such as we have referred to in Chapter II. Finally, it consists of certain habitual modes of action, acquired rather by half-unconscious imitation than by any distinct injunctions or efforts to copy an ideal pattern. In any given age and country these three elements of a social universe will nearly always be found in some more or less fully developed form; but often there is a very considerable divergence between the three. A people's ideal does not always bear a close resemblance to its

1 Even Carlyle partly admits this. See his *Heroes and Hero-Worship*, Lect. IV. "I do not make much of 'Progress of the Species' as handled in these times of ours. . . . Yet I may say, the fact itself seems certain enough. . . . No man whatever believes, or can believe, exactly what his grandfather believed: he enlarges somewhat, by fresh discovery, his view of the Universe; and consequently his Theorem of the Universe. . . . It is the history of every man; and in the history of mankind we see it summed up into great historical amounts—revolutions, new epochs. . . . So with all beliefs whatsoever in this world—all Systems of Belief and Systems of Practice that spring from these."

institutions or its habits; and sometimes even its habits are not entirely conformable to its institutions. A religion of peace and good-will has been found not incompatible with the thumb-screw and the torpedo; and the existence of the monogamic family is not always a guarantee of social purity. A large part of the moral development of peoples consists in the effort to adjust these three elements to one another; though it also partly consists in the effort to elevate their ideas, and improve their institutions and habits.

§ 3. Inner Contradiction in our Universe.—The mere want of adjustment between the various elements in our moral universe is often of itself sufficient to suggest the need of a new ideal or of new institutions. Institutions to which men's habits cannot be adapted are soon felt to be unsatisfactory, and have to be abolished. This was largely true, for instance, of the institution of celibacy among the clergy in the middle ages. So, again, if our institutions and habits are in contradiction with our ideal, this will sometimes be the means of enabling us to see that our ideal is too narrow. The early Christian ideal has been in this way expanded by the absorption of elements derived from the Greeks and other pagan peoples. On the other hand, our habits may become gradually reformed, so as to adapt themselves to the institutions among which we live; and our institutions may gradually be adjusted to our ideals. This is perhaps the more normal course of the two. Sometimes there is a crisis in a people's life, in which the question arises, whether the institutions are to be revolutionized or men's habits reformed. There seems to be such a crisis, for instance, at the present time with regard to our industrial system.

§ 4. SENSE OF INCOMPLETENESS.—Even apart, however, from those contradictions within our universe which drive us forward by a kind of natural dialectic, there is also a tendency to progress in our habits, institutions, and ideals, due simply to our consciousness of their incompleteness. This incompleteness is often first brought to clear consciousness by some reformer who points out a certain want of logic in our present system. Such a reformer points out, for instance, that we habitually act in one way under certain circumstances, but in quite an opposite way under other circumstances, when there is no sufficient reason to account for the difference. He may point out inconsistencies, for instance, in the way in which men commonly treat their children, being sometimes cruel and sometimes over-indulgent. Or he may point out the difference between the morality recognized in the relations between countries in their negotiations with one another and that recognized in the relations between individuals, and may ask whether there is any adequate reason for this contrast. Or he may point to the pains inflicted on animals in certain processes of vivisection, or in various forms of the chase, or in slaughter-houses, or even in the ordinary use of animals as instruments of human service; he may contrast this with the treatment accorded to human beings; and may ask whether, seeing that in respect of the suffering of pain there appears to be no distinction between men and animals, there is any sufficient reason for tolerating in the case of animals what would not be tolerated in the case of men. Or, again, he may turn to the *institutions* of social life, as distinguished from its habits, and may call attention to anomalies in the government of the country, in the regulation of family life, in the methods of industrial action, and in the various other organized forms in which the life of the community is carried on. He may thus criticise these institutions by means of themselves, showing that the principles underlying them are incompletely carried out. He may ask, for instance, upon what recognized principle women are excluded from certain functions and privileges which are universally open to men. Finally, such a reformer, carrying his weapon of criticism still higher, may attack our ideals themselves. He may ask whether we are quite consistent in our ideas of what constitutes the highest kind of life. Is there not a certain narrowness about them? Do we not apply principles in one direction which we omit to extend in another? If we attach so much importance to the tithing of mint and cummin, should we not be at least equally careful about some other weightier matters of the law? If the ideal man should be brave in battle and temperate in his food and drink, should he not also show fortitude under disaster and self-restraint in power? Such questions lead[1] to an extension of the conception of our duties and of the virtues which we ought to cultivate; and this aspect of moral development is so important that it may be well to consider it a little more fully.

§ 5. DEEPENING OF SPIRITUAL LIFE.—There is no respect in which moral progress can be more clearly seen than in the deepening views which men are led to take of the nature of the virtues and of the duties

1 Through the force of persuasion. It is here that Mr. Alexander's view of "Natural Selection in Morals" is in place. See above, pp. 243-246.

that are required of them. This has been illustrated in a most masterly manner by Green in that part of his *Prolegomena to Ethics* [1] in which he contrasts the Greek with the modern conceptions of virtue—perhaps the most original and suggestive chapter in the whole of that great work. He takes up the two most prominent of the personal virtues recognized by the Greeks, courage and temperance,[2] and shows how in modern times both the range of their application has been extended and the conception of the principle on which they rest deepened. With regard to temperance, for instance, he observes that the Greeks limited the application of this virtue to questions of food and drink and sexual intercourse; whereas, in modern times, we apply it to various other forms of self-denial. He urges, moreover, that even with regard to those particular forms of self-indulgence which the Greeks recognized as vicious, the principles on which they rested the claim for self-denial were not so deep as ours.

"We present to ourselves," as he says,[3] "the objects of moral loyalty which we should be ashamed to forsake for our pleasures, in a far greater variety of forms than did the Greek, and it is a much larger self-denial which loyalty to these objects demands of us. It is no longer the State alone that represents to us the *melior natura* before whose claims our animal inclinations sink abashed. Other forms of association put restraints and make demands on us which the Greek knew not. An indulgence, which a man would otherwise allow himself, he foregoes in consideration of

1 Book III., chap. v.

2 *Cf.* also Muirhead's *Elements of Ethics*, pp. 225—8.

3 *Loc. cit.*, p. 284.

claims on the part of wife or children, of men as such or women as such, of fellow-Christians or fellow-workmen, which could not have been made intelligible in the ancient world. . . . It is certain that the requirements founded on ideas of common good, which in our consciences we recognize as calling for the surrender of our inclinations to pleasure, are more far-reaching and penetrate life more deeply than did such requirements in the ancient world, and that in consequence a more complete self-denial is demanded of us." And Green goes on to add that even in respect of those aspects of life in which the Greeks did recognize the virtue of self-denial, their recognition is less complete and far-reaching than that of the moral consciousness in our own time. This is especially true with regard to self-denial in matters of sexual indulgence. And the change which has thus taken place in our moral consciousness does not mean merely that we have extended the range within which certain virtues are applicable. It involves also a deepening of our conception of the principles on which the virtue rests. "The principles from which it was derived"[1] by the Greek moralists, "so far as they were practically available and tenable, seem to have been twofold. One was that all indulgence should be avoided which unfitted a man for the discharge of his duties in peace or war; the other, that such a check should be kept on the lusts of the flesh as might prevent them from issuing in what a Greek knew as ὕβρις—a kind of self-assertion and aggression upon the rights of others in respect of person and property, for which we have not an equivalent name, but which was looked upon as the antithesis of

[1] *Loc. cit.*, p. 285.

the civil spirit." Another prevalent notion among Greek philosophers was "that the kind of pleasure with which temperance has to do is in some way unworthy of man, because one of which the other animals are susceptible." "Society was not in a state in which the principle that humanity in the person of every one is to be treated always as an end, never merely as a means, could be apprehended in its full universality; and it is this principle alone, however it may be stated, which affords a rational ground for the obligation to chastity as we understand it. The society of modern Christendom, it is needless to say, is far enough from acting upon it, but in its conscience it recognizes the principle as it was not recognized in the ancient world. The legal investment of every one with personal rights makes it impossible for one whose mind is open to the claims of others to ignore the wrong of treating a woman as the servant of his pleasures at the cost of her own degradation. Though the wrong is still habitually done, it is done under a rebuke of conscience to which a Greek of Aristotle's time, with most women about him in slavery, and without even the capacity (to judge from the writings of the philosophers) for an ideal of society in which this should be otherwise, could not have been sensible. The sensibility could only arise in sequence upon that change in the actual structure of society through which the human person, as such, without distinction of sex, became the subject of rights."[1] Thus we have here, not merely an extension of the range of the virtue, but also a deeper conception of the principle upon which it rests. And the same truth might be illustrated in the case of other virtues. The

[1] *Loc. cit*, p. 288.

principle of the virtues, in fact, becomes universalized, and ceases to attach itself simply to this or that particular mode of manifestation. And along with this universalization there comes a deeper consciousness of the inwardness of the virtuous life. So long as the virtues are connected only with particular modes of manifestation in social life (*e. g.* courage with the activities of war), they seem to be little more than outer facts. When, on the other hand, we see that the essence of the virtues consists in the application of a certain principle, whatever may be the sphere in which it is applied, we recognize at the same time that their essence lies rather in the attitude of the individual heart than in the particular forms of outward action. It is true that the Greeks were by no means ignorant of this essentially inward character of the virtues. They knew—*i. e.* their best thinkers knew—that the virtues are not virtues at all unless they are accompanied with purity of heart and will, unless they are done *τοῦ καλοῦ ἕνεκα*, for the sake of what is beautiful or noble. But the recognition of this has been very much deepened [1] by the growth of a clearer consciousness of the universality of the principles on which the virtues rest.

§ **6.** New Obligations.—In the preceding section we have seen that the deepening of the conception of the principle on which the virtues rest is accompanied by an extension of the sphere of their application. The expansion of our ideas of obligation which takes place in this way is of a comparatively simple kind. We

[1] It seems to me that Green somewhat exaggerates the unity of sentiment on this point in the Greek and Christian moral consciousness, *Ibid.*, p. 271 *seq.*, p. 288, &c. But no doubt there is greater danger in unduly emphasizing the divergence between them.

learn to recognize that what applies to the Greek applies equally to the Barbarian, that what applies to the Jew applies equally to the Gentile, that what applies to men applies equally to women. But along with this expansion there is another of a less simple kind, by which we become aware of obligations that present themselves to our minds as *new* rather than as mere extensions of the old ones. Thus, when the Christian conception of man's nature and destiny was introduced, it seemed to bring with it an obligation of propagandism which had not been felt in the same way before. The recognition of the infinite issues at stake in the moral regeneration of mankind, and of the interest in these issues which belongs to every individual soul, rendered it an imperative obligation on those who accepted the Christian doctrine to endeavour, to the utmost of their power, to "preach the Gospel to every creature." On the other hand, the knowledge which has been subsequently acquired of the gradual way in which the moral nature develops, has modified the obligation of preaching, and transformed it into the obligation to make intellectual and moral education universally accessible. Again, the knowledge that has recently been acquired of the relation between men and animals has led to a transformation of our view with regard to the way in which the latter ought to be treated. It would be going somewhat too far to describe this transformation by saying that we have extended to the lower animals the same conception of rights and obligations as we apply to men. In the case of some of the lower animals any such extension would be generally regarded as absurd; and even with respect to the highest of them, unless we allow that they are self-conscious, rational beings, with a moral life like that of man (which even their best friends scarcely claim for them), we cannot acknowledge that they possess rights, in any strict interpretation of the term. All that we seem entitled to say is, that we have begun to recognize that the animal consciousness has a certain kinship with our own, that we can discover in it traces of feelings, perceptions, and instincts that appear to be on the way towards the development of a moral life, and that consequently we feel bound to treat the animals, at least in their higher forms, in a way that is semi-human—in a way approximating to that in which we treat children, in whom also the moral consciousness, to which rights attach, is not fully developed.[1] But the acknowledgment of our relationship has, in recent times, extended even further than this. Even with inanimate nature we have begun to recognize a certain kinship; and this has given rise in some minds to a more or less vague sentiment that even natural scenery possesses a certain *quasi*-right to exist, and ought not to be wantonly outraged.

In noticing such extensions of our obligations as these, it ought not to be denied that there are also some obligations of which we are apt to lose the consciousness. Thus, it has often been pointed out that, in more primitive times, the consciousness of the mutual obligations of master and servant was much stronger than it is now. This must be fully admitted. At the same time it should be remembered that this

[1] I need hardly say that I do not intend this passage to be taken as a complete discussion of this difficult question. The *quasi*-rights of children, for instance, must differ widely from those of the lower animals, inasmuch as the former are actually on the way to become rational, whereas the latter are not.

partial obliteration of the consciousness of a duty is partly due to an extension of the sphere within which our obligations hold. The intensity of the personal relationship between master and servant (which, however, is often greatly exaggerated) was due in part to the fact that no human obligation was acknowledged except what was due to that particular relationship. The servant was supposed to owe a debt of gratitude to his master for the protection and patronage vouchsafed to him.[1] The obligation recognized on the side of the master was, I am afraid, generally of a much vaguer character. Now, on the other hand, we recognize the obligation of man to man, as such, independently of any special relationships. That this recognition of a wider sphere of duty has practically weakened the narrower ties, seems to be partly true. It is always more difficult to act up to the requirements of a large obligation than to those of a small one. But this ought not to prevent us from perceiving that there has been a great extension of the sphere of acknowledged duty.

§ 7. Moral Change and Change of Environment.— The question is sometimes raised[2] whether the extension which thus takes place in our view of moral obligation is in reality due to a development of our moral consciousness, or only to a change in our environment. Thus, it may be urged that the emancipation of slaves[3] in modern times may be accounted for by the general development of our industrial methods;

[1] *Cf.* Buckle's *History of Civilization*, Vol. III., p. 325. See also above, pp. 304, note 1, and 346, note 1.

[2] *Cf.* Muirhead's *Elements of Ethics*,, p. 229 *seq.*

[3] *Cf.* Adam Smith's *Wealth of Nations*, Book III., chap. ii.

and it may be suggested that the attempt to rest the movement in this direction on general considerations of the rights of men is merely an illustration of the cant and hypocrisy of the modern age. Now it seems clear that the general recognition of the possibility of abolishing slavery (which Aristotle could not acknowledge), and with this the recognition of the duty of actually abolishing it, was really due to the development of economic conditions. And a similar remark would apply in most other cases in which an extension of recognized obligations occurs. It is so, for instance, also with the movement towards the emancipation of women. New industrial conditions have pushed forward the demand for it. But this fact need not in any way stumble us, or make us hesitate the more to believe that there is a moral advance. Doubtless the moral life does not grow up *in vacuo*. It is relative throughout to the environment in which it is nurtured. It grows by the increase of our knowledge, by the increase of our power, by the increase of the possibilities of our action. The moral life is thus constantly being determined anew by the new conditions and combinations presented for solution, and by the new directions in which possible solutions appear.[1] But its growth is not therefore the less real. Those who know anything of the spirit in which the emancipation of the slaves was carried out, must be well aware that, however true it may be that industrial conditions made it possible, that industrial conditions first brought it to men's minds, and first won for it a general acceptance, how-

1 The spirit of man "makes contemporary life the object on which it acts; itself being the infinite impulse of activity to alter its forms." Hegel's *Philosophy of History* (English translation), p. 215.

ever true it may even be that commercial and merely political motives weighed most strongly with the rank and file of those who fought for its accomplishment, yet the inspiration of the great leaders of the movement, without which the necessary self-sacrifice would never have been undergone, was at bottom purely moral. Mere external changes may bring the need of a moral reform to light; but it is only in so far as they thus serve to awaken a moral consciousness that the world is moved by them.

§ 8. THE IDEAL UNIVERSE.—The fact of moral progress causes it to be not entirely true that the good man, and especially the moral genius (who is generally at the same time a moral reformer), lives within a universe constituted by actually existing habits and institutions, or even by ideals that are definitely acknowledged at a given time and place. What is said of Abraham may be applied to the moral life generally. "By faith Abraham, when he was called to go out into a place which he should after receive for an inheritance, obeyed; and he went out, not knowing whither he went. . . . For he looked for a city which hath foundations, whose Builder and Maker is God." The spirit of man, in its moral growth, looks continually for such a city. It is continually "moving about in worlds not realized." It is dissatisfied with the habits and institutions actually established at any time and place, and even with the ideals that are customarily recognized, and presses forward towards a form of life that shall be more complete, consistent, and satisfying.[1] Hence the perennial interest of Utopias and

[1] "That which gives life its keynote is, not what men think good, but what they think best. True, this is not the part of belief which

poetic dreams and anticipations of better modes of existence. The danger, in such dreams and anticipations, is that they are apt to represent only a partial and abstract phase in the development of life, and to involve some loss of hold upon its concrete content. In this sense, there is some truth in the saying that the world as a whole is wiser than its wisest men. The fresh intuitions of the prophets, who are as strangers and pilgrims on the earth, require to be reinterpreted in the light of the practical good sense of those who are at home on it. The prophetic seer is sometimes apt to be blinded by his own light, so that the rest of the world seems to him darkness. Hence the melancholy which Carlyle regarded as at the basis

is embodied in conduct: the ordinary man tries to avoid only what is obviously wrong; the best of men does not always make us aware that he is striving after what is right. We do not see people growing into the resemblance of what they admire; it is much if we can see them growing into the unlikeness of that which they condemn. But the dominant influence of life lies ever in the unrealized. While all that we discern is the negative aspect of a man's ideal, that ideal itself lives by admiration which never clothes itself in word or deed. In seeing what he avoids we judge only the least important part of his standard; it is that which he never strives to realize in his own person which makes him what he is. The average, secular man of to-day is a different being because Christendom has hallowed the precept to give the cloak to him who asks the coat; it would be easier to argue that this claim for what most would call an impossible virtue has been injurious than that it has been impotent. Christianity has moulded character where we should vainly seek to discern that it has influenced conduct. *Not the criminal code, but the counsel of perfection shows us what a nation is becoming;* and he who casts on any set of duties the shadow of the *second best*, so far as he is successful, does more to influence the moral ideal than he who succeeds in passing a new law." These suggestive, and even profound remarks are taken from Miss Wedgwood's work on *The Moral Ideal* (p. 373). The italics are mine.

of all true insight—the pessimism and despair which cloud the consciousness, so long as it sees only the imperfection and incompleteness of all actual achievement in the moral life, in contrast with the partial Pisgah-sight of something better to be attained; and does not yet perceive, what is often the deeper truth, that the germs of the better are already at work in the partly good, and may even be contained in what presents itself at first as simply bad.

The recognition, however, of this moral faith, this presence of the consciousness of an unattained and even unformulated ideal, leads us at once into the region of poetry and religion, which in a manner transcend morality. The consideration of these would carry us beyond our present subject; but we may conclude with a chapter on the relationship between Ethics and Metaphysics, in which the place of religion will be incidentally referred to.[1]

[1] The whole subject of the present chapter is most admirably treated in Muirhead's *Elements of Ethics*, Book V.

CONCLUDING CHAPTER.

ETHICS AND METAPHYSICS.

§ 1. General Remarks.—It must be evident to the discerning reader that, in what has gone before, we have occasionally been skating on rather thin ice. The ultimate questions to which we have been led have not received any quite satisfactory solution. We have perhaps seen the insufficiency of all other theories of Ethics more fully than we have seen the sufficiency of that which we have been led to adopt. The truth is that the theory of Ethics which seems most satisfactory has a metaphysical basis, and without the consideration of that basis there can be no thorough understanding of it. If we could have satisfied ourselves with a Hedonistic theory, a psychological basis might perhaps have sufficed. On the other hand, if one of the current evolution theories could be accepted, we might look for our basis in the study of biology. But if we rest our view of Ethics on the idea of the development of the ideal self or of the rational universe, the significance of this cannot be made fully apparent without a metaphysical examination of the nature of the self; nor can its validity be established except by a discussion of the reality of the rational universe. Some further examination of this point seems now to be demanded.

§ 2. Validity of the Ideal.—The general result of

our inquiry may be summed up as follows. We have seen that the moral consciousness presents itself first of all in the form of law, a supreme command or categorical imperative imposed on the will of the individual. Hence, when reflection begins on the nature of morality, the first theory which presents itself is one that conceives of it as an absolute law of Duty. But this breaks down, because, as we have seen, when this idea is carefully analyzed, it is found to yield no content. The next form in which the idea of morality presents itself is that of the Good; and this is naturally thought of at first simply as that which satisfies desire, *i. e.* as the pleasant. But the pleasant is formless, just as the law of Duty is empty; and we are thus led to look for a more adequate conception of the Good. This is found in the idea of the complete realization of the essential nature of mankind. But in order to understand this, it is necessary to study the nature of mankind in its concrete development. Accordingly, we have been led to notice, in a brief and summary fashion, the ways in which the realization of humanity may be regarded as accomplishing itself through the various institutions of social life, through the duties and virtues which grow up in connection with these, through the growth of the inner life of the individual, and through the progressive development of human history. Through these various activities mankind may be seen to be gradually attaining to that complete rationality which can only be reached through the complete grasping of the world of experience, and bringing it into intelligible relationship to ourselves. This process cannot be seen to complete itself within the actual moral life of mankind: and the ideal involved in the moral life is consequently unfulfilled. Life remains at the best incomplete—a noble work, it may be, but a torso. Now this incompleteness in the concrete realization of the moral ideal brings with it the further defect that the validity of the moral ideal is not fully made apparent in the course of its concrete realization. If mankind could be supposed actually to attain that complete development of human faculty, that complete bringing of the world into intelligible and harmonious relationship to the human consciousness, at which we may be said to aim, the result would no doubt be seen to be so satisfying in itself that it would be impossible to question the validity of the ideal as an object of human effort. But this complete justification is not possible so long as the process is not fully worked out. Now it is this insufficiency in the moral life that leads us to the point of view of religion; and perhaps some consideration of the latter may enable us to see more clearly the nature of the ultimate problem which is involved in the moral consciousness.

§ 3. Morality and Religion.—Matthew Arnold, as is well known, defined religion as "morality touched with emotion." "This," remarks Mr. Muirhead,[1] "does not carry us far. Emotion is not a distinctive mark of religious conduct. All conduct . . . is touched with emotion, otherwise it would not be conduct at all." This criticism is perhaps not entirely fair. All conduct is in a sense touched with emotion—*i. e.* it involves an element of feeling. So does all conscious life. But this need not prevent us from distinguishing between emotional and unemotional acts and states. In ordinary life the element of feeling is to all intents

[1] *Elements of Ethics*, p. 180.

in abeyance. It influences us quietly, but does not rise into prominence. We do what is in harmony with our habits and convictions; we shun what is in discord with them: but our attention is not specially directed to the agreeableness of the one or the disagreeableness of the other. The one does not thrill us, and the other does not jar upon us or shock us. This is the case so long as we are living steadily within the universe to which we have become habituated. And we are so living throughout the greater part of that conduct which we describe as moral. Even the saint or hero may perform saintly or heroic acts with no consciousness that he is doing anything particular, and consequently with no sense either of harmony disturbed or of harmony restored. The more entirely he is absorbed in his work, the more likely is this to be the case. Still more is it the case that the "good neighbour" and the "honest citizen" go about their avocations, for the most part, with no particular stirrings of the breast. On the other hand, Matthew Arnold was probably so far in the right, that the religious attitude, as distinguished from the simply moral, is at least generally characterized (as is also the artistic) by a more or less distinctly marked emotion. Still, I agree with Mr. Muirhead in thinking that Matthew Arnold's definition is inadequate, and this for more reasons than one.

In the first place, although it seems an exaggeration to say that *all* conduct is in any special sense characterized by emotion, yet conduct is frequently emotional without being, in any ordinary sense of the term, religious. Conduct becomes emotional whenever our attention is strongly directed to some end, affected by our conduct, which we have come to regard as supremely important. Now this end may or may not be of such a kind as we ordinarily designate religious. In a hotly-contested political election, a man may perform his duty as a citizen under a strong emotional influence, which in some cases has been so powerful as to produce death. Yet we should scarcely say that his conduct is more religious than that of the good workman who carefully finishes his job, without feeling that anything particular is at stake. Or again, when one of the parents of a large family suddenly dies, leaving the whole responsibility on the shoulders of the other, the sense of this new responsibility, in a conscientious person, will generally cause the ordinary duties of the family to be, for some time at least, performed with a keener feeling than before of the issues that are at stake. Yet we should scarcely say that it is thereby rendered more religious. The truth is that the emotional quality of our actions depends largely on the question whether they are habitual acts, acts that belong to the ordinary universe within which we live, or whether we are rising into an unfamiliar universe. Now it may be readily granted that religion, in any real sense of the word, can hardly be made so habitual as not to involve some uplifting of the soul, some withdrawal from the point of view of ordinary life to a more comprehensive or more profound apprehension of the world and of our relations to it. Hence it can hardly fail to involve emotion. Even the *Amor intellectualis Dei* of Spinoza, however purely intellectual it may be, is still *amor*. But conduct may involve strong and deep emotion and yet not be specially religious.

But, in the second place, Matthew Arnold's definition

seems to err not merely by including much which would not, in any ordinary sense, be regarded as religion, but also by excluding much which would naturally fall under that category. Some religions have scarcely any direct bearing on the moral life. Even the religion of the Greeks, one of the most beautiful and typical of all religions, was largely a worship of the powers of nature. Their gods were not conspicuously respectable; and though in an indirect way they had an ennobling influence on Greek life, yet they were not consciously set up as models of moral conduct, nor did the worship of them involve any direct incitement to virtue. They did indeed, stand to some extent as representations of the social bond; so that to violate social order was to offend against the gods of the society. But this was not perhaps their most prominent characteristic. And the same is true of many other forms of religion.[1] It cannot, therefore, be said that religion is always to be regarded as immediately connected with the moral life.

§ 4. THE RELATION OF RELIGION TO ART.—The connection of religion with Ethics, in fact, appears to be very similar to the connection of art with Ethics;[2] and we

[1] *E. g.*, the Scandinavian. The religion of the Romans, on the other hand, was strongly moral (*Cf.* Froude's *Cæsar*, p. 12). No doubt, even the Scandinavian and early German mythologies contained some strongly-marked ethical traits: *Cf.* Carlyle's *Heroes and Hero-Worship*, sect. I., and Prof. Pfleiderer's article on "The National Traits of the Germans as seen in their Religion," in the *International Journal of Ethics* for October, 1892 (vol. iii., No. 1, pp. 2—7).

[2] A chapter dealing with this subject, which appeared in the earlier edition of this *Manual*, has been omitted, partly from want of space, and partly because it was felt that the treatment of such a subject in a handbook like this is necessarily too slight to be of any value. The remarks in the present chapter will probably be found suffi-

may understand the connection better by noticing the relation of art to religion. Carlyle was fond of reminding us of the connection between the terms "Worship" and "Worthship." What we worship is what we regard as having supreme worth or value. Religion, in short, like art, is concerned with ideals. But while the ideals of art are beautiful objects that yield an immediate satisfaction, the ideals of religion are rather objects that are regarded as having supreme and ultimate worth. In their immediate aspect they may have "no beauty that we should desire them." For the same reason the ideals of religion must be regarded as *true.* Art, aiming at an immediate satisfaction, may be partly dream. No doubt, if it is to be great art, it must keep close to reality; and even its most imaginative creations must express some inner truth in nature or in morals. Indeed, in its highest forms art approaches very closely to religion. But still it is never necessary that the creations of art should be absolutely true. It is enough that they should be beautiful suggestions of truth. Even in the highest regions of art, such a work as Shakespeare's *Tempest* has no literal truth. There are no Calibans or Ariels; nor is it necessary for our appreciation of the play that we should actually believe that there are any. We can feel the whole beauty of it, and yet be well aware that all the creations in it are "such stuff as dreams are made of." Religion, on the other hand, gives us ideals which are regarded as realities, and even as the most real of things. The Homeric gods, as depicted in the poems, are poetic creations; and there is no necessity for supposing

ciently intelligible without reference to the preliminary chapter on Art.

them to be anything but dreams—*significant* dreams, no doubt, but still dreams. As worshipped by the Greek people, on the other hand, the gods were necessarily regarded as realities. Hegel, indeed, has contrasted the Greek with the Christian religion, by saying that the gods of the former were mere creations of the imagination.[1] This is partly true. The Greeks were an artistic much more than a religious people; and their gods never became, in any complete sense, definitely established objects of belief. But just to this extent they remained poetry rather than religion. So also in the Christian religion there are many mythical elements which have been made subjects of poetry and of various forms of artistic representation. We may admire the paintings of Jesus and of the Virgin, and feel an artistic pleasure in the contemplation of them, without believing that they are anything more than beautiful dreams.[2] But the man who takes Jesus

1 See Wallace's *Logic of Hegel*, p. 233.

2 No doubt there are stages of human development at which the distinction here indicated is scarcely perceived. To the Greeks, for instance, Homer supplied poetry, philosophy, and religion all in one. And so, no doubt, it was to some extent in the great ages of Mediæval art. At such periods the significance of art for a nation's life is much greater than it is after the three provinces have been more rigidly divided. "However excellent," says Hegel, "we think the statues of the Greek gods, however nobly and perfectly God the Father and Christ and Mary may be portrayed, it makes no difference, our knees no longer bend." See Bosanquet's *History of Æsthetic*, p. 344, and *cf.* Caird's *Hegel*, pp. 111–12. Of course, the clearer distinction in modern times between art and philosophy or religion need not in the end cause our art to be less perfect or less serious than that of the ancient world. For we may still recognize that art is the best expression of all that is deepest in philosophy and religion. But it is necessarily dethroned from its former unique position. Homer and Dante may have been treated as *authorities*:

as a supreme object of worship necessarily regards him as real and as the greatest of realities.

§ 5. THE NECESSITY OF RELIGION.—Religion, being thus akin to art, is related to Ethics in somewhat the same way as art is. It carries us, in a sense, beyond the moral life, by raising us to the idea of a sphere of attainment beyond the sphere of mere struggle. And this it does, not, like art, in the way of hint and suggestion, but rather in the way of definite conviction. Such convictions are a necessity of man's life—a necessity partly intellectual and partly moral.[1] Both on the intellectual and on the moral side this necessity may be said to arise from a consciousness of the incompleteness and inadequacy of our experience. On the purely intellectual side this presents itself as a feeling of wonder at the inexplicable in nature. Out of this wonder, as Plato taught, all science arises. But the imagination outruns science, and creates explanations for itself; and even after science has done its best, there remains a sense of unexplained mystery into which we still seek to press. On the moral side, in like manner, there is a sense of inadequacy in our ordinary experience—a want of completeness in our lives, a want of poetic justice in our fates. It is chiefly on this side that religion touches on Ethics. But even the demand for intellectual explanation expresses a moral need. It is the desire to be at home within our universe, and not to be confronted at every turn with alien mysteries. In an unintelligible world we could

Shakespeare and Goethe are regarded only as *exponents* and *illustrators*. But perhaps they have gained in breadth what they have lost in height. *Cf.* Bosanquet, *op. cit.*, p. 469.

[1] See Caird's *Philosophy of Religion*, chap. iv.

not lead a moral life, because we should not know what ends to propose to ourselves, or how to set about realizing them.[1] Hence even when the imagination constructs myths to explain the formation of the clouds or the motion of the sun, it is indirectly serving morality. It saves us from that prosaic abandonment in which the higher life expires—that state in which as Wordsworth complains, "Little we see in nature that is ours." Natural religions, like that of the Greeks, save us in some measure from this. They enable us in the presence of nature to

> "Have glimpses that may make us less forlorn;
> Have sight of Proteus rising from the sea;
> Or hear old Triton blow his wreathed horn."

Even here, then, the religious imagination comes to the aid of the moral life. Still, it is chiefly in so far as it supplies a relief from the inadequacy of the moral life itself that religion touches on Ethics. On this aspect we must now look a little more closely.

§ 6. THE FAILURE OF LIFE.—Those who fix their attention on the lives of individuals have always sufficient ground for Pessimism. Even the most favoured human beings attain only a small part of what they hope; and what they hope is generally but a small part of what they would wish to be able to hope. And a large proportion of the human race scarcely seem to get the length of hope at all. Nor is it merely

1 It is chiefly for this reason that intellectual scepticism is apt to have a detrimental effect on the moral life. This effect was strongly insisted on by Plato, and, in more recent times, by Carlyle. Descartes also, in the pursuit of his intellectual scepticism, felt the need of guarding himself against its moral accompaniment. See his *Discourse of Method*, Part III. Burke also emphasized this point.

that the average individual does not get so much out of life as he could wish. The apparent unfairness of fate is equally galling. Sometimes the sight of the wicked flourishing "like the green bay tree" offends the moral sense even more than the failures of the righteous; and this not from envy, but from a sense of injustice.

§ 7. THE FAILURE OF SOCIETY.—Some consolation may be found, indeed, for the failure of the individual life in the confidence that society at least goes on advancing. But the progress of society can scarcely be regarded as compensating for individual failure. Society is not an entity apart from the individuals who compose it; and if the individuals fail, society cannot have wholly succeeded. It might be argued, indeed, that it is moving towards success, towards some "far-off divine event." Still no such event could be morally satisfactory if it were reached, so to speak, by trampling over the fallen bodies of generations of men who "all died not having received the promises."[1] And even the poor comfort that society advances, does not seem an altogether certain hope. In nearly all ages wise men have been inclined to think that they and their generation were no better than their fathers; and even if we can on the whole trace a line of progress through the lives of nations, "yet progress has many receding waves,"[2] and in nearly every case it seems to be followed in the end by a period of cor-

[1] This point is strikingly emphasized in Prof. A. Seth's pamphlet on *The Present Position of the Philosophical Sciences*, near the end. *Cf.* also his *Hegelianism and Personality*, p. 228. With much of what is said in both these places, however, I do not agree.

[2] Sorley's *Ethics of Naturalism*, p. 272.

ruption and decline. And even such progress as there is, appears only to lead in an asymptotical way to the goal that we hope for. The highest civilizations that have ever been achieved, have been accompanied by corrupting luxury on the one hand and degrading toil and misery on the other; and there has never been a time at which the most deeply moral natures have not been made to feel that, in some important respects, the world was out of joint, and that neither they nor any others were born to set it right. Is there, it may well be asked, any sober and certain ground for supposing that it will ever be otherwise? If not, we must regard society as having failed, just as, for the most part, the individual life is perceived to fail.

§ 8. THE FAILURE OF ART.—Conscious of the failure of life and society, many of the finest natures have taken refuge in art. Matthew Arnold, in one of the most striking of his poems,[1] represents Goethe as turning from the vain strife of his age, after having exposed its weaknesses, and proclaiming to his contemporaries as their last resort—"Art still has truth, take refuge there." And indeed in the same poem Matthew Arnold describes the message of Wordsworth to his generation, though in very different language, as being yet substantially the same. Seeing the folly and confusion of the actual world around him, he taught his age to set it aside, and seek relief in feeling. But this is a somewhat treacherous refuge. "Art for Art's sake" is a shallow doctrine at the best.[2] It is true in a sense that art is play. *Ernst ist das*

[1] *Memorial Verses.*

[2] See Bosanquet's *History of Æsthetic*, p. 457.

Leben, heiter ist die Kunst.[1] Men may seek a temporary relief in it from the struggle of life; and it may be a not unworthy commendation to say of a great poet—

> "The cloud of mortal destiny,
> Others will front it fearlessly—
> But who, like him, will put it by?"

But even this service can be rendered to us by art only so long as it is believed by us to be a revelation of a deeper truth in things.[2] If it is taken merely *as* art, merely as a beautiful dream, it sinks into play, becomes a mere refined amusement, and loses all its real power over the human spirit.[3] There could hardly be any worse sign of an age than that it regards art as a mere amusement, as a mere escape from the graver problems of life. In the great ages of art, there has always been a faith behind the art—a belief that it symbolizes truths that are eternal, and that can be expressed, though with an unspeakable loss of adequacy and completeness, in sober prose[4] as well as in the form of artistic dreams. Their art was, indeed, in a sense, play; but it was a playful mode of giving utterance to the exuberance of a nation's faith, and as such it had the highest beauty and value.

1 "Life is serious, art is joyous."—Schiller. *Cf.* Bosanquet's *History of Æsthetic*, p. 296.

2 On the relation of Beauty to Truth, see Caird's *Essays on Literature and Philosophy*, vol. i., pp. 54–65, 151–154, &c.; and *cf.* Bosanquet's *History of Æsthetic*, pp. 336, 458–460, &c.

3 "We cannot give the name of sacred poet to the 'idle singer of an empty day,' but only to him who can express the deepest and widest interests of human life."—Caird, *loc. cit.*, p. 154. *Cf.* also Caird's *Critical Philosophy of Kant*, vol. ii., pp. 465–6.

4 Dante actually gave a prose interpretation of his *Divine Comedy.*

But as a desperate escape from scepticism it could have no such worth. Its dreams, if they were supposed to be altogether unreal, would only make the emptiness of life the more conspicuous.[1] We might still feel that they were beautiful; but it would be like the beautifying of a sepulchre full of dead men's bones. The soul would have gone out of them.

§ 9. THE DEMAND FOR THE INFINITE.—"Man's Unhappiness," says Carlyle, "comes of his greatness. It is because there is an Infinite in him which with all his cunning he cannot quite bury under the finite." The ideal unity of our self-consciousness demands a perfectly harmonious and intelligible universe; and this cannot be found so long as we see the world in its finite aspect, as a series of isolated events set over against each other. Art partly breaks down this finitude, and lets us see the infinite significance of it shining through.[2] But it does this in a form that is not quite adequate to the truth—a form that is partly playful; and we return from its ideals to the actual

[1] Some suggestive remarks on the possibility of making art a substitute for religion will be found in Dühring's *Erzatz der Religion*, pp. 106–111. See also Caird's *Hegel*, pp. 37–8.

[2] Carlyle says (*Heroes and Hero-Worship*, Lect. III.) that music is "a kind of inarticulate unfathomable speech, which leads us to the edge of the Infinite, and lets us for moments gaze into that." *Cf.* also Caird's *Hegel*, pp. 112–114; and see the passage quoted from Hegel in Bosanquet's *History of Æsthetic*, p. 361. "For in art we have to do with no mere toy of pleasure or of utility, but with the liberation of the mind from the content and forms of the finite, with the presence and union of the Absolute within the sensuous and phenomenal, and with an unfolding of truth which is not exhausted in the evolution of nature, but reveals itself in the world-history, of which it constitutes the most beautiful aspect and the best reward for the hard toil of reality and the tedious labours of knowledge."

world with all our discontent again—sometimes, indeed, with our discontent deepened and intensified. Art reaches its intuitions of truth, as Browning put it, "at first leap;" and often, when reflection supervenes, we find that what we have received is not a solution of our problems, but at most the suggestion of a solution. What we require is an ideal which shall at the same time be absolutely real.

§ **10.** THE TWO INFINITES.—Now there are two main forms in which we become aware of the infinite as a reality within our experience—what we may call the purely intellectual form and the moral form. These two are well expressed by Kant in a familiar passage, in which he states the two great objects of reverence.[1] "Two things fill the mind with ever new and increasing admiration and awe, the oftener and the more steadily we reflect on them: *the starry heavens above and the moral law within.* I have not to search for them and conjecture them as though they were veiled in darkness or were in the transcendent region beyond my horizon; I see them before me and connect them directly with the consciousness of my existence. The former begins from the place I occupy in the external world of sense, and enlarges my connection therein to an unbounded extent with worlds upon worlds and systems of systems. . . . The second begins from my invisible self, my personality, and exhibits me in a world which has true infinity, but which is traceable only by the understanding, and with which I discern that I am

1 Conclusion of *Critique of Practical Reason* (Abbott's translation), p. 260. *Cf.* also Janet's *Theory of Morals,* Book III., chap. xii., where the whole subject of the relation of Ethics to Religion is treated in a suggestive way.

not in a merely contingent but in a universal and necessary connection. . . . The former view of a countless multitude of worlds annihilates as it were my importance as an *animal creature*, which after it has been for a short time provided with vital power, one knows not how, must again give back the matter of which it was formed to the planet it inhabits (a mere speck in the universe). The second, on the contrary, infinitely elevates my worth as an *intelligence* by my personality, in which the moral law reveals to me a life independent on animality and even on the whole sensible world, at least so far as may be inferred from the destination assigned to my existence by this law, a destination not restricted to conditions and limits of this life, but reaching into the infinite." These two reverences, separately or in combination, may be said to furnish the basis of religious worship. When the first is taken alone, it gives rise to Pantheism or to Agnosticism: when the second is taken alone, it gives rise to Monotheism or to the Religion of Humanity. When the two are combined, we have a more complete form of religion.

§ 11. THE FIRST RELIGION.—The first form of reverence, then, in which the demand for the infinite is recognized, is the worship of Nature in the boundlessness of its extent and power. In its crudest form this religion is summed up in the saying that "All is God." This form of worship rises very naturally in our minds when we are brought face to face with the great elemental forces of nature. "What is man," we are then tempted to exclaim, "that he should be put in comparison with the infinity of the material universe!" This point of view is materialistic, and is scarcely distinguishable from Atheism. It is, however, a superficial view. The infinity which is reached by the mere adding on of an endless number of parts is what Hegel called "the bad infinite." Such an infinity is in no way more satisfying to our minds than the finite is. The mere fact that we cannot get to an end of a thing does not add anything to its value. The blank emptiness of space, for instance, has no worth for us. The deeper Pantheism is distinguished from this superficial one, in that its meaning is summed up, not in the saying that "All is God," but that "God is all"—*i. e.* that the finite world is an unreality, and that the ultimate reality is the spiritual power behind it. This view is developed, with great force and suggestiveness, in the *Ethics* of Spinoza.[1] Since, however, it rests on the mere negation of the finite, it ends either in the assertion of blank nothingness as the ultimate reality (the Nirvana of the Buddhists), or in the assertion of some ultimate reality of which nothing can be known (the Unknowable of Mr. Herbert Spencer). This infinity of emptiness is in the end quite as unsatisfactory (both from an intellectual and from a moral point of view) as the infinity of an inexhaustible aggregate.

§ 12. THE SECOND RELIGION.—The second religion is the worship of the moral law in the absoluteness of its authority. In order, however, that this may be made an object of reverence, it requires to be regarded as embodied in some concrete form. The simplest form is that of a supreme Law-giver, as in the religion of the Jews. The unsatisfactoriness of this view arises from the fact that such a Law-giver has to be thought of as external to that to which he gives the law. He

[1] There is, however, another side to the doctrine of Spinoza, which

deals with a refractory material. He requires, therefore, to be thought of as in some sense finite,[1] being limited by a world outside. Accordingly, this view leads readily to Manicheism, the belief in an infinite Devil as well as an infinite God. Other methods of escape are (1) to say frankly, like J. S. Mill, that God is not infinite at all,[2] which deprives us of that supreme satisfaction which the infinite alone can give; or (2) to abandon the idea of a personal God, and assert only a progressive realization of the moral ideal. This latter resource appears in the Religion of Humanity, instituted by Auguste Comte,[3] in which the human race as a whole is represented as a Great Being struggling forward against the opposing tendencies of an unintelligent and unintelligible nature. A similar view is to be found in Matthew Arnold's idea of a "Power, not ourselves, that makes for righteousness." The inherent weakness of any such position is that it leaves an irreconcilable dualism in our world. Evil is left unaccounted for, and we have no assurance that it will be finally overcome with good.

§ **13.** The Third Religion.—It is one of the supreme merits of the Christian religion that it combines these two infinites so completely. The God of Christianity is conceived at once as the infinite Power revealed in nature, and as the source and end of the moral ideal. It

is even more important and characteristic, and which brings it into connection rather with the moral point of view, referred to in the next section. The same may be said of Buddhism.

1 In which case this view would become identical with Mill's.

2 A similar view is developed in a recent book entitled *Riddles of the Sphinx.*

3 For an account and criticism of this, see Caird's *Social Philosophy and Religion of Comte.*

enables men to see in the world outside them the working out of their own moral aspirations,[1] to believe that "morality is the nature of things," and to have confidence, not indeed that "whatever is, is right," but that "whatever is right, is"—*i. e.* as Carlyle put it, that "the soul of the world is just," that in the last resort "the Good" (in Plato's phrase) is the only reality. Other religions have partly contained this same inspiring faith; but Christianity seems to bring it out most clearly.

§ 14. Religion and Superstition.—It has been frequently noted that ages of religious faith tend to be rapidly followed by times of doubt and disbelief. The cause of this is not far to seek. The religious imagination, as we have already remarked, in its effort after a final explanation of the mysteries of things, outruns science. It cannot wait for the plodding processes of reasoning and verification. But these come afterwards; and when they come, they generally find that the kernel of religious truth has been hastily wrapped up in a husk of superstition. The religions of the world have grown out of the buoyant faith of some imaginative and impassioned natures. To the founders of them they have nearly always been an inextricable blending of truth and poetry.[2] Those who came after

1 Beautifully expressed by Browning—*Epistle from Karshish*—

> "So through the darkness comes a human voice,
> Saying—'O heart I made, a heart beats here,'" &c.

2 *I. e.* their meaning takes the form of an image, which for them is inseparable from the meaning. As the Germans say, the *Begriff* (*i. e.* the conception or meaning) appears in the form of a *Vorstellung* (imaginative representation). *Cf.* Wallace's *Logic of Hegel* (First Edition), pp. 1–2, and lxxxvii.—lxxxix.

them have seldom been able to catch just that point of view at which insight passed into beauty. The poetry evaporates, and the truth does not remain. The happy intuition becomes a miserable creed; and the beautiful images that clustered round it turn into the spectres of superstition. Then, as soon as another man of real insight arises, the hollowness of the dogma is revealed, and with this revelation the entire religion appears to be exploded. The gods before which the rapt adoration of saint and poet once knelt become mere names that serve perhaps only to give gusto to an oath.

§ 15. THE ETHICAL SIGNIFICANCE OF RELIGION.—What remains essential in religion, however, is the conviction of the reality of the moral life; and this conviction it is which metaphysics is required to justify. In other words, it has to justify the belief that the moral life is worth living. From a practical point of view we may say no doubt that such a justification is hardly required. It is the faith which is inevitably involved in life itself, just as in science there is involved the faith that the world can be seen as an intelligible system. In a stirring article entitled "Is Life worth Living?" Professor James remarks—"If this life be not a real fight, in which something is eternally gained for the universe by success, it is no better than a game of private theatricals from which one may withdraw at will. But it *feels* like a real fight;" and he concludes by urging that our attitude on this matter is necessarily one of faith. "Believe," he says, "that life is worth living, and your belief will half create the fact. The 'scientific proof' that you are right may not be clear before the day of judgment (or some stage of Being which that expression may serve to symbolize) is reached. But the faithful fighters of this hour, or the beings that then and there will represent them, may then turn to the faint-hearted, who here decline to go on, with words like those with which Henry IV. greeted the tardy Crillon after a great victory had been gained: 'Hang yourself, Crillon! we fought at Arques, and you were not there.'"

The belief, then, that the moral life is in this sense real may be said to be the essential significance of religion; and without some such belief the moral life is hardly possible at all. In all spheres of thought, however, the human intellect demands proof; and the proof of this particular point can only be found in metaphysics.

§ **16.** The Ultimate Problems of Metaphysics.—We thus see how it is that the science of Ethics is incomplete in itself, and stretches out its hands to metaphysics. But in a sense this is true of all science, and we may even say, of all art. All positive science rests on the belief that the world can be seen as an intelligible system, and this belief cannot be justified except by metaphysical inquiry. All fine art, in like manner, at least in its higher and more serious forms, may be said to rest upon the conviction that "Beauty is Truth," that the point of view from which the beautiful is apprehended is a point of view which grasps a more essential form of actuality than that which appears in mere existence. Similarly, the moral point of view involves the conviction that Good is more real than Evil, that the moral ideal has a higher actnality[1] than the exist-

[1] In so far as such a point of view as that here indicated can be adopted, the Ideal becomes transformed into the Idea (in the sense in which that term was used by Plato and Hegel)—*i. e.* instead of

ing world as it appears to the ordinary consciousness of mankind.

How this can be established by metaphysical reflection it is not our business here to inquire. It may be possible, as in the system of Hegel, to show that "the actual is rational, and the rational is actual;" or again, it may only be possible, as in the view of Bradley, to show that the moral point of view contains a higher "degree of reality" than that to which it is opposed. Or it may be that we are left in a purely agnostic position. Such questions could not be answered here except in a purely dogmatic fashion, and a dogmatic answer is of course worse than none. It is enough for us to have indicated where the ultimate problem lies; and to have shown that Ethics, regarded as a separate science, is not complete in itself.[1]

being thought of teleologically, as the end or standard by which *we* are guided in the realization of the moral life, it would be regarded rather as the underlying principle by which reality itself is determined, in the process by which its inner significance is gradually unfolded. Thus, from the point of view of religion, or of a metaphysical system such as that of Plato or Hegel, the distinction between the Ideal and the Actual vanishes. The term *Idea*, expresses in this sense (which must be carefully distinguished from its use by Descartes, Locke, Berkeley, Hume, &c.), the point of view from which this transcendence of the opposition takes place. But it would obviously be far beyond the scope of such a work as this to consider whether this point of view can be justified. It would require a complete metaphysical system to deal with it.

1 Metaphysics is a subject which it is hardly worth while for any one to take up unless he intends to study it thoroughly. The student who takes it up in this way will soon find that the writer who is most important at the present time is Hegel. A popular introduction to Hegel has been written by Dr. Edward Caird (*Blackwood's Philosophical Classics*); and Professor Wallace has also written valuable *Prolegomena* to his Translation of the *Logic* and the *Philosophy of Mind*. The best introduction to Hegel in English is, how-

ever, Caird's *Critical Philosophy of Kant*, where the transition from Kant to Hegel is explained with the greatest thoroughness and clearness. Mr. McTaggart's *Studies in Hegelian Dialectic* and the Prefatory Essay to Dr. Bosanquet's translation of the Introduction to Hegel's *Aesthetik* may also be found helpful. As a more elementary introduction to the study of Metaphysics, Watson's *Comte, Mill and Spencer* may be recommended, with some slight reservations; and, for still more elementary purposes, Mr. W. M. Salter's *First Steps in Philosophy* may be mentioned. With special reference to the more religious aspect of the subject, Caird's *Evolution of Religion* will be found exceedingly instructive. Mr. Bradley's *Appearance and Reality* is the most important attempt at a metaphysical construction in English. It is largely, but not entirely in harmony with the Hegelian system. But perhaps it must still be sorrowfully admitted, as it was by Kant, that "Metaphysics is undoubtedly the most difficult of sciences; but it is a science that has not yet come into existence."

APPENDIX.

NOTE ON ETHICAL LITERATURE.

THE chief function of such a handbook as this must be, like that of Goldsmith's village preacher, to "allure to brighter worlds and lead the way." The "brighter worlds" in this case are the works of the great masters of the science. To these frequent references have been given throughout this sketch; but it may be worth while now to make a few general remarks upon them, and to indicate the order in which they may be most profitably read. The precise order in which they should be taken will of course depend partly on individual taste, and partly on the amount of time at the student's disposal.

For the majority of readers, I believe that Mill's *Utilitarianism* will be found one of the most easy and interesting books to begin upon; and it will give a good general impression of the Hedonistic point of view. If thought desirable, the concluding chapter on Justice may be omitted on a first reading. The study of the whole book may be accompanied by a reference to the criticisms contained in Sidgwick's *Methods of Ethics*.

Portions of Kant ought also to be read at an early date. The student will soon find that modern Ethics, like modern Philosophy generally, turns largely upon him. The first two sections of the *Metaphysic of Moral* (to be found in Abbott's *Kant's Theory of Ethics*) will be found comparatively easy, even by students who have not read anything on Metaphysics, and will convey a fair understanding of Kant's general position: but it is difficult to proceed far in Kant's ethical system without some knowledge of his metaphysical principles.[1]

The student who has mastered the general principles of Mill and Kant will have a fair idea of the bases of the Utilitarian and the

[1] Those who are prepared to go fully into Kant's point of view will find invaluable aid in Caird's *Critical Philosophy of Kant*.

Idealistic systems of morals. Those who wish to go more fully into the modern developments of these points of view must read Sidgwick's *Methods of Ethics* and Green's *Prolegomena.* Of these two, Green's is the more difficult to understand, on account of his strongly metaphysical point of view. Muirhead's *Elements of Ethics*, however, will give the student great assistance in following the line of Green's argument.

Sidgwick's book has the advantage of supplying the student not only with the best statement of the modern Utilitarian point of view, but also with the best criticism of Intuitionism. For a statement of the Intuitionist point of view by one of its own adherents, reference may be made to Martineau's *Types of Ethical Theory.* An elementary student, however, would probably find this book somewhat confusing.

The chief books written from the Evolutionist point of view are Spencer's *Data of Ethics*,[1] Stephen's *Science of Ethics* and Alexander's *Moral Order and Progress.*[2] Each of these possesses special merits of its own. Mr. Alexander's book seems to me the most profound of the three; but for this very reason it may perhaps be the most difficult for an elementary student. Mr. Stephen's book, being by a man of letters, is written in remarkably clear and vigorous English, and will probably be found the most pleasant to read. It is also in some respects the most suggestive. Mr. Spencer's work has the advantage of forming part of a complete and comprehensive speculative system; and the way in which he connects Ethics with the various other departments of knowledge gives his book a peculiar interest and stimulating power, especially perhaps for young students. Otherwise, it does not seem to me so satisfactory as the work of either of the other two.

While, however, the more recent books will naturally have a certain attraction for the student, he ought not to neglect the older masterpieces. Plato's *Republic* and Aristotle's *Ethics*[3] are still in many respects the greatest works on Ethics that we possess; and

---

1 Now Part I. of *The Principles of Ethics.*

2 Chapters v. and vi. in Darwin's *Descent of Man* may also be referred to. But the treatment of this subject there is slight and superficial.

3 In connection with these, Bosanquet's *Companion to Plato's Republic* and Muirhead's *Chapters from Aristotle's Ethics* may be used. See also the Commentaries by Nettleship and Stewart.

every serious student ought to read them at as early a point in his course as he finds possible. Spinoza's *Ethics* is a very difficult book, and can only be fully appreciated by an advanced student of Metaphysics.[1] The same remark is on the whole true of Hegel's *Philosophie des Rechts*—a great book of which at last there is a tolerable translation. Some of the most important points in Hegel's system are, however, reproduced in a simple and interesting form in Dewey's *Outlines of a Critical Theory of Ethics.*[2] Bradley's *Ethical Studies* also represents the Hegelian point of view; but this most interesting and stimulating work is unhappily out of print.[3] Among other works of historical importance, which the student may profitably read, may be mentioned Butler's *Sermons* and *Dissertation II.* ("Of the Nature of Virtue"), Hume's *Treatise on Human Nature,* Books II. and III., or *Dissertation on the Passions* and *Inquiry concerning the Principles of Morals,* Adam Smith's *Theory of Moral Sentiment,* Bentham's *Principles of Morals and Legislation,* Bacon's *De Augmentis,* Books VII. and VIII., and Hobbes's *Leviathan.*[4]

---

[1] Students who desire to read Spinoza will derive great assistance from Principal Caird's excellent monograph in Blackwood's "Philosophical Classics." Those who read German will find his whole system expounded very fully and with extraordinary clearness and brilliancy in Kuno Fischer's *Geschichte der neuern Philosophie,* I., ii. For a shorter account, students may be referred to the article on "Cartesianism" in the *Encyclopœdia Britannica.* Spinoza, as a pure Determinist, and as one who wholly excludes the conception of ideals or of final causes, may be said to begin by denying the possibility of Ethics. He treats it as a positive or natural history science, not as a normative science. *Cf.*. above, p. 92, *note* 1. But as he goes on with the development of his system, he is led, in spite of himself, to admit the conception of an ideal or end in human life, and even of a certain "immanent finality" in nature. This point is well brought out by Principal Caird (*op. cit.,* pp. 270, 304).

[2] Hegel's *Philosophy of History* (translated in Bohn's Series) will also be found very interesting.

[3] Bosanquet's *Civilization of Christendom*—a collection of Essays on Applied Ethics—is also written from this point of view.

[4] A fairly complete list of important English works on Ethics, arranged according to schools, will be found at the end of Muirhead's *Elements of Ethics.*

Many other useful books might be mentioned. Students who read German will find Paulsen's *System der Ethik*,[1] Höffding's *Ethik*, Wundt's *Ethik*, and Simmel's *Einleitung in die Moralwissenschaft*, of the greatest value.[2] In French, the writings of Guyau and Fouillée will be found particularly suggestive: Simon's *Du Devoir* and Renouvier's *La Science Morale* may also be referred to. For Social Ethics Comte's *Politique Positive* is invaluable.[3] I may also mention Sorley's *Ethics of Naturalism*,[4] Fowler's *Progressive Morality*, Clifford's *Lectures and Essays* (containing some extremely suggestive points), Lotze's *Practical Philosophy*, Janet's *Theory of Morals*, Royce's *Religious Aspect of Philosophy*, Edgeworth's *Mathematical Psychics* and *New and Old Methods of Ethics*. In the History of Ethics, in addition to Sidgwick's *History of Ethics* and to the short statements contained in General Histories of Philosophy (*e. g.* Erdmann's, Zeller's, and Kuno Fischer's), reference may be made to Lecky's *History of European Morals*, to Stephen's *English Thought in the Eighteenth Century*, and (for readers of German) to Ziegler's *Ethik der Griechen und Römern* and *Geschichte der Christlichen Ethik*, and to Jodl's *Geschichte der neuern Ethik*. C. M. Williams's recent work on *Evolutional Ethics* will be found useful with reference to that particular school. Notices of current literature on the subject, as well as discussions on particular points, will be found from time to time in the pages of *Mind*, of the *Philosophical Review*, and of the *International Journal of Ethics*.

---

[1] This is particularly valuable on the side of Applied Ethics.

[2] The last-named is almost purely critical.

[3] For a summary of Comte's point of view, see Caird's *Social Philosophy and Religion of Comte*. For the history of social Ethics before Comte, reference may be made to Janet's *Histoire de la Science Politique;* also to the same writer's *Philosophie de la Revolution francaise, Saint-Simon et le Saint-Simonisme*, and *Les Origines du Socialisme contemporain*. See also Mohl's *Geschichte und Literatur der Staatswissenschaften*.

[4] Containing extremely valuable criticisms of the Utilitarian and Evolutionist schools.

INDEX.